Plain ugly

Manchester University Press

Plain ugly

The unattractive body in early modern culture

Naomi Baker

Manchester University Press

Copyright © Naomi Baker 2010

The right of Naomi Baker to be identified as the author of this work has been asserted by her in accordance with the Copyright, Designs and Patents Act 1988.

Published by Manchester University Press
Altrincham Street, Manchester M1 7JA, UK
www.manchesteruniversitypress.co.uk

British Library Cataloguing-in-Publication Data is available

Library of Congress Cataloging-in-Publication Data is available

ISBN 978 0 7190 6875 1 *paperback*

First published by Manchester University Press in hardback 2010

This paperback edition first published 2015

The publisher has no responsibility for the persistence or accuracy of URLs for any external or third-party internet websites referred to in this book, and does not guarantee that any content on such websites is, or will remain, accurate or appropriate.

Printed by Lightning Source

Contents

List of illustrations	page vii
Acknowledgements	ix
Introduction: ugly subjects in early modern England	1
1 Theorising ugliness	11
What is ugliness?	11
Is ugliness in the eye of the beholder?	13
'There was never any thing ugly'	17
'Frightful pleasure': responding to ugliness	21
'Nature's ill-shap'd letters': mechanical philosophy	35
2 'Charactered in my brow': deciphering ugly faces	41
'A man may look a sentence'	41
The mark of Cain	57
'Empty men': *Bussy D'Ambois*	64
3 Opening the Silenus: gendering the ugly subject	69
'Loathsome loveliness': the odious female body	70
'Surface ugliness': the male Silenus	77
'Opacous' bodies: *Richard III* and *The Changeling*	80
Ugliness in the Age of Reason: William Hay	93
4 'Sight of her is a vomit': abject bodies and Burton's *The Anatomy of Melancholy*	97
'Still abusing women'	98
'Menstruous, plaguy, loathsome'	101
Old hags	107
'Vast virago[s]'	115
Abjection in *The Anatomy of Melancholy*	122
5 'To make love to a deformity': praising ugliness	131
Repairing the ruins: constructing beauty	132
'Fairing the foul': the deformed mistress	139
The limits of transformation: smallpox writing	151

6 Sacrificing beauty: defeatured women	158
'Flay my face': self-mutilation	165
'Eating poison': Parthenia and her sisters	178
Notes	189
Bibliography	228
Index	249

Illustrations

1 Domenico Ghirlandaio, *Old Man with a Young Boy*, c. 1490, tempera on wood, 62 cm × 46 cm. Musée du Louvre, Paris, 96-001427 © RMN/Hervé Lewandowski *page* 4
2 Conrad Goltzius, *Pride*, date unknown, National Gallery of Art, Washington, DC, Rosenwald Collection. Image courtesy of the Board of Trustees, National Gallery of Art 8
3 Leonardo da Vinci, *Two Grotesque Profiles Confronted*, c. 1485–90, pen and ink with wash, 16.3 cm × 14.3 cm. The Royal Collection © 2008 HM Queen Elizabeth II 24
4 Giuseppe Arcimboldo, *Winter*, 1573, oil on canvas, 66 cm × 50 cm. Musée du Louvre, Paris, 98-021468 © RMN/Jean-Gilles Berizzi 26
5 Hieronymus Bosch, *Christ Carrying the Cross* (detail), after 1500, oil on wood. Museum voor Schöne Kunsten, Ghent 28
6 Matthias Grünewald, Isenheim altarpiece (detail), c. 1512–15, oil on panel. © Musée d'Unterlinden, Colmar 30
7 Antonio Tempesta, 'The amorous Angelica' and 'The most beautiful Diana', *The Twelve Principal Roman Heroes and Heroines Drawn in a Grotesque Manner*, c. 1597. Bibliothèque nationale de France, Collection des Estampes, Paris 32
8 Leonardo da Vinci, *Study of Five Grotesque Heads*, c. 1493, 261 mm × 206 mm. The Royal Collection © 2008 HM Queen Elizabeth II 47
9 'Metoposcopie', Richard Saunders, *Physiognomie and Chiromancie*, 1653 © The British Library Board 719.k.7 49
10 '[T]he chinne decerned over long doth innuate a most wicked creature, very talkative, and a whisperer, yea his mynde altogither occupyed with deceytes', Thomas Hill, *The Contemplation of Mankinde, containing a Singular Discourse after the Art of Phisiognomie*, 1571, 61503, fol. 144r. Reproduced by permission of the Huntington Library, San Marino, California 50
11 'The eyes oblique, or lookyng crookedly: declare that man to be a deceaver', Bartholomew Cocles, *A Brief and most Pleasant Epitomye of the*

	whole Art of Physiognomie, gathered ... by that learned Chyrugian Cocles, and Englished by Thomas Hyll, 1556 © The British Library Board C.31.c.15	50
12	Hendrik Goltzius (1558–1617), Anger, no date, engraving, 139 mm × 107 mm, Brussels. The Illustrated Bartsch, Vol. 3, p. 87, Abaris Books	60
13	Philips Galle, Cain leaving the presence of God, c. 1565, engraving, 72mm × 84 mm, Vienna. The Illustrated Bartsch, Vol. 56, p. 12, Abaris Books	62
14	Quinten Massys, An Old Woman ('The Ugly Duchess'), c. 1513 © The National Gallery, London	100
15	Giorgione, La Vecchia, c. 1505–10. Gallerie dell'Accademia, Venice	109
16	George Wither, 'Deformitie, within may bee,/Where outward Beauties we doe see,' A Collection of Emblems, Ancient and Moderne, 1635, 601390, p. 229. Reproduced by permission of the Huntington Library, San Marino, California	110
17	Hans Baldung, The Three Ages of Man and Death, c. 1539, oil on panel, 151 cm × 61 cm. Museo del Prado, Madrid	112
18	Titian, Isabella d'Este, 1534–36, oil on canvas, 102 cm × 64 cm. Kunsthistorisches Museum, Vienna	135
19	Lucas Cranach, The Fountain of Youth, 1546, oil on limewood, 121 cm × 184 cm. Reproduced by permission of bpk/Gemäldegalerie, Staatliche Museen zu Berlin; photograph: Jörg P. Anders	138
20	Antonio Tempesta, 'The neat Marfisa' and 'The beautiful Bradamante', The Twelve Principal Roman Heroes and Heroines Drawn in a Grotesque Manner, c. 1597. Bibliothèque nationale de France, Collection des Estampes, Paris	148
21	Mummy of a two-year-old child who died of smallpox in Naples in the mid-sixteenth century, www.paleopatologia.it/immagini/faccia.jpg	156
22	Titian, The Flaying of Marsyas, c. 1570–75, oil on canvas, 212 cm × 207 cm. Kromeriz Archdiocesan Museum, Czech Republic. Reproduced by permission of the Archbishopric of Olomouc	164

Acknowledgements

My research for this book began with discussions at the University of Manchester with Gerald Hammond and the late John Stachniewski, both of whom offered inspiration and advice. Gerald Hammond also made many helpful comments on a draft of the manuscript, as did Jacqueline Pearson. I am very grateful to them both, and to Anke Bernau for her comments on particular chapters. I would also like to thank Nigel Smith for his encouragement and support. I am grateful to the librarians at the John Rylands University Library of Manchester for their assistance, particularly the staff at Deansgate, and to the staff at Manchester University Press. Finally, special thanks to my father, Bruce Baker, my mother, Sylvia Baker, Gideon Baker, Deirdre Boleyn, Jo Carruthers, Jeff Forshaw, Rachael Gilmour and Zoë Kinsley, all of whom read various versions of my work in progress and provided much encouragement. My research was supported by Arts and Humanities Research Council research leave and by research leave from the University of Manchester. An earlier version of part of Chapter 5 was published as '"To Make Love to a Deformity": Praising Ugliness in Early Modern England', *Renaissance Studies* 22:1 (February 2008), 86–109, (awarded the Society for Renaissance Studies Essay Prize 2009), reproduced here by permission of Wiley-Blackwell.

N.B.

Introduction: ugly subjects in early modern England

'What a piece of work is a man!' exclaims Hamlet, expressing the awe at the splendour and dignity of humanity with which the Renaissance is often associated: 'How noble in reason, how infinite in faculty, in form and moving how express and admirable, in action how like an angel, in apprehension how like a god – the beauty of the world, the paragon of animals!' The fact that to Hamlet this 'paragon' appears nothing but a 'quintessence of dust', the cosmic order a 'foul and pestilent congregation of vapours', is conclusive proof, even to the Prince himself, of his jaded perspective.[1] Whatever the glory of the human form presented in Italian Renaissance art, or declaimed on the early seventeenth-century English stage, however, 'foul and pestilent' bodies were inescapable in early modern England. Roy Porter describes the material reality of noisome, repugnant early modern flesh:

> To a degree that is hard to imagine nowadays, visible, tangible flesh was all too often experienced as ugly, nasty and decaying, bitten by bugs and beset by sores; it was rank, foul and dysfunctional; for all of medicine's best efforts, it was frequently racked with pain, disability and disease, and death might well be nigh.[2]

'Ugly, nasty and decaying' bodies appear regularly in writing and the visual arts from across Europe in this period. Far from being solely preoccupied with beauty, it was an age in which the human figure in all of its often repellent as well as potentially magnificent variety was an object of fascination. The ability to depict the singular, the eccentric and the downright ugly was in fact a marker of creative genius, as Leonardo da Vinci's celebrated grotesque drawings testify.[3]

In this book I investigate representations of the unattractive human body in early modern English culture, examining in particular the role played by depictions of the unsightly body in the construction of specific models of identity. I focus primarily on the ugly characters found in English literature and drama, but also refer to wider European texts and discourses, including Italian and other European visual art. Although many authors, readers and viewers in early modern England may not have encountered wider European visual or textual materials directly, cultural interchange between England and the rest of Europe, particularly Italy, played a dynamic role in shaping English visual, material and literary cultures, as recent scholarship highlights.⁴ The grotesque style was discussed and imitated in England after its revival in Renaissance Italy, for example, while the seventeenth-century English fashion for witty poetic celebrations of ugly women draws heavily on Italian burlesque traditions. Early modern English representations of the unattractive body are thus influenced by and potentially negotiate with other European textual and visual discourses of both beauty and ugliness.

With a few notable exceptions, the ugly subject in early modern English texts tends to be female, old, black, obese or from the lower social orders (or any combination of these categories). In line with Bakhtin's model of the grotesque bodily economy, the ugly body, when associated with such social groups, is typically represented as chaotic, unregulated and amorphous.⁵ It leaks polluted bodily fluids and is consumed with flesh-eating diseases, emphasising the extent to which the ugly subject, marked by his or her unruly corporeality, horrifically fails to maintain a discrete, clearly defined identity.⁶ Put simply, ugly figures in early modern texts often embody all that the emerging modern subject, a subject premised on self-control and the ability to transcend the body through the rule of reason, must not be. Ugliness is repeatedly seen to erase identity. 'Grief is the moth of Beauty,' states Thomas Jeamson in his cosmetic manual *Artificiall Embellishments* (1665):

> it frets out the characters of natures fairest Orthography; wearing off those ruddie and carnation flourishes which her skilfull pencil drew, it makes the face a discolourable blank; and renders those who over much indulge it, so wannish and pale, that they seem but walking shrouds to carry themselves to their own shadie sepulchres.⁷

While beauty is identified as a legible, meaningful text, the inscription of 'natures fairest Orthography', ugliness is a form of living death. 'The Girl is in a manner dead already,' observes the unsympathetic mother of the physically unattractive narrator known as 'Shocking Monster' in Sarah Scott's *Agreeable Ugliness* (1754).⁸ An ugly face thus potentially represents a space outside of recognisable, acceptable forms of modern subjectivity.

Historians argue that key changes in the conceptualisation of subjectivity took place in the early modern era, particularly in terms of perceptions of the relationship between the body and the self. Prior to this period, the body tended to be loaded with symbolic meanings. Indivisible from the self, it possessed its own agency and was understood to be a legible text, inscribed with divine signatures and with marks of character. After Descartes, and even for sometime before, however, selfhood began to be located in a rational consciousness which was understood to be somehow detached from the body.⁹ In Descartes's *Discourse on Method* (1637), for instance, 'I' is equated with the capacity for rational thought, explicitly distinguished from the body and its passions. The soul, asserts Descartes, 'is entirely distinct from the body': 'I could pretend that I had no body and that there was no world nor any place where I was, I could not pretend, on that account, that I did not exist at all[.]' The existence of the self does not depend 'on any material thing', he claims:

'this 'I', that is to say, the soul through which I am what I am, is entirely distinct from the body ... and even if there were no body at all, it would not cease to be all that it is'.[10] Observing such philosophical developments, alongside the rise of mechanical philosophy and a new emphasis on anatomical dissection, critics have suggested that this was an era in which the body became 'mere mechanism ... devoid of any spiritual essence or expressive dimension'.[11] Emptied of its previous significations, it was progressively 'silenced'.[12] A mute machine rather than a vehicle of symbolic meaning, the body could no longer easily be regarded as the window of the soul.

Representations of unattractive bodies in early modern texts provide one means of interrogating this narrative of the emergent nature of subjectivity in the period. As I discuss in the opening chapters, some depictions of ugly figures confirm that the body is becoming increasingly 'opaque', of ever-decreasing relevance to those who seek to understand the self within. In medieval texts, an ugly body is an instantly recognisable symbol of evil as well as of low social status, but ugly bodies in early modern literary and visual texts are often difficult to interpret in moral terms.[13] Domenico Ghirlandaio's *Old Man with a Young Boy* (c. 1490; Figure 1), a sensitive yet unflinching depiction of the physical deformity associated with old age and disease, provides an early illustration of some of the key changes taking place in representations of physical ugliness in the Renaissance. The child in the painting gazes intently at the older figure, possibly his grandfather, transfixed by the prospect of what he, too, will become with time. The lifelike depiction of the old man, whose condition, perhaps rhinophyma, has been the subject of subsequent medical diagnoses, illustrates the development in Renaissance portraiture away from idealised, symbolic representations of human figures towards more naturalistic depictions.[14] Situating ugliness as a natural, even inevitable, aspect of life, the painting does not impose a moral reading of the ugly face. The old man's deformity is skin-deep, in all senses of the term: literally exhibited in his skin, it does not bear witness to a corrupt character. Despite being stripped of its moral content, ugliness does not lose its power to arrest the viewer's attention. Capturing the old man in the moment that he is observed by the young boy, the painting draws attention to the ambivalent impact of ugliness on the beholder. The child looks affectionately at the older figure, yet his love is mixed with curiosity and perhaps even astonishment, evoking the multiple, contradictory responses generated by an unsightly face; responses which we, too, viewing the painting, perhaps uncomfortably share.

The difficulty of identifying the moral implications, as well as the emotional impact, of certain unattractive bodies in early modern texts to some extent confirms the rising prominence of the dualistic Cartesian self in this period. For male literary and dramatic characters, in particular, physical ugliness has the potential to be regarded as a misleading veneer, concealing rather than revealing the nature of the self within. As I demonstrate in Chapter 3, unattractive men are often depicted as Silenus figures, those whose lack of external appeal belies the nobility and wisdom of the self within. 'Thou art lame of body, deformed to the eye,' surmises Robert

Figure 1 Domenico Ghirlandaio, *Old Man with a Young Boy*, c. 1490

Burton, 'yet this hinders not but that thou mayst be a good, a wise, upright, honest man.' In a (male) context in which 'imperfections of the body do not a whit blemish the soul', ugliness, though displeasing, can garner a degree of compassion.[15] Other representations of ugliness from this era nevertheless qualify the model of the body as a newly silent, simply mechanical entity. As Stephen Pender argues, 'While the medical and scientific cultures attempted to remake the human body into an object of scientific scrutiny, in popular understanding the body remained a vast and insistent index of natural and political worlds.'[16] Physiognomy, the art of reading faces for signs of character, continued to be a popular and credible discourse, at least at a 'vulgar' level, throughout the seventeenth century and beyond, and physiognomical principles influence many depictions of unattractive characters in early modern English texts.[17] In relation to female, old and black characters, in particular, alongside figures from other marginalised groups, physical features deemed ugly often resonate as markers of the self.[18] Witches, for example, are seen to betray their evil nature in their twisted, warty bodies. Elizabeth Sawyer, the 'lean old beldame' in *The Witch of Edmonton* (performed 1621, publ. 1658) is 'shunned/And hated like a sickness' in large part because she is 'like a bow buckled and bent together.'[19] Anything but skin-deep, female ugliness, often located in excessive, contagious flesh, generates moral as well as aesthetic disgust.

Residual discourses thus circulate alongside emergent models of the self in the early modern era, often within single works.[20] 'Your face, my thane, is as a book,' Lady Macbeth warns her husband, contradicting Duncan's earlier statement that 'There's no art/To find the mind's construction in the face.'[21] The very texts that trumpet the emergence of new models of nature and philosophy in which the body is no longer the index of the mind often contain significant inconsistencies in their representation of unsightly bodies. Francis Bacon's essay 'Of Deformity' (1612) exemplifies the juxtaposition of incompatible perspectives on ugliness characteristic of the era. 'Certainly, there is a consent between the body and the mind,' asserts Bacon, noting that 'Deformed Persons' are commonly 'void of natural Affection'. He swiftly qualifies his argument, however, observing that 'it is good to consider of Deformity, not as a Sign, which is more deceivable, but as a Cause, which seldome faileth of the Effect'.[22] Seeking to reach an objective understanding of the ugly body, Bacon identifies social rather than material causes for the distorted personalities of the ugly. As Helen Deutsch observes, however, he remains dependent 'on a logic of resemblance, a mirroring of visible excess by interior lack'. His interpretation of deformity is thus characterised by 'narrative instability', reflecting and perpetuating the confusions of the age regarding the meanings of an unattractive face.[23]

One of the most startling points to emerge in this book is the difficulty, in the end, of distinguishing ugly women from their beautiful counterparts. Ugly hags at first glance appear to be the polar opposite of the icy beauties celebrated in Petrarchan love poetry, but time and again early modern writing works to erode this distinction, insisting that women are likely to be inverted Sileni, their veneer of beauty covering both physical and moral deformity. The 'Out-side silk and out-side Lawn' are 'Sceanes to cheat us neatly drawne', warns the speaker of Robert Herrick's 'Upon some Women' (1648): beneath their artfully constructed erotic allure, women are 'In-laid Garbage ev'ry where'.[24] So closely is ugliness aligned with female matter in early modern representations, in fact, that female beauty itself has the potential to be presented as a kind of deformity. Both the 'painted' Jone, who 'goes/Like one of those/Whom purity had Sainted', and the 'prittie' and 'wittie' Jane are 'tainted' and smelly.[25] Conrad Goltzius's *Pride* (date unknown; Figure 2) illustrates the commonplace assumption that beneath the sumptuous exterior of a woman, even a woman of high social status, resides a repulsive body, here represented by a skeleton. As the image of Eve feeding fruit to Adam reminds us, the ugliness of women betrays their fallen nature, dangerously disguised and thus in need of the physical and moral uncovering which this interactive picture literally allows. While the ugly male character cannot easily be equated with his physical presence, the script of an ugly body continues to define a female subject's identity, even if her unattractiveness lurks behind a superficial beauty.

At times a means of displaying the disparity between the body and the self while elsewhere drawing attention to the inseparability of the outer and inner person, ugly characters play a fascinating role in textual negotiations with identity in this era. Diseased, necrotic and perpetually transgressing its own borders, the ugly (female) body in early modern English writing rejects the 'entirely finished, completed, strictly limited body' identified by Bakhtin as an emergent ideal in dominant Renaissance culture. Early modern beldames and viragos recall the Bakhtinian grotesque, the senile pregnant hags whose exaggerated, exposed orifices oppose the 'impenetrable façade', the 'opaque surface', of the bourgeois individual. For Bakhtin, however, the grotesque body, a 'cosmic and universal' form that cannot simply be equated with the (ugly) bodies of individual subjects, is positive and subversive: it 'uncrowns' official culture from below.[26] While ugly characters in early modern texts hold subversive potential, they often work to shore up, rather than to dismantle, dominant forms of identity. Kristeva's theorisation of the abject illuminates the ambivalent processes at work in representations of ugly figures in this era. In *Powers of Horror*, Kristeva defines the abject as that which 'does not respect borders, positions, rules'. Anything that transgresses bodily boundaries, for example faeces or blood, represents the abject, as do deformed bodies and corpses, entities that confuse the borders of life and death. The abject compels and nauseates because it recalls an originary state of non-differentiation from the maternal body. Identity depends on the rejection of the abject: the subject must define himself in opposition to 'what, having been the mother, will turn into an abject'. Kristeva thus argues for the fundamental role of repulsion in the construction of identity. The abject is the place 'where meaning collapses', but is simultaneously that which, through its repudiation, allows meaning, identity and culture to exist. For Kristeva, abjection '[borders] the frail identity of the speaking being', enabling this speaking being to be defined while haunting it with its own precariousness, its potential to be 'pulverized'.[27]

Representations of 'menstruous' women, old hags and 'vast virago[s]' in early modern English texts exhibit the anxious and fragile processes of self-construction suggested by Kristeva's theories. As Chapter 4 highlights, the amorphous, contagious, transgressive ugly body poses an ever-present threat to models of subjectivity premised on clearly defined boundaries of the self and the rational self-regulation of the body. Generating extreme loathing, the deformed woman nevertheless fulfils a crucial function, potentially enabling the dominant subject to expel the disruptive bodily model that she represents. Constantly being told to 'Go!' and being subjected to fantasies of violence, the repulsive witch repeatedly reappears in early modern texts, betraying her continuing and necessary role in the construction of identity.[28] Representations of ugly women, in other words, have as much, if not more, to tell us about the formulation of male subjectivity in this era as they do about available models of female selfhood.

The usefulness of the ugly woman as a means of consolidating specific forms of masculine identity is particularly visible in the group of early seventeenth-century texts written in praise of unattractive mistresses that I investigate in Chapter 5. Apparently jettisoning the clichéd beauty demanded by Petrarchan poetic conventions, poets and dramatists taking part in this brief literary fashion champion mistresses whose 'eyes are nothing like the sun', whose breasts are 'dun', whose hair is like 'black wires' and whose cheeks fail to live up to any comparisons with roses.[29] Rather than granting new recognition to women who fall outside narrow canons of beauty, however, texts seemingly appreciating unattractive women are primarily concerned with the male speaker, he whose desire is not thwarted by the devastating effects of time, disease or even violence on the face of his beloved. Works 'celebrating' ugly women ultimately draw attention to the male creative genius that is capable of transforming even unsightly female matter into compelling art.[30] Beauty, these texts suggest, is that which is imposed by men, or more specifically by the male artist, on to 'naturally' ugly female matter. Texts praising ugly women thus perpetuate the identification of women with repulsive physicality, the negative status of which is never seriously reconsidered.

Despite its brief literary fashionability, then, female ugliness stubbornly resists rehabilitation in the writing of this era. Several female characters in early modern texts try to turn ugliness to their own advantage, seizing the opportunities seemingly offered by an unattractive face to escape the constraints of beauty and male desire. Praying to become ugly, or even resorting to self-mutilation, such characters, I argue in the final chapter, expose the difficulty of turning a repulsive female body into a vehicle of self-determination. Far from eluding male definitions of the female body, disfigured women become an obscene display of the unruly, defiled corporeality that is repeatedly identified as the truth of femininity in this era. While the ugly man in early modern texts potentially becomes a key representative of the modern subject, he who is no longer in thrall to his body, the ugly woman continues to be defined by a chaotic, repulsive body whose meanings cannot be positive.

The ugly body, at once titillating and nauseating, is thus the site where multiple cultural tensions are negotiated and where potential models of identity are interrogated and confirmed. Variously disturbing, comic, pleasurable and horrifying, an

Figure 2 Conrad Goltzius, *Pride*, date unknown. The image on the right shows the skeleton that is revealed when the paper flap is raised

ugly face has the power to evoke a range of responses, none of them straightforward. Eluding simple categorisations and dismantling the most fundamental of social and subjective binaries, even as they are at the same time deployed to support them, ugly figures burst repeatedly on to the scene in early modern texts, often in the most unexpected of places. Easy to dismiss as moments of bad taste in an era generally associated with the representation and adoration of beauty, depictions of unattractive faces and bodies in fact play a key role in the construction and representation of early modern subjectivities, confirming emergent models of the self at the same time as they reveal the fragility and selective application of these models. The rational, self-controlled early modern subject is perpetually and necessarily haunted by his terrifying opposite, the contagious, necrotic hag, a figure he at once detests and is fascinated by, as her compelling, ambivalent presence in numerous texts reveals.

1

Theorising ugliness

What is ugliness?

The term 'ugly' originates from the Old Norse *ugglig*, meaning 'to be feared or dreaded'.[1] Early modern English definitions of ugliness frequently focus on its power to disturb the viewer. 'Foulnesse is Lothsome,' states John Donne, and Robert Burton similarly defines ugliness by its ability to repulse: 'we contemn and abhor generally such things as are foul and ugly to behold, account them filthy, but love and covet that which is faire'.[2] Ugliness and beauty thus appear to be fixed properties of objects, generating natural and inevitable responses in the viewer. Definitions of ugliness were nevertheless undergoing important changes in early modern England, leading to a proliferation of contradictory statements regarding the nature and implications of unattractive human bodies, which did not, after all, provoke uniform responses in those who viewed or represented them.

Prior to the development of formal aesthetics in the eighteenth century, beauty and its inversions operated within wider moral and transcendent frameworks.[3] In classical and medieval thought, the ugly is the morally repellent. Evil is ugly, according to William of Auvergne, thirteenth-century Bishop of Paris, because it 'repels our mind and arouses aversion . . . and offends our inner sense with its sight'.[4] Reaching beyond the realm of superficial physical appearances, ugliness is sin, set against a beauty defined in terms of virtue. Into the early modern era, ugliness, like beauty, continues to be deployed in abstract terms. 'When I behold . . . the amiable countenance of Christ,' claims Joyce Lewes, one of Foxe's martyrs, 'the ugsome face of death doth not greatly trouble me.'[5] Milton's Adam recoils from his first glimpse of mortality with less serenity than Lewes but with an equally assured sense of its ugliness: 'O sight/Of terror, foul and ugly to behold,/Horrid to think, how horrible to feel!'[6] Sinful actions are repeatedly labelled ugly in this era, as are theological perversions. The 'monstrous error of atheism', for instance, is said to be 'most ugly'.[7]

To be ugly in these contexts is to deviate from a moral ideal. The spiritual and the physical are not clearly distinguished from each other, however, and moralised perceptions of ugliness inevitably shape responses to faces or bodies that are deemed to be less than attractive. Ugly faces, either in the flesh or in literary and visual texts, emblazon moral corruption for all to see. During the Italian Renaissance, and later in sixteenth- and seventeenth-century England, ugliness, like beauty, nevertheless begins to lose its transcendent referents and to be described in more reductively material terms. The Neoplatonist Agnolo Firenzuola's influential treatise *Dialogo delle bellezze delle donne* (*On the Beauty of Women*) (1541, publ. 1548) marks a key shift in theorisations of human beauty in Italy: 'it is not my intention to speak of beauty of the soul', states Celso, separating such questions from his interest in quantifying the beauty of the body. Beauty is treated in geometric terms in the text, where it is defined as 'nothing else but ordered concord, akin to a harmony that arises mysteriously from the composition, union, and conjunction of several diverse and different parts'.[8]

Potentially limiting ugliness, as well as beauty, to a material rather than a spiritual phenomenon, the early modern era witnesses a fundamental reconfiguration of the relationship between the natural and the ugly. In the medieval era, ugliness tends to be viewed as an unnatural intruder into a fundamentally beautiful universe. This perception persists into the sixteenth and early seventeenth centuries in England, where natural forms are often regarded as by definition beautiful, whatever their eccentricity. As the seventeenth century progresses, however, the material order begins to be reconceptualised as a regular, ordered machine, within which instances of disorder or irregularity cease to be pleasurable displays of nature's or God's creative ingenuity and become instead repellent physical aberrations.[9] The ugly, for a certain section of the intellectual elite at least, shifts from a metaphysical distortion of God's creation to a material irregularity generated by a blindly impersonal universe. While unpleasant, ugliness understood in such terms is not morally or spiritually legible. No longer necessarily viewed as purposive signs, distorted physical features, like other natural aberrations, become merely 'skin-deep', a term emerging for the first time in the early seventeenth century.[10]

The seventeenth century therefore witnesses significant changes in the theorisation of ugliness, the main themes of which I explore in this chapter. It will soon become apparent that the term 'ugly' is being used in many different ways in the discussions considered here. Rather than attempting to impose a watertight account of ugliness, a term that never achieves a single, agreed-upon meaning in this era, I aim to give some indication of the divergent concepts of ugliness circulating at this time. Speaking in broad terms, it is possible to trace a historical narrative in the development of the use and representation of ugliness. What is perhaps even more interesting, however, is the manner in which seemingly incompatible concepts of ugliness coexist in early modern texts from all levels of the social strata. Key changes are under way in this era, but much confusion and disparity of outlook remains. Illustrating the contradictory perspectives on ugliness characteristic of the moment, I turn now to a central question to which no one could provide a definitive answer: is ugliness an objective property or a subjective perception?

Is ugliness in the eye of the beholder?

In the medieval era, ugliness, like beauty, was held to be an objective property. Things are not beautiful because they please, but 'please because they are beautiful', stated Augustine.[11] The vital role of the perceiving subject in the recognition of beauty or deformity was noted, particularly by Thomas Aquinas, but beauty and ugliness were nevertheless understood to be intrinsic qualities of objects.[12] By the eighteenth century, however, beauty and ugliness were being defined as subjective perceptions. The first English treatise explicitly dedicated to aesthetic issues, Francis Hutcheson's *An Inquiry into the Original of our Ideas of Beauty and Virtue* (1725), defines beauty in seemingly subjective terms, as an 'idea raised in us'. This 'idea' is nevertheless provoked by the properties of objects, namely 'uniformity amidst variety'. Beauty and ugliness thus remain fixed qualities, generating necessary responses: 'Who was ever pleased with an inequality of heights in windows of the same range, or dissimilar shapes of them? With unequal legs or arms, eyes or cheeks in a mistress?' That which lacks proportion 'never fails to pass for an imperfection, and want of beauty ... as when the eyes are not exactly like, or one arm or leg is a little shorter or smaller than its fellow'.[13] Physical ugliness, defined here as disproportion, invariably generates pain and revulsion. By the mid-eighteenth century David Hume nevertheless states that it is 'certain, that beauty and deformity, no more than sweet and bitter, are not qualities in objects, but belong entirely to the sentiment.... One person may even perceive deformity, where another is sensible of beauty.' The properties of the object are not irrelevant ('some particular forms or qualities ... are calculated to please, and others to displease') but beauty and ugliness are now subjective perceptions, firmly located in the eye of the beholder.[14]

In the seventeenth century, questions regarding the potentially subjective or relative nature of beauty and ugliness surface repeatedly, suggesting that the issue generates some anxiety. The topic is often treated humorously. Wittily defending his choice of an ugly wife, for example, the speaker of Henry King's 'The Defence' (1664) emphasises the primacy of the viewer in deciding what is attractive:

> Nor can'st discern where her form lyes,
> Unless thou saw'st her with my eyes ...
> If lik't by me, tis I alone
> Can make a beauty where was none;
> For rated in my fancie, she
> Is so as she appears to me.[15]

The perverse nature of this poem, constructed in the classical rhetorical tradition of paradoxical praise, nevertheless undermines its argument: beauty is in the eye of the beholder, states the speaker, but this claim is made in order to justify the self-evidently preposterous suggestion that ugliness is preferable to beauty. Including the reader in the joke through the assumption of a shared aesthetic standard, the apparent recognition of the subjectivity of beauty ironically reinforces the idea that beauty, and ugliness, are objective, universally discernible properties.

One of the conversants in Firenzuola's *On the Beauty of Women* toys with the idea that 'everyone has his own opinion' of beauty: 'some like dark-skinned women, and others fair-skinned ones. When it comes to us women, it is the same as at the cloth market, where one sells even the rough wool cloth and inexpensive floss silk.' While less 'valuable' women may still have some worth in the sexual economy, however, their plainness remains a self-evident quality. Celso, the voice of masculine reason in the dialogue, insists that beauty and ugliness are objective properties, whatever the variety of response to them may be. 'Tommaso likes his Nora beyond all measure,' he admits, but 'she is still as ugly as can be.'[16] His subsequent elaboration of the geometrically quantifiable nature of feminine beauty gives detailed expression to the Renaissance emphasis on beauty as proportion, emphasising its status as a property of the object rather than a construction of the perceiver.

Elsewhere, however, the potential subjectivity of beauty and ugliness is taken more seriously. To Thomas Hobbes, 'beautiful' and 'ugly' are labels that we apply to entities that we either desire or loathe in accordance with our self-interest, rather than the nature of the objects themselves:

> the constitution of a mans Body is in continuall mutation; it is impossible that all the same things should always cause in him the same Appetites, and Aversions: much lesse can all men consent, in the Desire of almost any one and the same Object.
>
> But whatsoever is the object of any man's Appetite or Desire; that is it, which he for his part calleth Good: and the object of his Hate and Aversion, Evill; and of his Contempt, Vile and Inconsiderable. For these words of Good, Evill, and Contemptible, are ever used with relation to the person that useth them: There being nothing simply and absolutely so; nor any common Rule of Good and Evil, to be taken from the nature of the objects themselves; but from the Person of the man (where there is no Common-wealth;) or, (in a Common-wealth) from the Person that representeth it; or from an Arbitrator or Judge.[17]

Neoplatonic paradigms also potentially encouraged the perception that judgements of sensory beauty are matters of fleshly appetite, making it unsurprising that tastes vary from person to person. The Italian Neoplatonist Thomasso Buoni argues in *Problemes of Beautie* (1606) that we perceive objects to be beautiful not solely because of the properties that they possess, but as a result of our own bodily disposition:

> corporall Beauty is not onely placed in the due proportion, or site, or quantitie, or quality of the members, but much more in the appetite, which by reason of the diversitie of the complection where it resideth, willeth and desireth diversely.

The process of taking pleasure in material beauty is seen here to be primarily physical, governed by 'the diversitie of mens complections', which 'breeds a diversitie in their desires; wherby they judge diversly of things present, & follow those which doe best agree with their constitutions'. 'The Appetite doth accommodate it selfe to the temperature of the body,' states Buoni, a 'temperature' which is evidently determined by social status:

> for we see that as the country Swaine desireth grosse meates, such as agree best with the grossnesse of his nature, labours & education, as Onions, Leekes, Garlike, Beefe, Bacon, and such like: and these meates to him are sweete, and savory. So we see that men fitting themselves in their customes and carriages to their bodily temperatures, do ever desire to converse with their like, and therefore no marvell if the same happen in the election of Beauty.

In this treatise, then, cultural differences in ideas of beauty have a sociobiological origin. Our bodies suffer from a form of narcissism:

> And therefore to the eye of the Moore, the blacke, or tawny countenance of his Moorish damosell pleaseth best, to the eye of another, a colour as white as the Lilly, or the driven snowe, to another the colour neither simply white, nor black, but that well medled Beauty betwixt them both... for an absolute Beauty carieth away the bell. Or Perhaps because every like desireth and loveth his like.[18]

European colonial expansion in the sixteenth and seventeenth centuries brought new encounters (and stories of encounters) with a range of cultures and peoples, such that the cultural relativity of standards of beauty was hard to ignore. Manuel de Faria e Sousa's account of the Portuguese 'discovery and conquest of India... From the coast of Africk to the farthest parts of China and Japan', translated into English by Captain John Stevens in 1695, boldly turns the tables on Occidental presumptions of superiority, noting that the Chinese 'look upon [our noses] as deformed'.[19] The recognition of cultural difference in standards of beauty does not usually extend to an acknowledgement that an English readership may hold a variety of aesthetic opinions, however. 'Beauty is determined by opinion, and seems to have no essence that holds one notion with all,' declares the doctor and philosopher Sir Thomas Browne. 'Thus flat noses seem comely unto the Moore, an Aquiline or hawked one unto the Persian, a large and prominent nose unto the Romane, but none of these are acceptable in our opinion.'[20] 'We' are clearly believed to be united in 'our' definitions of beauty and of ugliness, and are thus assumed to be duly startled by the exotic and implicitly incomprehensible opinions of other cultures.

Some awareness of the global variety of ideas concerning beauty is not, moreover, necessarily accompanied by a recognition of fundamental aesthetic relativity. For the doctor John Bulwer, 'foreign' ideals of beauty are the very definition of deformity. The 'artificiall and affected Deformations' of non-English fashions are 'Monstrosities that have appeared to disfigure the Humane Fabrick', he proclaims in the title to his *Anthropometamorphosis* (1650). While the English have become degenerate through their aping of foreign cultures, categories of beauty and deformity, mapped on to national identities, remain objective and absolute, in theory at least. The beautiful is that which is natural, while artificial tampering with the body produces 'diverse depraved Figures'. Despite the inconsistencies in his argument, in which the division between the natural and the artificial cannot be maintained, Bulwer insists that beauty is an objective property, one that can be evaluated by the fact that the beautiful is synonymous with the efficient: 'true beauty is referred to the successe and goodnesse of utility', he asserts. While some may argue that the beauty of the nose is 'determined by opinion ... that seeming beauteous unto one, which hath no favour with another', Bulwer's conviction that all foreign fashions mutilate the body and thus compromise its God-given functionality militates against such foolishness. Flat noses are 'in request' in the 'great Turks Court', for example, but this trend compromises the function of the nose and must therefore be regarded as ugly:

> if their designe be to gaine beauty thereby, they are much out of the way, since the Nose is thereby hurt in its form, because it is hurt in its adorning and beauty, which is thereby blemished; and when its ornament and beauty is blemished, the very forme of it is hurt, and so consequently the instrument.[21]

Montaigne, however, draws very different conclusions from the variety of models of beauty that he perceives in various cultures. Non-European cultures are said in his *Essais* to hold standards of beauty which demand the mutilation of the body:

> For a painter in the Indies beauty is black and sunburnt, with thick swollen lips and broad flat noses; there, they load the cartilage between the nostrils with great rings of gold, so that it hangs right down to the lips ... for them it is elegant to lay their teeth bare exposing the gum below their roots. In Peru, big ears are beautiful: they stretch them as far as they can, artificially.... Elsewhere there are whole nations who carefully blacken their teeth and loathe seeming white ones. Elsewhere they dye them red.... The women of Mexico count low foreheads as a sign of beauty.... We would fashion ugliness that way.

While the strangeness and exoticism of such practices is implied in this description, Montaigne uses this evidence to assert the subjectivity of categories of the beautiful. 'We give human beauty any form we fancy', he observes:

> It seems we have little knowledge of natural beauty or of beauty in general, since we humans give so many diverse forms to our own beauty; if it had been prescribed by Nature, we would all hold common views about it, just as we all agree that fire is hot.

'We' do not share identical perspectives of the beautiful, he insists, a fact which seems to prove that beauty is not a natural or an objective quality. 'Anyone we dislike appears more ugly,' he observes.[22] Our tastes are not innate, moreover, but are shaped by particular rhetorical discourses. Elsewhere, Montaigne cites the Italian proverb that 'he who has not lain with a lame woman does not know Venus in her sweet perfection'. '[O]n the sole authority' of this saying, he confesses, 'I once got myself to believe that I had derived the greater pleasure from a woman because she was deformed, even counting her deformity among her charms.'[23] A crooked body can be perceived to be attractive, he argues, if cultural and linguistic discourses frame it so: beauty and ugliness, in the end, are rhetorical constructs.

The wide variety of approaches to the question of the objectivity or subjectivity of beauty and ugliness in the early modern period highlights the lack of consensus surrounding 'aesthetic' questions in an era before aesthetics was formalised as an area of philosophical enquiry. Particular beliefs regarding the nature of ugliness were nevertheless inherent in certain early modern English orthodoxies. Christian teachings, for instance, held that nature was the creation of a wise and benevolent deity, and, as such, must be fundamentally beautiful. While nature was seen to be a direct expression of God's creative ingenuity, it was difficult, in fact, to regard any natural form as truly ugly.

'There was never any thing ugly'[24]

From classical antiquity into the early modern period, ugliness was identified as a form of perversion, a deviation from a stated norm. An object in the wrong place, or the absence of a required entity, is ugly. William of Auvergne, a medieval philosopher who returned repeatedly to questions of the ugly, grounded ugliness in concepts of failure and transgression. Objects are ugly, he stated, if they diverge from their intended design, either through excess or lack: 'We should call ugly a man who had three eyes, and no less ugly one who had only one eye.' Ugliness, as a form of inappropriateness, also occurs when elements are wrongly situated:

> Redness is in itself pleasant-looking and is beauty; if, however, it were in that part of the eye which should be white, it would disfigure the eye.... The eye is in itself shapely and beautiful... but only when it is in its proper and rightful place. If, however, it were where the ear is, or in the middle of the face, that is, in an inappropriate place, then it would make the same face ugly.[25]

The beautiful object has an ideal structure; whole, discrete, coherent, defined, bounded. Ugliness is the negation of these properties: the erroneous, the mistaken, that which resists totality.[26] William Sanderson in *Graphice: The Use of the Pen and Pensil, or The Most Excellent Art of Painting* (1658) contrasts the inherent unity of beauty with the multiplicity and chaos of ugliness:

> Beauty should consist but of One at the most; and deformity contrariwise, measured by many: for the even Lineaments and due proportion of fair and goodly Persons, seem to be created and framed, by the judgement and sight, of one form alone, which cannot be in deformed persons, as with blub cheeks, bigg eyes, little nose, flat mouth, out chin, and brown skin, as it were moulded from many ill faces; and yet some one part considered about, to be handsome, but altogether become ugly; not for any other cause, but that they may be Lineaments of many fair women, and not of One.[27]

Ugliness is a principle of irrationality, the failure of purposeful or ordered form. Firenzuola states that white eyelashes are not beautiful, partly because they 'impair the sight'.²⁸ George Puttenham, meanwhile, regards disproportionate bodies as indecent, offending against the decorum of order, symmetry and purpose. Entities are 'unseemely'

> if they discover any illfavourednesse or disproportion to the partes apprehensive, as for example... the shape of a membred body without his due measures and simmetry, and the like of every other sence in his proper function. These excesses or defectes or confusions and disorders in the sensible objectes are deformities and unseemely to the sence.²⁹

If beauty is equated with unity, reason, form and decency, however, ugliness not only represents dysfunctional or obscene form but is opposed to the very possibility of form. The first Neoplatonist, Plotinus, stated that ugliness is 'the Principle contrary to Existence: and the Ugly is also the primal evil'.³⁰ To the twentieth-century art critic Mark Hutchinson, 'ugliness is not the failure of something to make sense but the lack of the possibility of significance'. 'A face with disproportionate features,' he comments, 'may not be considered beautiful but is not ugly: a face lacking in features... is what is ugly. It threatens to stop being a face at all.'³¹ The character of Margaret in George Chapman's *The Gentleman Usher* (1606) reaches the same conclusion. After mutilating her face with poison, she proclaims that 'this [u]gly thing is now no more a face'.³² Sacrificing the beauty of her face involves the loss of her face itself. Beauty, in this model, is a fundamental property of shape and being, so that the statement an 'ugly face' in some senses becomes an oxymoron.

While it is defined as an unnatural principle of negation and disorder, the opposite of form, ugliness cannot easily inhabit a material order believed to be designed and shaped by a divine Creator. To Browne, everything within the created order participates in a purposeful design. As a result, nothing that exists can properly be said to be ugly:

> I hold there is a generall beauty in the works of God, and therefore no deformity in any kind or species of creature whatsoever: I cannot tell by what Logick we call a Toad, a Beare, or an Elephant ugly, they being created in those outward shapes and figures which best express the actions of their inward formes. And having past that generall visitation of God, who saw that all that he had made was good, that is, conformable to his will, which abhors deformity, and is the rule of order and beauty; there is no deformity but in monstrosity, wherein notwithstanding there is a kind of beauty, Nature so ingeniously contriving the irregular parts, as they become sometimes more remarkable than the principall Fabrick. To speake yet more narrowly, there was never any thing ugly, or mis-shapen, but the Chaos[.]³³

Browne's celebration of the 'generall beauty' of creation, in which 'there was never any thing ugly', draws on a Christian philosophical tradition reaching back to Augustine. 'There is no form, nor any body at all lacking some trace of unity,' reasoned Augustine, arguing that every element of nature possesses a degree of beauty.³⁴ The binary opposition of beauty and ugliness is an unhelpful means of categorising objects which can more accurately be said to occupy different points on a sliding scale of beauty. 'The beauty of the human form is greater than that of the ape,' he concedes, 'so, by comparison with it, the beauty of the ape is called ugliness'. Labelling an ape ugly nevertheless blinds us to the 'appropriate harmony, the bilateral symmetry of members, the concordance of parts, the ability for self-defence' and other beautiful qualities that it possesses.[35] Beauty, here, is defined both as form and as fitness for function. Even 'the most imperfect creatures' are informed by a divine purpose that differentiates them from the ugly.

Until the second half of the seventeenth century, the dominant paradigm of a vibrant, diverse and constantly surprising natural order meant that even the misshapen could be seen as an expression of divine creativity.[36] Examples of physical irregularity that would later be regarded as meaningless and repellent were potentially identified as the 'speciall handyworke of God'.[37] 'God forbid that any one should be so besotted as to think the Maker erred in the creation of this,' thundered Augustine of a 'monstrous' birth, 'though we know not why He made it thus.'[38] To Thomas Fuller, likewise, in *The Holy State* (1642), deformed bodies are God's art-work:

> Mock not at those who are misshapen by Nature. There is the same reason of the poore and of the deformed; he that despiseth them despiseth God that made them. A poore man is a picture of Gods own making, but set in a plain frame, not guilded: a deformed man is also his workmanship, but not drawn with even lines and lively colours: The former, not for want of wealth, as the latter not for want of skill, but both for the pleasure of the maker.

Quotidian regularity does not exhibit divine wisdom any more than does an apparent deviation, nor can it necessarily be regarded as more beautiful. Beauty, then, is a characteristic of that which is created by God, leaving nothing in the material order outside its scope. Working from the premise of a fundamentally beautiful, because purposeful, natural order, ugliness is merely the perception of the short-sighted:

> if, for example, a man is placed like a statue in a corner of an extremely large and beautiful building, he will not be able to perceive the beauty of this building, of which he is a part.... And if the syllables in a poem were alive and able to perceive for as long as they sound, they would by no means be pleased with the rhythm and beauty of the poetic diction, which they are unable to perceive and appraise as a whole[.][39]

Fuller thus denies that beauty is ultimately defined by subjective sense impressions. If we could adopt a global perspective, we would recognise that those elements which appear to us to be ugly play a vital role in the unity and beauty of the universe.

A variation on the theme that nothing is ugly, then, is the recognition that while local objects may seem ugly, in the sense of irregular, they are crucial to the overall beauty of the natural order. Beauty inheres in design which can only be judged from an objective position. To Augustine, the universe is 'beautified' by 'opposition and diversity of parts': 'he that cannot contemplate the beauty of the whole stumbles at the deformity of the part, not knowing the harmony that it has with the whole'.[40] Montaigne follows Augustine in his insistence that beauty arises from an 'arrangement and relationship' of multiple parts, including those that appear to be unattractive:

> What we call monsters are not so for God, who sees the infinite number of forms which he has included in the immensity of his creation: it is to be believed that the figure which astonishes us relates to, and derives from, some other figure of the same genus unknown to Man. God is all-wise; nothing comes from him which is not good, general and regular: but we cannot see the disposition and relationship.... Whatever happens against custom we say is against Nature, yet there is nothing whatsoever which is not in harmony with her.[41]

Beauty, in fact, was often said to rely on the interplay of contrasting elements. Leonardo da Vinci worked according to the principle that 'beauty and ugliness seem more effective through one another'.[42] 'Black your haires are; mine are white;/This begets the more delight,/When things meet most opposite,' argues Herrick, wittily defending the value of his ageing appearance.[43] John Lyly repeats the sentiment in *Euphues: The Anatomy of Wit* (1579), stating that 'we commonly see that a black ground doth best beseem a white counterfeit, and Venus, according to the judgement of Mars, was then most amiable, when she sat close by Vulcan'.[44] In James Shirley's play *The Dukes Mistris* (1636, publ. 1638), an ugly woman is hired because she is 'Usefull at Court, to set of[f] other faces,/Especially the Duke's Mistres'.[45] The seventeenth-century female fashion of wearing artificial spots or moles was similarly generated by the belief, in the words of one critic of the practice, that 'contraries compared and placed neare one another, shew their lustre more plainely.... Imperfection can make perfect... the defect can encrease beauty.'[46] 'Through foule, we follow faire,' pens Richard Lovelace, delighting in the witty paradox that beauty cannot exist without ugliness: 'For had the world one face/And Earth been bright as Ayre,/We had knowne neither place.'[47] Arguing for the beauty of the natural against the deformity of the artificial, Bulwer rejects cosmetic improvements of the features, stating that

> The beauty of the Face of man is much advanced and heightned by the Cavities and Eminencies thereof; that as the greater world is called *Cosmus*, from the beauty thereof, the inequality of the Centre thereof contributing much to the beauty and delightsomeness of it: so in this Map or little beauty in the face, the inequality affords the prospect and delight. These Face-moulders, then, who affect a platter-Face, not only in their endeavour, overthrow the lawfull proportion of the Face, but demolish the most apparent eminency and extant majesty thereof.[48]

Edward Ward's 'Club of Ugly Faces' (1710) draws on similar arguments as it satirically 'praises' ugliness:

Should true Proportion e'ery Mortal grace,
And Simetry be seen in e'ery Face:
Beauty no longer would be thought Divine,
Nor would its Charms with half the Lustre shine:
No Courtly Dame a killing Look could boast,
If once the Foils of Homeliness were lost.
The dusky Sky sets off the silver Moon,
And Neighbouring Clouds add Blushes to the Sun:
So Ugly Faces make the Fair seem bright . . .
Therefore 'tis fit the Blare or Goggle Ey'd,
Should get his Likeness on his Shipton Bride,
And that the mighty Nose, enrich'd with Wines,
Which, like a glowing Lump of Coral shines,
Should on some drunken Bride's Pimgenet Face,
For the next Age beget a Monstr'ous Race;
That Beauty, when with homely looks compar'd,
May be for ever honour'd with regard . . .
But should one Level run thro' humane Race,
And neither Sex could shew a homely Face,
Beauty would lose its Power[.][49]

According to this common theme in early modern discussions of ugliness, then, beauty is not reducible to uniformity but relies on variety and contrast, requiring inequalities and seeming defects alongside more regular forms.[50] Misshapen forms play a vital part in the overall beauty of the universe. Instead of being seen as mistakes to be suppressed or ignored, irregularities could be viewed with fascination and even delight.

'Frightful pleasure':[51] responding to ugliness

The anomalous was frequently flaunted in sixteenth- and early seventeenth-century England, where the prodigious, displayed in curiosity cabinets and freak shows, made for potentially pleasurable viewing.[52] As Paula Findlen demonstrates, bizarre objects such as hermaphroditic snails or zoophytes were often interpreted as jokes of nature.[53] Nature, according to one early modern scholar, is capricious, prone to 'follow and fly from her self both at once, aping and imitating her own works'. She delights to break 'the plain ground of some common nature into an elegant variety of Individuals, different in shape and temper'.[54] Anomalies were freakish, the products of 'irregular fancy', but they were greeted with delight rather than with the fear and loathing that typically defines responses to the ugly.[55]

'Freaky' bodies presented for public consumption in fairs generated enormous attention from all sections of society until the end of the seventeenth century.[56] Samuel Pepys, for one, took unashamed pleasure in the display of human anomaly. On 21 December 1668 he went

> into Holborne, and there saw the woman that is to be seen with a beard. She is a little plain woman, a Dane: her name, Ursula Dyan; about forty years old; her voice like a little girl's; with a beard as much as any man I ever saw, black almost, and grizly; they offered to shew my wife further satisfaction if she desired it . . . . It was a strange sight to me, I confess, and what pleased me mightily.[57]

Daston and Park observe that the monstrous could generate pleasure alongside horror in sixteenth- and seventeenth-century England, and the same applies to the related category of the ugly.[58] One cause of desire, notes Edward Reynolds in his *A Treatise of the Passions* (1640) (although one he takes a dim view of) is 'admiration':

> a strange thing though monstrous and deformed calleth the eyes of every man unto it. Rarity is a marvellous *Lenocinium*, and inciter of Desire . . . strange things as they make stronger impressions upon the Retentive, so they do upon the Appetitive faculties.[59]

Reynolds's observation anticipates that of the Marquis de Sade, who later stated that 'beauty belongs to the sphere of the simple, the ordinary, whilst ugliness is something extraordinary, and there is no question but that every ardent imagination prefers in lubricity the extraordinary to the commonplace'.[60] Eighteenth-century philosophers of the aesthetic likewise incorporated the ugly into the sublime: 'Between beauty and ugliness there is a sort of mediocrity, in which the assigned proportions are most commonly found,' noted Edmund Burke, 'but this has no effect upon the passions.' Ugliness, meanwhile, provokes strong feelings: 'Ugliness I imagine likewise to be consistent enough with an idea of the sublime.'[61]

If God or nature can display creative genius through irregular or anomalous forms, generating pleasure in those who view them, so can the artist. In Ward's dissection of early eighteenth-century London life, *Satyrical Reflections on Clubs* (1710), the 'Club of Ugly Faces' overflows with 'uncooth-look'd Mortals' and 'Scare-crow Visages'. The founding member of this club, a 'Hatchet-fac'd Fellow' who 'lugg'd about with him at least two Pounds of Nose', is joined by a figure with 'a Mouth like a Gallon-Pot, when both sides are squeezed near close together', a man with 'as many Wens and Warts upon his Forehead as there are Knots and Prickles upon an old Thornback', a man with a 'Hair Lip, that had drawn his Mouth into as many Corners as a Minc'd Pye', and numerous other 'comical, clownish, surly, antick, moody, booby Faces'. Despite their repulsive appearance, the members of this club are said to be a source of inspiration for craftsmen who 'cut the Prints for the frightful Heads upon Stone Bottles' and carvers who 'notch out preposterous Cherubs upon Base-Viols'. Ugly faces, states Ward scathingly, are the 'new Originals', providing a 'Singularity' absent from the symmetrical sameness of the beautiful:

> Since British Ladies, skill'd in Features,
> Admire Dutch Dogs for handsome Creatures:
> And Men oft leave their beauteous Spouses,
> For nauseous Punks, and dowdy Blouzes:

> Why not great Fiddles please your Maids,
> For wearing strange prepost'rous Heads?
> Or Barber's Block be priz'd for having
> A phiz to humour Fools while shaving?
> For awkward Things effect the Eyes
> The most, by giving new Surprize.[62]

While Ward disapproves of the early modern taste for ugly representations, regarding it as evidence of a vulgar and degenerate culture, others defend the artistic merit of depicting ugly subjects. Leonardo da Vinci can see no reason why an artist should limit himself to the creation of beauty: 'if he wishes to see monstrous things that frighten, or those that are grotesque and laughable, or those that arouse real compassion, he is their lord and creator.'[63]

Even if ugly bodies in the flesh repel us, artistic depictions of these bodies have the potential to generate more ambivalent responses, not all of them negative. John Donne insists that art can make the ugly beautiful: 'doe wee not with pleasure behold the painted shape of Monsters and Divells', he contends, 'whom true, wee durst not regard?'[64] Aristotle argued that representations of the repellent could achieve a form of beauty: 'we enjoy contemplating the most precise images of things whose actual sight is painful to us, such as the forms of the vilest animals and of corpses.'[65] To Aristotle, the pleasure of viewing representations of ugly objects stems from the viewer's perception of the accuracy of the representation, a recognition of the skill of the artist which operates regardless of the subject matter in question. Aquinas agrees that 'an image is said to be beautiful, if it perfectly represents even an ugly thing.'[66] St Bonaventure elaborates on the theme, suggesting that a well executed depiction of the Devil can be beautiful, despite the intrinsic ugliness of this figure:

> Beauty refers to the model in such a way that it is to be found in the image too, and not solely in the subject that it represents.... the image is called beautiful when it is well painted, and it is also called beautiful when it is a good representation of the person whose image it is.... one [mode of beauty] can be present in the absence of the other: ... the image of the Devil is beautiful when it well represents the turpitude of the Devil and as a consequence of his aspect it is also repugnant.[67]

The argument that the pleasure, and hence the beauty, of art reside in the skill of the artist and the verisimilitude of his work rather than in the innate attractiveness of the subject matter leads to depictions of ugly subjects becoming limit cases for demonstrations of artistic ability. Leonardo insists that art must not seek to correct nature but must reproduce it in all its eccentricity: 'that painting is most praiseworthy which conforms most to the object portrayed. I put this forward to embarrass those painters who would improve on the works of nature.'[68] His grotesque drawings (e.g. Figure 3), ostensibly derived from his observations of real figures, give expression to this desire to capture the human form in all its potentially deformed variety rather than to be constrained by rigid canons of beauty.[69] These drawings

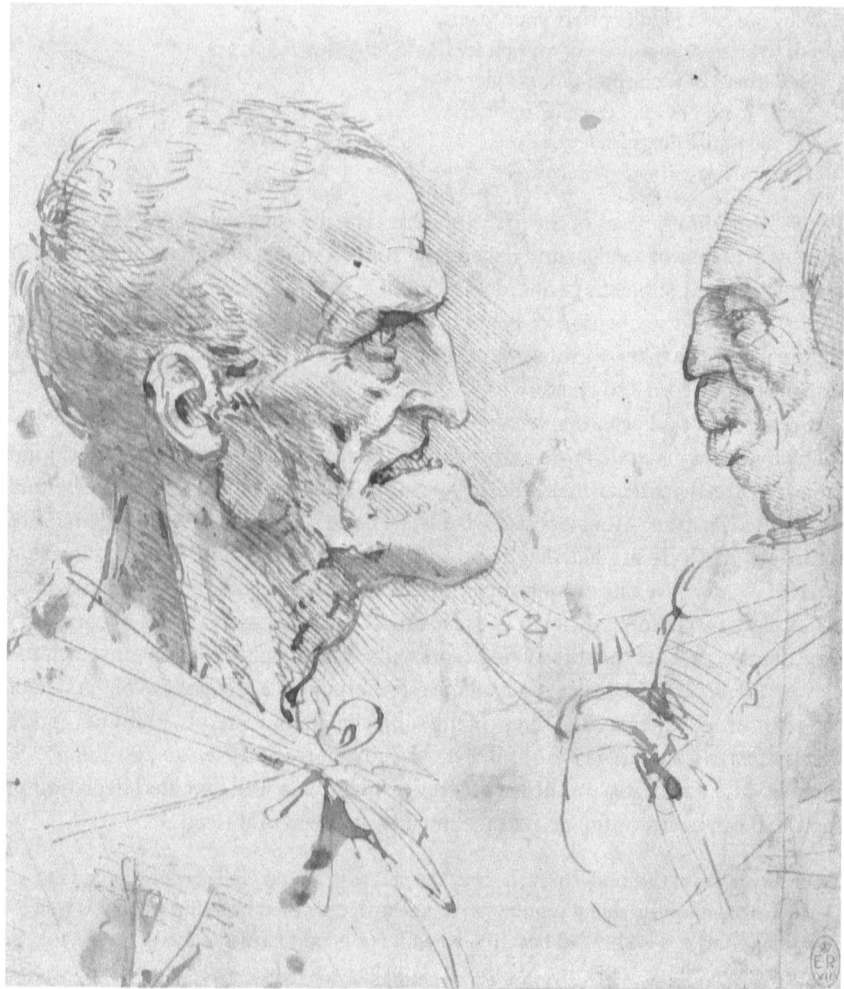

Figure 3 Leonardo da Vinci, *Two Grotesque Profiles Confronted, c.* 1485–90

were his most celebrated works in the seventeenth and eighteenth centuries, giving weight to his argument that an artist's reputation depends on his ability to depict nature truthfully, as well as illustrating the popular appeal of subjects which, when viewed in the flesh, might be expected to stimulate revulsion rather than delight.

Representations of unattractive bodies may generate pleasure, then, because of their accurate depiction of the world. Classical Renaissance aesthetics insisted that art must be true to nature, as Leonardo emphasised. Depictions of ugliness were one means of conforming to this dictum, of showing figures 'with roughnesse, pimples, warts, and everything', as Cromwell directed his portrait painter.[70] Lyly, in the prefatory material to *Euphues*, discusses the requirement for art to reflect reality in terms that make the representation of ugly features essential to a great work:

> Vulcan was painted curiously, yet with a polt foot; Leda cunningly, yet with her black hair. Alexander, having a scar in his cheek held his finger upon it that Apelles might not paint it. Apelles painted him with his finger cleaving to his face. 'Why,' quoth Alexander, 'I laid my finger on my scar because I would not have thee see it.' 'Yea,' said Apelles, 'and I drew it there because none else should perceive it, for if thy finger had been away, either thy scar would have been seen or my art misliked.' Whereby I gather that in all perfect works as well the fault as the face is to be shown. The fairest leopard is made with his spots, the finest cloth with his list[.] ... in every counterfeit as well the blemish as the beauty is coloured.... The Persians, who above all their kings most honoured Cyrus, caused him to be engraven as well with his hooked nose as his high forehead.[71]

The artist must incorporate the shade along with the light; as we have seen, the contrast between these elements is often seen as essential to the representation of beauty in this period. Through such juxtapositions, natural imperfections are incorporated into 'perfect works' of art.

As rule-bound classical Italian Renaissance aesthetics gave way to Mannerism, and later, in the seventeenth century, to Baroque, the creative power of the artistic imagination became ever more prominent in discussions of art and beauty.[72] Far from simply mirroring nature, creative genius was increasingly seen to be an alchemical force capable of transforming even (or perhaps especially) irregular forms into powerfully beautiful art. The fascination with anamorphic art, a genre which beguiles the viewer with fantastic distortions, illustrates the pleasure taken in wittily malformed representations in the seventeenth century.[73] The works of Arcimboldo, where human bodies are shaped out of non-human objects, suggesting strange and monstrous connections between different life forms, further illustrate the fashion for eccentric representations. Arcimboldo's *Winter* (1573) (Figure 4), according to Roland Barthes, depicts the face of a man who has just died, his lips a 'hypertrophied organ, cancerous and hideous'. *Autumn* (1573), meanwhile, is a 'sum of tumours: the surface is bibulous, turgescent: it is an enormous inflamed organ whose brown blood is becoming congested'. As Barthes observes, Arcimboldo's work 'disturbs and disaggregates the unitary development of form'. Echoing Bakhtin's description of the grotesque, 'Nature does not stop' in these figures, but multiplies, transgresses, protrudes, overtakes, inverting canons of beauty premised on closure, wholeness and the discrete, bounded self.[74] These images of excessive, diseased, decomposed and fragmented corporeality were nevertheless viewed with pleasure in the court of Rudolph II: 'in that milieu', as Tatarkiewicz comments, 'the *bizarre* was scarcely distinguished from the beautiful'.[75]

The delight generated by imaginative depictions of strange forms is also apparent in the grotesque style, an ancient ornamental art form depicting hybrid, monstrous figures that was revived in Renaissance Italy and mimicked across Europe in this

Figure 4 Giuseppe Arcimboldo, *Winter*, 1573

era.[76] The grotesque is by definition deformed, dissolving natural forms and categories, but this did not prevent it from being regarded by many in the early modern era as an appealing form of ornamentation.[77] Giovanni and Raphael were reportedly 'struck with amazement at the freshness, beauty and quality' of the grotesque.[78] Vasari meanwhile praised its beauty and inventiveness, while Inigo Jones introduced grotesque forms into his lavish, sensuous designs for seventeenth-century English masques.[79] The grotesque style was nevertheless viewed by others as a debased form of art.[80] For many, nature, not the imagination, remained the ultimate arbiter of beauty, and, in the words of Browne, there are 'no grotesques in nature'.[81] Vetruvius had condemned grotesque ornament: 'we now have fresco paintings of monstrosities, rather than truthful representations of definite things', and some Italian theorists echoed his disapproval of the unnatural and thus ugly forms.[82] Ben Jonson cites Vetruvius as he denounces the grotesque:

> he complaines of their painting Chimaera's, by the vulgar unaptly called Grottesque: saying, that men who were borne truly to study, and emulate nature, did nothing but make monsters against nature; which Horace so laught at.[83]

Variously celebrated and condemned, hybrid grotesque forms are characterised by the duality of response they evoke, encompassing both pleasure and disgust.[84] St Bernard captured the ambivalent status of the grotesque, implicitly acknowledging the sensuous appeal of ugly, unnatural forms of art even as he disapproved of their moral impact when he condemned the grotesque decorations of monasteries as 'deformed comeliness... comely deformity'.[85]

The equivocal delight generated by representations of ugly subjects is further apparent in the fashion for poetic celebrations of ugly women in seventeenth-century English poetry. 'Away with handsome faces, let me see/Hereafter nothing but deformity,' states James Shirley's 'To a Beautiful Lady' (1646), and John Donne, Thomas Carew and, most prolifically, John Collop, among other poets, participated in the trend for witty depictions of unattractive women.[86] As is typical of responses to representations of deformity, repugnance sits alongside enjoyment in the impact of these works. Far from genuinely praising the unattractive subject, or transforming her into an object of beauty, such depictions, as I discuss in Chapter 5, foreground the artist's creativity, titillating the reader through a demonstration of his ability to create an appealing work of art out of unpromising material. The beauty of the piece thus rests in the artist's display of his genius, his brilliance thrown into relief by the contrast between his lofty artistic achievement and the lowly, repellent subject of his work. Even when a representation of ugliness generates pleasure in the viewer, then, the status of the object as ugly is not necessarily called into question. The joke implied in the paradoxical praise of ugliness relies on the assumption that the reader and the author share the same definition of beauty, from which the subject described self-evidently deviates. Repulsion and admiration thus coexist in the response of the viewer to representations of ugly subjects, which rarely have a straightforward impact.

Multi-faceted responses to ugliness have long been elicited by Western religious visual arts. Medieval and Renaissance paintings often deploy ugliness as an instantly recognisable sign of evil. The tormentors of Christ in Bosch's representations of the Passion narrative, for instance, are depicted with monstrous appearances, their grotesquely distorted features, as James H. Marrow observes, giving visual form to biblical imagery describing the bestial natures of these persecutors (Figure 5).[87] Marrow nevertheless documents the manner in which the

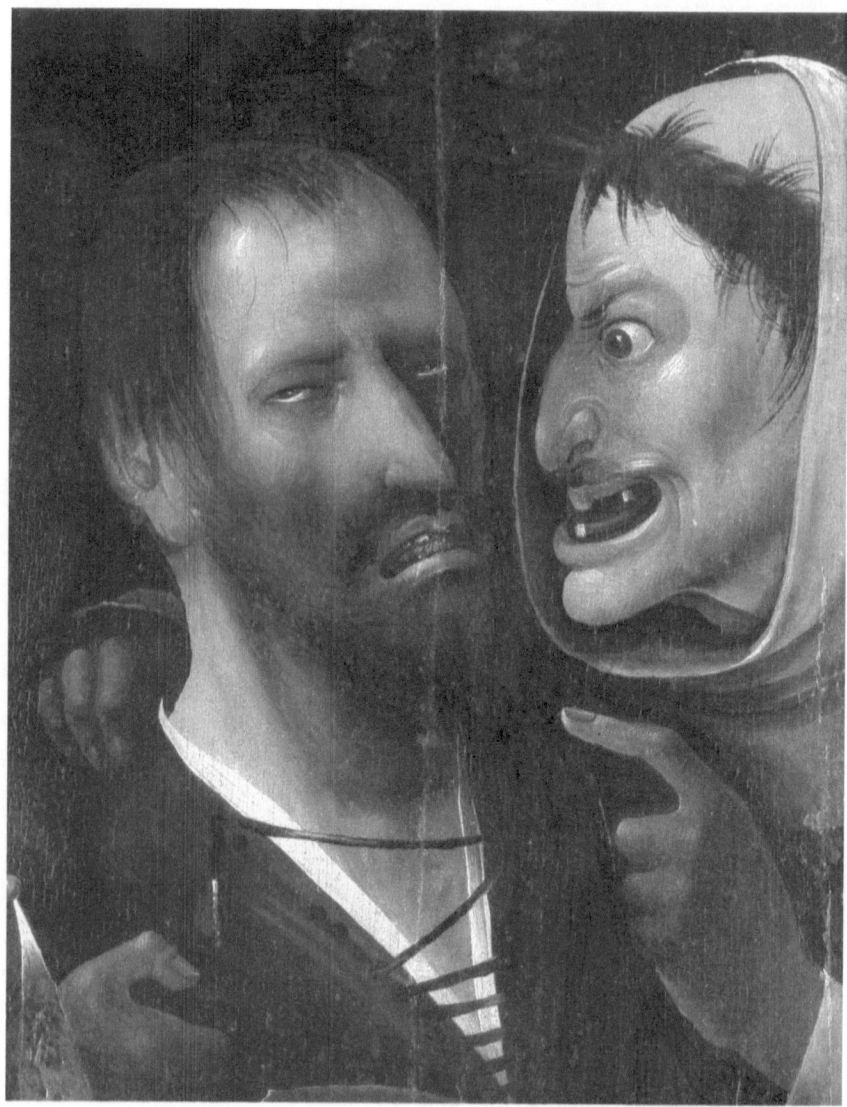

Figure 5 Hieronymus Bosch, *Christ Carrying the Cross* (detail), after 1500

'extraordinarily inventive expansion of passion imagery' in the late Middle Ages also emphasises the deformities of Christ's suffering body in order to provoke pathos in the viewer.[88] Instead of always being the embodiment of beauty, set against ugly persecutors, Christ is thus sometimes depicted in accordance with the Old Testament description of the Messiah as a figure with 'no beauty in him, nor comeliness' (Isaiah 53.2). Marrow notes that late medieval and early Renaissance depictions of Christ from the Low Countries in particular repeatedly draw on biblical accounts of the Messiah as scapegoat, an outcast described in Isaiah 53.4 as being 'like a leper' (Figure 6).

As Harald Hendrix demonstrates, many Neapolitan works of art from the first half of the sixteenth century also depict 'repulsive' portraits of Christian saints. The paintings of Jusepe de Ribera, for instance, in which the tortured, distorted figures of saints glare 'provocatively' at the viewer, stimulating admiration as well as horror, exemplify a 'taste for disturbing images' in this era.[89] Representations of both Christ's and the saints' twisted and suffering bodies are designed to evoke pity and devotion in their viewers: rather than simply provoking disgust, ugly bodies in this context arrest the observer's attention and elicit a spiritually edifying response.

The Reformation cast Passion iconography along with all forms of devotional visual representation in a suspicious light, so that the piety inspired by disfigured representations of Christ and the saints had no easy place in post-Reformation England. George Lauder's translation *The Anatomie of the Romane Clergie* (1623) mocks the role of visual representations of the broken body of Christ in Roman Catholicism, highlighting 'papist' devotion to images of suffering: 'O Sonne of God, why see I now thy face,/With bloudie wounds deformed all about/And skin so rent with scarres in every place.'[90] Representations of mutilated bodies nevertheless continue to be deployed in the service of Protestantism, most notably in the gruesome literary vignettes and woodcuts of John Foxe's *Actes and Monuments* (1563). Foxe rejects the sanctity surrounding the body of the martyr in Roman Catholic accounts, on the whole refusing to depict Protestant martyrs in miraculous or supernatural terms.[91] He nevertheless exploits the dramatic potential of spectacular torture to the full, using the saints' patient endurance of graphically depicted physical suffering as a means of testifying to the purity of the Protestant faith. Fuller, a moderate Church of England clergyman, muses in his popular work *The Holy State* on the positive emotions potentially evoked by the sight of the mutilated bodies of the godly:

> Confessours which wear the badges of truth are thereby made the more beautifull; though deformed in time of Persecution for Christs sake through mens malice. This made Constantine the Great to kisse the hole in the face of Paphnutius, out of which the Tyrant Maximinus had bored his eye for the profession of the faith, the good Emperour making much of the socket even when the candle was put out.[92]

A fierce opponent of the civil wars, Fuller expresses his horror of intolerance through his gruesome depiction of the physical consequences of tyranny and persecution. His identification of tortured bodies bearing 'badges of truth' draws on pre-Reformation iconographic traditions in which such bodies evoke devotion from those who view them, generating a desire to 'kisse' the disfigured forms as the pious context transforms repellent features into marks of beauty. Though the bodies of those suffering for their faith are 'Scar'd or Dismembred', notes 'N.H.', whose entry

Figure 6 Matthias Grünewald, Isenheim altarpiece (detail), c. 1512–15

on 'Deformity' in *The Ladies Dictionary* (1694) draws heavily on Fuller's tract, 'they look more Beautiful in the Eyes of their Maker, and likewise in the Esteem of all Good Men and Women'.[93] To John Donne, likewise, in 'What if this present were the worlds last night?', Christ's lacerated body remains a 'beauteous forme'.[94]

The compassion potentially evoked by representations of the twisted bodies of Christ and the saints and which Leonardo had envisaged as a possible response to the depiction of unattractive features was nevertheless in short supply outside of particular religious contexts in the early modern era. '[C]onsider the discomfort of Deformitie,' Bedford urges his congregation in response to the birth of conjoined twins in 1635, '[h]ow liable it is daily to exprobation through the evil custome of wicked men, more ready to cast it in the teeth, than condole or commiserate it, if God hath stampt a deformity upon the Bodie'.[95] Instead of eliciting pity, depictions of ugliness were likely to provoke laughter.[96] Antonio Tempesta, an Italian graphic artist, includes comically deformed figures among his popular designs (Figure 7).[97]

Ugly faces are repeatedly referred to as a laughing matter in early modern texts from across Europe.[98] Samuel Johnson's *Dictionary* (1755) defines deformity as 'the quality of something worthy to be laughed at'.[99] Ben Jonson notes that 'a wry face without pain moves laughter, or a deformed vizard',[100] echoing Aristotle, who remarked that laughter is generated by 'any fault or mark of shame which involves no pain or destruction: most obviously, the laughable mask is something ugly and twisted, but not painfully'.[101] Laurent Joubert's *Traite du Ris* (*Treatise on Laughter*) (1579) agrees: 'ugly things, unworthy of sympathy, are what we laugh at'. The laughter generated by unsightliness does not indicate that the ugly is simply pleasurable, however. As Joubert notes, 'inasmuch as laughter is caused by something ugly, it does not proceed from pure joy, but has some small part of sadness'.[102] Sir Philip Sidney, in *An Apology for Poetry* (c. 1581–83, publ. 1595), highlights the ambivalent, conflicted laughter generated by 'deformed creatures':

> Delight hath a joy in it, either permanent or present. Laughter hath only a scornful tickling. For example, we are ravished with delight to see a fair woman, and yet are far from being moved to laughter. We laugh at deformed creatures wherein certainly we cannot delight[.][103]

The laughter directed at the physically distorted or blemished in the early modern era thus differs from the renewing, inclusive, life-affirming laughter theorised by Bakhtin as an essential element of the grotesque.[104] Instead of being a form of laughter that includes all within its scope, this laughter is directed at the ugly body, which is satirised and mocked as an object of repugnance and contempt. *The Ladies Dictionary* sympathises with those whose 'want of Beauty . . . breeds discontent of mind': 'Some had as lieve not be at all, as be much deformed, to be made a Mock and Jest of by the unthinking Vulgar, or the sorted pretending Criticks in Beauty'.[105] Dryden is less compassionate. Comedies aim to 'produce laughter; which is occasion'd by the sight of some deformity', he notes. Burlesque poetry, moreover,

Theorising ugliness

Figure 7 Antonio Tempesta, 'The amorous Angelica' and 'The most beautiful Diana', *The Twelve Principal Roman Heroes and Heroines Drawn in a Grotesque Manner*, c. 1597

is like a picture of a deformed woman, 'as in that of a Lazar, or of a fool with distorted face and antique gestures, at which we cannot forbear to laugh, because it is a deviation from Nature'.[106] Laughing at ugliness in the early modern era is thus inextricable from the brutal condemnation and exclusion of those labelled ugly.[107]

Shadowing the laughter (and in many cases inseparable from it) is the fear prompted by the ugly, particularly in an era when irregular or monstrous forms are potentially identified as divine portents, signs of evil or of imminent judgement. Protestantism insisted that the inner truth of an individual did not necessarily accord with his or her outward appearance, but the belief that physical characteristics testified to the condition of the soul persisted in some quarters, and was taught from many pulpits, even after the Reformation. As Julie Crawford notes in her study of monstrous births, at a popular level 'physiognomy took on a kind of predestinarian legibility'.[108] In John Sadler's *The Sick Womans Private Looking-glasse* (1636), for instance, 'the outward deformity of the body' is said to be 'a signe of the polution of the heart, as a curse layd upon the child for the parents incontinency'.[109] If God lays upon us or our children 'the black-finger of Deformity', concurs Bedford in his sermon on the conjoined twins, he has 'written in great Letters the guilt of Sin, and in a deformed Body drawn a resemblance of the Soules deformity'.[110] In keeping with his equation of beauty with holiness, William Laud reportedly discouraged James Shirley, later a playwright and poet, from entering holy office because of a facial disfigurement: 'having a broad or large mole upon his left cheek, which some esteemed a deformity, that worthy Doctor would often tell him that he was an unfit Person to take the sacred function upon him, and should never have his consent so to do'.[111] Ugly bodies were thus by no means necessarily silent in this era. Deformed children are 'the subject matter, on which [God] stampeth the markes of his Providence', pronounces Bedford. '[A]ll monstrous and misshapen births,' he continues, 'though dead, yet speake for the Instruction of the Living.' Not all, he concedes, see the 'speciall hand of God' in deviant bodies. Some posit natural causes for deformity, while astrologers and philosophers work according to their own interpretive paradigms, citing 'reason' rather than looking 'higher' for spiritual causes. The 'common sort', meanwhile, often fail to recognise that the ugly body 'speaketh' at all, caught up as they are in its entertainment value: they 'make no further use of these Prodigies and Strange-births, than as a matter of wonder and table-talk'.[112] The meanings of deformity, though potentially ominous, then, are far from transparent. Even Bedford cannot reach a stable interpretation of the conjoined twins, deploying their malformed bodies as a symbol of brotherly unity as well as insisting that they are a manifestation of original sin. He is nevertheless certain that '[t]hese Births ... though dead, yet speake and preach to the world'.[113] Whether operating as evidence of God's or nature's playful creativity, as a stimulus for devotion or mockery or as a mark of sin, ugliness, for many, is a legible sign.

Despite the persistence in some quarters of the perceptions of ugliness discussed so far in this chapter, a new model of nature was nevertheless beginning to emerge in the seventeenth century in which regularity, order and symmetry displaced anomaly and eccentricity as meaningful, pleasurable qualities. With the dawn of the era of mechanical philosophy, definitions of ugliness, as well as the responses it generated, were to alter radically.

'Nature's ill-shap'd letters':[114] mechanical philosophy

Robert Boyle summarises the 'vulgar notion of nature' in the following terms:

> Nature is a most wise Being, that does nothing in vain, does not miss of her Ends; does always that which ... is best to be done[.]

To Boyle, however, advocate of the new mechanical philosophy, nature is neither so perfect nor so conscious a being. It is instead a passive, inanimate entity, a 'Compounded Machine' or a 'great Automaton' set in motion by a creator who does not intervene in its operations. The universe is 'like a rare Clock, such as may be that at Strasbourg',

> where all things are so skilfully contriv'd, that the Engine being once set a Moving, all things proceed according to the Artificers first design, and the Motions of the little Statues ... do not require, like those of Puppets, the peculiar interposing of the Artificer, or any Intelligent Agent imployed by him, but perform their functions upon particular occasions, by vertue of the General and Primitive Contrivance of the whole Engine.[115]

The mechanical model of the universe means that local anomalies are no longer celebrated as positive, even beautiful, instances of God's or nature's creative ingenuity. By the end of the seventeenth century, beauty is instead beginning to be equated with the principles of order and regularity believed to underpin natural processes. This emerging 'aesthetics of uniformity' has the effect of identifying all irregularities as ugly.[116] Most of nature is regular, insists Boyle, and mechanical philosophy generates a sense of wonder at the general subservience of brute matter to the elegantly ordered laws of nature. Instances of disorder, where they occur, however, are repugnant. Early proponents of mechanical philosophy do not hold identical perspectives on the meaning and nature of material ugliness. In Boyle's writing, local instances of ugliness are the inevitable by-products of the operations of the laws of nature. Elsewhere, as for example in the Hebraist John Spencer's defence of natural philosophy, ugly chaos characterises a nature innately prone to disorder, whose general conformity to mechanical laws is the result of direct divine intervention. Whether ugliness is the product of the laws of nature or the result of those moments where nature eludes such laws, however, it is now regarded as morally opaque, devoid of legible intent.

Boyle confronts questions of the beauty of the universe in his *Free Enquiry* (1686), asking 'Whether the world, and the Creatures that compose it, are as perfect as they could be made?' Clearly not, he concludes: 'it seems manifest, that many sorts of Creatures might have been more perfect than they are, since they want many compleating things, that others are indow'd with'. We need to reformulate the question, however, away from 'whether God could have made more perfect Creatures', to 'whether the Creatures were not so curiously and skilfully made, that 'twas scarce possible they could have been better made, with due regard to all the wise Ends He may be suppos'd to have had in making them'. God did not set out to create a natural order in which every detail was perfect or beautiful. He instead set in motion a universe whose laws as a whole work according to his intended design. Likening the universe to a passive, inanimate object, Boyle insists that 'the Plain Watch' answers 'the Artificer's Idea and Design in making it, as well as the more Compounded and Elaborate one did'. He also compares nature to divine handwriting, emphasising that an author is concerned with the functional purpose of his script rather than its aesthetic value. The divine inscriber did not intend to make each hand 'as Curious, Sightly and Flourishing as he could, but as Conformable to the true Idea of the sort of Hand he meant to exhibit'. Any attempt to prioritise beauty over functionality would have compromised his purposes: 'if he should have made a Text-Hand as fair as a Roman-Hand, by giving it more Beauty and Ornament, he would not have made it better in its Kind, but spoil'd it'.[117] Beauty, now defined in ornamental terms, is thus sharply distinguished from utility. Rational design, in other words, no longer precludes ugliness.

Margaret Cavendish likewise insists that the natural or functional is not necessarily beautiful. 'Some say there are no Monsters nor ugly Creatures in Nature,' she states, 'for a Toad, a Spider, or the like, are as beautifull Creatures in Nature, if it be according to their kind, as the lovelyest Man or Woman.' Such claims, she asserts, are patently ridiculous:

> a right-shap'd Toad may be of an ill favoured kind, as not being so handsom a kind as Mankind, or many other kinds of Animals; for I never heard any Poetical high expression of the Commendation of a Toad, as to say, that is a most beautiful, amiable, sweet, lovely Toad.

Ugliness, to Cavendish, is not precluded by fitness for purpose. It is instead defined by more objective material properties. The beautiful, she assumes, is the symmetrical: 'that which is ugly, is that which is deformed, and that is deformed that is misshapen, and that is misshapen, that is made crooked, or awry, or one part bigger or less than another'.[118]

Mechanical philosophy therefore radically reformulates the relationship between ugliness and the natural order. Rather than insisting that all natural phenomena participate in a fundamentally beautiful universe, Boyle presents nature as a blind, impersonal machine, indifferent to the local instances of ugliness that are occasionally generated by its conformity to immutable, divinely imposed laws. The author of all things 'comprehended, at once, the whole System of His Works', imposing laws for the good of the whole even though they sometimes produced abhorrent effects.

Divine provision 'is made with reference to what regularly, or what most usually, happens', states Boyle, 'not with regard to such things as may happen . . . irregularly, contingently, and (in comparison of the others) unfrequently'. The machine has been left to run its course, generating monstrous births and 'other Anomalies' which are 'not repugnant to the Catholick Laws of the Universe' even though they may seem to us to be 'mischievous Irregularities'.[119] Ugliness, then, is no longer the antithesis of divine design, but is its dark underside.[120]

The ugliness of much of nature is crucial to Boyle's argument, allowing him to emphasise the impersonal operation of the universe. In a model of nature governed by an interventionist deity (either God or Nature), every detail of the created order is infused with divine rationale. The purposive beauty subsequently seen to characterise every corner of the material world is far from obvious to Boyle, however. 'Nature seems to do Her Work very weakly, or bunglingly, in the Production of Monsters,' he sneers,

> whose Variety and Numerousness is almost as great as their Deformity, or their Irregularity; insomuch that several Volums have been written, and many more might have been, to give the Description of them. How these gross Aberrations will agree with that . . . exquisite Skill, that is ascrib'd to Nature, in her seminal Productions, I leave the Naturists to make out[.]

Rather than viewing 'gross Aberrations' as beautiful, meaningful instances of divine plenitude, he insists on their ugliness, using them as evidence that natural processes are immutably fixed, regardless of particular outcomes. Nature is just as likely to generate disease and disorder as it is to produce 'fit Colours, taking Features, just Stature, fine Shape, graceful Motions, and . . . other Accidents of the Human Body and its Parts'.

> Thus we see, that not only Wens and Scrophulous Tumours are nourish'd in the Body, but mis-shapen Mola's do by Nutriment grow in the Womb, as well as Embryo's feed there. . . . in Wounds, Proud-Flesh, and perhaps Fungus's, are as well produc'd and entertain'd by the Aliment brought to the wounded Part, as the true and genuine Flesh . . . . Nature is not so shy and reserv'd in Her Bounty, but that She sends Nourishment, to repair as well Things that do not belong to the Body, as genuine Parts of It . . . . I have seen a Woman, in whose Forehead Nature was careful to nourish a Horn, about an Inch and more in length.[121]

John Spencer, fellow of Corpus Christi, Cambridge, and proponent of natural philosophy, similarly insists on the naturalness of the ugly. Ugliness, to Spencer, is more natural, in fact, than is beauty. 'Natures ill-shap'd letters', as he describes instances of irregularity in *A Discourse Concerning Prodigies* (1663), are nature's own production,

> an assurance that she could not write so fairly and evenly as generally, had she not some Great Master to guide her hand, and bind in the powers of some causes apt to

exorbitate and flie out.... The exorbitances of Natural causes at sometimes, and their running (like unruly horses) out of that way ... resolve us that their general stillness and order is owing to Him who rideth upon the Heavens, whose Wisdom and power moderates all their blind impetuous forces.

When apparent aberrations occur, nature is not being acted upon by a force or consciousness external to the material order. In these instances, instead, 'nature suffers from it self, and is (in a sort) both victour and captive to its self'. Material deviations are no longer signs of divine intervention or even the conscious playfulness of nature, but illustrate the absence of such intervention or intent. 'There will perhaps appear more of Nature in a Prodigy, then in the more harmonious consort of Uniform Agents, to which common usage hath appropriated that name,' he observes.

> That nature in its production of the several kinds of creatures, should (as if they were all stampt with one common seal) give them forth in such equal and similar figures and proportions, is a more just object of wonder, then to see the natural Archeus sometimes to play the bungler, and to leave its work ... rude and misshapen.[122]

It is order and regularity, then, not anomaly and disorder, which are meaningful and awe-inspiring, pointing to a divine creator. The 'rude and misshapen', by contrast, are divested of any meaning or transcendent truth. To Hutcheson,

> that mind must be weak and inadvertent which needs [miracles] to confirm the belief of a wise and good Deity, since the deviation from general laws, unless upon very extraordinary occasions, must be a presumption of inconstancy and weakness, rather than steady wisdom and power, and must weaken the best arguments we have for the sagacity and power of the universal mind.

The equation of deviation with 'inconstancy and weakness' while order and regularity display 'wisdom and power', reveals the extent to which beauty is now defined in uniform, ordered terms. That which transgresses such ideals is repulsive: the disproportionate 'never fails to pass for an imperfection and want of beauty'.[123]

Within mechanical philosophy, ugliness is only meaningful in so far as it sheds light on the operations of the natural order. 'Seeming Anomalies', as Boyle terms them, are not, in the end, anomalous. That which appears incongruous, he states, the 'Cyphers' in the divine script that we have yet to decode, may in the end be seen to fit with 'the plainest Parts of the Epistle'.[124] Irregularities are part of the same script as the rest of nature, and therefore have the potential to be made subject to human knowledge. Their meanings, when we discover them, will relate to the nature of which they are a part, however, rather than to any transcendent order. Anomalies 'serve to lead us into a more distinct knowledge of the works of Nature', asserts Spencer: 'like tortur'd men', she 'discovers her secrets, when ... disturb'd'.[125] Ugliness is of no intrinsic interest: its sole value lies in its potential to illuminate the normative and the beautiful. 'He that knows the ways of Nature, he shall with more ease observe its deviations,' claims Bacon, '[a]nd again, he that understands its Deviations can better discover its ordinary ways and methods.'[126]

While mechanical philosophy works from the premise that all natural phenomena can ultimately be made subject to human understanding, the move towards a natural rather than a supernatural or moral interpretation of ugliness has the effect of rendering the uncomely body more opaque, less available for ready interpretation. When a repellent body was seen to be a legible text inscribed with divine signatures, the door was open for confident assertions of its significance. Addressing those credulous enough to give weight to physiognomy, Spencer warns the gullible masses that those who 'read and expound all the cryptick lines in your hands and face' are asserting 'an ability to know ... which hath the power of fascination upon weaker minds'. Spencer insists that deformed bodies are not as transparently legible as some would have us believe. He derides in particular the widespread belief that physical prodigies warn of impending judgement, scornfully asking whether we must 'look for such a Jewel as the intimations of the counsels of infinite Wisdom ... in the dunghill of obscene and monstrous births'. 'It is rashness to say the tree was rotten, because we see it blasted,' he argues, mocking those who claim that aberrant bodies are 'stampt with some Characters and touches of Divinity'. For the perceptive, implicitly, the deviant body is obtuse, perhaps holding the key to a deeper understanding of natural laws, yet not easily reducible to a single meaning. Ugliness, along with other apparently anomalous natural events, resists simple interpretation: 'if God do write *Fata hominum* in these mystick characters, there is none on earth found able to read the writing, and (with any certainty) to make known the interpretation thereof'.[127] Bacon agrees, attacking the doctrine of correspondences for 'dreaming up mutual imitations' based only on the 'obvious and superficial qualities of things'. Appearances cannot be conflated with reality, he warns: '[t]he evidence drawn from things is like a mask cloaking reality and needs careful sifting'.[128]

While ugly objects will ultimately shed light on the natural laws which have produced them, instances where nature appears to deviate from her ordinary course are in the end a reminder of the limitations of our understanding. 'Is it so great an inconvenience,' asks Spencer, 'to admit of some passages in the book of the creature, of which we are not scholars good enough to make a right and proper construction?'[129] It is the credulous, those who believe in the supernatural significance of prodigious or irregular occurrences, who jump to simple interpretations of the ugly or the anomalous. For the elite proponents of the new, rational science, any reliable interpretation of a specific instance of ugliness or apparent aberration demands a complete understanding of the laws of the universe, and is therefore, for the meantime at least, out of reach. Ugliness is natural, claim early expressions of mechanical philosophy, ultimately subject to human understanding, but not, for the time being, readily comprehensible. Science, maybe, would ultimately account for every visible irregularity of the flesh, but this project had only recently been initiated, and for the time being raised as many questions as it answered.

Spencer's scathing assault on the supernatural interpretation of prodigies illustrates the widening gap between popular and elite understandings of deformity in the latter half of the seventeenth century. Spencer is well aware that his rational approach is not shared by the majority, not even, necessarily, at Cambridge.[130] Whatever natural philosophers might say to the contrary, an ugly body continues to be interpreted as a marker of corruption, evil and danger into the eighteenth century and beyond. Thomas Knagg's early eighteenth-century sermon, for instance, proclaims that through 'barbarous desires' '[b]oth Body and Soul become odious and deformed'.[131] It would nevertheless be an oversimplification to attribute different interpretations of the significance of ugliness merely to divergences of opinion between social groups.[132] Confusions regarding the meaning of ugliness are frequently visible at the level of individual authors and texts, as I shall explore in the following chapter.

Despite the inconsistent statements of its early proponents, mechanical philosophy potentially transformed the terms in which ugliness was defined, interpreted and represented in this era. Insisting that the beauty of the universe lay in its rigid conformity to natural laws, all instances of apparent deviation became repellent while simultaneously being divested of transcendent meaning. The ordered universe opened up by natural philosophy inspired wonder in many, but its vision of an automatic, impersonal order in which ugly deformities are meaninglessly generated alongside beautiful forms also disturbingly undermined popular certainties regarding the legibility and significance of the natural order, including the human body. Literature, as we shall see, was one of the sites where such philosophical shifts were scrutinised and negotiated.

2

'Charactered in my brow':[1] deciphering ugly faces

Does an ugly face reveal a corrupt soul? Answers to this question in early modern England are strikingly various. Towards the earlier part of the era, the term 'character' refers to 'a face or features as betokening moral qualities'.[2] Persuading Techelles to join his camp, Marlowe's Tamburlaine, for instance, states that 'by characters graven in thy brows/And by thy martial face and stout aspect/[thou] Deserv'st to have the leading of an host'.[3] From the mid-seventeenth century, however, 'character' begins to denote 'moral and mental qualities', properties that are not necessarily linked to or visible in the body.[4] The body, in other words, is no longer held to be a transparent sign of the self. The belief that ugliness reaches beyond the physical order, representing a spiritual and moral malaise made tangible in the unattractive object, nevertheless proves remarkably persistent. While divisions between elite and popular opinions account for some contemporary differences of outlook, contradictory perspectives are often put forward by single authors, indicating a more complicated picture. Allusions to the mark of Cain in sermons and texts from the era, for instance, betray incompatible views of the significance of ugly bodies. Cain's blemish, a physical emblem of divine judgement, becomes a useful figure for those articulating a clear position in the religious and political schisms of the era, suggesting that perpetrators of evil are readily identifiable. Despite the reassuring implication that the morally corrupt cannot hide their 'naughtiness',[5] however, the symbolic meanings of the mark of Cain refuse to be stabilised, suggesting the wider difficulties encountered by those who seek to impose moral readings of the ugly body in this period. George Chapman's *Bussy D'Ambois* (c. 1603–04, publ. 1607), as we shall see later in the chapter, also exhibits an ambivalent perspective on the meaning of bodily appearances, placing emergent models of an indifferent natural order generating meaningless material forms in tension with residual philosophies of a morally transparent physical realm.

'A man may look a sentence'[6]

Ugliness, as we have seen, has a long tradition of being identified as a deviation from a natural, divinely created order and thus being linked with sin. In Neoplatonic thought, physical beauty is a manifestation of the beauty and goodness of Ideal Form. 'A good exterior springs from a beauty dominant within', states Plotinus.[7] Although physical charms are only shadows of true beauty, they have the potential to awaken desire for the spiritual beauty which is their source. These paradigms are influential in medieval formulations of beauty and ugliness, where the beauty of the body is repeatedly said to reveal an underlying goodness.[8] Bernard of Clairvaux describes the manner in which spiritual beauty irradiates the body:

> The body is an image of the mind, which, like an effulgent light scattering forth its rays, is diffused through its members and senses, shining through in action, discourse, appearance, movement[.][9]

Bernard's own appearance was said to illustrate this model. Despite his 'meagre and emaciated' frame,

> His body was marked by a certain grace rather spiritual than bodily . . . . Such was the beauty of the inner man, that it brake forth by manifest tokens to the sight, and even the outer man seemed bedewed with the abundance of his inward purity and grace.[10]

Within Neoplatonic structures, then, beauty is a spiritual quality, aligned with goodness, which can nevertheless be made visible in the material realm. Spenser's 'An Hymne in Honour of Beautie' (1596) draws on Neoplatonic discourses to establish a connection between physical and spiritual beauty:

> So every spirit, as it is more pure,
> And hath in it the more of heavenly light,
> So it the fairer bodie doth procure
> To habit bin, and it more fairely dight
> With cheerful grace and amiable sight;
> For of the soule the bodie forme doth take;
> For soule is forme, and doth the bodie make.[11]

While a beautiful body exhibits a pure soul, an ugly body is less easy to interpret in Neoplatonic terms. To Plotinus, an 'ugly thing' is 'something that has not been entirely mastered by pattern, that is by Reason, the Matter not yielding at all points and in all respects to Ideal Form'.[12] Resisting principles of reason and goodness, an ugly body may be at odds with the nature of the spirit within, as Spenser's 'Hymne' suggests:

> Yet oft it falles, that many a gentle mynde
> Dwels in deformed tabernacle drownd
> Either by chaunce, against the course of kynd,
> Or through unaptnesse in the substance fownd,
> Which it assumed of some stubborne grownd,
> That will not yield unto her formes direction,
> But is perform'd with some foule imperfection.[13]

The fact that deformed bodies, less 'apt' to be moulded by rational Form, are 'stubborne', refusing to 'yield' to the spirit, nevertheless attributes a moral culpability that undermines the suggestion that the 'foule imperfection' of the deformed may be a purely surface phenomenon. Bodies, as well as souls, in this poem, are moral agents, responsible for their receptivity, or otherwise, to principles of rationality, order and goodness. While ostensibly dissociating the deformed body from the nature of the soul within, Spenser's poem in fact perpetuates the widespread association of physical ugliness with evil character. A 'gentle mynde' may in theory be able to resist the contaminating influence of a 'deformed tabernacle', but it seems more likely that it will ultimately be 'infected with the taint of body'.[14] Resisting the shape of things as they should be, physical ugliness in Neoplatonic thought is largely synonymous with moral perversion.

The association of ugly bodies with evil in early modern English culture is also rooted in Christian doctrines of the Fall, in which the originally perfect, beautiful creation is said to have become both morally and physically deformed as a result of Adam's sin. The Bible states that man (and woman, although many in this era were less sure of this doctrine) is made in the image of God, and describes the body as a potential 'temple of the Holy Spirit'.[15] After the Reformation, however, and particularly within the Calvinist orthodoxy of the early seventeenth-century Church of England, the depraved, fallen condition of human nature received greater emphasis than did its potential holiness. Following the Fall, writes Calvin, nature is marked by 'uggly deformitie'.[16] By the 'uggly deformitie' of the 'flesh' (a term for human nature including, although not limited to, the body) Calvin is referring primarily to its moral status: even the superficially attractive would fall into this category. The fallen status of the flesh is nevertheless described in vividly material terms in sermons and texts from this era, in which repellent bodies are repeatedly identified as evidence of sinful corruption. '[W]e cannot conceive ... Deformity was made on purpose, but by cross Accidents obstructing Nature in her Operation,' states *The Ladies Dictionary*. Ugly bodies are by definition fallen bodies: 'in the Resurrection all Deformity shall be done away, the recollected Dust shall shape a perfect Body'.[17] 'True beauty in any Creature, is not to be found,' declares Sanderson in *Graphice*, 'being full of deformed disproportions, far remote from truth; for Sinne is the cause of deformity'.[18]

John Donne's sermons graphically highlight the marks of the Fall in the unattractive human body. 'Those Gummes, and spices, which should embalme thy flesh, when thou art dead, are spent upon that diseased body whilest thou art alive', he berates his congregation:

> Thou seemest, in the eye of the world, to walk in silks, and thou doest but walke in searcloth; Thou hast a desire to please some eyes, when thou has much to doe, not to displease every Nose; and thou wilt solicite an adulterous entrance into their beds, who, if they should but see thee goe into thine own bed, would need no other mortification, nor answer to thy solicitation. Thou pursuest thy works of the flesh, and hast

none, for thy flesh is but dust held together by plaisters: Dissolution and putrefecation is gone over thee alive; Thou hast over liv'd thine own death, and art become thine own ghost, and thine own hell.[19]

Donne's nauseating description of fallen bodies as rotting corpses illustrates the abject status of the flesh within Protestant frameworks. A principle of death in life, the flesh, identified in this sermon with the skin, is at once the physical border of the self and the site where both the body and the self break down. Kristeva identifies the corpse as a figure of 'fundamental pollution': 'if the corpse is waste, transitional matter, it is above all the opposite of the spiritual, of the symbolic, and of divine law'. The corpse dismantles boundaries between the self and the other, betraying the subject's terrifying lack of distinction from the material order: it is a 'decaying body, lifeless, completely turned into dejection, blurred between the inanimate and inorganic, a transitional swarming.... A body without soul, a non-body, disquieting matter, it is to be excluded from God's territory'.[20] Donne similarly evokes the horrific annihilation of identity represented by the corpse, warning that we will be 'mingled with the dust of every high way, and of every dunghill, and swallowed in every puddle and pond; This is the most inglorious and contemptible vilification, the most deadly and peremptory nullification of man, that we can consider'.[21] Rather than a future event, however, he insists that the rotting of our flesh through which our identity is nullified has already taken place. Death and life horrifically coexist in the fallen condition, in which our decomposing flesh, perpetually transgressing its own boundaries, is characterised by an ugliness which represents both a fallen identity and the loss of identity itself. Far from burying the abject figure of the corpse in order to identify the self in opposition as discrete, pure and whole, Donne's sermons symbolically excavate it, throwing back the 'silks' to reveal the decomposing body beneath. Through uncovering the repulsiveness of their bodies, Donne convinces his congregation of the fallen state of their souls.

Unattractive bodies thus have a long philosophical and theological history of being interpreted and represented in moralised terms. Classical rhetorical traditions invoked physical features as signs of moral character, praising the bodily beauty of the virtuous while verbally dissecting repellent bodies in order to encourage disgust for those deemed vicious.[22] Medieval literature follows in this rhetorical tradition, maintaining an almost inevitable relationship between physical unattractiveness and evil. 'The primary function of hideousness in the literature of the Middle Ages,' states Henrik Specht, 'may be summed up as that of arousing aesthetic disgust and moral aversion against the person (or being) who is described as physically repulsive.'[23] In *Wisdom*, for instance, Anima 'apperythe in the most horrybull wyse, fowlere then a fende', embodying her corruption by Lucifer. Her face unambiguously reflects her soul: 'Se howe ye have dysvyguryde yowr soule!/Beholde youwrselff; loke veryly in mynde!'[24] Gregory the Great further articulates the commonplace medieval identification of the physically ugly with the fallen natural order:

The crookbacked is one who is weighed down by the burden of earthly cares, so that he never looks up to the things that are above, but is wholly intent on what is underfoot in the lowest sphere. If at any time he hears something good about the heavenly fatherland, he is so weighed down by the burden of evil habit, that he does not raise up the face of his heart; he just cannot lift up the cast of his thought, being kept bowed down by his habitual earthly solicitude.[25]

Physical defect here associates its bearer with the tainted realm of matter, set against the beautiful spiritual order.

It is not until the early modern era, Susanne Fendler argues, that the 'allegorical meaning of beauty', namely the idea that beauty is 'a reflection of God's perfection in human beings', begins to be dismantled, as 'the existence of a transcendent referent, that is of a higher or hidden 'truth' behind earthly concepts, [is] increasingly questioned or even denied'.[26] An ugly body nevertheless often continues to be interpreted as a sign of a morally corrupt nature in the early modern period. 'Man is read in his face,' states Jonson.[27] '[I]n a faire body, I doe seldome suspect a disproportioned minde, and as seldome hope for a good in a deformed,' agrees Donne: 'from a ruinous weather-beaten building I turn away, because it seems either stuff'd with varlets as a Prison, or handled by an unworthy and negligent tenant, that so suffers the waste thereof.'[28] Constance's speech to her son Arthur in Shakespeare's *King John* (1596) meanwhile works from the assumption that unattractive bodies belong to morally and socially inferior subjects:

> If thou, that bid'st me be content, wert grim,
> Ugly, and sland'rous to thy mother's womb,
> Full of unpleasing blots and sightless stains,
> Lame, foolish, crooked, swart, prodigious,
> Patch'd with foul moles and eye-offending marks,
> I would not care, I then would be content,
> For then I should not love thee: no, nor thou
> Become thy great birth nor deserve a crown.
> But thou art fair, and at thy birth, dear boy,
> Nature and fortune join'd to make thee great.[29]

The figure in early modern texts most likely to be singled out as both ugly and morally corrupt is the ageing woman. Bosola's verbal abuse of the old lady in Webster's *The Duchess of Malfi* (c. 1614) draws on the widespread notion that an older person's body betrays the manner in which she or he spent her or his youth.[30] The perceived ugliness of the old body thus becomes a sign of depravity. The 'deep ruts and foul sloughs' of the old lady's face justify Bosola's attack on her character: the 'sin of your youth is the very patrimony of the physician . . . I do wonder you do not loathe yourselves.'[31] Often depicted as a living corpse, the unattractive older female body repeatedly evokes physical decrepitude, sexual transgression and moral turpitude.[32]

Shaped by Neoplatonic, Christian and rhetorical traditions of the moral depravity of ugliness, the perceived legibility of ugly features in the early modern era is also grounded in humoural models of the body. As Nancy Selleck summarises, 'it was the dominant preference of ancient, medieval, and Renaissance medicine to hold that both one's physical and mental conditions depend on the individual's overall "complexion" ... which depends on the balance or imbalance of the body's humours'.[33] Within this Galenic model, ugliness results from a lack of proportion in the humours by which the body is constituted. An overabundance of black bile, for instance, is visible in pale skin and a sorrowful manner. A sanguine personality, meanwhile, is linked to the dominance of the blood, explaining its association with the obese, whose fat is identified as a materialisation of excessive blood.[34] Bardolph's blotched face in *1 Henry IV* (*c*. 1596–97), meanwhile, is a sign of the 'hot [liver]' of those in whom 'choler', the humour aligned with an angry temperament, predominates, as well as the result of drink.[35] Leonardo da Vinci's *Study of Five Grotesque Heads* (*c*. 1493; Figure 8) has been interpreted as a depiction of subjects in whom each of the four humours predominates, surrounding a more balanced central figure.[36]

Premising ugly bodies and characters on physical imbalance, the humoural model pathologises ugliness as illness and thus initially appears to undermine moralised readings of unattractive features. The agency of the subject is nevertheless central to such accounts of the body, which do not posit the suffering body as the passive victim of externally acquired sickness but instead identify disease as an internally generated state. The maintenance of humoural balance, and thus both health and beauty, to a large degree remains within the subject's control. '[E]vennesse of Carriage' is a means of setting 'a fairer stampe' upon ourselves, claims Henry Peacham in *The Compleat Gentleman* (1622). 'Temperance and ... Moderation of the mind' act as a 'bridle' with which we can

> curbe and breake our ranke and unruly Passions, keeping as the Caspian Sea, our selves ever at one height without ebbe or refluxe. And albeit true it is that Galen saith, we are commonly beholden for the disposition of our minds, to the Temperature of our bodies, yet much lyeth in our power to keepe that fount from empoisoning, by taking heede to our selves[.][37]

While temperance is the path to a 'fairer' self, its absence results in an unruly ugliness of both body and mind for which the subject, again, is ultimately responsible. As Schoenfeldt observes, illness in this period is 'perceived as a symptom of immorality': humoural imbalance is the consequence of a moral lack which is subsequently made visible in unattractive physical features.[38] In Firenzuola's *On the Beauty of Women*, Celso describes the physical process by which iniquitous women become unattractive:

> all those women who have stained their conscience with that foulness that defaces and sullies the purity and cleanness of the will, a foulness caused by the misuse of reason ... these women fall into a certain disease of the soul that continually worries and

Figure 8 Leonardo da Vinci, *Study of Five Grotesque Heads*, c. 1493

upsets them. This upset and worry produces such an arrangement of the humors that with their vapors they soil and stain the purity of the face and especially of the eyes which, as was said before, are the ministers and messengers of the heart. These vapors produce such an expression in the eyes, or, as is generally said, a certain bad air that indicates and reveals the infirmity of the soul not any differently than the paleness of the cheeks and of other features indicates the diseases and imbalances of the body and the upsets and agitations of its humors.[39]

Departing from acceptable forms of female behaviour, in other words, leads inexorably to an ugly face. 'What is there that makes a Wife handsomely humor'd, but Industry, Fidelity, Humility, and Obedience?' asks one witty English author.[40]

The body does not determine the self in any simple manner in humoural models of the body, then, but instead reflects the nature of the self from which it is inextricable. Bacon's interpretation of the myth of Dionysus describes the sensual passions that distort the appearance of the body:

> every passion doth cause, in the eyes, face, and gesture, certaine undecent, and ill-seeming, apish, and deformed motions, so that they who in any kind of passion, as in anger, arrogancy or love, seeme glorious and brave in their own eyes, do yet appeare to others mis-shapen and ridiculous.[41]

Joubert's *Treatise on Laughter* meanwhile argues that a man 'sees and recognises himself' in his face, where his passions are inscribed:

> it is not possible for him to conceal totally what he has in his heart, clever, feigning, cunning, shrewd, and crafty as he may be. It is in the face that all the affections imprint some mark and sign of their movement, being like the face of a clock on which the hours are marked and indicated by its hands, the gears and movements being hidden within.... It is impossible that the affections, when vehement, not be revealed by some change imprinted in the face. For this reason this part is to be more esteemed and cherished than any other, just as one loves and holds in high esteem an open person that is naïve, without falseness and dissimulation.[42]

While character, within humoural frameworks, is visible in the face, this character is not fixed or stable.[43] 'Grief hath changed me since you saw me last,' states Egeon in *The Comedy of Errors* (c. 1590–93), drawing attention to the malleability of a subjectivity in which body, mind and soul are intertwined: 'carefull houres with times deformed hand,/Have written strange defeatures in my face'.[44] As Selleck notes, it was not until the end of the seventeenth century that the term 'humour' shifted 'from its concrete reference to a psycho-physical condition to an abstract reference to an individual's mood or inner personality', indicating the development 'of a newly abstract and interiorised conception of self'.[45] In the meantime, subjectivity, reflected in and constituted through the fluid, changing vagaries of the body, was inevitably visible in – indeed, was indistinguishable from – physical features.

Physiognomy, the art of reading faces, retained popular credibility until the end of the seventeenth century and beyond.[46] Superficially, the principles of physiognomy reinforce a Platonic equation of beauty with goodness and ugliness with evil. The just man's body is 'commensurately proportioned', states one mid-seventeenth-century treatise, *Physiognomie and Chiromancie*, and the honest man possesses a 'face fair and amiable', but an impious character is not too subtly betrayed by a 'deformed' face, with long, narrow ears, bulging eyes, a hairy mono-brow, small, protuberant mouth, long protruding teeth, a 'neck awry', a crooked back and 'bunched' feet.[47] (Figure 9.) Its author, Richard Saunders, momentarily allows the possibility of well

Figure 9 'Metoposcopie', Richard Saunders, *Physiognomie and Chiromancie*, 1653

proportioned, 'amiable' bodies in his treatise, but the disfigured, the bloated, the contorted and the crooked overwhelmingly dominate the pages of physiognomical treatises in this era. The asymmetrical figures populating these texts point to the fact that the physiognomer is chiefly preoccupied with the fleshly inclinations of his subjects. To the Roman Catholic priest Thomas Wright, anatomising *The Passions of the Minde* in prison at the end of the sixteenth century, physiognomy is the study of 'the inordinate motions of Passions', those fallen elements of man that obstruct reason and rebel against virtue. The signs being read by physiognomers are the 'thornie briars sprung from the infected root of original sinne', which explains why physical features nearly always point in the direction of vices such as deceit, anger, folly and pride.[48] Moral corruption is thus given visual form in the ugly, misaligned bodies glaring from the pages of the physiognomer's text (Figures 10 and 11).

The Passions of the Minde holds that the morally unsavoury are likely to be physically unattractive. We are right to suspect that a child will be corrupt 'if his parents were base, wicked, or infected with any notorious vice; if deformed in body, or marked by any monstruositie of Nature'. Wickedness is a hereditary disease, passed on from parents whose monstrous 'imprint' is at once physical and spiritual:

> men know full well, that waters, which runne thorow stinking soyles, carrie an unsavoury smell . . . in like manner, Parents naturall propensions to wickednesse, imprint for most part in their children, a certaine resemblance: wherefore as these externall respects be not invincible arguments to convince a vitious nature, or a corrupted soule: so when in the progresse of life, we infallibly discover an exorbitant badde carriage and brutish demeanour, then we may well inferre, that the first staines and infections were ominous presages of future malice: as if Nature had foreseene that an infamous guest was to lodge in that body, and therefore prepared a lodging correspondent.[49]

Figure 10 '[T]he chinne decerned over long doth innuate a most wicked creature, very talkative, and a whisperer, yea his mynde altogither occupyed with deceytes', Thomas Hill, *The Contemplation of Mankinde, containing a Singular Discourse after the Art of Phisiognomie* (1571)

Figure 11 'The eyes oblique, or lookyng crookedly: declare that man to be a deceaver', Bartholomew Cocles, *A Brief and Most Pleasant Epitomye of the whole Art of Physiognomie*, trans. Thomas Hill (1556)

While 'external respects' are not 'invincible arguments', the synthesis between physical and spiritual resemblance in this passage suggests that a reading of physical 'stains' as signalling an unsavoury disposition is unlikely to be wide of the mark.

Despite the persistence with which physical ugliness was interpreted as the manifestation of an evil character, however, fundamental shifts in the conceptualisation of identity were taking place in this era, changes which undermined the certainty with which the body could be read for signs of the self. As historians of the subject argue, the shift to modernity in the seventeenth century was marked by a movement away from the conception of the body as an entity loaded with transcendent resemblances and signs towards a model of the body as a machine, radically divided from the mind or soul.[50] Insisting that we cannot be identified with our bodies, Descartes argues that we must in fact define ourselves in opposition to them:

> those in whom the will can naturally conquer the passions most easily and stop the accompanying movements of the body have the strongest souls. . . . even those who have the weakest souls could acquire a quite absolute dominion over all their passions if one employed enough skill in training and guiding them.[51]

Giving dark voice to the alienation of modern subjectivity, Iago articulates ideal identity as that which is distanced from the 'raging motions' of a body which must be controlled through reason. 'Our bodies are gardens, to the which our wills are gardeners,' he insists, emphasising the gap between a physical nature defined by 'blood and baseness' and the 'power and corrigible authority' of our mind and will.[52] John Milton's *Paradise Lost* (1667) similarly trumpets the rule of the mind over the body, positing that 'rational liberty' is the prize to be won when the 'inordinate desires/And upstart passions' of the body are mastered and silenced.[53]

Rather than being understood to be the product of body, soul and mind working inextricably together, then, selfhood began increasingly to be located in the internal depths of an individual, an authentic, rational space set against external appearances.[54] Increasingly divorced from the self, appearances were seen to be open to manipulation. As Katherine Eisaman Maus demonstrates, the impact of 'rapid urbanization', together with the upheaval of the Reformation, in which most sections of the community at one time or another experienced the potential for religious persecution, meant that the 'art of self-deployment' became newly prominent in this period.[55] If the front that we present to the world can be a performance, our bodies clearly do not necessarily betray the truth of our selves. Protestantism encouraged believers to focus attention on their inner selves, insisting that the spiritual status of an individual could not be discerned by his or her exterior. Calvinism, in particular, accentuated the potential disparity between the inner and outer nature of any given individual, warning that honest and virtuous living, let alone mere physical beauty, offered no reassurance that one was among God's chosen elect. Fruit may be 'beautyfull to the eye . . . but in no wise good', counselled Calvin. 'It is to be accompted nothing worth, whatsoever semeth prayse worthy in ungodly men,' he insisted: a 'Hidra' of corruption 'lurketh in the heartes of all men', whatever their outward charms.⁵⁶

Dislocating spiritual identity from appearances, Protestantism enables a subject's identity to be constructed in opposition to his or her carnal nature. Donne's sermons, in which the rottenness of the flesh symbolises the fallen state of man, also open up the possibility of a gap between the flesh and the redeemed spirit. 'This flesh ... is but the loame and plaster of thy Tabernacle, thy body, that, all that, that in the intire substance is corrupted,' he declares. Depicted in alienated terms, the 'loame and plaster' of fleshly identity, identified with the body, is distanced from an alternative, redeemed identity, shaped in the image of God. God hath 'walled us with mud walls, and wet mud walls, that waste away faster, then God meant at first, they should', he continues. Skin, the site of our fallen, condemned self, is set against an alternative script of the 'book of God, the Law, written in our own hearts', an externally inscribed, universal text, yet one which constitutes a more authentic form of subjectivity.⁵⁷ Within Protestantism, then, ugly, twisted, rotting bodies may symbolically represent the sinful state of humanity, but an unattractive physical form does not preclude the presence of grace. Physical beauty and ugliness are irrelevant to the final truth of our identity: for the Protestant subject, a perpetual conflict is established between the flesh and the true self, posited as somehow detached from that flesh.⁵⁸

Perhaps surprisingly, the increasing contemporary emphasis on a self able to master and control an alienated body is apparent even in early modern physiognomical treatises, in which the equation of the body and the self is often not as simple as it first appears.⁵⁹ The distorted bodies anatomised in physiognomical treatises may point to deceptive, angry and proud temperaments, but the texts explicating the signs of the body grant access to the 'natural disposicion' alone, their authors repeatedly acknowledging the limitations of an occult knowledge which is able to dissect the visible world of vicious inclination with a far greater accuracy than the less tangible, but ultimately more significant, order of grace and virtue. 'Although a man may perfectly by Physiognomy declare the natural inclinations of any man,' asserts *A Brief and Most Pleasant Epitomye of the whole Art of Physiognomie* (1556), 'yet may he not perfitly judge hym except he know whether he have grace or no'. Socrates' response to the physiognomer who seemed to misidentify him as a 'great leachour, a craftye felow, subtyle, and geven to all wyckednes' is repeatedly cited to qualify physiognomical claims. 'Such I am by nature,' granted Socrates, 'but I have (as al other men may have if they wyl) a reason and grace that ruleth above nature.'⁶⁰ The fact that individuals can 'brydle nature' is one of the reasons why physiognomy is seen by some to be a valuable skill.⁶¹ The 'Art we teach is able to bring a man to the knowledge of himself', claims the English translation of Cureau de la Chambre's *The Art How to Know Men* (1665), implying that such self-understanding will lead to self-improvement.⁶²

William Berkeley's *The Lost Lady* (1638) illustrates the extent to which physiognomical readings, even when they predict the future, are not seen to override personal responsibility. In the play, Hermione, thwarted in love, consults an 'Egiptian lady' skilled in 'devination', including the art of reading faces. The 'Moor' Acanthe (a disguised character) qualifies her interpretation of Hermione's face with the caveat that her knowledge 'is but conjectured, for our starrs incline not force us in our actions'. Far from instructing Hermione to resign herself to her fate, Acanthe helps her to contrive a scheme to bring about her own desires, leaving Hermione 'determin'd for knives fire & Seas,/Shall lose their quallities ere fate shall make mee his'.[63] Faces, then, and the cosmic signs that they embody, are not in any fixed way determinative of either character or destiny. Through 'Temperance' and 'Moderation of the mind', affirms Peacham in *The Compleat Gentleman*, we are able 'to correct the malignitie of our Starres, with a second birth'.[64] For Bacon, moreover, the fact that 'there is in man an election touching the frame of his mind, and a necessity in the frame of his body' means that 'the stars of natural inclination are sometimes obscured by the sun of discipline and virtue'.[65] An ugly body, in the end, is no excuse for an ugly soul.

The signs of the body, particularly the ugly irregularities focused upon by the physiognomer, cannot therefore be taken at 'face value' as a transparent text of the self. They require sophisticated interpretation. 'Wise men often, thorowe the windowes of the face, behold the secrets of the heart,' asserts Wright, but he swiftly concedes that hearts are, in fact, 'inscrutable and only open unto God'. Physiognomers can only ever 'aime well at them'. It is as if we are looking at faces in water, where we see 'rather a shadow, than a face':

> even so he, that by externall physiognomy and operations, will divine what lyeth hidden in the heart, may rather conceive an image of that affection that doth raigne in the minde, than a perfite and resolute knowledge.

Wright thus recognises the limitations of hermetic systems of correspondence, stating that the face is 'onelie the rhinde and leaves'.[66] Porter cites this text, authored by a Jesuit priest and thus emerging from a community well versed in new scientific developments, as an example of the impact of natural philosophy, which undermined hermetic discourses.[67] Even within physiognomical writing, then, tensions regarding the legibility of the human body are beginning to surface in this period.

Despite the fact that physiognomical texts engage with the contradictions of their age in their representations of the ugly body, many in the seventeenth century, particularly amongst the intellectual elite, vigorously refuted the veracity of the art of reading faces, associating such techniques with a credulous 'vulgar' outlook. Bosola in Webster's *The Duchess of Malfi* scathingly rejects physiognomy as a redundant art:

> Doth he study physiognomy?
> There's no more credit to be given to th' face
> Than to a sick man's urine, which some call
> The physician's whore because she cozens him.[68]

As early as the late sixteenth century, in fact, Thomas Nashe lambasts physiognomical fortune-telling, arguing in *The Terrors of the Night* (1594) that it is 'absurd ... by the external branched seames of furrowed wrinckles in a mans face or hand, in particular or generall to conjecture and foredoome of his fate'. The lines on our faces and hands, Nashe states, have more tangible causes than is presumed by those who would read our nature and fortunes in them:

> According to everie ones labor or exercise, the palme of his hand is wrythen and pleyted, and everie daye alters as he alters his employments or pastimes: wherefore well may we collect, that he which hath a hand so brawned and enter-lined, useth such and such toyles or recreations; but for the minde or disposition, we can no more looke into through it, than wee can into a looking Glasse through the wooddden case thereof.

Far from being the window of the soul, the face, or the palm, to Nashe, is a 'wooddden case', an opaque object masking, rather than revealing, the self within. Undermining physiognomical connections between an unattractive exterior and a corrupt soul, Nashe identifies external causes for ugliness:

> So also our faces, which sundrie times with surfets, greefe, studie, or intemperaunce, are most deformedlye welked and crumpled; there is no more to bee gathered by their sharpe embossed Joyners anticke worke, or ragged over-hangings or pit-falls; but that they have beene layd up in slovens presse, and with miscarriage and mis-government are so fretted and galled.... those fatall brands of phisiognomie which condemne men for fooles and for idiots, and on the other side for treacherous circumventers and false brothers, have in a hundred men I know been verefied in the contrarie[.][69]

Despite such efforts to rescue ugliness from a necessary connection with a flawed personality, however, Nashe's preoccupation with physical imagery elsewhere leads him to represent evil in grotesque corporeal terms.[70] Citing 'the Philosopher', there is 'no place', he states, where devils cannot be found:

> (bee it no bigger than a pockhole in a mans face) but is close thronged with them. Infinite millions of them will hang swarming about a worm-eaten nose.
>
> Don Lucifer himselfe, their grand Capitano, asketh no better throne than a bleare eye to set up his state in. Upon a haire they will sit like a nit, and over-dredge a bald pate like a white scurffe. The wrinkles in old witches visages, they eate out to entrench themselves in.[71]

Ugliness therefore carries multiple meanings in Nashe's text: the passage above depicts evil in graphic, comic terms, where it is closely associated with the physically repellent, while elsewhere in the same tract ugliness is simply a surface appearance with no necessary connection to moral or spiritual orders.

Echoing Nashe's ambivalence, leading seventeenth-century proponents of mechanical philosophy sometimes display a surprising tolerance for physiognomical principles. Arguing that 'irregular accidents' of nature cannot simply be reduced to ominous portents, Spencer, for instance, suggests some alternative ways of interpreting the unshapely body. One possibility, unexpectedly, is that ugliness is the manifestation of sin:

> Many of these Errata (in the book of the Creature) lead us to an understanding of the evil of sin which hath made the creatures thus subject to vanity and miscarriage.... in the matter whereof natural things consist, there is ... much of it which is unwieldy, too stiffe and stubborn to be turned to the seal of Nature, to receive those signatures and impresses, which are best, and primarily intended to be stampt upon it. A defect which escapt not the notices of many contemplative Heathens, who could not resolve themselves of the proper cause thereof [Divine malediction layd upon the creatures for the sin of man].

Despite Spencer's invective against prophetic interpretations of the ill proportioned body, moreover, he also concedes that specific physical conditions may testify to particular sins:

> [Judgement] bears upon it the evident portraitures and figures of the sin. The cross men bear (like that of our Saviour) often carries the inscription of the crime in such plain and legible characters, that he that runs may read it.... the cross is (as it were) shap'd out of the forbidden tree whereby they offended.... In such examples of Divine justice, God's rod hath a voice as well as a smart, and it becomes us to be his notice-takers.

Deciphering the meaning of aberrant or suffering bodies is no easy matter, however, since it is also the case that 'a great judgement on [our brother's] body, may be intended a great mercy to his soul'.[72] Ugly and prodigious bodies are not wholly reduced to material errors or 'natural miscarriages' in his treatise, then. They also occasionally emerge as forms of divine communication, albeit obscure scripts demanding scrupulous interpretation. The variety of meanings ascribed to physical anomaly in the tract is partly a deliberate strategy, a means of countering the naive certainty of 'superstitious' interpretations of irregularity. The contradictory discourses on which Spencer draws nevertheless illustrate the variety of ultimately incompatible discourses concerning unattractive bodies circulating in English culture in this era. Even at the level of the intellectual elite, an assumption that ugliness is infused with moral and supernatural meaning repeatedly collides with an emergent understanding of ugliness as a purely physical phenomenon, devoid of spiritual significance.

One of the early architects of the Royal Society, John Evelyn, further illustrates contemporary inconsistencies in the perception of ugliness, even amongst the elite advocates of mechanical philosophy. Evelyn's late seventeenth-century treatise *Numismata* (1697) includes a substantial section on physiognomy, signalling the coexistence of seemingly contradictory discourses of nature in his work. An empirical rationalism prone to emphasise the role of nurture and environment in shaping both subjectivity and the body clashes unevenly with occult principles of natural signatures in the text, which retains a commitment to principles of correspondence at the same time as it betrays the influence of new paradigms where the body is of dubious relevance to the self within. 'I am sufficiently sensible,' he states, 'that to judge, and pronounce from Externals, is very liable to great Mistakes, and Consequently to Censure'. 'Not without reason,' on the other hand,

> have some named the Countenance, the Mirror of the Soul, as reflecting all our Passions and Affectations ... unless ... where Education, and Philosophy have superinduced a Change, or the Christian Institution interpose, undertake, and effect the Cure[.]

Oscillating between perceptions of the body as natural sign and as cultural artefact, Evelyn's kaleidoscopic work testifies to the multiple, and not, to his mind at least, entirely incompatible discourses of the body in circulation in the late seventeenth century.

Physiognomy tends to work from the assumption that the bodies which it interprets are both natural and stable entities. Physical characteristics that emerge as a result of interaction with the environment cannot be afforded the same status as natural features: only marks present from birth inscribe divine signatures. Evelyn's empiricist inclinations lead him to ruminate on the problem that this disjunction between the natural or divinely ordained and the merely environmental poses for physiognomy. Pointing to persistent associations between ugliness and moral decrepitude, Evelyn, like Nashe before him, is at pains to emphasise the critical difference between an innate and an acquired ugliness:

> [M]uch we confess is to be attributed to Age, Infirmities, cruciating Pains, macerating Studies and Elucubrations; hard, and bodily Labour; to outward Losses and Afflictions; inward Remorse, religious Severities; to Want, Poverty; much to Diet, and other Usages: All of them Abatements in these Conjectures, and without prejudice to the Virtue and worthy Inclinations of many Persons, whose Looks may seem to bear the Characters of vitious and immoral Men; when all this while, they spring only from Impressions caused by unavoidable Accidents; besides such adscititious Habits, as may possibly be contracted by Institution, Discipline and Custom: One is therefore first to inquire into the Conversation, Education, Condition, and other Circumstances of their Lives; before we give hasty Sentence of their Natures and Dispositions. Every hard-favoured Man should not presently be concluded a Cruel and Ill-natur'd Person[.]

Evelyn's awareness that ugliness may be merely skin-deep, a surface condition rather than a fixed, innate state, constitutes a decisive challenge to physiognomical premises. His scepticism emerges repeatedly in the account, for instance as he notes that 'some (perhaps innocent poor People) have been accused for Witches and Evil-lookers as they call them'. He nevertheless also propagates physiognomical aphorisms, claiming that 'Strokes and Figures ... are Ingraven in the Countenance' and that 'a great regard should be had to ... Externals'. King Charles's features, for instance, reveal that 'Majesty does not consist in a grim and crabbed Look . . . but in a grave, staid, and unelated amiability'. 'In a word,' he concludes, 'very serious, and thinking Persons, have commonly serious and composed Looks; and the Light, the Trifling, and the Wanton, is discovered in the Face'.[73] 'Looks' in Evelyn's treatise sometimes refer to natural signatures, embodying the truth of a person's character, and at other times represent the flexible surface of a person's body, detached from spiritual or mental qualities. Evelyn's treatise thus illustrates the growing prominence of a 'silenced' body in this period while simultaneously revealing the persistence of residual understandings of the importance of physical appearance for acquiring knowledge of the self.

Literary and dramatic texts from the era also register the interweaving of alternative discourses of the ugly body's legibility. Engaging with contemporary debates regarding the transparency of the body, early modern texts often continue to draw on long-established rhetorical conventions in which physical features operate as the index of the mind. Red hair, for instance, widely regarded as ugly in this era, continues to be used as a sign of evil in early modern literary and visual texts, as it had been since classical times. The hero of George Chapman's *Bussy D'Ambois*, for example, refers to flattery as 'worse than the poison of a red hair'd man'.[74] Sycophants are aligned with Jews in this speech, following an English tradition of depicting Jews as evil redheads, a recurrent theme in representations of Judas.[75] Significant developments in the construction of ugliness can be traced in this era, then, but the close reading of texts from seventeenth-century England brings to light the coexistence of multiple, often incompatible, conceptualisations of ugliness, drawing on a variety of philosophical, cultural and rhetorical traditions. Contradictory interpretations of ugly bodies are particularly evident in contemporary discussions of the mark of Cain.

The mark of Cain

Following Cain's lament that his punishment for murdering Abel (to till the land to little effect and to be 'a fugitive and a vagabond') is effectively a death sentence, Genesis states that 'the Lord set a mark upon Cain, lest any finding him should kill him'.[76] As Henry Glover candidly admits in a 1663 sermon, 'What this Mark was, is very uncertain.' Glover's statement condenses centuries of various, often highly imaginative, solutions to the puzzle of the mark of Cain. Among other possibilities, the mark has been identified as a sign (perhaps an alphabetic character, a star or a cross) on Cain's forehead, an uncontrollably shaking body, the trembling of the ground beneath Cain's feet, a dog preventing anyone from approaching him, or a physical blemish, perhaps horns, beardlessness or, conversely, excessive hairiness.[77] Some Jewish sources identified Cain's mark with black skin, an interpretation subsequently taken up by apologists for slavery and racial segregation.[78] A seventeenth-century Cornish play draws on several of these traditions, depicting a physically repulsive, hairy and horned Cain, portrayed in dehumanised terms:

> Hairy, quaint he is and ugly;
> I know not what beast it can be:
> It should seem by his favour
> That he is some goblin of night[.][79]

As Ruth Mellinkoff comments, 'no matter how the mark of Cain was conceived... it was also construed as part of his punishment.... [I]t identified Cain as someone who must not be touched; degraded and dishonoured, but strictly off limits and taboo.'[80] A visual stigma, his mark guaranteed his isolation from human society, repelling all who viewed him. He became a 'horrible spectacle of God's wrath and fury',[81] an 'Example and Terrour to others', a 'living, walking Monument of vengeance', inspiring 'greater terrour' than death itself.[82] Generating fear and repulsion, Cain's abject body was marked as ugly.

The story of Cain is repeatedly put to political use in the seventeenth century. Glover's sermon compares Abel to the 'martyred' Charles I, and, almost twenty years later, the Church of England clergyman David Jenner follows suit. Jenner's sermon, delivered, like Glover's, on the anniversary of the king's execution, was published as *Cain's Mark. And Murder. K. Charles the I his Martyrdom* (1680). Commenting on the inadequacy of Cain's sacrificial offering, which despite its 'pompous shows' could not compete with the 'honest simplicity' of Abel's sacrifice, Jenner proclaims that Cain's story illustrates the biblical principle that 'God Almighty looks not at the outward Features and Beauty of the Body, but at the inward accomplishments and Rectitude of Mind, at the Sincerity, Uprightness, and Integrity of Heart.'[83] Having insisted on the irrelevance of external appearances, however, he proceeds to examine the significance of the body in great detail, engaging in a lengthy, digressive discussion of the nature and implications of the mark of Cain. Jenner seeks to impose a meaningful reading of the mark through situating it within a physiognomical context. Interpreting Cain's blemish as a facial feature equivalent to those bodily signatures read by the physiognomer does not resolve its ambiguities, however, demonstrating the confusion surrounding attempts to decipher the ugly body in seventeenth-century England.

Jenner admits that 'we are at a loss' regarding the nature of the mark of Cain and has little time for most of the historical 'fancies' which have attempted to pin it down. One opinion arrests his attention above all others, however, touching as it does on the wider question of the legibility of the body. This interpretation states that 'God did not set on Cain any other visible... Mark or Sign... but what did appear unto the view of every one, in his Physiognomy, frightful gashly look, and dejected countenance.'[84] Rather than an externally imposed sign, the mark is the natural physical outworking of Cain's moral character. His face betrays his corruption well before the murder of Abel, as suggested by the fact that he is 'wroth', with a 'fallen' countenance, after his sacrifice is rejected.[85] The term 'wroth', signifying anger, could also refer more specifically to that which is marked by anger in this period, betraying the widespread assumption that the passions and humours are visible in the features.[86] As Jenner points out, 'the Countenance is *ira index* ... the Discoverer of a Man's inward wrath and Anger'. He elaborates on the sparse biblical account in order to give weight to this physiognomical reading, speculating that it is Cain's face that gives him away to God himself, who states:

> I know by thy knitted Browe and frowning countenance, that thou hast not done well ... thy mad hellish look discovers the naughtiness of thy heart; thy very Fore-head speaks thy guilt[.]

If murderous intentions are written all over Cain's forehead, how much more legible in his features is the act itself?

> Well then might his Fore-head wrinckle it self into a Thousand Furrows, and his whole Face become the Scene; On which you might at the first view behold the Prologue and Epilogue, the first and the last part of so direful a Tragedy.

Cain's face publicly performs the truth of his inner self:

> who ever saw him might easily conjecture him to be the Murtherer, none ever looking with such an unkind Aspect and frightful hue as did Cain, in so much as that his Murther might be read in his Eye, and by the wretched forlorn cast thereof, Men might soon perceive the late Murtherous Act, bad habit and intent of his Mind: For ... the Mind dwelleth in the Eye, and by the several Aspects and Casts of the Eye, many intrinsecal Vices (as well as Virtues) are commonly discerned ... and from hence (I mean from the Evil, Cruel, Envious, and Malicious Cast of the Eye) Murtherers of old were usually called ... Men Sour, Grimm, Fierce, and Savage in Countenance.[87]

Jenner thus perpetuates physiognomical assumptions, following the pseudo-Aristotelian tradition that character is apparent in the face, particularly the eye.

Hendrik Goltzius's engraving *Anger* similarly situates the narrative of Cain and Abel within a pseudo-Aristotelian physiognomical framework (Figure 12). The female figure of Anger is depicted with Cain's murder of Abel and subsequent banishing by God being played out in the background. Anger's long, straight nose, fierce eye and open mouth echo the features of the lion and the bear at her feet, animals believed to have an angry temperament.[88] The narrative of Cain, where the presence of anger is marked on the features of the protagonist, is thus seen to accord with the physiognomical tradition where human features resemble those of the animals whose temperaments they share.[89]

Cracks nevertheless soon start to appear in Jenner's argument. After insisting on the public visibility of Cain's murderous nature, he stumbles upon the problem of Cain's wife, who was willing to associate intimately with Cain 'after he was thus stigmatised by God'. This troubling exception to the repellent nature of Cain's transparently evil character cannot be assimilated into the argument and so is abruptly brushed aside: 'But to wave this, the generality of writers conclude, that God did set some peculiar and visible Mark on Cain.' Cain becomes the first subject to be

Figure 12 Hendrik Goltzius (1558–1617), *Anger*, no date

susceptible to physiognomical reading, the sign on his body instigating a tradition of marked and consequently legible subjects:

> God did set some peculiar and visible Mark on Cain, and ... from hence after Ages (in imitation of the Divinity) did fix Marks on persons, as Characteristical notes and signs, sometimes of their Honor and Renown, other while, of their Shame and Naughtiness. And these Marks were either Divine, Ecclesiastick, or Civil[.]

It is as a result of Cain, according to Jenner, that criminals are branded, that Christian subjects are marked with the sign of the cross, and that foreheads receive divine inscriptions in order to make vice and virtue visible. Narratives tracing the legibility of bodies back to the mark of Cain play a part in the early modern physiognomer's tendency to see physical characteristics as indicative of iniquitous inclinations. Identifying the mark of Cain as the first physiognomical sign establishes that divine signatures on the body are necessary only because of sinful behaviour. Ugliness, from the first, possessed unique legibility.

Despite his insistence on the scrutability of the features, however, Jenner cannot reach a stable interpretation of the mark of Cain. Following centuries of paradoxical biblical exegesis, he is unable to resolve the question of whether Cain's mark is a sign of judgement or of forgiveness: 'it was either a Mark of Punishment, or (Secondly) a Token of great Favour and Mercy towards him', he rather unhelpfully concludes.[90] After focusing on the 'ignominy' of the sign for much of the sermon, he arrives at 'one opinion more (the most probable of all)', which states that Cain's forehead was inscribed with the Hebrew letter Tau, the first letter of the word for repentance.

Prefiguring the protective divine sign described in Ezekiel 9.4–6, where an angel marks the foreheads of those who are to be spared judgement, the mark of Cain could point to the divine blessing of long life, perhaps bestowed in order to allow Cain time to repent.[91] In this reading, he can act in line with the murderous nature inscribed in his features or can 'expiate and wash out . . . the stain of his Blood-guiltiness in the Tears of godly Sorrow'. The sign on his forehead does not, after all, determine his fate. Its meaning, perhaps, is deliberately open-ended, placing the responsibility for its final significance with Cain himself. This interpretation accords with contemporary physiognomical writings in which, as we have seen, the ugly body accounts for nefarious inclinations alone, allowing room for a self posited as separate from this body to resist such urges and to fashion itself in alternative terms.

Regardless of the meaning which Cain's choices may have secured for it, the mark is open to later interpretations and appropriations which potentially invert its earlier resonances. Jenner notes that the Phoenicians paint their foreheads with a star:

> 'tis probable after Ages did this in honor and in imitation of Old Cain, whom Tradition makes to be thus Stigmatized and Marked, in the Fore-head, with a Star: And thus Cain's posterity made and accounted that Mark a Badge and Emblem of honor, which God instituted to be not only a Token of future security and preservation, but also a signal Mark of present Guilt and of Divine displeasure.[92]

The divine inscription of Cain's shame has become a free-floating signifier whose significance is determined historically and culturally. The meanings of the mark of Cain thus proliferate endlessly in this sermon as elsewhere in the culture, resisting any attempt to secure a single, authoritative, interpretation.

Figure 13 Philips Galle, *Cain leaving the presence of God*, c. 1565.

The slippery nature of Cain's mark is indicative of the elusive meanings of physical ugliness more generally in this period. Jenner's sermon demonstrates that categories of beauty and ugliness play a crucial role in the mediation of wider social categories of purity and pollution. As Mary Douglas argues, bodily categories are symbolically deployed in a culture in order to police binaries of the pure and the impure.[93] The mark of Cain, to Jenner, is a means by which the corrupt can be distinguished from the godly, establishing the presence of clearly defined boundaries between the virtuous and the vicious:

> as soon as Cain's Murther is Revealed and proved, God out of Hatred and Indignation to that his Sin, turns him out of his Favor, and Churches Communion, and all because Virtue and Vice, Light and Darkness, God and Belial, may not cohabit, and dwell together. All care then, is to be used for the preserving Gods Church pure and spotless, without Wrinckle or Blemish: For as God Almighty at the Judgment Day will make a Separation between the sheep and the Goats: So does he authorize his Bishops, Pastors, and Governors of the Church Militant here upon Earth, to Separate the Notoriously Bad from the Eminently Good.

The body of Christ, the Church, is characterised by her purity, a state aligned with beauty and defined against 'Wrinkle[s] or Blemish[es]'. Jenner's sermon on the 'martyrdom' of Charles identifies religious Dissenters with the visibly marked and exiled Cain, as he deploys metaphors of physical blemish in order to insist upon an absolute, self-evident and fundamentally necessary division between the godly and the ungodly, defined as such according to his Royalist sympathies. Other Church of England clergyman at this time were making a case for concessions to Dissenters, a position hotly rejected by Jenner in his 1683 tract *Beaufrons, or, A New-discovery of Treason under the Fair-face and Mask of Religion, and of Liberty of Conscience*. The title of this tract deploys discourses of beauty and ugliness in order to establish an innate difference between the godly and the evil. In the absence of clearly established social binaries between these categories of subject, Jenner argues, anarchy will ensue. The mark of Cain, in his earlier sermon, provides a reassuring metaphor of the transparency and visibility of murderers and sinners, those Dissenters, in other words, who must remain exiled from the Church. As the title of his later tract reveals, however, 'fair-face[s]' are not always as self-evidently indicative of goodness as they initially seem to be. The Church must be preserved 'pure and spotless, without Wrinkle or Blemish', he had preached earlier, necessitating its dissociation from those with the 'mark of Cain'. The divisions which the bodily metaphors of beauty and ugliness imply are both innate and universally discernible are sometimes far from obvious, however:

> As for Hypocrites and such Wicked Men, whose Naughtiness cannot be discovered nor proved, they being Masked over with an outward Profession and Form of Religion, and so lying undiscovered, must be tolerated in the Church, for they are the Tares which will grow up with the Wheat: But as for all Cain's who are openly wicked, whose Villanies may be read in their Fore-heads, they are not to be permitted to enjoy so transcendent a Priviledge as Church Fellowship, but ought to be presented in due Course of Law.[94]

Regicides, implicitly, fall into the category of those whose 'Villanies may be read in their Fore-heads'. The violent branding of the state, marking them physically as criminals, merely echoes the divine signatures inscribing their murderous natures. Given the existence of 'masks' for such 'naughtiness', however, and in the light of the confusions surrounding the meaning and visibility of the mark on Cain himself, this easy coincidence of social and moral identity emerges as something of a forlorn aspiration. The mark of Cain, indicative in Jenner's sermon of physiognomical principles more generally, initially offers the reassuring prospect that evildoers are immediately identifiable. The badge of dishonour imprinted on the body of Cain nevertheless collapses into a proliferation of contradictory meanings and obscurities, suggesting, on closer examination, that bodies, even when inscribed by the hand of God, do not easily yield their secrets.

'[N]o Man's Face is Actionable,' concludes Jeremy Collier, late seventeenth-century polemicist and later bishop in the nonjuring Church of England.[95] Those who identify 'Cain's Mark' in the faces of others are making subjective judgements: the 'singularities' which people conclude are 'either a Caution given us by Providence, or the natural Effect of a crafty and suspicious Mind' are also 'interpretable, from more innocent Causes'. Displaying the scepticism regarding the moral legibility of physical signs to which natural philosophy gave rise by the end of the seventeenth century, Collier's musings on 'the Aspect', one section of his *Miscellanies upon Moral Subjects* (1695), nevertheless reveals a persistent confusion in the culture regarding the interpretation of bodily features. An author of antitheatrical pamphlets, Collier seems reluctant to let go of the notion that the 'countenance' is 'designed ... for Information'. 'A face well furnish'd out by Nature, and a little disciplined,' he notes, 'has a great deal of Rhetorick in it.' We 'see the Soul flash in the Face', he states, insisting that

> the Language of the Face is fixt, and universal. . . . Tis the Short-hand of the Mind, and crowds a great deal in a little room. A Man may Look a Sentence, as soon as Speak a Word. . . . [T]hough I cannot tell what a Man says, if he will be sincere, I may easily know what he Looks.

Despite his faith in the universal legibility of the features, Collier is thus all too aware that accurate readings of 'Looks' are dependent on features being natural and 'sincere', a quality evidently in short supply in this corrupt, shape-shifting age. The face is 'the Short-hand of the Mind', but it may display an inaccurate message:

> since tis in our Power not to give a wrong Sign, we should not pervert the Intendments of Providence. To wash over a coarse or insignificant Meaning, is to counterfeit Natures Coin. We ought to be just in our Looks, as well as in our Actions; for the Mind may be declared one way no less than the other. A Man might as good break his Word, as his Face.

Having conceded that the signs of the face are open to manipulation, Collier goes one step further: even natural signs themselves are open to multiple interpretations. 'Whether Honesty and Dishonesty are discernable in the Face, is a Question which admits of Dispute,' he concedes. Social interaction depends on the fact that the 'Soul can't be all forced into the Face': if this were the case, 'People would chuse to converse in the dark, rather than trust themselves with the Sight of each other.' At once insisting on the inscrutability and the legibility of the features, Collier, echoing many in this era, ultimately refuses to come off the fence: 'Whether Men ... have Signatures to discover their Natures by, is hard to determine.'[96] Literary and dramatic texts frequently echo this ambivalence, as *Bussy D'Ambois* illustrates.

'Empty men':[97] *Bussy D'Ambois*

George Chapman's *Bussy D'Ambois* (c. 1603–1604, publ. 1607) presents a disjointed vision of the body and the self that is at once a lament for an older order in which bodies were transparent vehicles of moral and symbolic meaning and an exposé of the naivety of this philosophy. The play is set in the French court, but the world of the play is not as far removed from English circles as it seems, given the play's pointed commentary on the English propensity to ape French fashions (1.2.50). Court life, we are told, revolves around manipulated and illusory appearances: 'brave barks, and outward gloss/Attract Court eyes be in-parts ne're so gross' (1.1.109–10). Bussy's 'Metamorphosis' following his acquisition of a 'brave suit' (1.2.118) bears witness to the centrality and emptiness of visual signifiers in this society. On one level satirising the hypocrisy of a world where an 'Asse' can think himself a 'Lion' (1.2.161), the play nevertheless fails to offer a stable, natural alternative to this superficial, amoral order.

Articulating a deep nostalgia for an 'old humanity' (5.3.274) in which bodies and selves were translucent texts as he depicts a world in which the physical order has been emptied of moral meaning, Chapman holds the contradictory positions of his age regarding the legibility of the body and the construction of identity in unresolved tension. It is this irresolution which makes it notoriously difficult to interpret the 'hero' of the play, Bussy D'Ambois. Celebrated by the French king as 'Man in his native noblesse', 'that in himself/(Without the outward patches of our frailty,/Riches and honour) knows he comprehends/Worth with the greatest' (3.2.91–95), Bussy appears to be idealised as the one natural, authentic man in a world of mirrors. Standing 'bare' before the court, Bussy proclaims that he is 'free', 'King [to him] selfe (as man was made)' (2.1.194, 198). Jane Melbourne identifies him as 'an anachronism', caught tragically in a nihilistic new order in which his transparent, unaffected heroism can no longer survive.[98] The elegiac aspect of the play, in which Bussy represents a natural ideal supplanted by corruptions and confusions, is nevertheless undermined by Bussy's own emphasis on the instability of appearances. Perspective is everything, he teaches Tamyra, as he represents guilt as a trick of vision: 'like empty clouds/In which our faulty apprehensions forge/The forms of dragons, lions, elephants,/When they hold no proportion' (3.1.21–4). His rise in the world of the court depends on the careful manipulation of appearances: whatever his rhetoric to the contrary, he is perfectly prepared to 'strew [his] hate with smiles' (4.2.155). He is a willing student of Friar Comolet, who teaches him to 'seem' (2.2.193), and he recognises that he must conduct himself like a politician who 'must like lightening melt/The very marrow and not print the skin:/His ways must not be seen' (4.2.168–70). Seen in this light, the 'man in his native noblesse', supposedly the embodiment of a lost order in which bodies figured forth natural, untainted selves, is merely another optical illusion.[99]

An apparently female propensity to disguise reality beneath deceptive appearances generates much anxiety in the play. 'Adders lie a-sunning in their smiles' (5.1.79), states Montsurry. As Tamyra recognises,

> We cannot keep our constant course in virtue:
> What is alike at all parts? every day
> Differs from other: every hour and minute:

> Ay, every thought in our false clock of life,
> Ofttimes inverts the whole circumference:
> We must be sometimes one, sometimes another[.]
>
> (3.1.53–8)

Bussy's identity is nevertheless also seen to be changeable and deceptive: repeatedly likened to the sea, he is dangerously mutable in both appearance and motive.[100] 'None can be always one' (4.1.25), he states, at once a lament and an observation. As its ambivalent attitude towards its valiant, self-important, compelling and flawed hero suggests, the play is caught between the recognition that identity is an illusion, a malleable performance which cannot be authenticated via the body, and a yearning for a more stable, fixed order in which the body, like the self, is intelligible, fixed, open to ready understanding. Recognising the naivety of this utopian ideal, moral judgements are necessarily deferred.

While Henry III may be enamoured of Bussy's heroism, others, notably Monsieur, interpret him very differently. Monsieur's dissection of Bussy's character relies on his body as a readable text, but reaches conclusions very different from those put forward by Bussy concerning his own nature. Far from embodying the ideal, rational, self-regulating man, Bussy, according to Monsieur, is driven by 'humours, that are more absurd/Childish and villainous than that hackster, whore,/ Slave, cut-throat, tinker's bitch, compar'd before'. He is more 'impudent/Than any painted bawd', his external presentation masking a physical repulsiveness which betrays more accurately the state of his soul:

> Thou eat'st thy heart in vinegar; and thy gall
> Turns all thy blood to poison, which is cause
> Of that toad-pool that stands in thy complexion;
> And makes thee (with a cold and earthy moisture,
> Which is the dam of putrefaction,
> As plague to thy damn'd pride) rot as thou liv'st.
>
> (3.2.351–68)

Complying with a humoural model of the body in which body and self, appearances and reality, cannot be distinguished, Monsieur's reading of Bussy's moral and physical ugliness contradicts Bussy's self-presentation as heroic, noble and straightforward. Bodies and selves are at once legible and opaque in this play.

Tamyra's body becomes the site where contradictory understandings of the body are violently played out. Seeking to justify her adulterous desire for Bussy, Tamyra presents herself as helplessly shaped by her physical passions, even as she suggests that her essential self is distinct from the humours of her body: 'Our bodies are but thick clouds to our souls;/Through which they cannot shine when they desire' (3.1.59–60). Positing a separation between the body and the soul, in other words, does not necessarily privilege the soul, or the mind, as the shaper of subjectivity. In the case of women, at least, 'passions fumes' have the potential to outweigh the feeble efforts of 'our souls'. The violent culmination of the play confirms that the body, not some nebulous inner self, is the location of female identity: 'Ile write in wounds (my wrongs fit characters),' announces Tamyra's cuckolded husband, mutilating her body in order to make her an 'image' of 'Adultery' (5.1.131–2). She thus becomes a 'killing spectacle', a 'prodigie' (5.3.181), a figure whose moral status is inscribed in her flesh for all to see.[101] Forced by her husband to write Bussy a letter which will entice him to his death, Tamyra assumes that her mutilated features speak a clearer, more powerful language than the words on the page. She writes 'in my blood that he may see/These lines come from my wounds and not from me' (5.1.168–9). Maintaining a distinction between her body and her self, Tamyra nevertheless assumes that the text of her body possesses clear meanings. Bussy's tragedy, however, and, through it, the wider tragic outlook of the play, resides in the fact that bodies are not so readily legible. The signs of Tamyra's body, translated literally into text in the letter penned in her blood, are fatally opaque to the hero: 'O tis a sacred witnesse of her love,' concludes Bussy, even after being warned that the letter is a trap (5.2.90).

The tragic denouement of the play is thus generated by its recognition that the 'old humanity', one in which 'bare' bodies testified to transparent selves, has been displaced by a material order in which physical entities have been divested of divinely inscribed or moral meaning. Guise tries to counter the cynical perspective that 'nature workes at randome', but Monsieur's darker acknowledgement that 'Nature hath no end/In her great workes' holds greater resonance in the final scenes (5.3.29, 1–2). As Melbourne notes, 'The Nature Monsieur announces... is deformed, but it prevails.'[102] The bleak vision with which the play concludes thus gives terrifying voice to the emergence of a new mechanistic model of the universe, a universe in which

> Nature lays
> A masse of stuff together, and by use
> Or by the mere necessity of matter,
> Ends such a work, fills it, or leaves it empty,
> Of strength, or virtue, error or clear truth;
> Not knowing what she does.[103]
>
> (5.3.12–6)

Even Bussy, for a time ostensibly the embodiment of an older, more noble order, is ultimately forced to acknowledge that his body is 'but penetrable flesh' (5.3.126). The fabric of the body, along with humanity itself, has been drained of meaning. The paragon has become a 'masse of stuff', inglorious, ugly: 'So this full creature now shall reel and fall/Before the frantic puffs of purblind Chance/That pipes through empty men, and makes them dance' (5.3.46–8).

The relationship between 'character' and 'brow' is thus far from straightforward in early modern England. Persistently operating as a sign of the self, physical appearance at the same time becomes increasingly detached from a subjectivity located within, out of sight of the casual observer or even, perhaps, the physiognomer. Thrown into new perspectives by natural philosophy and by dualistic models of the self, ugly faces, disturbingly, are emptied of legible meaning. *Bussy D'Ambois* captures the anxiety generated by such developments. The widening gap between the body and the self, and thus the growing opacity of the ugly body, nevertheless offer the possibility of escape from the fixed and necessarily negative implications of an unattractive face. As will soon become apparent, however, modern subjectivity, defined in opposition to the body and thus potentially enabling the renegotiation of the meanings of ugliness, was not a model of identity to which all had equal access.

3

Opening the Silenus: gendering the ugly subject

As the material realm is imagined in increasingly mechanistic terms during the seventeenth century, the physical order, including the human body, begins to be seen as that which can and must be mastered by a self posited as somehow detached from this order. Charles Taylor identifies 'the growing ideal of a human agent who is able to remake himself by methodical and disciplined action', highlighting the crucial role of a 'disenchanted' material order in the new focus on internalised self-fashioning.[1] An ugly body, within this formulation, does not determine or exhibit the self, but is an entity to be controlled by the detached rule of reason. Protestant discourses emphasise the operations of grace more than those of autonomous reason, but Protestant demands for self-control, for the mastery of the wayward yet ultimately conquerable flesh, reiterate the same key principles. Models of identity in which the self is opposed to the flesh are nevertheless a stubbornly masculine preserve in this era. For women, as for those of low social status and other marginalised groups, the body, constructed in disorderly terms, continues to be perceived to play a key role in defining the self. Early modern depictions of ugly characters are therefore uneven. While a physically ugly male character has the potential to be virtuous despite the irregularities of his body, an unattractive female character possesses an excessive, unregulated corporeality that is inseparable from moral depravity. Ugly men are often represented as Silenus figures, their unappealing exteriors belying their inner nobility. Women, on the other hand, are more likely to be depicted as inverted Sileni, those whose ostensibly attractive forms disguise their true deformity.

The gendered frameworks structuring representations of physical ugliness in this era are particularly visible in Middleton and Rowley's *The Changeling* (1622), a play in which the meanings of male ugliness are opaque while female beauty is represented as an artificial cover for a deformity whose moral and physical referents are inextricably linked. 'Enveloped in a Calvinist miasma', with an acute sensitivity to the misleading nature of appearances, the play is also influenced by physiognomical principles, illustrating the multiple, contradictory discourses shaping representations of physical ugliness and beauty in early seventeenth-century England.[2] Asking whether or not evil takes visual form in human features, and proposing various, inconsistent answers to this question, *The Changeling* reveals contemporary fears surrounding the legibility of faces as well as the gendered terms through which some of these anxieties are negotiated.

William Hay's *Deformity: An Essay* (1754) further illustrates the crucial role of gender in the generation of a modern subjectivity able to reformulate the significance of ugliness. In this startling text, the short MP with a 'bent' back rejects any necessary link between physical deformity and moral depravity. Representing himself as a rational and virtuous subject, Hay insists that his identity is not determined by his twisted physique: his subjectivity, defined in opposition to his body, is instead shaped by his own choices. Hay's ability to renegotiate the meanings of his deformity follows a tradition of masculine self-representation that received new emphasis in England in the previous century. As we shall see, ugly women in this era were not generally offered the same opportunities to redefine the significance of their 'repulsive' forms.

'Loathsome loveliness':[3] the odious female body

Physiognomy claims to be able to penetrate the hearts of all: no one can think themselves beyond the reach of an art which teaches 'how to discerne the dispositions of al men by their fourme and shape'.[4] On closer examination, however, it becomes clear that some bodies are particularly suitable texts for physiognomical reading. 'Passions have certayne effectes in our faces; howbeit some doe shew them more evidently than others,' states Wright, betraying the fact that bodies are not equally legible.[5] The best way to shield one's heart and soul from the eye of the physiognomer is to resist the carnal tendencies inscribed in the body. Virtuous subjects are inscrutable:

> Now keep pure and sincere hearts.
> If nature's crooked, streight your souls
> By heavenly vertue that controles
> And gives mistake to those of skill.
> Not by inclination, but by will
> You virtuous are. So you shall be
> Free from the Laws of Palmestry.[6]

Those who blindly act in line with the crookedness of their nature, on the other hand, are transparent texts, open to accurate physiognomical interpretation. Hill openly states that his aphorisms are relevant only to 'those, which lyve after their affection, and appetites, rather than governing themselves by reason'. Physiognomical principles

> are ment rather to happen and come to passe on the brutishe sort: which for the lacke of grace, and being not regenerated by Gods holy spirit . . . are mooved to follow their sensuall will and appetites.[7]

The 'brutishe sort', those who are in thrall to their 'sensuall will and appetites,' include women as well as those from the lower social orders. As Wright elaborates,

> Superiors may learne to conjecture the affections of their subjectes mindes, by a silent speech pronounced in their very countenances. And this point especially may be observed in women, whose passions may easily be discovered, for as harlots by the light and wanton motions of their eyes and gestures may quickely be marked, so honest matrons, by their grave and chaste lookes, may soone be discerned.... The Scriptures also teach us, in the face of a harlot, to reade the impuritie of her heart. The fornication of a woman shall be knowen by the lifting up of her eyes, and in her eye-bries.[8]

As those prone to displaying their 'passions' (and, implicitly, being enslaved by them), women are ideal objects of physiognomical observation, 'quickely' and 'soone' betraying their nature through their features. The 'face of a harlot' is particularly open to scrutiny: at once female and morally defective, and thus emphatically defined by her nature, a 'fallen' woman is the most accessible of all physiognomical texts. The ability to read the female body nevertheless relies on an accurate interpretation of the beauty with which women were increasingly identified in this era. Far from a clear sign of goodness, female beauty is likely be identified in this period as an artificial cover for both physical and moral deformity. The legibility of the female body, then, depends on the viewer's ability to see through its apparent charms to the ugliness that lies beneath.

Western philosophy has a long tradition of regarding physical beauty with suspicion. In Platonic discourses, physical beauty is a mere shadow of true beauty. Keen to emphasise the disparity between spiritual and earthly orders, medieval philosophers often focus on the relative poverty of physical attractions. 'The sleek looks of beauty are fleeting and transitory, more ephemeral than the blossom in spring,' warns Boethius:

> If, as Aristotle said, we ... could see right though things, even the body of an Alcibiades, so fair on the surface, would look thoroughly ugly once we had seen the bowels inside. Your own nature doesn't make you beautiful. It is due to the weak eyesight of the people who see you.[9]

Rather than providing a window to a pure soul, a beautiful body is likely to be a dangerously misleading illusion, deathly negation posing as its opposite. Renaissance Neoplatonism, under the influence of Marsilio Ficino, placed renewed emphasis on the incorporeal nature of beauty: the 'body and beauty are different'.[10] According to Ficino, beauty is not defined by properties within the material object but resides in the form of a rational idea, a memory of the spirit's place of origin. A 'certain lively and spiritual grace', beauty can be visible in the body but cannot be reduced to physical features alone.[11]

In *Problemes of Beautie*, Buoni sets the material against the spiritual order, bleakly stating that 'there is no earthly thing whatsoever, that hath not some imperfection annexed unto it'. Bodily charms are corrupt, distracting from rather than reflecting or leading to true beauty:

> How should a man that hath abased his lips, by inordinate lust to the standing, and stinking poole of a rotten Beauty, dippe them in the pure fountaine of the onely fayre

> ...? How should he gazing, by a sensuall, and brutish love, upon a corporall, and corruptible Beauty, fasten the subtilitie of his understanding, upon the first fayre, who is meerely spirituall, and heavenly? What proportion hath the Sunne with darknesse; the day with night, truth with a lye ... vertue with vice, order with confusion[?]

In the light of heavenly beauty, the most appealing features of this world are transformed into ugly negations:

> the glittering rayes of the Sunne are darkned; the Starres lose their light; the sparkling Diamond is defaced, the flashing Ruby shineth not, the white Lilly is black, the Spring not beautifull, Laughter not pleasant, Musick not delightfull[.]

Buoni's vivid depiction of earthly beauties nevertheless betrays the continuing appeal of the physical order he is ostensibly denouncing. While insisting on a clear hierarchy of worldly and heavenly beauty, his treatise reveals the ambivalence of Neoplatonic attitudes to physical beauty. After setting the physical against the spiritual, he insists on the value of physical beauty as the manifestation of 'divine splendour ... in thinges naturall'. 'The fairer a man is,' he states, 'the nearer he cometh to the divine Nature.' Material beauty exhibits spiritual goodness:

> the face is the true resemblance both of the Beauty of the body, and of the minde, for in the face as in a living figure are seene, those livelie colours.... And as for the Beauty of the minde it is manifest in the face, as it were in a cleare looking glasse: For in it are seene the vales of shamfastnesse, the true ornaments of an honest minde, the treasures of chastity[.]

After reiterating the principle that 'Beauty of the body [is] an outward signe of the inward Beauty of the minde', Buoni nevertheless once again reveals the (typically gendered) suspicion of physicality generated by Neoplatonic binaries: the beauty of a sinful woman is a 'cloke for sinne'. Giving concise expression to the paradoxical position of physical charms within Neoplatonic thought, Buoni asserts that 'bodily Beauty is a cleare signe (if Malignity bee not hidden under it) of a faire (that is) of a vertuous mind'.[12]

Neoplatonic theories of beauty were particularly influential in seventeenth-century England in the Caroline court under the influence of Henrietta Maria.[13] The Queen promoted 'preciositie' in the court, emphasising the beauty of women as an essential aspect of their virtuous, socially cohesive influence. As Erica Veevers demonstrates, courtly attempts to reconcile beauty and virtue were manifest in the court masques of the 1630s. Inigo Jones's masque *Tempe Restored* (1631), for example, is premised on the principle that 'Corporeall Beauty ... may draw us to the contemplation of the Beauty of the soule, unto which it hath Analogy.'[14] The promotion of sensuous beauty as a means of stimulating spiritual contemplation was also central to the controversial efforts of Archbishop Laud and his supporters in the 1630s to reintroduce the arts and beauty into Church of England worship.[15]

Denouncing what they perceived to be the worldly corruption of 'papist' principles, Protestant reformers on the other hand rejected the deployment of visual stimuli in Christian worship, associating sensuous displays with corruption, pride and false religion. Any philosophy that denies the value of beauty is 'inhuman', reducing man to a senseless 'block', concedes Calvin, but 'excessive elegance and superfluous display' nevertheless 'arise from a corrupted mind'.[16] The biblical figure of the 'Whore of Babylon', deployed in Reformed discourses as an image of Roman Catholicism, disguises her monstrosity beneath resplendent clothing and accessories.[17] Attachment to earthly beauty is inextricable from idolatry in Protestant discourses: 'many give all their senses to bodily delytes, that the mind lyeth overwhelmed', notes Calvin elsewhere, 'many are so delited with marble, golde, and paintings, that they become as it were men made of marble ... turned and be like unto painted images'.[18] A love of beauty thus betrays a fascination with artificial representations which has the potential to dehumanise the self. The 'Bower of Bliss' episode in Spenser's *The Faerie Queene* (1590–96) lends subtle imaginative realisation to this strand of Protestant thinking. Acknowledging the powerful allure of sensory beauty, Spenser nevertheless elides the beautiful and the artificial, ultimately exposing its malignancy. Succumbing to the allure of the beautiful threatens emasculation and dehumanisation: as Greenblatt demonstrates in relation to the episode, feminine sensuous appeal must be violently (and constantly) repudiated if 'gentlemanly' virtue and power are to be constructed and maintained.[19]

The Puritan polemicist Phillip Stubbes harbours no doubts whatsoever about the moral status of physical charms. Any interest in external appearance, to Stubbes, is a form of devil worship: 'those that looke in [mirrors] may be said to looke in the Deviles arse, whilest he infuseth the venomous winde of Pride into their soules'.[20] The pursuit of beauty, inextricable from artificial beauty in his treatise, necessarily signals a rejection of virtue: 'Whosoever do colour their faces, or their haire, with any unnaturall colour, they begin to prognosticate of what colour they shalbe in hel.' Physical charms are set against spiritual beauty and are aligned with the corruptions of the flesh:

> [Women] busie themselves in preserving the beautie of their bodyes, which lasteth but for a time, & in time is cause of his own corruption, & which in effect, is nothing else then putrification it self, & a dunghill covered with white & red; but for the beautie of the soule they care nothing at all.[21]

Debates regarding the moral value of beauty thus strike at the heart of religious, political and gendered discourses in this era. Contrasting representations of the biblical character of Esther highlight the tensions mediated through depictions of female beauty. Francis Lenton echoes the Catholicism of Henrietta Maria's court in his poem 'Queene Esters Halliluiahs' (1638), in which Esther's beauty is presented as a divine gift, virtuously enhanced through cosmetics in order to achieve the noble goal of influencing the king and hence preventing the genocide of the Jews.[22] The Protestant Francis Quarles, writing in 1621, takes a different view of Esther's physical appeal:

> Now when the turne of Ester was at hand
> To satisfie the wanton Kings command,
> Shee sought not (as the rest) with brave attire,
> To lend a needlesse spurre to foule Desire,
> Nor yet indeavours with a whorish Grace,
> T'adulterate the beauty of her face;
> Nothing she sought to make her glory braver,
> But simply tooke, what gentle Hege gave her:
> Her sober visage daily wan her honour:
> Each wandering eye inflam'd, that look'd upon her.²³

While Esther's 'sober visage' initially appears to be opposed to the 'whorish Grace' with which artificial beauty is associated, the division between natural and artificial beauty breaks down in this passage. In line with the misogynist bent of the poem, female beauty is identified as the source of 'foule Desire'. Esther's refusal to 'adulterate the beauty of her face' does not prevent her from provoking lust in all that 'look'd upon her': as Jo Carruthers observes, her beauty, rather than male desire, is held responsible for this sinful response. The very fact of Esther's beauty, for Quarles, calls her virtue into question.²⁴

In Thomas Cooper's *The Churches Deliverance, containing Meditations and Short Notes uppon the Booke of Hester* (1609), a text written to celebrate the thwarting of the Catholic Gunpowder Plot, Esther's beauty appears in a different light again. Retelling the story of Esther with copious commentary in order to instruct his own age, the Church of England clergyman describes the manner in which the tyrannical King Ahasuerus is driven by a lust for beauty as he searches for Vashti's replacement. Far from a divine blessing, Esther's beauty is the curse that draws her into the evils of the court. 'Wel fare then deformities,' concludes Cooper,

> for beauty bringes bondage: here's no seeking for foule ones, the faire must serve the Court; So doe the best giftes of the wicked tend to their distruction, and no marvaile: For as they are given of God in anger and not in mercy, so they are desired of the wicked, for they though seeming good, yet indeed are for true hurt & distruction.

Beauty, here, is inextricably linked with the 'bondage' of tyrannical, corrupt, courtly society. It is a quality 'cast upon the wicked to their greater condemnation: Therefore lette us not be discouraged if wee are scanted of [beauty], but rather lette us seek after durable riches.'²⁵ Liberty and virtue consist in rejecting that which appeals to the flesh, as Cooper aligns physical ugliness with a laudable disregard for worldly pleasures. In *Comarum Akosmia: The Loathsomenesse of Long Haire* (1654), the clergyman Thomas Hall, ejected after the Restoration for nonconformity, echoes the sentiment. Those qualities deemed attractive by the world are by definition sinful:

> Observe which way is most pleasing to flesh and bloud, which course takes most with the world, and hath most carnall inducements to draw the heart after it, and then know, that this way lyes most under suspition, to be the worst way.²⁶

Hall lived according to his principles, wearing his hair unfashionably short. '[W]hen Christ is once entertained in the soule,' he opined, 'it will soone appeare in the haire, habit, attire, in an humble, modest, mortified, self-denying walking.'[27] For some Puritans, beauty is so problematic that its absence almost becomes a prerequisite for virtue.

Protestant suspicion of physical beauty, particularly female beauty, is apparent in the numerous instances in early modern English texts where the apparent charms of a woman are exposed as a dangerous disguise for her true deformity. So common is the identification of female beauty with artificiality, in fact, that the natural state of womankind implicitly emerges as one of disfigurement.[28] Aristotle had argued as much: 'just as it sometimes happens that deformed offspring are produced by deformed parents, and sometimes not', he commented, 'so the offspring produced by a female are sometimes female, sometimes not, but male.... the female is as it were a deformed male[.]'[29] 'Shew me a Woman, I'll a Monster find,' agrees the anonymous *The Female Monster* (1705). All women, according to this tract, are both physically and morally twisted, whatever their initial appearance. The work depicts two sisters, one 'as Ugly as the other's Fair', who are nevertheless 'form'd in the same crooked Mold,/Both are Ill-natur'd, both are Vain and Old'.[30] In *Morbus Anglicus* (1666) the physician Gideon Harvey also rehearses misogynistic perceptions of an innate female ugliness lurking beneath deceptive exteriors. Infatuation with a woman is easily remedied, according to Harvey, by a glimpse of her true repulsiveness. He relates the case of a chemist, Raimundus Lullius, who was 'furiously taken with the beauty of a certain young woman' until the 'fair lady' 'flung open her bosome, and offer'd a most filthy, stinking, ulcer'd Cancer of her Breast to his view' in order to 'break the strings of his Satyrick passion'. The 'incomparable wit and excellent beauty' of Hypatia, meanwhile, were 'doted upon by a young scholar', until she

> muster'd a great bundle of her menstruous rags together ... and spread them all open before him; saying, you men that do so admire at the Elegant Shape, and Nitourous Complexion of Womens upper parts, behold now, O Scholar! The constitution of their lower ... what a filthy, nasty, detestable sight is here?

The scholar is disabused of the notion that 'whatever is above is like to what is below', and 'ever after ... abhorred the sight of a Woman'. 'If arguments of this kind, drawn from the false appearance of Women, would take with the generality of men, there's enough to be said to fling 'em all out of favour,' concludes Harvey.[31]

Female beauty is often regarded with such wariness, in fact, that it becomes itself a form of ugliness. The conduct book *The Mothers Counsell, or Live within Compasse* (1631), for instance, presents apparent beauty both as a misleading cover for the 'odiousness' of the female body and as an inherently repulsive quality. Presented as the final testament of a mother to her daughter (although women are referred to as 'them' in the text), the work defines appropriate feminine behaviour according to four binary oppositions. Women must be chaste (not wanton), temperate (not mad) and humble (not proud). Living 'within compasse' also requires beauty: 'a beautifull countenance is a silent commendation'. Despite its structural positioning as a positive quality, however, beauty emerges in the work as an ambivalent property, one more closely aligned with sin and transgression than with appropriately restrained feminine conduct. Women are 'blinded with beautie and self-love', the section rather unpromisingly opens, and the author seems more keen to warn of the perils of beauty than to extol its virtues. 'Trust not beauty, for it never payeth what it promiseth,' the reader is instructed, as physical beauty emerges as an untrustworthy, false quality. External attractiveness is no guarantee of goodness: 'the fairest cheeke hath often times a soule/Leprous as sin it self, than hell more foule'. The supposed opposite of beauty in *The Mothers Counsell* is 'odiousnesse', defined in the work as transgressive behaviour, that which exceeds nature through 'lust, apparel, or other ornament'. Rather than establishing a clear distinction between beauty and ugliness, then, the tract suggests that a woman is liable to be 'odious' even if at first glance she appears attractive: 'A painted womans face is a liver smeared with carrion, her beauty baits of dead wormes, her lookes nets, and her words inticing charmes.' 'Odious is that beautie which sleepeth not with the face,' the author states, revealing the extent to which female beauty, understood to be essentially artificial, is categorised as a form of ugliness in the text. Make-up ultimately reveals rather than conceals an ugly face: 'painting hastens wrinkles before old age comes'. The moral depravity betrayed by face painting is materialised in a repulsive body, the 'dead wormes' which comprise the feminine form.[32]

The anonymous *The Wonders of the Female World, or A General History of Women* (1682) also blurs the distinction between beautiful and ugly women. The work initially appears to establish a clear binary of 'fair Women and Deformed'. Associated with 'railing Tongues', deformed women are presented as socially and sexually as well as physically transgressive figures. Their apparent opposites, the fair women, are nevertheless by no means straightforward embodiments of virtue. Labelled 'Devils' and 'the great Tempters of Mankind', beautiful women generate disruption and misery. Those 'whom Nature hath endowed with beautifull Bodies, should endeavour after Humility the Beauty of the Soul', the speaker declares, suggesting that the two are by no means inevitable companions. In common with numerous early modern works, the work insists on the temporary nature of corporeal beauty, emphasising that even the greatest beauty will end up 'old, lean, withered and dried up; nothing left but riveled Skin and hard bone'. A temporary veneer, female beauty is inherently artificial, as is revealed by a group of women who washed their faces in public and 'had their artificial Beauties turned into Deformity by the water, and so were exposed to the Laughter of the Company'. Even when not explicitly associated with the use of cosmetics, female beauty is presented as somehow less natural, and certainly less appealing, than the beauties to be found elsewhere in nature. 'What Rose in the Cheek can countervail the Rose in the Garden, or what Azure-Vein in the

Temples the blew Flower of the Field?' asks the speaker as he insists on the 'Vanity of Beauty, and how little reason any have to be proud thereof'. Set in opposition to the true beauties of nature, female attractions emerge as a form of ugliness.[33]

As the above examples illustrate, early modern representations of the deformity of womankind interweave physical and moral qualities. John Hagthorpe's 'Sinne and Vertue' (1623) represents Sin as a painted harlot whose repellent 'Ethiopian' body betrays her viciousness:

> Trust not her painted brow, her blandishment;
> Her beauties but a vizor paisted on,
> A cunning baite to catch th'improvident;
> She's under it an Ethiopian:
> And though she smoothes her wrincles all she can,
> Shee's filthy, cruel . . .
> Under her Silke and Purple braverie,
> Unpartiall eyes shall find with perfit sight,
> Her members spotted with ranck leprosie;
> Her fingers armed with Harpies clawes for fight
> And rapine; cloven beast-like both her feete;
> A Dragons tayle which venombd foynes uncases
> At her fond lovers, in their deare embraces.[34]

Once the veneer of artificial beauty has been scraped away, the black, diseased, dehumanised female form betrays the moral degeneracy of its possessor.

Women's apparent beauty does not therefore preclude an ugliness that, once brought to light, is likely to be interpreted in morally significant terms. A woman's body may be inherently deceptive, but for those with the discernment to see beyond its artificial veneer, its loathsomeness carries transparent meanings. The physically unattractive male character in early modern texts, meanwhile, potentially accrues very different symbolic associations.

'Surface ugliness':[35] the male Silenus

Early modern women, like the lower social orders, black people and the obese, categories of the population likely to be seen to be defined less by autonomous rationality or self-control than by a stubborn, unruly corporeality, were problematic modern subjects, unlikely to be held to possess the fortitude to disengage their minds from the order of the body and its passions.[36] The ugly male character, on the other hand, potentially becomes the epitome of the alienated modern individual, he whose subjectivity is constructed in opposition to his body. '[T]hough/Your Person is none of Natures exactest Peeces,' Lady Prudence tells a suitor in Margaret Cavendish's *The Publick Wooing* (1662), 'yet your Mind doth seem to/Be compos'd with all her best Ingredients . . . for though you seem but poor and mean,/Your Soul appears to me sublime.'[37] Evelyn cites Seneca's description of Claranus to illustrate the fact that physically ugly features do not always signify an evil nature. 'Nature, I confess,' states Seneca,

> has dealt a little unkindly with him, in lodging so great a Soul in so homely a Cottage, unless perhaps it be to shew us that the greatest, and happiest Wit, may lie under any the coursest outside.... A great Man I see, may come forth of a little Hovel, and a bright and magnanimous soul, from a mean, and ill-framed Body.... it must be confess'd, that the Countenance is not always an infallible Guide.[38]

Similarly insisting that the relationship between the ugly body and the self is not clear-cut, Montaigne, quoting Cicero, establishes a distinction between 'surface ugliness' and true deformity:

> There is nothing more probable than the conformity and correspondence of the body and the mind.... The author here is talking about unnatural ugliness and physical deformity. But we also use ugliness to mean an immediately recognizable uncomeliness, which is lodged primarily in the face and which we often find distasteful for quite trivial causes: for its colouring, a spot, a coarse expression.... Such surface ugliness ... is less harmful in its effects on a man's mind and is not, in people's opinion, by any means a certain prognostic. The other kind, which is strictly speaking deformity, is more substantial and more inclined to turn its effects inwards.[39]

While unattractive women in early modern texts are deformed, in Montaigne's sense of the term, physically ugly men are more likely to be identified as superficially unsightly, and thus to remain in control of their own identities.

Physically repulsive men in literature in this era are repeatedly likened to Silenus figures. Named after the outwardly risible, portly tutor of Dionysus, a Silenus has an ugly and foolish exterior which masks its inner beauty and wisdom. According to Rabelais,

> *Silenes* of old were little boxes ... painted on the outside with wanton toyish figures ... to excite people unto laughter ... but within those capricious caskets were carefully preserved and kept many rich jewels, and fine drugs.[40]

Alcibiades described the outwardly ugly Socrates as 'one of those little Sileni that you see on the statuaries's stalls' and many early modern texts echo this description of the philosopher:[41]

> Just such another thing was Socrates, for to have eyed his outside, and esteemed of him by his exterior appearance, you would not have given the peel of an Oinion for him, so deformed was he in body, and ridiculous in his gesture: he had a sharp pointed nose, with the look of a Bull, and countenance of a foole ... now opening this boxe you would have found within it a heavenly and inestimable drug.[42]

Erasmus describes Christ as a Silenus figure, emphasising the extent to which his humble appearance belies his inner majesty. To Erasmus, treasure is more valuable if it is hidden beneath a coarse shell, all the more precious for not being freely and shamelessly available to the masses: 'The more significant something is, the deeper it is hidden, the more effectively it is concealed from prying eyes,' he reasons. Physical beauty is cheap and showy, appealing only to those who lack spiritual discernment. 'The mask is preferred to the face,' he laments, drawing on Platonic imagery:

> the shadow to the reality, the artificial to the natural, the fleeting to the substantial, the momentary to the eternal.... Ordinary people pay much more attention to what they see with their eyes than to those things which are all the more real for being less exposed to view.

Erasmus thus sets beautiful physical appearance against spiritual beauty: 'In this world there are really two worlds, in conflict with each other in every possible way. One is gross and physical, the other heavenly and already straining every nerve to practice being what it one day will become.'[43] The trope of the Silenus is thus premised on an intense suspicion of external beauty, a suspicion that chimes with Protestant sensibilities. The moral goodness of Sileni figures such as Socrates and Christ is bound up with their physical ugliness, their lowly external appearance marking their humble and spiritually superior disregard for the gross and the physical. To Erasmus's Folly, for instance, 'prudence' is a 'vice' that is visible in the 'rough features' of men.[44] Rabelais meanwhile suggests that Socrates' famed unattractiveness was a conscious decision, 'the better by those meanes to conceale his divine knowledge.'[45] Ugliness, in these terms, is presented as a virtuous choice, an expression of personal agency and rational self-control.

Even when a man cannot be said to have chosen his unattractive appearance, it is not necessarily seen to determine his identity. Fuller notes in *The Holy State* that 'Nature oftentimes recompenceth deform'd bodies with excellent wits. Witnesse Aesop, then whose Fables children cannot read an easier, nor men a wiser book.' 'Their souls have been the Chappells of sanctity,' he continues, 'whose bodies have been the Spitolls of deformity':

> An Emperour of Germany coming by chance on a Sunday into a Church, found there a most misshapen Priest, *pene portentum Naturae*, insomuch as the Emperour scorn'd and contemn'd him. But when he heard him reade those words in the Service, For it is he that made us and not we our selves, the Emperour check'd his own proud thoughts, and made inquiry into the quality and condition of the man, and finding him on examination to be most learned and devout, he made him Archbishop of Colen, which place he did excellently discharge.[46]

The 'quality and condition of the man' evidently remains under his own control, even if he has been dealt his 'misshapen' body by external forces. The body does not make the man: the potential for self-fashioning means that a virtuous soul can inhabit a twisted physique.

Not all male subjects in early modern texts have equal access to this paradigm of subjectivity. Othello, whose 'sooty bosom' within the racialised terms of Shakespeare's play is seen to be ugly, possesses an inner beauty at odds with his 'fearful' exterior: 'If virtue no delighted beauty lack/Your son-in-law is far more fair than black.' The perception that Othello's nature is not defined by his physical appearance is not universally shared in Venetian society, however. *Othello* (1602–03) stages the collision between emergent perceptions of the body's irrelevance to the self and residual beliefs in the congruity of physical and moral deformity, tracing the tragic fate of a 'Silenus' caught in a social context where external appearances are not readily ignored. As the 'white Devil' Iago betrays, the insistence that the outer figures forth the inner is hopelessly misguided, yet Othello ultimately internalises wider narratives of his 'black' identity, coming to recognise himself in terms which allow no space between the body and the self. 'I am black,' he states, a designation he begins to deploy as a marker of moral taint: 'Her name . . . is now begrimed and black/As mine own face.' Identifying himself in terms of particular constructions of his body, Othello begins to be defined by unruly passions, losing grip of his 'masculine' self-control. Likening himself to the sea, his nature, which 'passion could not shake', is overtaken by a monstrous, feminised, irrational enslavement to his 'blood'.[47] Disastrously, the 'ugly' black body, like the 'ugly' female body in numerous other texts, ultimately comes to define the self. *Othello* thus exposes the extent to which its own apparent recognition of the superficiality of appearances has not displaced wider cultural perceptions of the coincidence of the body and the self, particularly, it seems, when the body in question is black.[48]

Representations of physical ugliness in early modern texts are therefore marked by inconsistency. In some contexts appearing skin-deep, a misshapen form elsewhere operates as the sign of a morally depraved character. Constructions of unattractiveness as a surface condition, potentially detached from inner character, illustrate the emergence of new forms of subjectivity. The ideal subject within both Protestant and early modern physiognomical discourses is not enslaved by the flesh but transcends it, forging a rational or spiritual identity (or having one forged by God) at odds with the carnal tendencies of the body. The disparity between representations of female and male ugliness in early modern texts nevertheless highlights the extent to which such models of subjectivity are unevenly applied in this era. For women, as for black subjects and the 'brutish sort', the body is unlikely to be constructed as an object that can be either mastered or ignored. Instead, the humoural chaos of female flesh continues to define a transgressive, irrational and implicitly ugly nature. Shakespeare's *Richard III* (*c*. 1591) reveals the potential difficulty of interpreting the ugly male body in this era, while Middleton and Rowley's *The Changeling* illustrates the extent to which disparate representations of deformity often coexist within single texts.

'Opacous' bodies:[49] *Richard III* and *The Changeling*

Shakespeare's Richard III, the most notorious of all ugly characters in early modern literature, initially seems to contradict the model of the male Silenus. Apparently inhabiting an earlier universe where the material order is spiritually meaningful, Richard's moral depravity appears to be inscribed in his hideous looks. Anne denounces him as a 'foul devil' and a 'lump of foul deformity', reading his body, as do other female characters in the play, as a sign of his perversity.[50] As critics have noted, however, Richard has a compelling ability to renegotiate the meanings of his ugliness.[51] In the 'general censure' his deformity secures his social and sexual exclusion.[52] 'So long as his body is regarded as "evidence" of his identity,' Charnes observes, 'he can have no "legitimate" authority.' As she states, however, 'the fascination Richard holds for the audience lies in his attempts to resist and escape the deformed and deforming signification the play insists upon – his attempts to counteract the Richard of Tudor legend . . . with his own version'.[53] To draw on Taylor's models of pre-modern and modern subjectivity, rather than being 'attuned to the order of the things [he finds] in the cosmos', Richard occupies a position closer to that of the emergent subject who disengages from the body and attempts to shape his life 'according to the demands of reason's dominance'.[54]

Michael Torrey notes that 'the play's relationship to physiognomy is more nuanced than we might initially assume':

> complicating any simple correlation between Shakespeare's play and physiognomy is the fact that Richard is a successful deceiver; despite the obvious signs of his wickedness, he repeatedly ensnares his victims . . . his body alternately does and does not seem to give him away.[55]

From the first scene of the play, Richard is preoccupied with the significance of physical appearances. Initially producing a reading of the changing face of the nation, where 'grim-visaged war hath smoothed his wrinkled front', he moves on to peruse the signs of his own body:

> But I that am not shaped for sportive tricks
> Nor made to court an amorous looking-glass,
> I that am rudely stamped, and want love's majesty
> . . .
> I that am curtailed of this fair proportion,
> Cheated of feature by dissembling nature,
> Deformed, unfinished, sent before my time
> Into this breathing world scarce half made up,
> . . .
> Why, I in this weak-piping time of peace
> Have no delight to pass away the time,
> Unless to spy my shadow in the sun
> And descant upon mine own deformity.
>
> (1.1.14–27)

Richard performs the self-reading which early seventeenth-century physiognomical treatises assume will inspire self-improvement.[56] Buoni suggests that the 'famous

Philosopher' instructed his followers to 'take a view of their owne Beauties in a glasse' so that

> If they should not finde that exquisite Beauty in themselves which they saw in others, they should endeavour to awaken themselves to all honourable exercises, and by their inward vertues supply their outward defects.[57]

In *The Mothers Counsell*, the woman who appears 'foule' when she sees herself in the mirror is instructed to 'make good with good manners the beautie which her face lacketh'.[58] Richard is not inclined either to 'awaken' himself or to 'make good' in such terms, however. 'I am determinèd to prove a villain,' he pronounces, implying that his body, shaped by 'nature', has left him little choice in the matter (1.1.30). Rather than an expression of indomitable will, this statement, following in the wake of Richard's self-pitying description of his deformity, can be interpreted as an attempted abdication of personal responsibility. The flaw in this approach would have been glaringly obvious to a physiognomically literate audience, however, since physiognomy insists that the body possesses no such powers of determination. Interpreted within this framework, Richard is freely choosing to act in line with the evil inclinations suggested by his body and thus remains culpable for his depraved moral development.

Richard's insistence that his deformity leaves him no alternative but to be vicious is the first of many wilful misinterpretations of his body in the play. Far from being 'determinèd' by his 'curtailed' form, he manipulates it for his own purposes.[59] Several critics have commented on the manner in which Richard displaces his deformity on to female characters, claiming that his 'blasted' and 'wither'd arm' results from Elizabeth's and Mistress Shore's witchcraft rather than originating in his own depravity (3.4.73–4).[60] Marking him as the victim of scheming women, his twisted shape ironically confirms his innocence. Richard is thus able to obscure the meanings of his ugliness, redefining it in external or surface rather than inner or substantial terms. Despite his ugliness, his body fails to display his evil. 'Hid'st thou that forehead with a golden crown,' observes Elizabeth, 'Where should be graven, if that right were right,/The slaughter of the Prince that owed that crown' (4.4.135–6). Richard's forehead, crucially, is not branded with his crimes, either as a result of state punishment or, it seems, through the presence of universally legible natural signatures.

Richard is consequently able to convince Anne that he is 'a marv'lous proper man' (1.2.239). Drawing attention to his ability to refashion the meanings of his body, he boasts that he will

> be at charges for a looking-glass,
> And entertain some score or two of tailors
> To study fashions to adorn my body.
> Since I am crept in favour with my self
> I will maintain it with some little cost.
>
> (1.2.240–4)

Splitting 'I' from 'my self', a self-alienation given fuller expression in his final soliloquy, Richard objectifies his body, which becomes an instrument under his control. '[B]odies are not, properly speaking, perceived by the senses or by the faculty of imagination,' argues Descartes, 'but by the intellect alone, and . . . they are not perceived through their being touched or seen, but only through their being understood[.]'[61] Richard's senses continue to register his physical repulsiveness: he cannot believe himself 'a proper man'. He insists on a different understanding of his appearance, however, one in which it ceases to be 'a setter of ends' and becomes 'a domain of possible means'.[62] As an entity at his own disposal, his body can even become a mask of virtue: 'O that deceit should steal such gentle shapes,/And with a virtuous visor hide foul guile' (2.2.26–7), laments the Duchess. The fact that the 'rudely stamp'd' Richard can 'seem a saint', that a hunchback can 'steal . . . gentle shapes', reveals that physical ugliness does not possess singular or universally negative meanings in this era, at least not for a male subject. The play presents a morally and physically crooked man, yet suggests that the parallel between the two states is far from straightforward. Richard's body, startlingly, is as much a mask as it is a window of his soul. A modern subjectivity hidden beneath the surface meanings of the body offers the opportunity for empowered self-fashioning, for an identity not fixed or determined by the script of the deformed body. Richard's terrifyingly successful ability to manipulate the terms of his identity reveals the potential dangers, as well as the intoxicating appeal, of the alienated modern subject.

Anxieties regarding the opacity of the body take centre stage again in Middleton and Rowley's *The Changeling*, a play in which deceptive female beauty is set against a male ugliness whose readability is called into question. Infused with Protestant sensibilities, the play sets a distinctively modern perspective of the impenetrability of the body in tension with continuing popular beliefs in the legibility of beauty and ugliness, throwing neat certainties regarding the significance of physical appearance into doubt. Presenting us with a beautiful heroine, first glimpsed in church, and a physically repellent anti-hero, *The Changeling* sets itself up within conventional classical and medieval rhetorical frameworks, suggesting that virtue and villainy are visibly inscribed in the features of the characters. Such paradigms are soon disrupted, however, as the play destabilises visual categories, revealing the dangerous naivety of belief in the body's transparency. The audience, along with Alsemero, must learn to 'check the eyes and call them blind' as easy reliance on conventions where character is inscribed in external appearance is at least partially displaced by the painful awareness that bodies are, in fact, 'opacous', resistant to visual interpretation.[63] Much of the play's dramatic tension derives from the collision of incompatible models of the body which it stages. Recalling stock literary figures and rhetorical conventions in which the body is a symbol of moral meaning, the play charts how ugly and beautiful characters fare within an early modern, specifically Calvinist, context in which the body can no longer be relied upon to be a transparent sign of the self. *The Changeling*, in Montaigne's terms, probes the difference between an 'immediately recognizable uncomeliness' which is not 'a certain prognostic' and an 'unnatural ugliness' or 'deformity' whose moral meanings are more certain.[64] Physical ugliness, it suggests, may be simply skin-deep, while 'more substantial' deformity may initially be invisible to the eye. The key factor determining the meanings of ugliness in the play is gender. Beatrice-Joanna cannot define her identity in her own terms and is instead constructed by others as deformed. De Flores, on the other hand, despite his ugly face, demonstrates a shocking ability to manipulate the terms of his own identity. Female ugliness, even when not immediately apparent in the face, constitutes the female subject, whereas male physical ugliness is no barrier to male agency or self-fashioning, and may even be a useful tool in the male subject's ability to shape his own identity.

Following the play's dissection of deceptive female beauty ('O cunning devils!/ How should blind men know you from fair-faced saints?' 5.3.108–9), much recent critical attention has focused on its depiction of the duplicitous female body.[65] De Flores's repulsive appearance and depraved character conversely seem to suggest that ugly male bodies are more transparent. Despite initial appearances, however, the play explores the impenetrability of unattractive male bodies as well as the hypocrisy of feminine beauty. In a play 'obsessed by images of the secret recess and the forbidden interior', both men and women possess hidden subjectivities, natures that not clearly visible in their features.[66] Their interiorities are not evenly aligned, however. Female secrets are the site of 'unnatural ugliness', while, for male characters, even an external ugliness does not guarantee the deformity of what lies within. Female interiority is a source of danger and pollution, an 'ulcer' that must be probed, revealed and condemned (5.3.7, 8). Male ulcers, on the other hand, are lodged 'in the face': they may coincide with moral depravity, as De Flores ultimately confirms, but they are not 'by any means a certain prognostic'.[67]

Beatrice-Joanna's beauty is initially presented within a framework of courtly love, nostalgically evoking an order in which beauty and virtue cohere which only enhances the nausea of the breakdown of such epistemological certainties:[68]

> Modesty's shrine is set in yonder forehead –
> I cannot be too sure though.
>
> (4.2.125–6)

The visual sign of beauty has become detached from its moorings, as have other conventional features in the discourse of courtly love:

> 'Twas in the temple where I first beheld her,
> And now again the same; what omen yet
> Follows of that? None but imaginary.
>
> (1.1.1–3)

Alsemero instinctively retains faith in an older order where foreheads reveal modesty, yet is simultaneously aware that all may not be so simple. A character on the cusp of modernity, yet reluctant (or unable) to inhabit it entirely (and, as such, an apt representative for the play as a whole), Alsemero straddles old and new mentalities. The uneasy juxtaposition of incompatible philosophical systems is revealed in his science. Acknowledging that visual clues alone are insufficient for the interpretation of women, he nevertheless refuses to abandon the belief that the female body can be made to reveal its secrets. Determined to acquire empirical evidence of the truth of women's bodies, he draws on occult knowledge, '[b]y a Chaldean taught' (4.2.112), in order to attain this.

Critics have been quick to label the virginity test a failure: Beatrice-Joanna is able to fake the required 'symptoms' of virginity and thus to nullify the diagnostic power of the test.[69] The play thus satirises gullible reliance on occult physiognomical principles, suggesting that the body can conceal its true meanings. The play does not call into question the fundamental viability of the test, however. Diaphanta, after all, has a textbook reaction. It requires cautious application, but hermetic knowledge remains capable of forcing the female body to reveal its truths. Rather than setting itself against physiognomical forms of knowledge, then, the virginity test episode echoes contemporary physiognomical texts, preaching caution, aware that the signs of the body may be misleading, yet upholding the belief that the skilled practitioner can accurately read the signs of the body.

Elsewhere, Tomazo is (sometimes) able to read the signs of the body correctly, producing an accurate interpretation of Beatrice-Joanna as he notes the 'small welcome' (2.1.106) for Alonzo in that most crucial of physiognomical signs, the eye. Beatrice-Joanna acknowledges that her body will betray her secrets, even as she plots to circumvent this fact. She fears her wedding night because Alsemero is

> clear in understanding...
> Before whose judgement will my fault appear
> Like malefactors' crimes before tribunals,
> There is no hiding on 't.
>
> (4.1.6–9)

Although the meanings of women's bodies are undoubtedly 'elusive' in this play, they are not, then, altogether 'undecipherable'.[70] At times revealing and elsewhere concealing the truth within, they are instead unstable signs requiring sophisticated interpretation. Awkwardly positioned on the brink of a new recognition of the obscurity of the body while residual models of its legibility continue to circulate, the play presents the female body as the site of anxious uncertainty. It nevertheless works to counter such indeterminacy, reassuring the audience that the female body cannot, in the end, remain 'impervious to scientific and occult investigation'.[71]

The truth of the female body is subject to knowledge in this play because its meanings, though not immediately apparent, are already fixed. As Arthur L. Little states, 'The Changeling works towards Beatrice's confession of her infirm (female) self'.[72] Little argues that femininity, in whatever guise it presents itself in this play, is ultimately defined by deformity. In order to pass the virginity test (and thus avoid being labelled a morally deformed whore), Beatrice-Joanna must perform a 'grotesque display' of hysteria.[73] The play moves inexorably towards its hellish conclusion, when her true nature is exposed: 'thou art all deformed!' (5.3.77). De Flores's misogynistic statement that all women are physically ugly in the end, when 'they're so old their chins and noses meet,/And they salute witches' (4.2.53–5), reinforces the play's construction of femininity as deformity. His comment suggests, moreover, that the ostensibly moral category of feminine deformity cannot finally be divorced from the unattractiveness of the female body, even if this physical ugliness is temporarily obscured by the apparent beauty of youth.

Beatrice-Joanna makes some attempt to impose her own reading of her body: "Tis innocence that smiles, and no rough brow/Can take away the dimple in her cheek' (5.3.24–5), she asserts. Alsemero nevertheless rejects her right to interpret herself, insisting that her external appearance is irrelevant to the truth of her self:

> Neither your smiles nor tears
> Shall move or flatter me from my belief
> You are a whore.
>
> (5.3.30–1)

Her body is a mask: 'there was a visor/O'er that cunning face, and that became you;/now impudence in triumph rides upon 't' (5.3.46–8). Initially referring to that which was worn over the head or face, 'visor' from the late sixteenth century could also refer to the face itself.[74] The shifting meanings of the term reflect the extent to which the body was newly conceptualised as an alienable, artificial cover for the self in contemporary models of identity. Beatrice-Joanna's beauty allows her to impersonate virtue, as her body masks the 'cunning face' of her deformity. Ultimately, however, the play reassures us, the truth will out: Beatrice-Joanna's face may be a 'visor', but the innate truth of her character will eventually be revealed. Female bodies are 'occult' in more than one sense of the term: they contain secrets and yet are also that which is revealed to the initiated. It is only 'blind' men, after all, who are unable to distinguish 'cunning devils' from 'fair-faced saints' (5.3.108–9).

In the end, as Sara Eaton notes, 'men see what they want to see'.[75] Alsemero describes the process by which Beatrice-Joanna's body is forced to expose that with which it has been pre-inscribed:

> I'll all demolish and seek out truth within you
> If there be any left. Let your sweet tongue
> Prevent your heart's rifling; there I'll ransack
> And tear out my suspicion.
>
> (5.3.36–9)

The truth of Beatrice-Joanna is defined by his 'suspicion': "Twas in my fears at first, 'twill have it now:/oh, thou art all deformed' (5.3.76–7).

Beatrice-Joanna draws attention to the socially constructed nature of deformity, commenting that the label 'whore'

> blasts a beauty to deformity;
> Upon what face soever that breath falls,
> It strikes it ugly.
>
> (5.3.32–4)

Recognising the constructed nature of her deformity does not make it open to negotiation, however. Once revealed, ugliness becomes the 'truth within' her, a truth which neither she nor any of the other characters can question or deny: 'Oh, you have ruined/What you can ne'er repair again' (5.3.34–5). The play's collusion in the revelation of feminine deformity is such that even Beatrice-Joanna internalises the script of her own incurable corruption.[76] Beauty and health, she realises, can be restored only through her elimination:

> I am that of your blood was taken from you
> For your better health; look no more upon 't
> But cast it to the ground regardlessly.
> Let the common sewer take it from distinction.
>
> (5.3.150–3)

'What an opacous body had that moon/That last changed on us!' concludes Alsemero, 'Here's beauty changed/To ugly whoredom' (5.3.196–8). The female body seems changeable, but it is not, ultimately, opaque: it has been deciphered, its 'ugly whoredom' dragged into public view. The visor of the female face has not in the end disguised what was already known to lie beneath: 'The black mask/That so continually was worn upon 't/Condemns the face for ugly ere 't be seen' (5.3.3–5).

It is not only the female body that is subject to scrutiny in *The Changeling*, however. Beatrice-Joanna is constructed as a 'patriarchal object',[77] but the play initially presents her as a viewing subject, one, moreover, with a clearer understanding of the subtleties of sight than Alsemero. 'Be better advised, sir,' she cautions,

> Our eyes are sentinels unto our judgments
> And should give certain judgment what they see;
> But they are rash sometimes and tell us wonders
> Of common things.
>
> (1.1.73–6)

'You read me well enough,' he later acknowledges (5.3.16). The play thus repeatedly emphasises Beatrice-Joanna's gaze, one in which men are constructed as objects of desire:

> Methinks I love now with the eyes of judgement
> And see the way to merit, clearly see it.
> A true deserver like a diamond sparkles.
>
> (2.1.14–16)

'I have within mine eye all my desires' (2.2.8), she states, as her gaze comes to stand for her assertive sexuality. Beatrice-Joanna is particularly presented as a viewing subject in her encounters with De Flores: much as he seeks to objectify her, it is because of the emphasis on her perspective that we are made so aware of his physical shortcomings. 'She turns her blessed eye upon me now' (2.1.50), he drools, only to be told to 'leave [her] sight' (2.1.59).

Beatrice-Joanna's 'eyes of judgement', like the men's, are nevertheless occasionally inadequate for the task. 'Mine eyes were mistaken,' she concedes with regard to her first betrothal, and, despite her initially perceptive insights into De Flores's nature, she catastrophically misreads her father's servant later in the play, believing that his 'looks promise cheerfully' (3.4.21) when he returns after murdering her fiancé, before realising that she is 'in a labyrinth' (3.4.72). Male bodies, it seems, are no easier to read than are their female counterparts. The failure to interpret them accurately, moreover, may be equally dangerous: Beatrice-Joanna ultimately lays the blame for her tragedy on the fact that she failed to perceive the significance of her initial 'loathing' of De Flores (5.3.156).

Alsemero's inscrutability is established in the opening scene, when Jasperino misinterprets him ('Lover I'm sure you're none' 1.1.36). He cannot even plumb his own depths, stating that there may be 'some hidden malady/Within me that I understand not' (1.1.23–4). As Boehrer establishes, Alsemero's 'secret study', one of several 'private architectural spaces, reserved for the business of men' in the play, represents his 'mental space':

> all the material enclosures constructed in *The Changeling* are officially masculine ones: the physician's closet of Alsemero, the madhouse of Alibius, the fortification and passageways of Alicante castle, and the church in which Alsemero gets his first view of Beatrice.

Commenting on the lack of equivalent female spaces, Boehrer argues that the play 'is all about feminine secrecy: what goes on within the parallel enclosures of women's bodies and minds'.[78] Instead of being substitutes for mental enclosures, however, the masculine confined spaces in the play focus attention on male interiority, an elusive entity whose secrets cannot be deduced from external appearances.

The repulsive De Flores appears to contradict this model of masculine opacity. 'An ominous ill-faced fellow' (2.1.52), a 'standing toad-pool' (2.1.58) and a 'viper' (3.4.166), his 'dog-face' (2.2.146), it seems, visibly emblazons his depravity. His 'scurvy' face (2.2.77) evokes both disease and moral contemptibility, apparently synthesising inner and outer qualities. 'Blood-guiltiness becomes a fouler visage' (2.2.40), assumes Beatrice-Joanna, and the play, on one level, does not appear to disagree. Although De Flores unites physical ugliness with moral deformity, however, the two forms of ugliness are not fully equated in the play. Obvious to some, including the audience, as a mark of his perversity (thus recalling earlier models of the self), his physical ugliness is in fact an ambivalent sign. Unexpectedly, a gap opens up between the body and the self, even in relation to this apparently caricatured, folkloric arch-villain.

De Flores connects his physical ugliness with his socially disempowered status, referring to them as inextricable aspects of his 'hard fate'. He moves seamlessly from a consideration of his 'bad' face into an account of his fall from gentlemanly status into 'servitude' (2.1.48, 36). Linked with his social decline, his unattractive appearance is implicitly an acquired, temporary, feature, rather than an expression of the innate truth of his character.[79] His ugliness is located in his face, and specifically in his skin, again suggesting both its superficial, and perhaps its reversible, nature. Despite the audience's knowledge of his moral deformity, De Flores's outward appearance therefore falls into Montaigne's category of superficial 'uncomeliness, which is lodged primarily in the face', and its meanings are not immediately obvious to other characters in the play.[80]

In line with a rising, if unsystematic, contemporary emphasis on the role of the perceiver in the construction of beauty and ugliness, *The Changeling* explores the idea that De Flores's physical ugliness is subjectively defined. De Flores admits that he has a 'bad' face, but reactions of disgust and the interpretation of his appearance as a sign of evil stem from those viewing him, rather than from his features themselves. He identifies the origin of Beatrice-Joanna's loathing as her own 'peevish will' (1.1.108), and she largely agrees:

> 'tis my infirmity,
> Nor can I other reason render you
> Than his or hers, of some particular thing
> They must abandon as a deadly poison,
> Which to a thousand other tastes were wholesome.
> Such to mine eyes is that same fellow there,
> The same that report speaks of the basilisk.
>
> (1.1.110–16)

The 'frailty' and 'imperfection' referred to in this passage belong to Beatrice-Joanna rather than De Flores. 'This ominous ill-faced fellow more disturbs me/Than all my other passions' (2.1.52–3), she admits, locating the source of the disturbance within her own body.

The possibility that the object which 'poison[s]' her sight might appear 'wholesome' to 'other tastes' introduces a note of subjective perception which raises question marks over the true status of De Flores's ugliness. Alsemero draws comparisons between Beatrice-Joanna's revulsion and an irrational dislike of 'roses', 'oil' or 'wine', entities 'which to infinites/Most pleasing is' (1.1.117–23). 'There's scarce a thing but is both loved and loathed' (1.1.126), he concludes, undermining the concept of beauty or ugliness as intrinsic properties of an object. De Flores notes that 'far worse' faces than his are 'doted on':

> And yet such pick-haired faces, chins like witches',
> Here and there five hairs, whispering in a corner,

> As if they grew in fear one of another,
> Wrinkles like troughs, where swine-deformity swills
> The tears of perjury that lie there like wash
> Fallen from the slimy dishonest eye –
> Yet such a one plucked sweets without restraint
> And has the grace of beauty to his sweet.
>
> (2.1.40–7)

'[T]here's daily precedents of bad faces/Beloved beyond all reason,' he reiterates later, 'these foul chops/May come into favour one day 'mongst his fellows' (2.1.83–5).

Beauty and ugliness are therefore contested, subjective categories in the play, at least in relation to De Flores. His ugly male body is open to positive as well as negative readings: Alonzo designates him 'kind De Flores' (2.2.164), while Tomazo mistakenly believes him to be '[h]onest De Flores', insisting '[t]hat De Flores has a wondrous honest heart' (4.2.37, 57). Beatrice-Joanna's judgement, as the audience is aware, is the correct one, yet the inability of other characters to perceive his true nature indicates that a 'bad face' (in a man) is not a readily legible sign of evil. Reflecting the wider cultural shift away from moralised readings of ugliness to a perception of its material superficiality, and pointing to the anxieties generated by that shift, De Flores's body, dangerously, is not as easy to decipher as we might initially assume.

Tomazo's later, more accurate, physiognomical reading of De Flores seems to return us to a simpler order where outer appearance is a clear indication of moral disposition:

> The fellow that some call honest De Flores;
> But methinks honesty was hard bested
> To come there for a lodging – as if a queen
> Should make her palace of a pest-house.
> I find a contrariety in nature
> Betwixt that face and me;
> 					. . . he's so foul,
> One would scarce touch him with a sword he loved
> 		. . . so most deadly venomous,
> He would go near to poison any weapon
> That should draw blood on him.
>
> (5.2.9–19)

This speech is nevertheless comically undermined by the fact that it was Tomazo himself who previously labelled De Flores 'honest'. Middleton and Rowley moreover emphasise the arbitrary nature of this judgement. Frustrated by his inability to identify his brother's murderer (thus revealing the difficulty of reading others), Tomazo impetuously decides to rely on blind chance: 'the next/I meet (whoe'er he be) the murderer/Of my most worthy brother' (5.2.6–8). Determined to see a villain, Tomazo sees one. Once again, the evil supposedly signposted by De Flores's ugliness is less transparent fact than wilful projection. Despite the fact that his description, at it happens, is accurate, Tomazo himself places no value on it: 'A brother may salute his brother's murderer/And wish good speed to the villain in a greeting' (5.2.47–8), he laments immediately after the encounter, no closer to being able to see through the opaque bodies with which he is surrounded.

The fact that male physical uncomeliness is unstable in its meanings is central to the play's action, enabling Beatrice-Joanna to deploy flattering interpretations of De Flores's features as she manipulates him into acting on her behalf in the murder of her fiancé. Playing on the potentially insubstantial nature of his ugliness, she suggests that his appearance has improved: 'What ha' you done/To your face alate? You've met with some good physician' (2.2.72–3). ''Tis the same physnomy,' retorts De Flores, yet Beatrice-Joanna disagrees, reminding him that it is all a matter of perspective:

> When we're used
> To a hard face, 'tis not so unpleasing.
> It mends still in opinion, hourly mends,
> I see it by experience.
>
> (2.2.87–90)

Detached from absolute values, ugliness has become a fluid property, subject to the whims of the viewer. Physical unattractiveness can even be interpreted in positive terms:

> Hardness becomes the visage of a man well;
> It argues service, resolution, manhood,
> If cause were of employment.
>
> (2.2.92–4)

Beatrice-Joanna's reinterpretation of ugliness as a badge of manliness draws on wider discourses of early modern masculinity. Fuller, for instance, insists that

> wounds in warre are most honourable: Halting is the statliest march of a Souldier; and 'tis a brave sight to see the flesh of an Ancient as torn as his Colours.[81]

'How lovely now/Dost thou appear to me!' (2.2.135–6) lies Beatrice-Joanna, yet her manipulation is possible only because of the potential plausibility of her statements. Later on, moreover, he does indeed seem 'lovely' to her:

> How heartily he serves me! His face loathes one,
> But look upon his care, who would not love him?
> The east is not more beauteous than his service.
>
> (5.1.70–2)

'His face' alone, then, does not define him as ugly: if one chooses to 'look' differently, his physical shortcomings do not preclude him from being 'beauteous'.

The equivocal status of De Flores's ugliness is partly responsible for the tendency among twentieth- and twenty-first-century critics and directors to present De Flores as the object of Beatrice-Joanna's desire. Felicity Rosslyn, for example, comments on the 'intense attraction' between De Flores and Beatrice-Joanna, noting his 'intelligence and nobility', and reading his ugliness in positive terms:

> Middleton takes us into a suggestive grey area, where the first real security the heroine knows is with a villain who has no illusions about her, and whose ugliness seems to be a guarantee for his realism and effectiveness in the world.[82]

Modern directors have also tended to interpret the play as a 'dark love story about the bond between two well-matched demon lovers', reading sexual attraction rather than physical revulsion in Beatrice-Joanna's vehement responses.[83] While such readings, as Barker and Nicol argue, involve an intensely problematic reinterpretation of Beatrice-Joanna's 'no' as really meaning 'yes', the indeterminacy of De Flores's physical ugliness in the play partly accounts for this ambivalent critical response to his self-appointed role as lover.

Physical ugliness, then, does not fix, determine or reveal masculine identity in this play. Once Beatrice-Joanna's deformity is exposed, her identity and fate are both secure: she is 'common [sewage]' (5.3.153). De Flores's ugliness, on the other hand, while it may be connected with his social fall, does not preclude him from renegotiating his social position. Bacon discusses the possibility that (implicitly male) deformity can be turned to social advantage:

> in their superiors, it quencheth jealousy towards them, as persons that they think they may at pleasure despise; and it layeth their competitors and emulators asleep, as never believing that they should be in possibility of advancement, till they see them in possession. So that upon the matter in a great wit deformity is an advantage to rising.[84]

De Flores's ugliness likewise in some ways works to his advantage, falsely suggesting to Beatrice-Joanna that he is someone she 'may at pleasure despise', and thus blinding her to his growing hold over her, until, too late, she sees him 'in possession'. De Flores is consequently able to refashion the terms of his social identity, making himself 'one' with his master's daughter (3.4.139). It is partly because of his ugliness, then, that De Flores is able to work his way back, if temporarily, into the aristocratic community from which he had been excluded. As Calbi argues, he effectively repositions himself in relation to Beatrice-Joanna as a superior 'judgemental super-ego', thus recovering 'his ideal self . . . the self he once was before the "expulsion"'. The abject is remoulded as the voice of moral judgement: it is De Flores, supposedly the amoral outsider, who purges the patriarchal body through letting Beatrice-Joanna's blood in the final scene.[85] Getting his revenge 'on nature', De Flores indicates the protean possibilities of a male ugliness whose meanings refuse to be stabilised.

More innocuously, Antonio also illustrates the surface and opaque nature of male ugliness in this play. Disguising himself as insane (and thus as ugly, since 'handsomest ... madman' is as much an oxymoron as 'understanding madman' in the play, 3.3.30–1) in order to woo Isabella, deformity and handsomeness are clothes to be worn or discarded at will:

> Look you but cheerfully, and in your eyes
> I shall behold mine own deformity
> And dress myself up fairer; I know this shape
> Becomes me not, but in those bright mirrors
> I shall array me handsomely.
>
> (3.3.187–91)

Once again, perception, rather than intrinsic quality, determines beauty and ugliness: we must '[t]ake no acquaintance/of [the] outward follies' of men (3.3.140–1).

The Changeling thus displays the extent to which representations of ugliness are inflected by gender in this era. Those who best disguise their deformity in the play, ironically, become those whose ugliness is most exposed to public view: surface beauty is no barrier, in the end, to a conclusive reading of feminine deformity. Once revealed in women, moral deformity carries clearly defined meanings. '[Blasted] to deformity', not even Beatrice-Joanna questions that she must be 'cast ... to the ground regardlessly'. Despite the potential duplicity of feminine beauty, then, women, as physiognomical texts promised, are ultimately legible: their ugliness is ready to be uncovered. Haunted by a Calvinist awareness that the truth of one's identity is dangerously hidden from view, the play thus attempts to provide some consolation through physiognomical discourses in which the female body, at least, can ultimately be forced to reveal its secrets.[86] Outward appearances nevertheless require careful reading, and are not equally legible. Potentially suggestive of evil, the meanings of male ugliness, in particular, are shown to be radically unstable. A surface, possibly transient, condition, rather than an inner truth, male ugliness is not, with any certainty, indicative of character. *The Changeling* therefore engages with contemporary anxieties as it explores the redundancy of simple visual categories of knowledge.[87] The sinister impact of the play, in which the audience remains as much in a 'labyrinth' (3.4.72) regarding moral judgements as are many of the characters on stage, reveals the dark fears surrounding the emergence of modern subjectivity in this era.

Ugliness in the Age of Reason: William Hay

Describing himself as an 'ill-tuned Person', 'scarce five Feet high' with a 'bent' back, William Hay, MP, tackles the 'uncommon' yet for him highly personal subject of bodily deformity in *Deformity: An Essay* (1754).[88] Pender claims that the essay is a milestone in the rejection of the notion that moral qualities can be 'accessed and assessed anatomically', while Felicity Nussbaum and Helen Deutsch have both identified the text as a key moment in the construction of disability as identity.[89] Question marks over the ugly (male) body's ability to figure the soul, as we have seen, were evident in literature long before the mid-eighteenth century. Hay's essay nonetheless illustrates the renegotiation of the meanings of physical ugliness generated by modern forms of subjectivity, a renegotiation that by this later date was beginning to be open to female as well as male characters in texts. Popular distrust and mockery of the deformed continue to be visible in the eighteenth century: to the masses, states Hay, ugliness is an '[apparition] of ill' (33). He nevertheless insists on the social determination of deformity, rejecting any necessary connection between a twisted body and a corrupt soul.[90] Deutsch observes in relation to Hay's work that the eighteenth century

> was divided in its representations of disability between two ideas of agency – one divine and insurmountable, one human and exceptional. In the earlier model the body is God's sign. In the later the body is transformed into a sign by the subjectivity it both obscures and creates.[91]

Many still deride and fear the deformed, but Hay imposes an alternative reading of his crookedness, suggesting that a defective body is in fact emblematic of the ideal rational and virtuous subject.

Following Bacon, even as he contests some of his key assumptions, Hay insists on the advantages of deformity, a physical condition which he presents as a spur to educated self-improvement. Deformity, in this essay, as Kathleen James-Cavan observes, turns out to be 'a civilizing influence'.[92] Hay dissects his physical shortcomings with clinical detachment, noting that his 'Spider-like Shape' inhibits his ability to buckle his shoe or pick up a lady's glove, limits the occupations to which he is suited and provokes the mockery of the 'vulgar'. The only relation his body bears to his spiritual, emotional or intellectual capacities, however, is to encourage him to develop his moral and cognitive 'Qualities'. Sarah Scott's *Agreeable Ugliness*, published the same year as Hay's essay, reaches a similar conclusion, emphasising the self-control and intellectual focus of its unattractive narrator, qualities stimulated by her lack of physical appeal, and detailing her consequent social and moral superiority to a sister who has the 'unlucky Destiny' to be beautiful.[93] Far from signifying an immoral character, an ugly body in mid-eighteenth-century writing has the potential to be an object that the subject negotiates and ultimately turns to his or her own benefit. 'Deformity is a Protection to a Man's health and person' (27–8), asserts Hay, citing his own temperament and avoidance of accidents to back up this thesis.

Rather than innate or transcendent states of being, beauty and ugliness are identified in the essay as cultural constructs, defined by the cultivation of the mind and the civilisation of the body (or the lack thereof). While conceding the natural limitations of his physical form, Hay considers both his body and his identity to be entities at his own disposal. He laments the 'awkwardness' of 'some part of [his] outward Gesture and Behaviour', but this ugliness of bearing results from his failure to deploy the 'Care and Habit' necessary to 'correct' such carelessness rather than an accident of birth. His embarrassment at his twisted shape is also identified as a social rather than a natural phenomenon, stemming from a childhood in which he was 'taught ... to be ashamed of [his] Person' (7). As an adult, he is able to construct his body in alternative terms, re-inscribing himself as beautiful through insisting on his civilised self-control. The 'Stamp of a Man's character' (10), he insists, inheres not in the shape of his features but in the evidence of his educated civility. Instead of being marked as vicious by the signs of his body, Hay's subjectivity is alienated from the body whose corruptions it is capable of correcting: 'I may pluck the Villain from my own Breast ... I may cleanse my own Heart from Filth and Impurity: I may demolish the Hydra of Vices within me' (71). He displaces monstrosity away from the deformed body, and from his own well regulated body in particular, identifying it with the sinful passions that he has overcome. True ugliness is projected on to those who fail to rein in their brutish passions: 'the Mob' may mock those with crooked backs, but 'one would think a prominent Belly a more reasonable Object of it; since the last is generally the Effect of Intemperance, and of a Man's own Creation' (35).

While female authors such as Scott were exploring the new possibilities for unattractive female characters opened up by modern reconfigurations of the relationship between the body and the soul, Hay's essay illustrates the stubborn persistence of gendered models of ugliness. Like the obese, ugly women in his essay exhibit their subordination to a corrupt physical order. The ugly female subject cannot renegotiate the significance of her own unattractiveness: 'if plain', he states, 'she cannot be transformed' (62–3). Hay thus redefines ugliness as enslavement to the body, a condition he emphatically distances from his own subjectivity. Rather than accepting the popular perception that his shape aligns him with 'the Hydra of Vices', Hay inverts his deformity into a sign of his rational self-control. Defined in opposition to the gross physicality of women, the obese and the vulgar, Hay's presents his self-cultivated body as possessing an alternative form of beauty. Hogarth's *The Analysis of Beauty* 'proves incontestably' that beauty 'consists in Curve Lines' (82), he remarks in his postscript.[94] 'O Temperance,' he apostrophises, 'Thou Patroness of Health! Thou Protector of Beauty! Thou Prolonger of Life! ... Thou Guardian of the Person! ... Thou Parent of every intellectual Improvement, and of every moral Virtue!' (25). Far from confining him within his physical form, his limitations have taught him to disregard corporeal concerns. As Deutsch comments, Hay 'draws on a tradition of exceptional bodies that bear the signs of corporeality conquered.'[95] He '[consecrates] to fame' a deformed auctioneer of Seville, thrown to wild animals by the Roman Balbus simply because of his ugliness, identifying him as 'foremost in the glorious List of our Martyrs' (40). Defined in vulgar opinion by their bodies, the deformed, for Hay, heroically transcend the physical order.

The modern man, Hay insists, is not created by his body; he creates himself. '[U]se Stratagem,' he advises his 'fraternity': 'call in the Aid of the Taylor, to present them with better Shapes than Nature has bestowed' (36). The body is not simply that which can be disguised through clothes, however, but is itself nothing more than an outward show, a mask. A 'Man's Person... is the Dress of his Soul', he states (39). Physical appearance, in other words, is no longer an essential aspect of the self; it has become an alienable property.[96] 'Is the Carcass the better Part of the Man?' he asks incredulously. Objectifying and neutralising the body, Hay refers to it as a 'Habitation: which is sometimes not lodged according to its Quality' (72). Noble minds can be made to dwell in 'inconvenient' bodies, but this is of little consequence, since this 'accommodation' is merely 'an Inn upon the Road' (72).

Hay therefore '[writes] of Deformity with Beauty', seeking to prove that 'Persons so oddly (I will not say unhappily) distinguished' are as capable of self-improvement, noble sentiment and civility as their more handsome neighbours, if not more so (3, 2). Deformity 'tends to the Improvement of the Mind': those who cannot rely on physical charms 'attempt to adorn that Part... which alone is capable of Ornament' (68). 'The more a Man is unactive in his Person, the more his Mind will be at work,' he claims, implying that the ugly have greater self-awareness than the beautiful, a sharper sense of detachment from the body which situates them more decisively as its master rather than its slave. Cultivating their 'true Qualities', distancing themselves from an objectified body whose appetites they bring under the control of virtuous reason, the deformed (that is, deformed men), to Hay, are ideal Enlightenment subjects.

4

'Sight of her is a vomit':[1] abject bodies and Burton's *The Anatomy of Melancholy*

The representation of ugly women in early modern texts not only betrays the extent to which women occupy an uneasy position in relation to emergent forms of subjectivity, but also exposes the role that the figure of the repulsive woman plays in the construction of dominant models of the self.[2] The early modern subject is increasingly defined by his rational self-control, his ability to regulate and thus to transcend the body and its potentially chaotic fluids. The ugly woman, as she emerges in literary and visual portraits from the period, operates as this subject's diabolical opposite. Possessing a body whose gross excesses refuse to remain within normative boundaries, she threatens to dissolve into amorphousness, beyond human recognition. Aligned with animals and corpses, her status as a human subject is called into question. Carrier of diseases and transgressor of sexual, social and physical norms, she horrifies and nauseates, provoking a violent response. Rather than simply subverting normative forms of identity, however, depictions of unattractive women frequently shore up the fragile boundaries of these identities.

Kristeva's theorisation of the abject sheds light on the function of representations of ugly characters in the maintenance of early modern subjectivity. The abject, recalling a state of non-differentiation from the mother, encompasses the deformed or defective body, a body which draws attention to its own materiality and thus recalls for the ego 'its source on the abominable limits from which, in order to be, [it] has broken away'. Ugly bodies, for Kristeva, evoke 'the impure, the non-separate, the non-symbolic, the non-holy'. As such, they are potentially subversive. Abjection is nevertheless defined in *Powers of Horror* as a mechanism through which both subjectivity and society are constructed. The abject is opposed to the symbolic order of language and identity but is also a necessary point of departure for the subject: 'I give birth to myself amid the violence of sobs, of vomit.' Identity depends upon nausea, on the rejection of the abject. The abject is thus the 'horror that [civilisations] seize on in order to build themselves up and function'.[3] To draw on the spatial terminology of Judith Butler in *Bodies that Matter*, an 'outside' must be constructed in order to make the 'inside' of subjectivity possible. The 'inside' depends on the 'outside' for its existence even as it relentlessly and necessarily seeks its expulsion:

This zone of uninhabitability will constitute the defining limit of the subject's domain; it will constitute that site of dreaded identification against which – and by virtue of which – the domain of the subject will circumscribe its own claim to autonomy and life. In this sense, then, the subject is constituted through the force of exclusion and abjection, one which produces a constitutive outside to the subject, an abjected outside, which is, after all, 'inside' the subject as its own founding repudiation.[4]

While the repulsiveness of the ugly woman in early modern texts is exposed and dissected in order to secure the 'pure' self as her opposite, her exaggerated, inchoate form perpetually undermines the boundaries of the self which she helps to constitute. Aggressive, demonic, lustful, the loathsome woman as she is constructed in the writing of the period plays a necessary role in the construction of dominant forms of identity but simultaneously betrays masculine anxiety regarding the power of the 'other' to encroach upon and dismantle the self, exposing the insecurity attendant upon the male subject's processes of self-differentiation.[5] Many of these tensions surface in Robert Burton's *The Anatomy of Melancholy* (1621), as we shall see later in the chapter. As critics note, the speaking subject of this text (like the text itself) fails to maintain a secure hold on the self-regulation, bodily integrity and rational control by which an acceptable masculine self is defined in this era. The unattractive female body meanwhile continues to be projected, indeed violently constructed, as a necessary 'other' to ideal forms of masculine subjectivity in the work. Ugliness works very differently for men and for women in *The Anatomy of Melancholy*, complicating recent critical readings of its 'delirious disfiguring'.[6]

'Still abusing women'[7]

Classical rhetorical traditions invoked physical features as signs of moral character, and such conventions were perpetuated in the middle ages. Matthew of Vendome's *Ars versificatoria* (c. 1175), for example, draws on the rhetorical techniques established by Horace and other classical figures. Helen of Troy's golden hair, milky forehead, snowy neck, starry eyes, rosy cheeks and lips, white teeth, dainty breasts and narrow waist embody perfect beauty in the treatise, while the 'mangy cur' Beroe, old, disfigured, hairy, 'filthy to look at and repulsive to touch', is an early instance of the literary ugly woman.[8] Helen's perfection is inextricable from the tight, polished and controlled boundaries of her body: 'Neither the shapely leg, nor the trim knee, nor/The small foot, nor the smooth hand hangs with loose/Skin.' Beroe, on the other hand, is characterised by foul and excessive bodily excretions. 'Slime drips' from her eyes, which 'have bloody matter running from them' and 'rheumy sickness welling up in them'. Her 'fetid flat nose . . . drips pestilential mucus', a 'flow' that 'keeps her upper lip wet as the thick froth/From her nose returns to its diseased host'. In a hideous parody of beautiful features, 'Stygian saliva' is said to '[manure] her mouth's/Curving lines'. Her neck is a 'repulsive mass of knots,/Sores, and streaming corruption'. In line with his focus on Beroe's uncontrolled, fetid bodily fluids, the speaker then emphasises the horrors of her 'chamber pot', a 'turbulent lake', a 'sulphurous whirlpool' that '[runs] red'. Even her knees are 'steeped in a painful flow of burning pus'. In sum, she is 'a lake brimming with filth'.[9] Helen is an icy, stony, discrete whole, whereas Beroe is a 'wretched chaos of a woman', dissolving bodily boundaries with appalling abandon. The description of Beroe accords with the open bodily orifices and protuberances described by Bakhtin as the grotesque bodily economy.[10] While the Bakhtinian grotesque straddles life and death, however, operating as a positive symbol of fertility, renewal and rebirth, Beroe is more narrowly associated with disease, decomposition and death. The fluids dripping from her body are 'pestilential', pus-filled and contaminating rather than renewing and regenerating. Flies buzz around her putrid form, which has already begun to be consumed by worms. More akin to a rotting corpse than Bakhtin's senile pregnant hag, she is depicted in entirely negative, satirical terms. A 'pallid social outcast', she embodies gendered and class-specific cultural anxieties.[11] In her old age and with her foul bodily emissions and diseased, necrotic body, Beroe prefigures the ugly woman as she is represented in scurrilous early modern descriptions.

The ugly woman in early modern English literature largely perpetuates established literary and rhetorical models of female ugliness. As in classical and medieval rhetorical traditions, for example, the ugly woman's sexual organs are frequently the focus of the viewer's disgust, the repellent sexuality they evoke bearing witness to the woman's moral depravity. No one remains in any doubt about 'fowle' Duessa's character in *The Faerie Queene*, for example, after 'her misshaped parts' are stripped for all to see. She is exposed as a 'loathly, wrinkled hag, ill favoured, old', her physical appearance materialising her corrupt nature: 'such is the face of falsehood'.[12] Early modern visual arts also tend to reproduce stereotypical patterns of female ugliness. Quinten Massys's *An Old Woman* ('*The Ugly Duchess*') (c. 1513; Figure 14), for instance, draws explicitly on Leonardo da Vinci's drawings of grotesque figures.[13]

Early modern English poems depicting ugly hags are often framed as a male speaker's response to a sexual or verbal assault (the two are usually indistinguishable) by a repulsive woman. Despite the fact that the works are invectives against a typically silent female figure, the woman is usually cast as the aggressor, the male speaking subject as the passive victim. The startling opening of Samuel Wesley's (equally strangely entitled) 'On a Discourteous Damsel that call'd the Right Worshipful Author – (an't please ye!) Sawcy Puppy' (1685) illustrates the widespread association of female ugliness with verbal and sexual assertion: 'Ugly! Ill-natur'd! impudent, and proud!/Sluttish! Nonsensical! And idly loud!'[14] The term 'slut' refers both to a woman of lower social status who is considered 'dirty, slovenly' or 'untidy' in appearance and to a woman 'of loose character', betraying the manner in which discourses of ugliness are deployed to demonise marginal and deviant figures and to police acceptable boundaries of gendered and social behaviour.[15] The ugly woman is a vulgar, outrageous character, in body, word and deed overstepping the boundaries of social and physical decorum. In rejecting her, and the bodily,

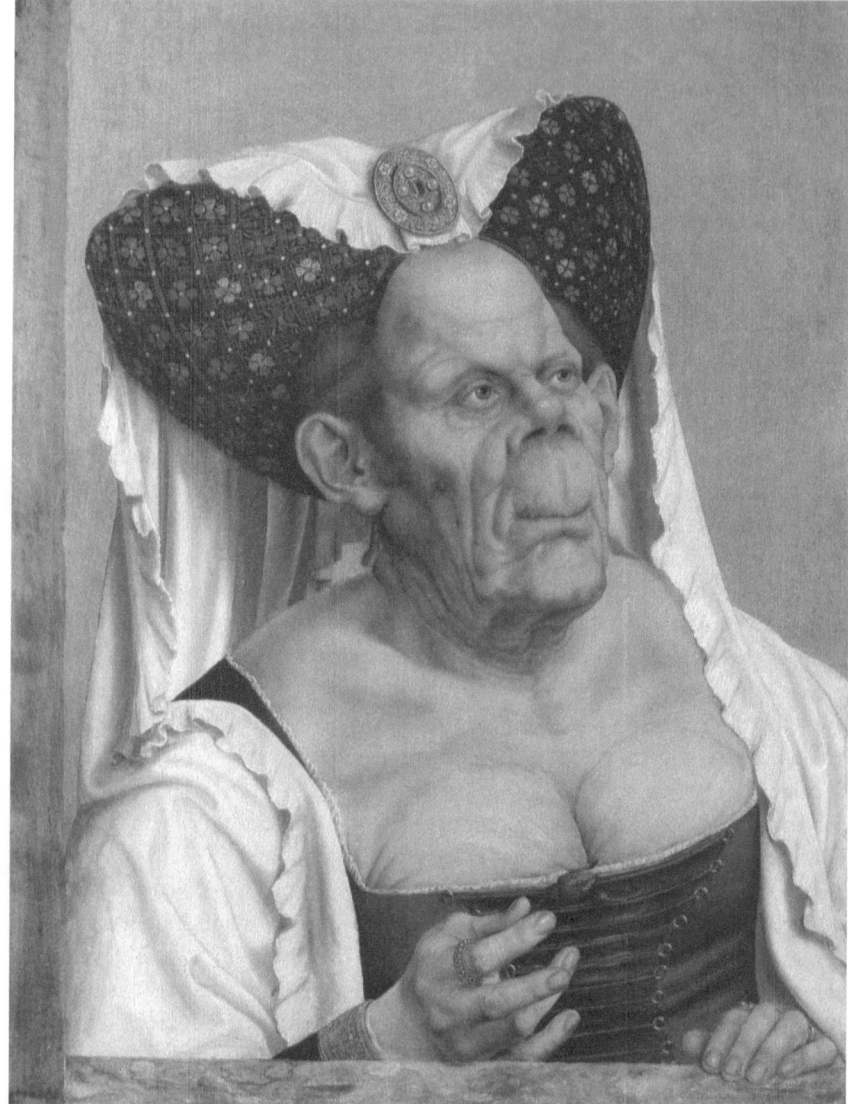

Figure 14 Quinten Massys, *An Old Woman ('The Ugly Duchess')*, c. 1513

social and sexual violation she represents, the male subject maintains his own identity, revealing the role that this grossly material 'other' plays in the formation of the male speaking subject's transcendent sense of self.

Representations of extreme repulsiveness attempt to keep the threatening ugly woman at a safe distance through rendering her unmistakable in her ugliness. The terms in which the ugly woman's body is depicted nevertheless tend to be grounded in more general constructions of the female body, undermining the distinction between beautiful and ugly femininity that the works are at the same time anxious to construct. *A Character of an Ugly Woman* (1678) by George Villiers, second Duke of Buckingham, describes its subject in the following terms:

> Her plaistred Face drops against ill Weather, and when she laughs, it looks like a Ruffled Boot, or an old Candle in the middle of it; she is Pigg-eye'd, Beetle-brow'd, Horse-tooth'd, Woodcock nos'd, as crooked in Body as in Mind, her Skin Pease-porridge Tawney, or somewhat inclining to the oriental Complexion of Rusty Bacon, beset with natural Rubies, and Carbuncles, yet always bare, always down to the Centre, and two or three huge black patches to cover the puny Gurncetts, and shin scabs into Beauty spots; as for the other infernal Parts, the Divel deals their altogether: For they lye under the Torrid Zone, and therefore utterly uninhabitable, only some bold Travellers that have ventur'd, represent them much like the Desarts of Arabia, horrible Wild and Barren.[16]

This description inverts and parodies the conventions of Petrarchan love poetry, drawing on the same imagery and techniques of fragmented description that construct the 'cruel fair', even as the terms in which this conventional beauty is represented are comically displaced. The desirable mistress is often depicted in love poetry from the era as colonial territory conquered by the male lover, and this imagery is parodied here as a means of evoking sexual loathing for the woman's body. Despite her repulsiveness, then, the ugly woman is a reworking of conventional literary models of beauty. Both beautiful and ugly women are subject to the same techniques of description, suggesting that the difference between them is not as great as we might assume: rearrange the imagery slightly, and one slips easily into the other.[17]

Donne's 'The Comparison' similarly insists on a stark polarity between his beautiful mistress and another man's unattractive conquest which soon becomes unstable. The 'other' woman is stained by 'ranke sweaty froth', her body defined by defiling waste products, 'like spermatique issue of ripe menstruous boiles'. The 'beautiful' woman, on the other hand, has 'sweat drops' like 'pearle coronets'.[18] The fact that both women are defined by leaky bodies marked by extraneous, impure bodily fluids undermines the distinction between them.[19] Maintaining a division between beauty and ugliness is beyond the reach of this poem, whose implicit argument is that all women's bodies, in the end, are excremental, fluid, 'odious'.[20] The equation of the monstrously ugly woman with womankind as a whole is a subtext throughout vituperative depictions of unattractive women from this era, undermining the efforts of these works to establish a clear gap between repulsive, unacceptable ugliness and pure, wholesome beauty.

'Menstruous, plaguy, loathsome'[21]

'This [u]gly thing is now no more a face,' says Margaret of her self-mutilated features in Chapman's *The Gentleman Usher*, drawing attention to the formlessness that frequently characterises female ugliness in early modern depictions.[22] Donne's 'The Comparison' likens the ugly mistress's head to 'a rough-hewne statue of jeat,/Where marks for eyes, nose, mouth are yet scarce set;/Like the first Chaos'.[23] '[C]anst thou finde in all that Masse/Of monstrous ugliness, one peece that can/Render thee fit for the most sinful man[?]' asks the speaker of Edmund Prestwich's 'On an old Ill-favoured Woman, become a young lover' (1651). '[T]hy shapeless age/Allowes thee not of mortall Parentage,' he continues. 'Thou'rt a meer Chaos, which I am content/To grant that nature for a Woman meant.'[24] 'I did once think thou hadst a face,' wryly states the speaker of James Shirley's 'To the Proud M.' (1646), implying that an ugly face is no face at all.[25] 'What Tytian lump is here? what form? what fashion?' agrees the speaker of Hugh Crompton's 'Deformity' (1657), incandescent at the prospect of sexual intimacy with a deformed woman.[26] The inchoate, repulsive female body is the polar opposite of the well defined and strictly self-policed early modern subject. Peter Stallybrass notes the growing enclosure of the body in this era: the 'cleansing of the orifices' that increasingly demarcated 'the social elite from the "vulgar"' emphasised the borders of a closed individuality.[27] The repellent woman in texts from this era embodies all that is being rejected by this emergent, class-specific, discrete modern self, highlighting through her amorphousness the extent to which an acceptable identity is grounded in a sense of boundedness.

Standing in opposition to emergent models of the self, female bodies, as Gail Kern Paster demonstrates, were associated with an embarrassing leakiness in this period. In the Galenic model of the body, both male and female bodies are constituted of humours, but female bodies are understood to be 'more' humoural. Associated with cold and wet humours, they are more fluid, open and porous than their male counterparts.[28] John Johnstone, a seventeenth-century physician and naturalist educated at the Universities of St Andrews, Cambridge and Leiden, whose Latin treatises on nature were highly regarded in England in this era, recounts the endlessly surprising manner in which the female body is liable to exceed its borders:

> A Maid of Saxony had her Terms come forth of her eys. A Nun had them come forth of her ears. Pareus his Wife had them by her nostrils: A Maid at Sturgard vomited them up: A Maid in the Island Chios, spit them up. Amatus speaks of some that voided them by their Teats: A woman, of Trent, voided them by her Navel; and which is wonderfull, a Nun voided them every month by her little finger, and ring finger of her left hand.[29]

The ugly woman once again emerges as an exaggerated version of wider models of femininity. In *A Character of an Ugly Woman*, for example, the woman is mocked for stating that her fictitious husband has died at sea: 'indeed, 'tis no wonder he should be cast away in such a filthy leaky Bottom; for all those must needs be Ship-wrack'd, that cast Anchor in her Embraces'.[30] In the broadside ballad *The Olde Bride, or The Gilded Beauty* (c. 1635), the woman's repulsive sexuality is evoked in the statement that 'all the issue can be given/Is that which runneth in her leg'.[31] *The Merry Dutch Miller* (1672), an anonymous tract which constructs a fantasy of men dragging their ugly, scolding wives to a windmill to be 'ground' into younger, better-behaved and more beautiful versions of themselves, includes the case of 'Kit the Cooper' who hauls his 'old wife Joan' to the miller because 'she cannot hold her Water . . . all that ever I can do will not stop her old Leak'.[32] Constructions of the uncontrolled lower social orders intersect with gendered models in descriptions of unregulated, fluid bodies. John Skelton's tavern woman, Elynour Rummynge, has 'lewde lyypes' that 'slaver', a hooked nose 'never stoppynge/but ever droppynge', while 'Dronken Ales' in the same poem 'pyst where she stood./Then began she to wepe'.[33] Herrick's epigrams also present an underclass whose bodies are perpetually seeping. In 'Upon a cheap Laundresse', 'Feacie . . . doth wash her clothes I' th' Lie/ That sharply trickles from her either eye', while 'Upon Dol' mocks a woman whose 'cheecks wo'd soon rost dry,/Were they not basted by her either eye'. 'Old Widow Shopter', meanwhile, 'when so ere she cryes,/Lets drip a certain Gravie from her eyes'.[34] The chaotic fluids characterising the ugly female and lower-class body pose a dangerous threat to emerging models of self-controlled, rational identity, disturbingly reminding the elite masculine subject of the precarious basis of his own carefully regulated physicality.[35]

Revealing the anxiety it generates, the fluid female body is often represented as a noxious source of contagion. A Puritan tract describes a 'vicious venomous humour' in the female body which 'glues together . . . the haire of the head with a prodigious ugly implication and intanglement' so that female hair represents the serpent-infested head of Medusa, 'full of nastiness, vermin, and noysome smell'.[36] Writing in 1615, Helkiah Crooke states that women overflow with vile and poisonous humours, like the bodies of 'those that have the French disease and the Leprosy, considering that in such bodies the Excrements of vicious humours are exceeding aboundant'.[37] '[A]re not your kisses then as filthy, and more,/As a worme sucking an invenom'd sore?' asks the speaker of Donne's 'The Comparison', while *A Character of an Ugly Woman* is more prosaic: 'where ever she comes, Diseases as naturally follow her'.[38] Lower-class female characters are represented as particularly filthy and contaminating, associated with the dirt, lice and scabies of bodies that are not subject to the hygiene with which the upper classes are increasingly aligned in the early modern era.[39] Elynour Rumming, for example, 'ugly of chere/Droupy and drowsy/ Scurvy and lowsy', has tavern customers who are '[a] sorte of foule drabbes/All scurvy with scabbes./Some be flybytten'.[40] The ageing female form is also associated with polluted excrement and disease. Rotten teeth and gums were a fact of early modern life, as Herrick's epigrams so often remind us, but the bad breath of the older woman receives particular attention in scurrilous descriptions of women.[41] Francis Lenton, in *Lentons Leisures Described* (1636), for example, delineates a host of characters, including the 'old bawd', 'a menstruous beast, engendred of divers most filthy excrements, by the stench of whose breath the Ayre is so infected, that her presence is an inevitable contagion, her eyes more poisonous than the Basilisk; her nose (if any) most pestilently pocky'. She is a 'defiled Carkasse'.[42] 'Prepare for to encounter Death,/And try to blast him with thy breath,' instructs the speaker of Samuel Sheppard's 'An old Woman Letcherous' (1651), while in Prestwich's 'On an old Ill-favoured Woman' the woman's 'sable teeth made of unpolish'd jet' are likened to 'jewels in a Dunghill set'.[43]

The diseases and infestations associated with unattractive figures suggest the ugly body's refusal to recognise limits, its dangerous, defiling capacity to bleed into its surroundings. Lady Would-Be, in Jonson's *Volpone* (1606), who 'hath not yet the face to be dishonest', is threateningly talkative and is consequently described as contagious: 'I do feel the fever/Entering in at mine ears,' laments Volpone as he anticipates being swamped by 'another flood of words'. Prestwich's 'On an old Ill-favoured Woman' similarly depicts a sexually aggressive older woman as infectious:

> For when thou opes thy sore, and dost relate
> Like a curst shrew the rigour of thy fate,
> Telling what flames are in thy bosom bred,
> A Feaver entertains him in his bed:
> If thy wan lookes for pitty seem to call,
> Into a deep consumption he doth fall; ...
> When thy rude cough doth shake each aged limbe,
> An Ague, or the Palsie shaketh him.
> Then if from thy pale Lips he drink a kiss,
> Without an Antidote he poyson'd is ...
> And for the Plague, there's none will doubt, but he
> In a full measure hath it, who hath thee.[44]

Mitigating the anxieties evident in depictions of contagious female bodies, other works cast the male speaking subject in a more empowered position, likening him to a surgeon. Wesley's 'On a Discourteous Damsel' deploys this image, as the speaker condescends 'to touch thee, tho' I'm forc'd to turn my face;/Touch thee as a Surgeon touches rotten sores'.[45] Rather than being threatened by the woman's contaminating, porous corporeality, the male subject here becomes the means of its excision and cure.

Elsewhere, however, the fluid, and particularly the menstruating, female body retains a terrifying power. Menstrual blood has 'a venemous quality in it', asserts Johnstone, citing Pliny that:

> You shall not easily find any thing that is more monstrous than the terms of women: new Wine will grow sowre by them, Corn will wither by touching them, plants will dye, the buds of Trees will be burnt by them, and fall; Looking-glasses grow dark by their very looks. The edge of Steel and the brightnesse of Ivory is mad[e] blunt, swarms of Bees dye, Brasse and Iron will presently rust, and a stinking smell corrupts the ayre: Dogs run mad that tast them, and bite deadly with venome incurable.[46]

Menstrual blood has a 'malignant quality', agrees Crooke: it is 'an excrement vomited out by Nature'. Crooke argues that the infant's exposure to this humour in the womb later manifests itself in 'Meazels and small Pocks', when 'the impurity of the menstrual blood, which humours boiling and being offensive to nature, are thrust out into the skin'.[47] It is no coincidence that the 'poysonous' quality of menstrual blood generates skin conditions in the child. Symbolising the transgressive, fluid, unregulated female body, menstruation finds its counterpart in contagious diseases characterised by skin eruptions, where the boundaries of the body are also breached.

Leprosy is a recurrent theme in depictions of ugly women from this period. 'Close keep your lips, if that you meane/To be accounted inside cleane,' instructs Herrick's 'To Women, to hide their Teeth, if they be Rotten or Rusty' (1648): 'For if you cleave them, we shall see/There in your teeth much Leprosie.'[48] Prestwich's 'On an old Ill-favoured Woman' asserts that "tis not time or age could change thee thus;/Thou wert by Nature made so leprous'.[49] The speaker of Thomas Jordan's 'To a Black-moor that had married a Deformed Spanish Woman' (c. 1680) expresses his horror of miscegenation in similarly pathological terms: 'Dost think I'll have my Heyr look like a Leper? ... Shall I pollute my Limbs with an embrace/For a py'd Kitling with a dappled face?'[50] Leprosy had largely been eliminated from Europe by the early modern period, but the discourses surrounding the complaint were resurrected in relation to a horrifying new disease, syphilis, which also manifested itself in disfigured skin. Early descriptions of syphilis evoking leprosy help to consolidate the significance of the 'heavily stigmatized' 'pox', seen as 'a supreme manifestation of disorder'.[51] Putrifying skin conditions are evidence of divine judgement in the Old Testament. Miriam, for instance, is punished with leprosy for questioning Moses's authority. King Uzziah, meanwhile, presumptuously enters the temple of the Lord, with the result that 'the leprosy even rose up in his forehead ... and they thrust him out from thence'.[52] Impiously crossing the line dividing the consecrated from the unconsecrated, Uzziah's transgression is figured in a flesh-eating disease which itself deconstructs borders, necessitating his removal from the community and thus enabling the re-imposition of clear lines between the holy and the tainted. Drawing on these biblical traditions, leprosy is frequently used as a metaphor for sin in early modern England. The righteousness of the best man is 'spotted and defiled with the Leprosy of his originall corruption', states Arthur Hildersam in one of his sermons on Psalm 51.[53] Hobbes speaks of the 'Leprousie of sin', while Miles Hogarde's *The Displaying of the Protestantes* (1556) figures Protestants as rotten flesh threatening to poison the entire body and hence requiring excision.[54] Skin conditions were not the unique preserve of the ungodly: Job's boils provide a biblical model of a righteous man suffering from a skin disorder. Even in this case, however, as Healy argues, skin lesions retain their association with the generally fallen state of mankind if not with the specific culpability of the sufferer: the 'historie of Job', notes Calvin, illustrates God's ability to 'throw men downe with knowledge of their owne follie, weakenesse, and unclennesse'.[55]

Characterised by the disintegration of the body, putrefying skin complaints disturbingly undermine corporeal identity, reducing figures to a horrifying facelessness.

In her discussion of abjection, Kristeva identifies leprosy as an 'impure' condition. The visible skin disease affects 'the essential if not initial boundary of biological and psychic individuation. From that point of view, the abomination of leprosy becomes inscribed within the logical conception of impurity . . . intermixture, erasing of differences, threat to identity'.[56] Symbolically aligned with lepers, menstruating women similarly evoke a horrific state of non-differentiation which marks them as 'non-holy'. Our righteousness, 'spotted and defiled' with leprosy, is likened in Hildersam's sermon, following Isaiah 30.22, to 'filthy (menstruous, plaguy, loathsome) raggs'.[57] Katherine Sutton, in *A Christian Womans Experiences of the Glorious Working of Gods Free Grace* (1663), similarly likens 'man's righteousness' to 'filthy raggs', which she also depicts as 'monstrous cloathes', silently eliding the 'menstruous' and the 'monstrous'.[58] To William Cowper, in *Pathmos* (1619), sin is

> A vile and lothsome filthiness. Oh that we could see it as it is . . . . It is that leprosie, which infecteth the bloud, the skin, the garments, the house, and all that a man hath. It is more ugly and abominable then a menstruous cloth.[59]

Robert Bolton's *Certaine Devout Prayers of Mr. Bolton* (1638), meanwhile, includes 'An Evening Prayer' where the speaker beseeches God to remove sin, to take away 'all the menstruous filthiness of our abominable nature'.[60] Aligned with transgression and expelling 'plaguy, loathsome' humours, the female body is both source and symbol of physical and moral contagion, its horror and ugliness, like that of the decomposing body of the leper, located in its failure to maintain discrete boundaries of the self.

Abusive descriptions of repulsive women from the early modern era therefore focus on the unattractive woman's tendency to breach the borders of subjectivity. Characterised by amorphousness, by unrestrained fluidity, by marked, broken and diseased skin, the particular characteristics of the ugly woman in these invectives point to the anxieties that she is deployed to negotiate. Foundational as the 'other' against which the dominant subject constructs himself, the ugly woman is a perpetual reminder of the illusory nature of this subject's sense of wholeness and completion. Failing to maintain a discrete corporeal integrity, she embodies a region beyond order, beyond identity, serving as both the necessary outside of the self and its potential point of collapse. The vehement loathing expressed for the unattractive old, female, lower-class body betrays the fear provoked by the horrific corporeal model that she represents. '[T]hy ugly face would fright/The Div'l himself,' states the speaker of Robert Heath's 'To Megaera' (1650).[61] 'Shield me, good Venus, from this ugly ghost/Else I am ruin'd, and for ever lost,' exclaims the speaker of Crompton's 'Deformity'. 'I am beset about/With snakie-hair'd Medusa,' he continues, but the most sinister threat of all is the fact that this monstrosity cannot be securely differentiated from the self: 'What monster in my breast would make invasion?'[62] Medusa elides with a monstrosity within: a safe distance between the two entities cannot be preserved.

The compulsion to expel the terrifying principles embodied in the repulsive woman is evident in the fantasies of violence that haunt early modern descriptions of ugly women.⁶³ The 'old damnable hag' Putana in Ford's *Tis Pity She's a Whore* (c. 1629–33) meets a violent end when Vasques commands men to 'carry her closely into the coal house, and put out her eyes instantly. If she roars, slit her nose.'⁶⁴ Expressing his loathing in slightly less gruesome terms, the speaker of Thomas Randolph's 'Upon a very deformed Gentlewoman' (1652) articulates a similar desire for the 'Gentlewoman's' elimination, suggesting that she 'dye! Resign [her] selfe to death... Turn only voyce.'⁶⁵ Thomas Freeman's epigram 'In Miluum' (1614) also constructs a fantasy of a woman 'in ev'ry part ill-fashioned by nature' killing herself, as he ostensibly warns the woman against looking at her own reflection in case she is driven to 'drowne the object of thy selfe so fowle'.⁶⁶ Addressing the 'proud M.', the speaker of Shirley's poem of that title threatens to 'laugh thee into age/Strike wrinkles on thy brow... Till thou, thy Witches face despise'. Having 'jeered thee into dead and rotten', he will 'throw thee into quite forgotten'.⁶⁷ Shirley's speaker illuminates the extent to which the violence articulated in scurrilous descriptions participates in the same process as the descriptive dissection and display of the woman's unattractive body, an act which aims to exclude and ultimately to eliminate the grotesque corporeal object in order to found the rational, self-controlled, disembodied early modern subject. Longing to 'throw [the ugly woman] into quite forgotten', the speaking subject in these works paradoxically focuses upon her repulsive, defiling body. Despite his apparent desire to turn away, the construction of his identity depends on the verbal anatomising of her deformity. The ugly woman, in other words, can never be 'forgotten': her presence, in the end, is vital to the early modern subject's sense of self.

Old hags

As the above examples suggest, the ugly woman in early modern literature and visual art is frequently elided with the old woman. Old age is synonymous with disease in many texts.⁶⁸ 'I am shunned/And hated like a sickness,' laments the 'lean old beldam' Elizabeth Sawyer, the 'ruined cottage ready to fall with age' in *The Witch of Edmonton*.⁶⁹ The old tend to be regarded as those 'over whose declining splendour, time has drawn a Cloud that will Skreen it till it sets in the shades of the grave'.⁷⁰ The speaker of Herrick's 'To a Gentlewoman objecting to him his Gray Haires' is conscious that he is 'despis'd' for his ageing appearance, indicating that the indignities suffered by the old are not unique to women in this era.⁷¹ Both Herrick's poem and the wider culture place particular emphasis on the physical horrors awaiting women as they age, however. Beautiful (young) women are often told to contemplate the defects of old age as a means of checking their vanity.⁷² Moral failings were believed to become increasingly visible in features as they aged. 'What youth does, age shows,' went the medieval proverb, and this belief extended into early modern

England.⁷³ Women, said in one late sixteenth-century tract to 'begin to wrinkle apace' after their fortieth birthday, are thus condemned as well as denigrated for the loss of beauty associated with their ageing bodies.⁷⁴

Verbal assaults on the old reached 'unprecedented' levels of violence in early modern England.⁷⁵ Vasques's brutal condemnation of Putana in *Tis Pity She's a Whore* ('I'll help your old gums, you toad-bellied bitch!') illustrates the abuse often meted out to the older woman in texts from this era.⁷⁶ Seeking an explanation for the 'hatred which the men of letters expressed towards old women', Georges Minois notes that women began to outlive men for the first time in the fifteenth century. 'Having discovered the old woman,' he surmises, men from the sixteenth century onwards 'pitted themselves against the scandal of hideous femininity'.⁷⁷ Demographic changes do not fully account for the construction of the older female body as 'hideous', however, nor for the specific terms in which this loathsome form is depicted.

Outlining the typical demeanours of men and women of different ages for painters, Leonardo da Vinci advises that 'old women should be represented with aggressive, quick, and wild gestures, like infernal furies'.⁷⁸ The ageing woman in both visual and literary texts is often depicted as a transgressive figure, possessing threatening powers. De Flores's comment that all women will eventually be 'so old their chins and noses meet/And they salute witches' illustrates both the vindictive treatment of the ageing female in early modern England and her alignment with evil powers.⁷⁹ The 'foul witch Sycorax', 'with age and envy grown into a hoop', in Shakespeare's *The Tempest* (c. 1610–11) and the beggar woman whose 'ancient and deformed withered face had made her a long time suspected for a Witch' in Richard Head and Francis Kirkman's *The English Rogue*, Part 4 (1671) further indicate the terrifying malevolence imputed to older women.⁸⁰

As with abusive descriptions of ugly women more generally, poems portraying unsightly ageing women are often framed as the response of a beleaguered male speaker to a verbal assault by the woman. 'Peace Beldam ugly,' begins John Hall's 'To an Old Wife talking to him' (1646–47), a poem in which the woman's speech, never directly reported, is inextricable from her ugliness.⁸¹ The term 'beldam' refers to 'a loathsome old woman, a hag, a witch, a furious raging woman . . . a virago', betraying the association of old women with transgressive power as well as the manner in which outspoken women are stigmatised as deformed.⁸² Giorgione's *La Vecchia* (c. 1505–10; Figure 15) displays a dishevelled, decrepit old woman captured, crucially, mid-speech.⁸³

Old age presented women in early modern England with many social and economic challenges but also potentially brought with it new opportunities for legal and economic independence. A widow in some instances gained control of the financial and business domains previously governed by her husband, as well as his property.⁸⁴ The mockery of aggressive, outspoken figures in texts depicting older women testifies to the anxieties provoked by the potential autonomy of the older

Figure 15 Giorgione, *La Vecchia*, c. 1505–10

woman, particularly the widow, a figure no longer legally 'covered' by father or husband and one more likely than any other woman to pursue her claims in court in this period.[85]

As well as potentially representing a culturally problematic female independence, the old female body provokes loathing because of its supposed ability to hide its hideousness. Female physical and moral ugliness, as we have seen, is often anxiously identified in early modern texts as that which is dangerously hidden or concealed. The abject, as Kristeva states, is 'immoral, sinister, scheming, and shady: a terror that dissembles, a hatred that smiles'.[86] Verbal assaults on older women who

Figure 16 George Wither, 'Deformitie, within may bee,/Where outward Beauties we doe see,' *A Collection of Emblems, Ancient and Moderne* (1635)

use cosmetics to disguise their ugliness betray the anxiety generated by newly available mechanisms for altering the features, suggesting a deeper terror of the potential for deceit contained in the female body. George Wither's 'Looke well, I pray, upon this Beldame here' (1635) deploys the ageing woman as an emblem of those 'Who making faire, and honest outward showes,/Are inwardly deform'd': 'in her habit, though shee gay appeare,/You, through her youthfull vizard, may espy,/Shee's of an old Edition, by her Eye'.[87] (Figure 16.)

Literary and artistic representations of the painted woman counter such anxieties by insisting on the self-evident, immutable nature of female ugliness. Bosola abuses the old lady who has come from painting her 'scurvy face-physic' in Webster's *The Duchess of Malfi* with disgusting images of cosmetically altered faces: 'There was a lady in France, that having had the smallpox, flayed the skin off her face to make it more level; and whereas before she looked like a nutmeg-grater, after she resembled an abortive hedgehog.'[88] 'The Gipsie seeks to wash away/Original Dirt, and Adams Clay', sneers the speaker of Richard Leigh's 'On an old Beldame, washing her Face' (1675). The ageing female body is demonised through association with foreign 'others', the gypsies, as well as becoming the embodiment of original sin. Nothing can disguise her repellent physicality, the speaker reassures himself: 'Would she a likelier Course pursue/She must put off, th' old Woman too.'[89] The tendency of these works to strip, reveal and expose the ugly female body is an attempt to fix the abject, to identify and thus to neutralise the threat that it poses.

The old woman also disturbs because of her liminal status as one who straddles life and death. Humoural theory explains ageing as the drying up of bodily fluids, suggesting that the old body is already, in some senses, dying.[90] 'Deaths character's in her face,' states *The Olde Bride, or the Gilded Beauty*.[91] Prestwich's 'On an old Ill-favoured Woman' meanwhile describes the older woman as a living corpse, capturing the nauseating manner in which the abject disrupts fundamental categories, including those of life and death:[92]

> some grave, fruitfull with dead mens bones,
> Hath teem'd the off-spring of her Skeletons.
> Thou art of such a dirty mol'd; a thing
> Already so like earth, the grave can bring,
> No change to thy complexion. I dare sweare,
> The wormes would scorn to touch thee wert thou there.[93]

Hans Baldung depiction of *The Three Ages of Man and Death* (c. 1539; Figure 17) again captures the old woman's liminal position. The old woman in this painting is more closely aligned with the figure of death than with the younger woman whose clothing she clutches in a vain attempt to remain associated with the living. Rather than a period of life in itself, old age is equated with the moment of death. The horror of the painting lies in the ability of the 'corpse' to reach out and grasp hold of the living, disturbing the boundaries of life and death which the work on another level attempts to construct.

Creating a terrifying link between life and death, just as she potentially collapses the distinction between male and female legal status, the old woman refuses to 'know her place', resisting stable or identifiable categories of being. Her characterisation as a figure likely to traverse acceptable physical and social limits is apparent in the frequency with which she is depicted as a sexual aggressor, a monstrous would-be seductress of young men. The desiring woman is repeatedly indistinguishable from the deformed woman in this period, and this equation comes to the fore in

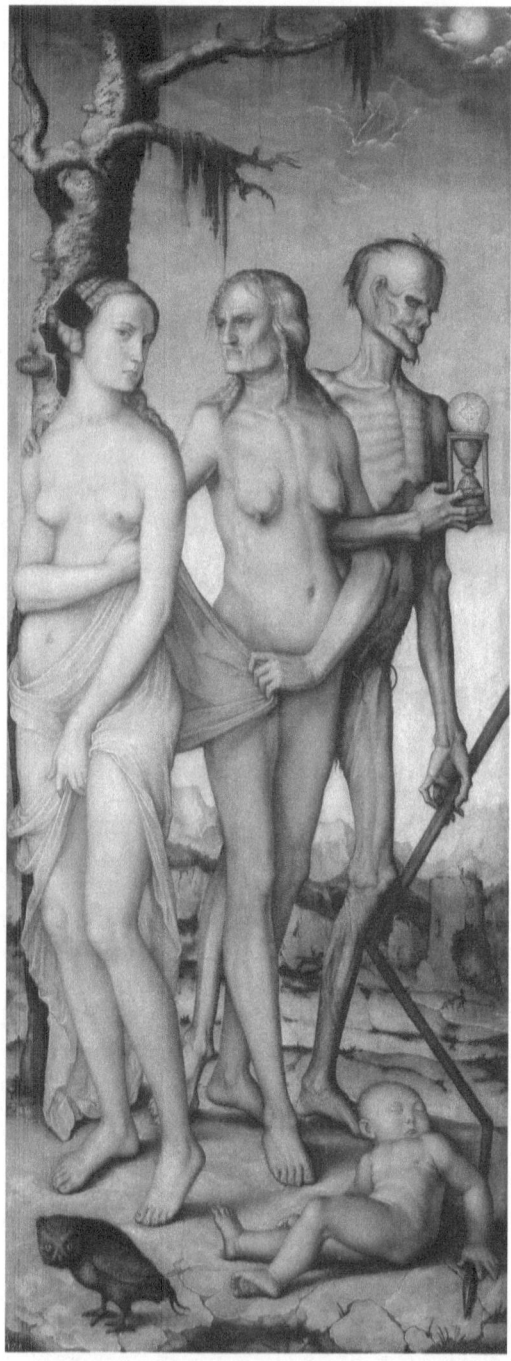

Figure 17 Hans Baldung, *The Three Ages of Man and Death*, c. 1539

representations of older women's sexuality.⁹⁴ The 'gilded beauty', in the ballad of that title, for instance, generates loathing because she is presenting herself as a 'bride': 'What hath been spoken is not meant/Any old woman to disgrace/But she who is to marriage bent.'⁹⁵ Even more disturbing to the speaker than the woman's advances is the possibility that he might fall victim to her seduction. The horror generated by the desiring older woman's body is thus partly the fear of her uncomfortable proximity to the self, the potential desire rather than revulsion that she might provoke. 'If my affection thou would'st win,' states the 'young man' in John Cleveland's 'A young Man to an Old Woman courting him' (1647), acknowledging, fleetingly, the possibility that the old woman could succeed in her quest, even as the concept generates disgust. He subsequently insists on the absolute 'discord . . ./Betwixt thy Skeleton and me', locating her beyond the grave and therefore attempting to place her safely out of reach. The speaker insists that the two figures are polar opposites:

> When th' heavens shuffle all in one;
> The Torrid with the Frozen Zone;
> When all these contradictions meet,
> Then (Sybill) thou and I will greet.⁹⁶

Cleveland's poem illustrates the manner in which descriptions of old women participate in a wider attempt to establish a clear division between the subject and the ugly 'other', a boundary that is clearly under threat. The nauseatingly sexualised images of corpses and the suggestion of the potential for contact between the male speaker and the repellent female body contained in these works evoke the horror of the abject's undermining of categories and binaries, its terrifying ability to make 'contradictions meet'.

John Donne's 'The Autumnall' (1633) brings to the fore many of the tensions characterising vitriolic depictions of ugly ageing women in early modern English writing. As with many early modern depictions of the unattractive body, the poem constructs a series of contrasts, ostensibly establishing clear polarities between different states of being.⁹⁷ In typically witty, paradoxical manner, however, Donne subverts normative categories, praising the older body and disparaging younger, conventional beauties. From the opening lines, the vulgarity of 'spring' and 'summer' beauties is set against the 'grace' of 'one Autumnall face'. Courting an older woman, the speaker insists, places the lover in a superior position to those enamoured with younger flesh: 'Faire eyes, who askes more heate, then comes from hence,/He in a fever wishes pestilence.' While young women are sources of disease and violation (they 'force our love, and that's a Rape'), the old woman is associated with wisdom. She is 'no voluptuousnesse, yet all delight'. 'This is loves timber, youth his underwood,' the speaker continues, as the advantages of an ageing object of desire emerge in opposition to the poor joys offered by a younger model.⁹⁸ Celebrating a quality usually deemed inferior, 'The Autumnall' shares many characteristics with the paradoxical praise genre that I discuss in the next chapter.

The poem nevertheless disturbs the binaries that it superficially constructs.[99] The distinction between youth and age is undermined in the reference to the 'Platane tree', which 'being young, nature did blesse/... with ages glory, Barrennesse'. Youth can possess the attributes of age, destabilising the distinction between the states that the poem has worked to establish. The opposition of the two conditions is further blurred by the fact that the young beauty with whom the ageing woman is compared is her own younger incarnation: 'That was her torrid and inflaming time,/This is her tolerable Tropique clyme.' Youth, the poem is unable to forget, inevitably slides into age, undermining stable oppositions between ugliness and beauty as much as between youth and age, life and death.

After setting age against youth, moreover, the speaker contrasts the 'autumnall' face with 'winter faces', indisputably ugly figures of deep old age,

> whose skin's slacke;
> Lanke, as an unthrifts purse; but a soules sacke;
> Whose Eyes seeke light within, for all here's shade;
> Whose mouths are holes, rather worne out, then made
> Whose every tooth to a severall place is gone,
> To vexe their soules at Resurrection.[100]

Initially exploring the unconventional beauty of old age, the poem abruptly and unexpectedly launches into a more orthodox condemnation of the repellent older woman's body. In doing so, it evokes absolute categories of ugliness in a manner that it elsewhere undermines. The distinction between 'autumn' and 'winter' cannot be maintained, however, any more than can the divide between the attractive and the hideous. The 'living Deaths-heads' whose repulsiveness momentarily accentuates the 'grace' of the autumnal face inescapably haunt her features. 'Call not these wrinkles, graves,' the speaker insists, only to consider them immediately as 'Loves graves'. Death cannot ultimately be divorced from the 'autumnall' woman's body, dissolving the opposition of life and death that the contrast between autumn and winter, evening and night attempts to establish. The poem thus sets up neat oppositions only to confuse them. As Dubrow observes, the central opposition between male speaker and female object of description also breaks down in the poem, which concludes with the speaker acknowledging his own journey towards death, identified with, rather than differentiated from, the repellent bodies of the 'living Death-heads'.[101] The blurring of conceptual categories and subject positions is echoed in the poem's elusive generic identification, straddling both the praise of unconventional beauty and the abusive description of the ugly old female body. The coexistence of disgust at the ageing female body and its ostensible celebration undermines the distinction between beauty and ugliness in relation to the female body, as does the poem's critique of youthful beauty, likened, as we have seen, to infectious disease.

The elusive, destabilising tone and effect of 'The Autumnall', where ugliness is reconsidered only to be insisted upon, age celebrated only to be condemned, categories opposed only to be blurred, draws attention to the contradictions surrounding depictions of the ageing female body in this era. Receptacle for the projected fears of her culture, the older woman's 'repulsive' body, brutally dissected in male descriptions, ostensibly works to distance the male speaker from the liminal state she represents. Fluid and leaky, straddling life and death, at once the site of lack and excess, her unsightly body is opposed to emergent modern forms of subjectivity. Her ugliness, moreover, secures the beauty of her younger counterparts, those objects of Petrarchan display whose flinty, polished features oppose her uncontrolled, badly smelling body in every respect. As Donne's poem reminds us, however, beauty slides into ugliness, youth into age. Rather than the opposite of youthful beauty, the ugly old woman reveals the temporality, the superficiality of that beauty.

The 'living Deaths-heads' of 'Winter-faces' are repeatedly revealed beneath the surface of female youth and beauty in early modern texts. The Cardinal in Middleton's *Women Beware Women* (*c.* 1620–24) fantasises about the disease and death to which all women are ultimately subject as a means of exposing the superficiality of their beauty:

> Is she a thing
> Whom sickness dare not visit, or age look upon,
> Or death resist? Does the worm shun her grave?
> If not, as your soul knows it, why should lust
> Bring man to lasting pain, for rotten dust?[102]

The Cardinal's morbid imaginings associate desire for a woman with desire for a corpse. Donne similarly suggests in 'The Comparison' that the other man's mistress is 'like worme eaten trunks, cloth'd in seals skin,/Or grave, that's dust without and stinke within'.[103] Mocking the 'Vanity of Courtship', John Collop's male speaker parodies the folly of male desire: 'sometimes a deaths head a devotion rears/. . . I never see the ruines of a face/But dust to dust I cry, and straight embrace.'[104] The ugly woman, the living corpse, does not readily stay removed from other women or, more disturbingly, from the male subject.[105] The old hag represents the terrifying mortality not only of all women but ultimately of all men, too. In the end, far from the 'other', she is the monster within.

'Vast virago[s]'[106]

The ugly body in early modern texts is often fat. The speaker of Ben Jonson's 'Epistle: To my Lady Covell' (1640) does not blame the object of his desire for rejecting him,

> being a tardie cold
> Unprofitable Chattell, fat and old,
> Laden with Bellie, and doth hardly approach
> His friends, but to breake Chaires, or cracke a Coache.
> His weight is twenty Stone within two pound.[107]

In 'My Picture left in Scotland' (1619) Jonson's speaker again laments the undesirability of his considerable girth, as well as his rugged features, noting that his beloved has 'Read so much waste, as she cannot embrace/My mountain belly, and my rocky face'.[108] Whatever the potential ironies of Jonson's self-representation, such depictions point to dominant perceptions of the unattractiveness of a corpulent form.[109] Weight-related anxieties are not therefore restricted to women in the writing of the era. The compiler of *The Ladies Dictionary* nevertheless identifies body weight as an issue of particular concern to its readership. The entry 'Body when too Fat, How to reduce it to a Beautiful Form and handsom Proportion' states that:

> Bodies of an unwieldy Bulk are to many unpleasing... no one can think it a very pleasing Sight to see a Soul struggling under a mountainous Load of Flesh and the Body stretched to such Dimensions, as renders it almost out of shape.[110]

While extreme forms of corpulence are regarded by many as repulsive, however, to be fat is not necessarily to be ugly. One of the key properties of the Englishman as he is imagined in patriotic early modern images is his ample flesh.[111] In John Fletcher's *Bonduca, or The British Heroine, a Tragedy* (1696), for instance, 'a hungry Roman soldier' salivates at the prospect of 'A good fat corpulent well-cramm'd Britain', who 'is Provision for a Prince'.[112] Fatness potentially signified wealth and affluence and could be regarded as beautiful.[113] Sanderson's *Graphice* delights in a Van Dyck portrait of a 'goodly Plump, Fat, Well Favoured, well formed Figure [... with] full and fat fleshed shoulders, plump breasts, well coloured skin, and altogether, able to indure a man's handling'.[114] Bartholin similarly notes that fat 'renders the Body smooth, white, soft, fair and beautiful', while George Keith's *The Arguments of the Quakers* (1698), an unlikely source for a celebration of corpulent beauty, states that 'what feeds the Body, doth Refresh and Comfort it, maketh it Lively and Vigorous, Fat and Beautiful'.[115]

Skeletal figures, meanwhile, are repeatedly said to be unattractive. 'Persons in a Consumption and decrepit old women are deformed for want of Fat,' declares *Bartholinus Anatomy*.[116] Jeamson's cosmetic manual *Artificiall Embellishments* notes that the

> contrary extreame to corpulency are those breathing Skeletons that carry Lent in their face at a Christmas feast.... No part about them thrives so well as their bones, and these look as lustie, as if they had eaten up the flesh and were readie to leap off the skin to fall upon others.[117]

Such women, he presumes, are desperate for cosmetic advice. *The Ladies Dictionary*, which draws on Jeamson's manual, agrees that 'Bodies that are very Lean and Scragged, we all must own, cannot be very Comely.' The text recommends that women with such figures eat sweet food, including a preparation of Almonds, 'Pistach-nuts', sugar and white poppy seed, which 'will not only make you Fat, but give you a good Complexion'.[118] Men, as well as women, were potentially disparaged for being too thin. The apothecary in Shakespeare's *Romeo and Juliet* (*c*. 1595), for example, betrays a contemptible destitution in his 'meagre ... looks'. '[S]harp misery [has] worn him to the bones,' observes Romeo. 'Famine is in [his] cheeks/Need and oppression starveth in [his] eyes.'[119]

Statements regarding weight often switch from one extreme body size to the other as though they are synonymous in their departure from beauty: 'extream Fat, dropsied Persons, such as are very lean etc are deformed', states Bartholin.[120] Robert Burton's anatomisation of ugly mistresses, moreover, slides seamlessly from a 'vast virago ... a fat fustilugs' to a 'truss, a long lean rawbone, a skeleton, a sneaker ... whom thou couldst not fancy for a world'.[121] Firenzuola's *On the Beauty of Women* cites Aristotle that 'if the good habits of the body are evident in the firmness and thickness of the flesh, the bad habits then be evident in its flabbiness and thinness'.[122] Avoiding the pitfalls of either extreme, beauty is the perfect mean between obesity and scrawniness: 'Beauty, no other thing is, then a Beame/Flasht out between the Middle and Extreame,' states Herrick.[123] The 'fair Lucina' in Laurence Twyne's *The Patterne of Painefull Adventures* (*c*. 1594) has a body 'of comely stature, neither too high nor too lowe, not scregged with leanenesse, not undecently corpulent, but in such equality consisting, that no man could wish it otherwise'.[124] Firenzuola's Mona Amorrorisca, meanwhile, possesses a form 'somewhere between lean and fat, plump and juicy'. She is thus 'of the right proportions, one in which we find agility and dexterity'.[125]

While excessive thinness potentially suggests consumption or the ravages of poverty and age, obesity is also linked with disease in early modern writing. Fat bodies were said to be particularly susceptible to smallpox.[126] Overeating, notes Richard Baxter,

> doth by degrees first alter and vitiate the temperament of the blood and humours making it a crude unconcocted unnatural thing, unfit for the due nutrition of the parts; turning the nourishing mass into a burdensome excrementitious mixture, abounding with saline or tartareous matter, and consisting more of a pituitous slime, or redundant serosity, than of that sweet nutrimental milk of nature ... which should make it the oyl of life.[127]

Shakespeare's *2 Henry IV* (*c*. 1598–99) is pervaded with images of unhealthily engorged bodies, as Rhodes observes.[128] In the play, the Archbishop of York diagnoses England's pathology: 'we are all diseased/And with our surfeiting and wanton hours/Have brought ourselves into a burning fever/And we must bleed for it.' In order to be wholesome, the humours of the body must flow freely, as they cannot do when the body is swollen through excessive consumption: we must 'purge th' obstructions which begin to stop/Our very veins of life'.[129] Obesity is therefore aligned with a pathological humoural stasis, as Healy contends.[130] *The Ladies Dictionary* recommends that the overweight 'purge pretty strongly' in both spring and autumn, as well as taking weekly laxatives.[131] Dieting, as well as purging, is crucial to the maintenance of physical health. Samuel Rowlands's poem in praise of tobacco, 'The Devil's Health-drinker' (1611), cites its ability to suppress appetite: 'you shall find it physical/A corpulent fatman/Within a yeare will shrinke so small/That one his guts may span,/Tis full of phisick rare effects.'[132]

As well as suggesting an unhealthy physical state, fatness is linked to unpleasant character traits in early modern English texts. To be plump, potentially, is to be fertile, rich and majestic, but it is also, in the eyes of many, to be indolent, greedy, stupid or plain evil. Falstaff, 'that swollen parcel of dropsies, that huge bombard of sack, that stuffed cloak-bag of guts', reflects his excessive physique, to Hal, in his 'fat-witted' mentality.[133] *The Ladies Dictionary* meanwhile contends that:

> If it were nothing more than the Incumbrance, it were sufficient to deter any one from so unwieldy a Magnitude, yet here in too Legible Characters those that can Read, conclude Sloth and Voluptuousness occasioned it; for when e're the Carcase swells it self into a bulk too Voluminous: Idleness is there described in Folio.[134]

John Norden, author of devotional Protestant texts, presents obesity as a sign of moral and physical deformity in his poem *The Labyrinth of Man's Life* (1614). Envy, for instance, is a 'hidious hagge', 'ougly, colour'd pale, and wan;/Her face puft up ... her belly bigge, she must disgorge or break'. The poem laboriously explicates its own symbolism, noting that 'her swolne cheeks, shewes her puft up with spight'.[135] John Reynolds's moralistic collection of narratives, *The Triumph of God's Revenge*, Book 2 (1622), also deploys body weight, among other physical characteristics, as a marker of character. Relating the fate of two sisters in one of the narratives, he outlines their 'perfections and imperfections', their 'vices and vertues, their beautie and deformitie: that as objects are best knowne by the opposition of their contraries: so by the way of comparison wee may ... know how to distinguish of the disparitie of these two sisters'. Berinthia is tall, slender, fair, 'modestly courteous, gracious and religious', while Catalina is short, 'corpulent of body', 'of taint and complexion, more browne than faire', with a disdainful eye and 'of humour extreamely imperious, ambitious and revengefull'. Categories of otherness overlap in the demonisation of Catalina, who deviates in behaviour, skin colour and body shape from the desired ideal of virtuous, beautiful femininity. Jealous of her sister, she 'runnes ... wilfully hood-winked from God to the devil ... and disdaines to retire, till her malicious ... thirst be quenched with her sisters blood'. After attempting to poison Berinthia, Catalina is struck and killed by a 'Thunder-bolt' that leaves 'all her body above her wast ... cole-blacke', in a further corporeal display of her moral taint. Less expectedly, however, Berinthia is also finally revealed to be a figure of moral opprobrium. Plotting the murder of her brother, her 'former vertues' are 'disgraced' with a 'foule ... vice', as beauty, after all, fails to preclude moral deformity: 'oh that a face so sweetly faire should be accompanyed and linked with a heart so cruelly barbarous, so bloudily inhumane!' Her punishment is to be 'immured betwixt two walls, and there, with a slender diet, to end the remainder of her days'.[136] While

Catalina's moral deviance is inscribed in her obese, dark and short body, Berinthia's carnal nature, less obviously displayed, must also ultimately be reigned in through imprisonment and the restriction of food. Both women, in the end, are too grossly physical, and must be materially reduced, either through death or through social invisibility and a starvation diet.

To be corpulent, in the end, is to be emphatically, excessively, unforgivably carnal. 'Never was humane soule so overgrown/With an unreasonable Cargazon of flesh,' states the anonymous author of 'Aldobrandino, a fat Cardinal' (1656).[137] Exorbitant in his or her corporeality, the fat character is opposed in essence to spiritual virtues. The Roman Catholic priest Thomas Wright observes in *The Passions of the Minde* that

> a fat belly engendreth not a subtile wit: for as if a man were drowned in a puddle of mire, he could not perceive the light of the Sunne; even so, a soule drowned in meat, fat, and blood, cannot behold the light of God; . . . there riseth from a gluttonous stomacke, a multitude of vapours to the braine, which causeth such a mist before the eyes of the soule, that she cannot possibly speculate any spirituall matter, concerning herself or the glory of God.[138]

To feed the spirit, implicitly, we must starve the flesh. Echoing this principle, Shakespeare's *1 Henry IV* sets the stubborn materiality of Falstaff's excessive flesh against abstract spiritual principles: 'there's no room for faith, truth, nor honesty in this bosom of thine; it is all filled up with guts and midriff'. Presented in an ambivalent light in the play, Falstaff's excessive body from another perspective represents a material reality that deflates hypocritical pretensions. The abundantly corporeal retains its association with sinful carnality, however: 'I have more flesh than another man,' admits Falstaff, 'and therefore more frailty.'[139] 'Make less thy body hence, and more thy grace,' he is instructed in *2 Henry IV*.[140] Milton's poetry also deploys images of superfluous flesh to signify immoral deviance. Set against the airy transcendence of the forces of good, figures of evil in *Paradise Lost* are depicted with a repulsive, engorged materiality. During the war in heaven, for instance, the good angels see their foe 'with heavie pace . . ./Approaching gross and huge'.[141]

Ursula, the 'pig-woman', in Ben Jonson's *Bartholomew Fair* (first performed 1614) articulates and embodies an alternative discourse, setting her own 'juicy and wholesome' nature against the 'lean playhouse poultry' of the playhouse prostitutes, with their 'bony rump sticking out like the ace of spades or the point of a partisan'. The play largely agrees that her joyous physical excess is infinitely preferable to life-denying and hypocritical Puritanical doctrines of self-restraint. To the elite visitors at the fair, however, Ursula's fatness is by no means wholesome. 'How she drips!' exclaims Quarlous: 'She's able to give a man the sweating sickness with looking on her.' To the 'fair-folk', corpulence is potentially life-affirming, but to the voices of legal and religious authority it is indisputably carnal and corrupt: Zeal-of-the-land Busy's perspective is not to be trusted, but he nevertheless highlights the widespread early modern correlation of excessive flesh with sin as he exclaims that 'the fleshly woman [...has] the marks upon her of... the world... the devil... and the flesh'.[142]

George Herbert's 'The Size' (1633) similarly deploys fatness as a figure for worldly indulgence. Confessing his yearning to be 'full' with earthly joys, the speaker reminds himself that

> A Christian's state and case
> Is not a corpulent, but a thin and spare,
> Yet active strength: whose long and bony face
> Content and care
> Do seem to equally divide,
> Like a pretender, not a bride.[143]

The 'thinne' and the 'spare' in the poem evoke 'care' and thwarted desires, but also signify an 'active strength' and 'content' which opposes the sensual pleasures, indolence and sloth of the corpulent.

Transgressively associated in dominant discourses with both sin and disease, fat characters in early modern texts are often depicted as inordinately oily and greasy. Falstaff, notably, 'sweats to death/And lards the lean earth as he walks along'.[144] Nell, in Shakespeare's *The Comedy of Errors* is also described as 'all grease': 'She sweats, a man may go over-shoes in the grime of it.'[145] Ursula is described in similar terms: 'An inspired vessel of kitchen-stuff' who will 'make excellent gear for the coach-makers ... to anoint wheels and axletrees with', she is 'oily as the King's constable lamp'. She describes herself as

> all fire and fat ... I shall e'en melt away to the first woman, a rib, again, I am afraid. I do water the ground in knots as I go, like a great garden-pot; you may follow me by the S's I make.[146]

On the one hand associated with an unhealthily glutted solidity, corpulence is thus also paradoxically aligned with a dripping, humoural body which fails to maintain polite, hygienic or self-contained borders.[147] Fat, states Bartholin, is 'the thinner and more oyly part of the blood': it is 'not a part, but rather an humour'.[148] Joubert's *Treatise on Laughter* also aligns fatness with excessive humours, notably blood. Joubert links the physical imbalance represented by fatness with a predisposition to laughter:

> fat people are very sanguine (if their stoutness comes, as we believe it does, from an abundance of blood) and such people are naturally joyous, foolish and laughing .... For it is the abundance of blood and of heat that makes us quicker to laugh, as on the contrary the cold and dry melancholic people are inept in laughter. This same heat, enveloped in a great and gentle moisture, makes fat in abundance ... having been softened by a great amount of humours, and inasmuch as abundant material is not lacking.

The overabundant humours of the fat body, moreover, tend to disregard constraints. Joubert's depiction of obese, laughing figures emphasises their inability to control their bodies and the breach of physical borders that results. The lungs of such people 'become heated and melt their mucus' which 'forces coughing in order to eject it', while they can laugh themselves sick or become incontinent: 'this great upset empties everything from it.... Whence it comes that one pisses, shits, and sweats by dint of laughing ... the bowels and the bladder ... give up their contents (as it happens in laughter), if there is a quantity of liquid matter, all escapes us indecorously'.[149] Fat people, then, are immoderately humorous, in more than one sense of the term. In its lack of self-control and tendency to leak, the obese body is aligned with both the lower-class and the female body. Falstaff, 'that trunk of humours', is explicitly feminised in *2 Henry IV*: 'had I but a belly of any indifferency, I were simply the most active fellow in Europe: My womb, my womb, my womb undoes me'.[150] Johnstone meanwhile describes the case of a thirty-four-year-old man, 'fat of body', who 'had as much Milk in his brests as would suckle a child'.[151]

Evoking a potentially positive fertility, the feminised fat body is thus also a site of emasculation, transgression and deviance, potentially generating repulsion. As *The Ladies Dictionary* states, the fat are 'almost out of shape'.[152] Like ugliness of other types, obesity is characterised by a formlessness which exceeds and denies clear human boundaries. The description of the 'kitchen wench' Nell in *The Comedy of Errors* illustrates the manner in which fatness operates alongside other markers of ugliness to identify the abject body:

> a very beastly creature [...] yet is she a wondrous fat marriage. [...] she's the kitchen wench, and all grease [...] No longer from head to foot than from hip to hip; she is spherical, like a globe; I could find out countries in her.... [Where America, the Indies?] O, sir, upon her nose, all o'er embellished with rubies, carbuncles, sapphires .... To conclude, this drudge, or diviner laid claim to me, called me Dromio, swore I was assured to her... I, amazed, ran from her as a witch. And I think if my breast had not been made of a faith, and my heart of steel,/She had transform'd me to a curtal dog, and made me turn i' th' wheel. [...] As from a bear a man would run for life,/So fly I from her that would be my wife.[153]

The comic anti-blazon anatomises Nell according to the conventions of Petrarchan description, with its imagery of new worlds and gem stones, yet applies such images incongruously in order to emphasise her inversion of ideals of beauty. A fat woman of low social status, she disturbs with her advances, '[laying] claim' to a male subject who must '[run] from her as a witch'. The comedy of this description is in part an effort to defuse the threat that Nell, a desiring, aggressive and deformed woman, poses. Unless he 'fly ... from her', an act achieved through his description as much as through the physical fact of leaving her presence, Dromio fears that he will be transformed into something less than human. As is the case in many early modern descriptions of ugly women, it is male, not female, subjectivity which is the true concern here. Projecting the ugly, obese woman as the opposite of all that he must be, the male speaker's sense of threat in the face of this figure betrays the insecure foundations of his own identity.

Abjection in *The Anatomy of Melancholy*

The compulsion to construct the ugly woman in order to shore up an unstable male identity is conspicuous in Burton's *The Anatomy of Melancholy* (1621). Mark Breitenberg argues that melancholy functions in the *Anatomy* as a 'repository for those elements deemed contrary to a specifically masculine vision of social order and individual rationality'.[154] Melancholy is feminised, but is also acknowledged by the male speaker as an ever-present 'enemy within': the Galenic humoural model of the body prominent in the text suggests that the male body is perpetually threatened by the possibility of degenerating into a terrifying, uncontrolled, effeminate fluidity.[155] Inscribing the male body's potentially chaotic passions within the lofty discourse of melancholy, however, while simultaneously projecting corporeal disorder onto a feminised 'other', the male speaking subject defends himself against such threats, re-establishing the rational self-mastery by which ideal masculinity is characterised.[156] In other words, as Breitenberg states, it is precisely through staging the fearful limits of masculine identity that the *Anatomy* is able to regulate masculine anxieties. Although posing a severe threat to male models of the self, melancholy ultimately operates in the work as 'an enabling discourse for the masculine subject', a 'mutable category against which masculinity may then (anxiously) define and defend itself'.[157] Christopher Tilmouth concurs that Burton's work maps melancholy in order to shore up a masculine identity perpetually threatened by dissolution and chaos. The work's ever-growing, excessive form points, for Tilmouth, to an 'urge to be comprehensive' grounded in the desire to impose order on a disease whose primary characteristic is the loss of control.[158]

Despite Burton's efforts to reassert masculine subjectivity, however, the fraught, contradictory nature of the enterprise, as both Breitenberg and Tilmouth emphasise, is evident throughout the work. Imposing an illusion of control in its apparent structure, the sheer overflowing verbosity of the *Anatomy* betrays the futility of mapping a condition this slippery, while rational autonomy remains an elusive ideal for male subjects in the work more closely aligned with humoural chaos than intellectual detachment. R. Grant Williams is forthright in his assessment of the failure of the *Anatomy* to impose any kind of regulatory order on its subject matter. He questions its status as an anatomy: the anatomised object is projected as 'a corporeal unity', granting 'epistemological mastery', whereas Burton's work is an 'epistemological aberration', constituting not 'a body of knowledge' but 'a delirious disfiguring'. Its digressions and lengthy lists in which 'unsubordinated parts ... do not comprise a comprehensible order' render the *Anatomy* as a 'mass of dislocations', a 'monster of knowledge' that reminds the reader of their 'helplessness in the face of undifferentiated difference'. Drawing on Lacan's theories of the fragmentary pre-imaginary subject, Williams claims that Burton's work 'resists the imaginary order', refusing the 'imaginary gestalt of the body' through which the subject, at the mirror stage, gains a sense of self-mastery.[159] To deploy Kristeva's terms, *The Anatomy of Melancholy* is an abject text, refusing binary and logical oppositions, evoking a disturbing state of non-differentiation. In the voice of Democritus Junior, Burton describes his work as 'a rhapsody of rags gathered together from several dung-hills, excrements of authors, toys and fopperies confusedly tumbled out . . . harsh, raw, rude, phantastical, absurd, insolent, indiscreet, ill-composed, indigested, vain, scurrile, idle, dull, dry'. Disfigured, swollen, amorphous, the monstrous form of the work fails to separate itself from the irrational state it ostensibly dissects. As such, Burton's compendious work emerges as a potentially subversive text, disrupting the foundations of (patriarchal) psychic and social order.

Highlighting the disfigurement of *The Anatomy of Melancholy*, Williams nevertheless fails to acknowledge the manner in which the work continues to abject the female body, and thus to participate in the regulatory system which its form and at times its content simultaneously disrupts. Abjection in the work is not limited to the deformation of the body of knowledge but also operates in relation to representations of the female body. As we have seen, Democritus Junior at times defines his creation as monstrous. He claims, for instance, that he was 'enforced, as a bear doth her whelps, to bring forth this confused lump; I had no time to lick it into form'. Shapeless, inchoate, nauseating, the work is abject, while the speaker is also placed in a feminised position. Elsewhere, however, the speaker is at pains to differentiate himself and his musings from the ugly and the abject. '[N]*on sum adeo informis* [I am not so ugly], I would not be vilified,' he asserts. Beauty and ugliness, moreover, are matters of perspective: 'Our writings are as so many dishes, our readers guests, our books like beauty, that which one admires another rejects; so are we approved as men's fancies are inclined.'[160] No longer repulsive, the work is now potentially an object of beauty, albeit one whose value cannot be objectively quantified.

Burton oscillates between presenting his speaker and his work as feminised and ugly and projecting ugliness as the property of the 'other', specifically a feminine other. Williams cites the work's account of the Basil gentlewoman who is told that she is as 'full of filthy excrements' as is the hog whose gruesome butchering she has just witnessed. Causing her to vomit, such remarks make it impossible to 'restore her to herself again' for many months afterwards.[161] To Williams, 'the remark that beneath her skin the gentlewoman resembles such putrid amorphousness shatters her imago', aligning her with the reader of the work whose recognition of his failure to possess 'mastery over learning' forces a confrontation with the misrecognition on which his illusion of subjective coherence is based.[162] Aligning the gentlewoman and the reader nevertheless elides the crucial role of gender in this account. Far from a subject position (or non-subject position) with which the reader can identify, the gentlewoman is depicted in terms that participate in the exclusion of the female body in the *Anatomy*, an entity repeatedly evoking the loathing of the male speaker and, implicitly, that of the reader. It is the female body which is identified as the repulsive, contaminating origin of melancholy, a condition which by this means is fundamentally differentiated from the male body and self. Through gaining mastery of their passions, the work argues, men will transcend a gross, repulsive corporeal identity from which woman are offered no escape.[163] Principles of disfigurement and horror are thus deployed in the service of hierarchical relationships in the *Anatomy*, even as the work at times fails to maintain the differentiations upon which these relationships depend. It is the absence of clearly defined boundaries, in fact, which generates the work's obsessive attempts to police binaries, of which beauty and ugliness become a key marker.

Gender divisions, while crucial to the representation of ugliness in the *Anatomy*, are by no means secure in the text. Describing the frustrated female sexuality that generates 'much discontent, preposterous judgement' and the inability to speak, for example, Burton's persona in the text appears once again to be projecting melancholic disorder onto a feminised body. He suddenly feels the need to dissociate himself from a condition which he has been describing with a potentially dangerous empathy, however:

> But where am I? Into what subject have I rushed? What have I to do with nuns, maids, virgins, widows? I am a bachelor myself, and lead a monastic life in a college ... I confess 'tis an indecorum, and as Pallas, a virgin, blushed when Jupiter by chance spake of love matters in her presence and turned away her face, *me reprimam* [I will check myself]; though my subject necessarily require it, I will say no more.[164]

The humour of this passage exposes the tensions it is deployed to defuse, as Burton's compulsion to differentiate himself from the feminine territory into which he has wandered is articulated through an abrupt assertion of his exclusively masculine existence. The mental instability generated by frustrated desire must remain a female experience, divorced from male spheres. Yet this differentiation cannot be maintained: Burton's attempt to reassert his masculine identity collapses into an image of himself as a blushing, female virgin. The need to separate the male self from sexualised and effeminate forms of madness is thus thwarted by the impossibility of maintaining the necessary boundaries.[165] Burton's proximity to the condition from which he is so keen to divorce himself is further evident in his opposition of his bachelor 'monastic' life to the secluded life of nuns; a binary which undermines, rather than secures, any ultimate difference between the two states.

Representations of ugly women in the text attempt to reinforce the evidently insecure division between male and female. Once again, however, the tensions in this enterprise are more apparent than its success. Constructed within wider literary and cultural discourses of the repulsive female body, sharing much in common with the poetic and dramatic depictions I have been discussing in this chapter, the ugly woman in *The Anatomy of Melancholy* is a figure of obscene materiality, poised in opposition to the ideally rational, self-controlled male self. As such, she is outside all possible reach, one would assume, of male desire. Intriguingly, however, the lengthiest portraits of repulsive women in the text depict women who are, indeed, desired by men. 'Every lover admires his mistress,' laments the speaker,

> though she be very deformed of herself, ill-favoured, wrinkled, pimpled, pale, red, yellow, tanned, tallow-faced, have a swollen juggler's platter face, or a thin, lean, chitty face, have clouds in her face, be crooked, dry, bald, goggle-eyed, blear-eyed, or with staring eyes, she looks like a squish'd cat, hold her head still awry, heavy, dull, hollow-eyed, black or yellow about the eyes, or squint-eyed, sparrow-mouthed, Persian hook-nosed, have a sharp fox-nose, a red nose, China flat, great nose, *nare simo patuloque* [snub and flat nose], a nose like a promontory, gubber-tushed, rotten teeth, black, uneven, brown teeth, beetle-browed, a witch's beard, her breath stink all over the room, her nose drop winter and summer, with a Bavarian poke under her chin, a sharp chin, lave-eared, with a long crane's neck, which stands awry too, *pendulis mammis*, 'her dugs like two double jugs', or else no dugs, in that other extreme, bloody-fallen fingers, she have filthy, long unpared nails, scabbed hands or wrists, a tanned skin, a rotten carcass, crooked back, she stoops, is lame, splay-footed, 'as slender in the middle as a cow in the waist', gouty legs, her ankles hang over her shoes, her feet stink, she breed lice, a mere changeling, a very monster, an oaf imperfect, her whole complexion savours, an harsh voice, incondite gesture, vile gait, a vast virago, or an ugly tit, a slug, a fat fustilugs, a truss, a long lean rawbone, a skeleton, a sneaker ... *remedium amoris* [a cure for love] to another man, a dowdy, a slut, a scold, a nasty, rank, rammy, filthy, beastly quean, dishonest peradventure, obscene, base, beggarly, rude, foolish, untaught, peevish[.][166]

Initially concentrating on physical characteristics, this monstrous conglomeration of repulsive femininity elides protuberant, grotesque bodies with particular social designations, as suggested, for example, in the fact that 'she breed lice'. An ugly body inevitably signals moral and gender transgression: terms such as 'virago', 'truss' and 'scold' evoke aggressiveness and sexual looseness alongside physical filth and carelessness. Physical appearance, social position and sexual morals are also inextricably fused in the label 'slut'. The unregulated bodies of the women thus merge seamlessly with their characters, behaviour and social status.

The chief fear driving this outburst is not the ugliness of the women in question, however, but the failure of men to identify this ugliness. 'If he love her once, he admires her for all this,' exclaims the speaker; 'he takes no notice of any such errors or imperfections of body or mind ... he had rather have her than any woman in the world.' The deceptiveness of the female body, a recurrent theme in the *Anatomy*, plays a part in generating the anxiety expressed in this passage. The emphasis here is less on female deception than on the male lover's disastrous propensity for self-deception, however, his ability to be so overrun by passionate desire that reason, judgement and even, it seems, reliable vision are entirely overthrown. Driven by the need to secure his own position in contradistinction to sufferers of love-melancholy (a distinction clearly in doubt given the speaker's repeated admission of his own propensity to melancholy), the speaker insists that a well regulated male subject, that is, the implied reader as well as the speaker, possesses clearer insight: the mistress for whom the lover pines 'to thy judgment looks like a mard in a lanthorn, whom thou couldst not fancy for a world, but hatest, loathest, and wouldest have spit in her face, or blow thy nose in her bosom'. Through the eyes of clear and rational judgement, the speaker insists, ugliness is self-evident, generating a natural repulsion: 'we contemn and abhor generally such things as are foul and ugly to behold, account them filthy, but love and covet that which is fair', the text states elsewhere.[167] Ensuring the revulsion which is the only justifiable response to such a monstrous spectacle, the speaker's lengthy, breathless act of description nevertheless betrays the difficulty of enforcing the correct or natural responses of desire and repulsion through which beauty and ugliness are defined. Male self and female other, as well as the beautiful and the ugly, cease to be clearly demarcated, generating an over-insistent description in which the sheer obviousness of female ugliness is secured. Instead of simply exhibiting an aberrant aesthetic sensibility, then, the perverse desire berated in this passage bespeaks the difficulty of maintaining the wider divisions which ugliness and beauty mediate in this work. Distinctions between male and female, sanity and insanity, reason and passion, and ultimately self and other are all at stake here, hence the frantic need to reinstate clear categories in the face of evident precariousness and confusion. The drive to identify and exclude the ugly in the text is thus an integral part of a wider negotiation of binary divisions on which the privileging of the self-controlled, rational, transcendent male subject depends.

In line with the need to reinforce divisions between mind and flesh, reason and passion, male and female, all women, in the end, must be aligned with the repulsiveness of chaotic, fleshly humours. The work repeatedly strips the female body bare, going beneath the clothes, even beneath the skin, to expose the horrific reality of a figure who continues to be projected as the site of the exorbitant, unregulated, undifferentiated elements against which the male self must be defined. Asking why men marry, the speaker concludes that 'her beauty belike, and comeliness of person, that is commonly the main object, she is a most absolute form, in his eye at least'. The eyes of desire are not to be trusted, however, as we should have learned by now: 'our eyes and other senses will commonly deceive us; it may be, to thee thyself upon a more serious examination, or after a little absence, she is not so fair as she seems'. The speaker encourages men to fantasise about their prospective partners, to undress them mentally, although not in the manner that we might expect:

> It may not be she that is so fair, but her coats . . . suppose thou saw her in a base beggar's weed, or else dressed in some old hirsute attires out of fashion, foul linen, coarse raiment, besmeared with soot, colly, perfumed with opoponax, sagapenum, asafoetida, or some such filthy gums, dirty, about some undecent action or other . . . . Suppose thou beheldest her in a frosty morning, in cold weather, in some passion or perturbation of mind, weeping, chafing, etc, rivelled and ill-favoured to behold. She many times that in a composed look seems so amiable and delicious . . . if she do but

laugh or smile, makes an ugly sparrow-mouthed face, and shows a pair of uneven, loathsome, rotten, foul teeth: she hath a black skin, gouty legs, a deformed crooked carcass under a fine coat. It may be for all her costly tires she is bald, and though she seem so fair by dark, by candle-light, or afar off at such a distance, as Callicratides observed in Lucian, 'if thou should see her near, or in a morning, she would appear more ugly than a beast' ... [if you reflect what issues from her mouth and nostrils and the other orifices of her body you will say that you have never seen worse filth]. Follow my counsel, see her undressed, see her, if it be possible, out of her attires ... [stripped of her stolen colours], it may be she is like Aesop's jay, or Pliny's cantharides, she will be loathsome, ridiculous, thou wilt not endure her sight[.][168]

The text enacts what it recommends, stripping a woman of her artificial finery (the only source of female beauty, according to the *Anatomy*) in order to expose her 'natural' repulsiveness.[169] Securing the dangerously deceptive female body as ugly, the text insists that with the correct judgement the truth of the female body can be known. Its abject status, its leaking, transgressive, excessive physicality, is revealed and can be maintained as that which opposes the unpolluted, self-controlled, transcendent male subject. Pursuing this goal, the speaker suggests that the hapless lover go so far as to imagine his ostensibly beautiful mistress as a rotting corpse:

> or suppose thou saw'st her sick, pale, in a consumption, on her death-bed, skin and bones, or now dead ... [she whose embrace was so agreeable], ... [her aspect will be horrible].... As a posy she smells sweet, is most fresh and fair one day, but dried up, withered, and stinks another. Beautiful Nireus, by that Homer so much admired, once dead, is more deformed than Thersites, and Solomon deceased as ugly as Marcolphus: thy lovely mistress that was erst ... dearer to thee than thine eyes, once sick or departed, is ... worse than any dirt or dunghill. Her embraces were not so acceptable as now her looks be terrible: thou hadst better behold a Gorgon's head than Helena's carcass.[170]

The fact that it is necessary for the lover to imagine his beloved as a stinking corpse in order to be convinced of her ugliness betrays the extent to which this supposedly self-evident repulsiveness is being projected on to a body which even on close examination does not easily yield to such a label. Aligning the female body with the corpse establishes its abject status as that which provokes nausea and loathing.[171] Burton's shocking depiction nevertheless evokes images of sexual contact with a corpse, betraying again the confusion of desire and loathing evoked by the abject as well as the impossibility of maintaining an absolute distinction between the abject 'other' and the self.

Instead of a fixed or an innate state, ugliness emerges as the end product of a process:

> a little sickness, a fever, a small-pox, wound, scar, loss of an eye or limb, a violent passion, a distemperature of heat or cold, mars all in an instant, disfigures all; childbearing, old age, that tyrant time, will turn Venus to Erinnys; raging time, care, rivels her upon a sudden; after she hath been married a small while, and the black ox hath

trodden on her toe, she will be so much altered, and wax out of favour, thou wilt not know her. One grows too fat, another too lean, etc.; modest Matilda, pretty pleasing Peg... will quickly lose their grace, grow fulsome, stale, sad, heavy, dull, sour, and all at last out of fashion.

Disease or time are not the only forces able to wreak havoc with a woman's features, however. The work repeatedly encourages the male imagination to deface the object of his desire. Rather than instinctively recognising and being repulsed by an ugliness with an objective material existence, the male subject must work at achieving his revulsion:

> when thou seest a fair and beautiful person... bethink with thyself that it is but earth thou lovest, a mere excrement which so vexeth thee, which thou so admirest, and thy raging soul will be at rest. Take her skin from her face, and thou shalt see all loathsomeness under it, that beauty is a superficial skin and bones, nerves, sinews; suppose her sick, now rivelled, hoary-headed, hollow-cheeked, old; within she is full of filthy phlegm, stinking, putrid, excremental stuff: snot and snivel in her nostrils, spittle in her mouth, water in her eyes, what filth in her brains[.]

In the *Anatomy*, then, ugliness is located less in the female body and more in the male imagination. Rather than uncovering a woman's repulsive corporeality, the text draws attention to the process by which her ugliness can be constructed, revealing the necessity of this process for the self-construction of masculine subjectivity. The ideal male subject, the 'good judge', is he who can mentally disfigure women. If he is perceptive, he will

> find many faults in physiognomy, and ill colour: if form, one side of the face likely bigger than the other, or crooked nose, bad eyes, prominent veins, concavities about the eyes, wrinkles, pimples, red streaks, freckons, hairs, warts, naeves, inequalities, roughness, scabridity, paleness, yellowness, and as many colours as are in a turkey-cock's neck, many indecorum's in their other parts... you find some things lacking, others superfluous, one leers, another frowns, a third gapes, squints etc... seldom you shall find an absolute face without fault.

Female beauty, Burton insists, can only ever be artificial, but female ugliness is similarly shown to depend upon art, this time, a male art which projects particular images of the female body in order to shape masculine subjectivity. 'Finding' faults, the text has revealed, is less an act of observation than one of imagination. It is an act, moreover, on which the establishment of ideal forms of male identity depends.

The urgency of the need to repudiate the repulsive female other and the transgressive, unregulated corporeality she represents is evident as Burton continues to rhapsodise on the inevitability of being confronted with female ugliness beneath shows of beauty. Desire must end in repulsion, he insists:

> [When the skin shrivels and hangs loose, and the teeth blacken], when they wax old and ill-favoured, they may commonly no longer abide them:... [thou art distasteful

to me], begone; they grow stale, fulsome, loathsome, odious; thou art a beastly filthy
quean... thou art... withered and dry... [savourless and old].... [Because you are
wrinkled, ugly, and grey], I say... [there is the door, go!]¹⁷²

Shifting from a detached third-person narrative to a first-person invective, the
impulse of the work as a whole to identify and expel the repulsive woman erupts
here on to the surface of the text. As with depictions of abject women in poetry,
prose and drama elsewhere in the early modern period, the 'wrinkled, ugly, and
grey' woman, the site of the abject, is fundamental to the construction of the male
self and therefore cannot ever 'begone'. Burton's dizzying prose, piling description
upon description as he insists upon the repellent female body, exhibits the paradox
at the heart of the manoeuvre: determined to identify the unattractive woman as
'wrinkled, ugly, and grey' and therefore to secure her exclusion, he simultaneously
demands her frightening but necessary presence. *The Anatomy of Melancholy* thus
reveals the violence at the heart of the construction of early modern subjectivity, its
reliance on the endless abjection of the female body, which becomes the mutilated
receptacle for all that the transcendent male self repudiates.

Burton disingenuously claims that his discussion of ugliness could as equally
apply to men as to women: 'read him for her, and tis all one in effect', he states.¹⁷³ As
we have seen, however, gender plays a crucial role in the deployment of ugliness in
the text. While female ugliness evokes an inability to regulate the body, male physical deformity operates in a very different manner in the work. Rather than defining
the man who possesses the unattractive body as out of control of his body and therefore his mind, Burton deploys the familiar figure of the male Silenus to argue that a
physically ugly man potentially displays a virtuous disregard for the physical order.
The male subject of Burton's text is a humoural subject, threatened by the body's
potential for chaotic passions, but he aspires towards a different model of subjectivity where the self transcends the body:

> Deformities and imperfections of our bodies, as lameness, crookedness, deafness,
> blindness, be they innate or accidental, torture many men: yet this may comfort them,
> that those imperfections of the body do not a whit blemish the soul, or hinder the
> operations of it, but rather help and much increase it. Thou art lame of body, deformed
> to the eye, yet this hinders not but that thou mayst be a good, a wise, upright, honest
> man.... A silly fellow to look to, may have more wit, learning, honesty, than he that
> struts it out... and is admired in the world's opinion.... How many deformed princes,
> kings, emperors, could I reckon up, philosophers, orators?... 'the night hath his pleas-
> ure', and for the loss of that one sense such men are commonly recompensed in the
> rest; they have excellent memories, other good parts, music, and many recreations:
> much happiness, great wisdom[.]¹⁷⁴

In the case of ugly men, then, the body is set against the spirit: 'the flesh rebels
against the spirit; that which hurts the one, must needs help the other'.¹⁷⁵ There
is an obvious overlap between deformity and melancholy in the above passage:

deformity, like melancholy, can be appropriated for the masculine subject as a sign of privilege.[176] Deformed men are 'martyrs', deserving 'honour and immortality'. They are likely to be notable philosophers and statesmen, just as Aristotle commented that 'all men who are outstanding in philosophy, poetry or the arts are melancholic'.[177] Women, meanwhile, as the gentlewoman of Basil discovered, are 'full of filthy excrements', an object of necessary loathing for the male subject/reader. The Duke of Muscovy, said to be 'instantly sick' if he sees a woman, is not so much an aberrant figure in the text as a symbol of the male subject it constructs.[178]

Burton's *Anatomy* thus highlights the role played by abusive descriptions of ugly women in the construction of early modern subjectivity. The typical features that recur in scurrilous depictions from this period reveal the anxieties negotiated in literary and visual displays of repellent women. Ugliness rarely appears in early modern texts in a more overt form than it does in descriptions of old hags, 'vast virago[s]' and 'ugly tit[s]' of the type discussed in this chapter. Such representations are nevertheless driven by a suppressed recognition that the border between beauty and ugliness, as between the categories of rationality and madness, male and female, self and other that the binary of ugliness and beauty mediates, is not secure. The 'beldam', consequently, must be excessive in her repulsiveness, must generate the immediate fear and loathing which defines 'natural' responses to the ugly and polices other categories of the natural and the necessary. 'There is the door, go!' these works insist, yet their reiteration of this command defers the ugly woman's expulsion, revealing the manner in which her compelling presence shores up the early modern self.

5

'To make love to a deformity':[1] praising ugliness

Descriptions of ugly women, I have been arguing, have as much, if not more, to tell us about (insecure) constructions of male subjectivity in the early modern period as they do about representations of female identity. The role played by depictions of the unattractive female body in the consolidation of particular models of male subjectivity becomes further apparent in this chapter. Female ugliness in Burton's *Anatomy*, as we have seen, depends on the male creative imagination for its realisation: without the male subject's active efforts to visualise the female body as repellent, it is in danger of seducing rather than repulsing. Burton also insists that female beauty is 'more beholding to art than nature', however. 'Art', in the form of outward ornaments, improves on nature to the extent that 'the veriest dowdy' can be transformed into 'a goddess'.[2] In this chapter, I explore a series of literary texts where authors put this claim to the test, rhetorically attempting to transform the ugly into the beautiful as they praise the charms of the unattractive woman. The ironic blazon of the foolish and ugly Mopsa in Sidney's *The Countess of Pembroke's Arcadia* is an early instance of this witty fashion in early modern English writing:

> What length of verse can serve brave Mopsa's good to show,
> Whose virtues strange, and beauties such, as no man them may know?
> Thus shrewdly burden'd then, how can my Muse escape?
> The Gods must help, and precious things must serve to shew her shape:
> Like great God Saturn fair, and like fair Venus chaste:
> As smooth as Pan, as Juno mild, like Goddess Iris fast.
> With Cupid she foresees, and goes God Vulcan's pace:
> And for a taste of all these gifts, she steals God Momus' grace.
> Her forehead Jacinth-like, her cheeks of Opal hue,
> Her twinkling eyes bedeck'd with Pearl, her lips as Sapphire blue:
> Her hair like Crapal stone, her mouth O heav'nly wide!
> Her skin like burnished gold, her hands like silver ore untry'd.
> As for her parts unknown, which hidden sure are best:
> Happy be they which well believe, and never seek the rest.[3]

As this mock praise of Mopsa suggests, the literary and dramatic vogue for the deformed mistress in early modern England celebrates masculine creativity at the expense of the (ugly) female body. Far from being given new recognition and acceptance in these modes of writing, the ugly woman is relocated within the bounds of literary descriptions of the beautiful which denigrate and effectively silence her. Through presenting the ugly woman as an object of desire, the texts appear to reject dominant aesthetic norms. They nevertheless reproduce the literary and cultural models of beauty and ugliness that they seem to interrogate, revealing the extent to which beauty is a masculine construct, imposed onto what is perceived to be a naturally ugly female body.

Repairing the ruins: constructing beauty

While Burton puts his faith in art to beautify the female form, beauty was more commonly identified in this era with divinely designed natural forms, any alteration of which was liable to result in horrible deformity. The term 'counterfeit', tellingly, referred to ugliness as well as to artificiality in this period.[4] Giving vocal support to this equation of the unnatural with the repellent, Bulwer issued a diatribe in 1650 against the 'foolish Bravery, ridiculous Beauty, filthy Finenesse and loathsome Loveliness of most NATIONS, fashioning and altering their Bodies from the mould intended by NATURE'.[5] Bulwer's oxymoronic formulations 'filthy Finenesse' and 'loathsome Loveliness' nevertheless suggest that the categories of the beautiful and the ugly are not as watertight in his work as his argument seems to demand. Whatever the morally repugnant status of artificially shaped objects, their visual appeal, it seems, remains all too potent.

Despite the fact that nature is often invoked as an unequivocal positive in early modern discussions of the natural and the artificial, Christian doctrines of the Fall complicate the beautiful and even the authentic status of the natural body.[6] Before the Fall, states Calvin, the image of God was visible in both the body and the mind of man. Adam's sin nevertheless caused this original beauty to become 'so corrupted, that all that remaineth, is but uggly deformitie'. Nature has been 'defaced, that nothyng remaineth since that ruine, but disordered, mangled, and filthily spotted'. Far from an original or perfect state of being, nature is marked by corruption. Women occupy an awkward position in this narrative of the descent of the created order from beauty to ugliness. The 'man alone is in Paule called the Image and glorie of God', notes Calvin, 'and the woman is excluded from that degree of honor'.[7] Even before the Fall, feminine nature is marked by lack, failing to embody full spiritual or physical beauty. It is perhaps unsurprising, then, that it is the female form which most powerfully evokes the 'uggly deformitie' of postlapsarian nature in early modern culture and literature. Milton's *Paradise Lost* depicts Sin in feminine terms, her monstrous physicality revealed in her repulsive genitalia: she 'seemed woman to the waist, and fair,/ But ended foul in many a scaly fold/Voluminous and vast'. Her body has been disfigured through childbirth, when her 'odious offspring' '[t]ore through [her] entrails, that with fear and pain/Distorted, all [her] nether shape thus grew/Transformed'.[8]

Corrupt nature is thus aligned with repellent female physicality and sexuality, the female body symbolising the twisted perversion of an originally beautiful creation.

So catastrophic were the effects of the Fall that some argue that the ugliness of nature is beyond repair. Nature, in these arguments, is synonymous with perversity: 'Thrust out nature with a croche, yet woll she styll runne backe agaune,' states Richard Taverner in his *Proverbes and Adagies with Newe Addicions gathered out of the Chiliades of Erasmus* (1539):

> A croked bough of a tree, be it never so much dryvene an other waye with a forke, or crotch, yet yf thou ones take awaye the forke, anone it returneth to that owne nature & course agayne. So in lyke wyse, yf man....[9]

To others, however, ugliness, as an aspect of the Fall, demands redress. Milton thinks it self-evident that we should endeavour to 'repair the ruins of our first parents'.[10] He promotes education as the means to achieve this goal, but the effects of the Fall could also, perhaps, be reversed by art. Sidney implies as much, celebrating the regenerative powers of poetry: 'as Aristotle saith, those things which in themselves are horrible, as cruel battles, unnatural monsters, are made in poetical imitation delightful'.[11] To Sidney, in fact, art is not limited either to copying or to transforming nature. Instead, it allows creation to take place all over again:

> [T]he poet ... lifted up with the vigour of his own invention, doth grow in effect another nature, in making things either better than nature bringeth forth, or, quite anew, forms such as never were in nature, as the Heroes, Demigods, Cyclops, Chimeras, Furies, and such like: so as he goeth hand in hand with nature, not enclosed within the narrow warrant of her gifts, but freely ranging only within the zodiac of his own wit. Nature never set forth the earth in so rich tapestry as divers poets have done; neither with so pleasant rivers, fruitful trees, sweet-smelling flowers, nor whatsoever else may make the too much loved earth more lovely. Her world is brazen, the poets deliver only a golden.[12]

Complicating categories of nature and artifice, nature becomes 'brazen', that is, fallen, shameless and, crucially, artificial, while poetic creations are elevated to the same level as God's original, beautiful creation. Masculine art, in other words, in line with Neoplatonic principles, is synonymous with ideal forms of nature, creating forms that are more beautiful than anything to be found in the corrupt material order.[13] Embodying this principle, the character of Parthenia in Sidney's *Arcadia*, a model of perfect beauty before her features are destroyed by a jealous suitor, is represented as even more beautiful (having a 'more pure and dainty complexion') after her poisoned features are restored by a male physician than she was before the assault occurred.[14] Far from creating an inferior, secondary copy of nature, masculine artistic constructions somehow recapture a more authentic, less tainted form of beauty than exists in (female) nature itself.

The ugly nature in need of masculine creative repair in Sidney's *Apology for Poetry* is represented in explicitly feminine terms:

as to a lady that desired to fashion her countenance to the best grace, a painter should more benefit her to portray a most sweet face, writing Canidia upon it, than to paint Canidia as she was, who, Horace sweareth, was foul and ill favoured.[15]

Titian provides a model for this approach to portraiture, depicting Isabella d'Este (Figure 18) as she looked a quarter of a century earlier, in a portrait by Francia, itself a copy of an earlier portrait, rather than as she appeared at the time of his portrait in 1534–36, when she was around sixty years old.[16]

As Elizabeth Cropper demonstrates in relation to this work and other portraits of women from this era, the true subject is not the beautiful woman in question but the nature and limits of artistic representation. Depictions of beauty, which reference wider debates regarding the relative (in)abilities of poetry and the visual arts to capture the beautiful, belong 'to a distinct discourse from which the woman herself is necessarily absent'.[17] 'Canidia as she was', in the words of Sidney, is largely irrelevant to the artist's construct of Canidia. In both Sidney's *Apology for Poetry* and Titian's portrait of Isabella d'Este, however, male creativity, far from recognising its own limitations, consciously transforms a female nature aligned with ugliness into a figure of beauty. In order to capture beauty, it seems, art must imitate (male) art, not (female) nature.

Debates surrounding the relative beauty of art or nature, as well as the gendered dynamics informing these debates, are particularly visible in the controversy surrounding women's use of cosmetics in the early modern era. Cosmetic arts 'do rather deform and misshape thee, than beautify thee', pronounced one moraliser, illustrating the manner in which female art is often depicted as destructive in its effects.[18] Efforts to improve the appearance of the body could nevertheless also be presented as virtuous attempts to resist the encroachments of sinful corruption, that unwelcome, unnatural intruder into God's creation. To the virulently anti-cosmetic author 'Miso-Spilus', nature, specifically female nature, is that which is fallen and corrupt. The effort 'to correct Nature', he grudgingly concedes, 'in some sort may be tolerable': made-up women 'having for the most part hard favours, [aim] chiefly to correct their deformities', and 'to correct or cure any deformity or blemish in Nature by lawfull means, not accompanied with sinfull actions, is tolerable', even if he is not optimistic about the end results.[19] N.H.'s entry on 'Painting' in *The Ladies Dictionary* agrees that efforts to 'repair by Art the Defects of Nature' in the female face are no different in essence from attempts to cure disease, to 'quench those fires which casually seize on our houses', to 'Row against the Stream, or ascend upwards by any Stairs or degrees, when our Native Tendency is downward'. Fallen nature, and specifically female nature, is perverse, and we are duty-bound to 'excite our invention and Industry' to redress its inadequacies, to

> enliven the Pallid deadness of it, and to redeem it . . . to pair and match the unequal Cheeks to each other, or to cover any Pimples and Heats, or to remove any Obstructions, or to mitigate and Quench excessive Flushings, thereby to set off

Figure 18 Titian, *Isabella d'Este*, 1534–36

the Visage to such a Decency and Equality as may innocently please our selves and others.[20]

Jettisoning commonplace anxieties about unnatural beauty in order to promote his collection of cosmetic recipes, Jeamson's manual *Artificiall Embellishments* also presents artificially acquired beauty as a necessary, indeed heroic, act of resistance to a wayward material order. Left unattended, any vestige of beauty will 'degenerate into a deformed nature':

> The Body, that weak and moving mansion of mortality, is exposed to the treacherous underminings of so many Sicknesses and Distempers, that its own frailty seems Petitioner for some artificial Enamel, which might be a fixation to Nature's inconstancy, and a help to its variating infirmities. For he that narrowly observes that fading house of distemper'd clay, will soon find that it emulats the Moon in mutability; that though today it be varnisht with a purple and lively blush, tomorrow it will be so white washt with a meager paleness, as if Death had took it to hire, and made it a whited Sepulchre[.]

Inverting the anti-cosmetic discourse of a stable nature corrupted by shape-shifting culture or art, Jeamson presents nature as the mutable, implicitly feminine entity whose errancy must be corrected by 'some artificial Enamel'. Nature herself, he states, pleads for the intervention of art. Art is cure and redemption, that which resists the encroachments of death. His task, he claims, is to 'fix the Complexion of the Body so that it be not too frequent in its variation; or to keep the fair and damask skin from being too much sullied with Deformities filthy fingers'. Female nature inexorably declines into ugliness: art, on the other hand, works to preserve an original state of beauty.

There is no question in Jeamson's mind that artificial beauty outshines the feeble charms to be found in nature. '[C]onceited beauties craven'd with their own defects shall crouch in your presence,' he promises the unattractive female reader whom he imagines benefiting from his recipes:

> When once your artificiall roses display themselves, others shall seem pale . . . their naturall vermilion shall only serve them to blush that their features are outvied by yours. Other Ladies in your company shall look like brown-bread sippets in a dish of snowie cream, or . . . like blubberd juggs in a cupboard of Venice glasses, or earthen Chamberpots in a Goldsmiths shop. . . . Be not banisht company for want of Beauty, when Art affords an innocent supply; . . . Borrow our ruddie vermilion, and become purple-plusht roses to be gatherd by the hand of some captivated Hero, least in the green-sicknesse livery of your own swarthy complexions, you be taken for thistles and crapt by Asses.[21]

Natural and artificial entities are confused in this passage: the artfully beautiful are transformed into 'purple-plusht roses', while those without 'artificiall embellishments' are reduced to unattractive inanimate objects such as chamberpots. It is art that now sets the standards of ideal 'natural' beauty, wresting the privilege from a nature which can produce only inferior copies.

Although women are to apply these recipes, Jeamson, as Frances E. Dolan observes, presents an ugly feminine nature heroically redeemed through masculine intervention.[22] The author's voice is unusually prominent for a collection of recipes, forming an authoritative framework that is an essential ingredient of the work. The male provider of cosmetics is a chivalrous hero: deformity is 'a single name, yet a complicated misery', but the author will 'quit you Ladies from the loathsome embraces of this hideous Hagge'. The recipes will 'transforme the wrinkled hide of Hecuba into the tender skin of a tempting Helena'.[23] The female body is thus a passive, malleable medium, to be shaped and reshaped by the male author in line with moulds of beauty established by male literary tradition.

Beauty in the early modern era is thus repeatedly presented as a masculine construct, an artful quality imposed onto women whose nature is aligned with ugliness. The anonymous tract *The Merry Dutch Miller* (1672) provides a comically extreme illustration of the gender dynamics informing models of beauty and ugliness in the period. As its subtitle informs us, the tract describes the Miller and his 'New Invented Windmill'

> Wherewith he undertaketh to grind all sorts of Women; as the Old, Decreped, Wrinkled, Blear-ey'd, Long-Nosed, Blind, Lame, Scolds, Jealous, Angry, Poor, Drunkerds Whores Sluts; or all others whatsoever. They shall come out of his Mill Young, Active, Pleasant, Handsome, Wise, Loving, Vertuous and Rich; Without any Deformity, and just suteable to their Husbands Humours.

The natural state of women, the tract suggests, is a physical ugliness inextricable from socially transgressive behaviour. Husbands drag their old, leaking, farting, scolding wives, their 'abominablest load of Foul-stuff', to the windmill, a place where 'no Woman is to make use of her tongue'. Male agency, the creativity of which is revealed here to be indistinguishable from violence, transforms these 'parcel[s] of old decay'd' femininity into suitably silent and obedient objects of virtuous beauty: 'though she were as old as Charing-Cross, or as crooked as Mother Shipton, or the arrantest Scold that ever came from Billingsgate, I will Ingage to make them Young, Active, Pleasant, handsom, Modest loving kind and Rich'.[24] If female beauty relies on male agency, however, male art, the tract suggests, is equally dependent on female ugliness. Providing the material for the men to 'grind', the ugly female body is presented in the moment of its transformation but is never finally transformed. As Jeamson's tract also reveals, the portrayal of heroic male agency relies on the construction of a hideous female body which is then available to be reshaped into an object of beauty. The representation of (female) physical ugliness is thus crucial to the construction of (male) art and the male artist, a prerequisite for the display of his redemptive creativity.

The contradictions surrounding the construction of female ugliness and redemptive male art are explored visually in Lucas Cranach's *The Fountain of Youth* (1546; Figure 19). The ugly old women on the left of the picture are isolated, poor and

Figure 19 Lucas Cranach, *The Fountain of Youth*, 1546

yearning figures, depicted against a bleak landscape and excluded from the pleasures of society. Doctors openly peer at their bodies, as the objectified, repellent nature of ugly female old age is unflinchingly portrayed. After the pool has enacted its metamorphosing power, however, beautiful young women emerge to become celebrated members of courtly society. As well as a powerful illustration of the significance of ugliness and beauty, mapped on to age and youth, in the construction and representation of early modern women, this arresting work metaphorically depicts particular constructions of artistic creation in this era. The process of passing through the pool evokes the sacrament of baptism, in Christian theology symbolising the death of the old, fallen subject and the resurrection of the new. In this painting it also symbolises the redemptive power of art, working against the corruption of the fallen order, most powerfully embodied in the unattractive female body, in order to recreate divinely beautiful objects. As the painting reveals, however, male art continues to require the ugly female objects that it ostensibly seeks to transform. Depicting on several levels at once the transformation of ugly female matter, the painting, like the pool, creates beautiful art out of unattractive female bodies. Caught in the moment of its metamorphosis, and thus its obliteration, the ugly female body continues to be represented, its presence providing male creativity with the opportunity to showcase its brilliance.

Texts from a range of contexts and settings therefore illustrate the gendered dynamics informing the representation of female ugliness and beauty in this era. For the rest of this chapter, I explore a group of early seventeenth-century English texts where male artists consciously engage with and seek to transform female ugliness. This body of writing, sometimes referred to as 'deformed mistress' or 'ugly beauty' writing, includes poetic, dramatic and prose works where men ostensibly celebrate or proclaim their desire for unattractive women. On the surface, such works appear to reappraise aesthetic norms and the constraints they place upon women, arguing for the appeal and value of features generally considered ugly. As we shall see, however, this form of writing ironically works to confirm the ugliness of the female body further, once again locating beauty in male art rather than in female nature. As in Cranach's painting, the ugly female body is stripped bare and exposed to public view in order that the transformative power of art (or, more accurately, that of the male artist) can subsequently be celebrated.

'Fairing the foul':[25] the deformed mistress

'Away with handsome faces,' opens James Shirley's 'To a Beautiful Lady', 'let me see/ Hereafter nothing but deformity.'[26] Possibly written for Horatio, a character with a perverse predilection for ugly women in Shirley's *The Dukes Mistris*, the poem illustrates the 'somewhat recondite taste for the beauty of deformity' that flourished briefly in seventeenth-century writing and drama.[27] Following the Italian burlesque tradition established by Francesco Berni, examples of the deformed mistress tradition include, among other works, John Collop's poems praising a 'Crooked Lady', a 'plump Lady', a woman with yellow skin and one with 'enammell'd Teeth, black, white and yellow', Donne's 'The Anagram', ostensibly celebrating Flavia (who 'hath yet an Anagram of a good face') and Shakespeare's sonnets addressed to a black and ageing mistress whose 'eyes are nothing like the Sunne'.[28]

Apparently rejecting the weary clichés of Petrarchan conventions, the deformed mistress motif has been seen to reflect the broadening of concepts of beauty taking place in the seventeenth century. Mannerist and Baroque aesthetics across Europe in this era celebrated 'the bizarre, the unusual and the witty'.[29] Reflecting the less rigid model of beauty that seemed to be emerging, Bacon commented that 'There is no excellent Beauty that hath not some Strangeness in the Proportion.'[30] Authors began to dismiss classical Renaissance ideals of the blonde, fair woman in favour of the possibilities offered by black beauty: 'In the old age black was not counted fair,/ Or if it were, it bore not beauty's name;/But now is black beauty's successive heir,' states Shakespeare's Sonnet 127.[31] While a few poems in the tradition praise what could be termed unorthodox beauty rather than ugliness, however, the deformed mistress tradition more characteristically operates within clearly defined frameworks of beauty and ugliness, wittily 'celebrating' features, including blackness, which it assumes the reader will find repellent.

Mock encomia of ugly women are a sub-set of the paradoxical praise tradition revived in the Italian Renaissance and subsequently in early modern England.[32] Originating as classical rhetorical exercises, paradoxes defend seemingly outrageous propositions, for instance that poverty is preferable to riches, sickness to health, or ugliness to beauty. 'Love is our Reasons Paradox, which still/Against the judgment doth maintain the Will,' declares Henry King in 'Paradox: that Fruition destroyes Love' (1664), drawing attention to the manner in which a paradox flies in the face of rational judgement.[33] As arguments, paradoxes seem designed to implode: 'If they make ye to find better reasons against them they do there [sic] office,' declares John Donne in an apologetic defence of his own juvenile foray into the briefly fashionable mode.[34]

A heavily ironic form of writing, paradoxes are nevertheless more elusive in tone and approach than Donne's statement suggests. As the *OED* notes, a paradox could refer to something 'intrinsically unreasonable' (*OED* 2b), as it does in *Love's Labours Lost* (c. 1593–94), where Biron states that 'No face is fair that is not full so black,' to which the King replies, 'O paradox, Black is the badge of Hell.'[35] It could also, however, refer simply to a statement that is contrary to received opinion, regardless of the truth or falsity of this opinion (*OED* 1a). To Thomas Hobbes, 'a simple reader' may 'take a paradox either for Felony or some other hainous crime, or else for some ridiculous turpitude; whereas perhaps a Judicious reader knows ... that a Paradox is an opinion not yet generally received'.[36] The truth-status of a paradox is liable to change: 'This was sometime a paradox,' states Hamlet, 'but now the time gives it proof.'[37] Whatever the status of the initial proposition, moreover, the arguments deployed in its support must at least appear to be credible. The largest early modern collection of paradoxes, *Athenian Sport* (1707), a volume containing many seventeenth-century examples of the genre, includes the paradox 'That it is better to be Half-starv'd than to fare Sumptuously'. 'I verily believe,' claims the author,

> however I have titled this Opinion, yet it will by no means be allow'd for a PARADOX by a number of those, whose Judgment ought to bear the greatest Sway.... [I]t would seem to me very uncouth, that any Man that makes profession of more Understanding than a Beast, should open his Mouth to the contrary, or make any scruple at all of readily subscribing to the Truth and Evidence of this Position[.][38]

'Paradox' is used in this passage to mean an untruth, yet the author suggests that this label does not preclude a convincing argument. Such posturing is part of the rhetorical game through which the author seeks to make an outrageous thesis persuasive, yet this invective against gluttony does indeed cite much common sense wisdom in defence of its cause. Although paradoxes defend apparently ridiculous propositions, then, the line between self-evidently false and plausible arguments within this mode of writing is not always clear-cut. Such ambivalence characterises poetic defences of ugly women. John Suckling's 'The Deformed Mistress' (1659), for example, suggests that the reader will not necessarily condemn the speaker's desire for an ugly woman. Declaring his predilection for a woman with a nose 'a foot long ... with pimples embro[i]der'd', the speaker asks the reader to 'Judge whether I am happy, yea or no.'[39] The (implicitly male) reader is primarily invited to congratulate Suckling for his wit rather than to reassess the merits of female deformity, but the poem consciously plays with the equivocal status of a paradox in its pretence of an appeal for a verdict. Early modern defences of ugliness consequently create a tone that is often difficult to interpret. Varying widely in approach, they frequently incorporate multiple, apparently contradictory, perspectives on ugliness simultaneously.[40]

Regardless of their apparently perverse stance, deformed mistress poems and prose arguments illuminate key changes taking place in the literary representation of ugliness in this era. Most notably, the moral status of deformity is unclear in these texts. The unattractive woman's body 'All revelation unto Man denys,' states Herbert of Cherbury in 'Another Sonnet to Black itself' (1665).[41] Suckling's 'The Deformed Mistress', meanwhile, leaves the reader in the dark regarding the moral or social status of the woman described. The 'comely Pearl of Snot' that is 'Considering whether it should fall or not' from her nose and her neck 'with yellow spots enamell'd' remain purely physical descriptions.[42] No longer the index of the mind, physical ugliness, the poems and prose texts ostensibly celebrating it suggest, is stubbornly opaque.

Although the moral and social meanings of the ugly body are open to interpretation within this mode of writing, its repulsiveness, perhaps surprisingly, is not. Living up to their status as paradoxes, poems or prose arguments presenting the ugly body as desirable nearly always depict it as visually disgusting, thereby enhancing the shocking impact of the speaker's apparently perverse desire. In the ironic blazon of Dipsas in John Lyly's *Endymion* (1591), an early example of the mode in English writing, for instance, the repulsiveness of the character described is never in question:

> O, what a fine thin hair hath Dipsas! What a pretty low forehead! What a tall and stately nose! What little hollow eyes! What great and goodly lips! How harmless she is, being toothless! Her fingers fat and short, adorned with long nails like a bittern! In how sweet a proportion her cheeks hang down to her breasts like dugs, and her paps to her waist like bags! What a low stature she is, and yet what a great foot she carrieth! How thrifty must she be in whom there is no waste! How virtuous is she like to be, over whom no man can be jealous![43]

Suckling's portrayal of a woman whose 'snout' meets her 'furrow'd chin, and both together/Hem in her Lips' in 'The Deformed Mistress' further illustrates the extent to which texts in this tradition reveal and expose the ugliness that they ostensibly exalt.[44] Like the comical anti-blazon of Mopsa in Sidney's *Arcadia*, a woman of a 'right base nature' who has 'a foul complexion upon a filthy favour, setting forth both in sluttishness', Suckling's portrait relishes its extreme depiction of the revolting body to which the speaker claims to be attracted.[45] 'In Praise of a Deformed Woman', published in *Choyce Drollery* (1656), similarly depends for its comic value on the disparity between the speaker's dissection of a repellent female body and the preposterous suggestion of male desire for this body: 'I love thee for thy blobber lips/Tis good thrift I suppose/They're dripping pans unto thy eyes/And save-all's to thy nose.'[46] Henry King's 'Madam Gabrina, or The Ill-favoured Choice' (1664) also insists upon the repulsive appearance of its subject, 'a thing/Made up, when Natures powers lay slumbering'. Fragmenting her body in a parody of the conventional blazon, the speaker itemises her 'teeth of jet', 'sallow' complexion and sour breath, leaving the reader in no doubt that she is 'ill-favoured'. The only 'defence' of an ugly mistress put forward in this poem is that she is unlikely to inspire either jealousy or lust: 'Thou cur'st thy appetite by a disease,' the speaker suggests to her lover.[47] The paradox on ugliness in Munday's translation of *The Defence of Contraries* (1593) similarly notes 'the good and profit ensuing by deformitie, when all they in generall ... doe openly confesse, as nothing hath like force in them, to tame and check the pricks of the flesh ... as one only looke upon an il-favoured and counterfeit person'.[48] The terms of this defence of female ugliness, echoed in many deformed-mistress works, exaggerate rather than reconsider the ugly woman's worthlessness in the sexual economy. It is male desire for the ugly body, or, more precisely, the wit displayed in the articulation of this desire, that is being defended in this tradition, not the unattractive body itself.

Instances of paradoxical praise are premised on authorial self-display. Synesius's praise of baldness, a classical example of the genre translated into English in 1579 by Abraham Fleming, states that the rhetorician's ability to praise that which is self-evidently unappealing generates 'much praise' and 'credit'.[49] Nashe agrees:

> Euery man can say Bee to a Battledore, and write in prayse of Vertue and the seuen Liberall Sciences, thresh corne out of the full sheaues and fetch water out of the Thames; but out of drie stubble to make an after haruest, and a plentifull croppe without sowing, and wring iuice out of a flint, that's Pierce a Gods name, and the right tricke of a workman.[50]

'Madam Gabrina' likewise draws attention to the benefits for the poet of demonstrating his ability to defend the indefensible: 'to make love to a Deformity/Only commends thy great ability/Who from hard-favour'd objects draw'st content/As Estriches from iron nutriment'.[51] For the author to get full credit for his ingenious ability to shape beautiful rhetoric out of unprepossessing material, the deformity of the object must be beyond doubt. Far from questioning the repugnant status of the unattractive woman's body, then, this paradoxical tradition is heavily invested in establishing its repulsiveness.

Female ugliness within this tradition is not limited to the deformed mistress in question but extends to the entire sex. 'That it is better to be fowle than fair' in *The Defence of Contraries* focuses far more attention on the shortcomings of female beauty than it does on the supposed benefits of ugliness. 'Beawty is an unknown detriment,' declares the speaker. '[N]othing else but secret deceit', it is both artificial and superficial: 'borrowed corporall beauty', as the author refers to it, 'so easily corrupteth, even by the least touch of any fever'. The paradoxical defence of ugliness is thus grounded in a more orthodox critique of beauty, as the author sets spiritual beauty in direct opposition to physical charms: 'if we shall compare and unite together, the beawty of the mind with that of the body: shall we not finde a greater number of deformed people, to be more wise and ingenious than the faire and well formed?'[52] As Shirley's 'To a Beautiful Lady' succinctly states, the choice, it seems, is 'betwixt misshape and perjury'.[53] Emphasising the supposed superiority of the ugly is a means of exposing the viciousness of the beautiful:

> deformed people deserve more praise than the beawtifull ... considering such as are hard favoured, are commonly chast, humble, ingenious, holy, and have ever some sweet appearance of most commendable grace.... But for them that boast of beautie, I leave to you to consider of their behaviour, which is often times so counterfeit, as nothing can be saide to agree lesse with nature.[54]

The extent to which the 'praise' of one ugly woman works to expose the moral and physical deformity of apparently beautiful women is apparent in the anonymous paradox 'That a Black-a-moor Woman is the greatest Beauty; in a Letter to a Lady exceeding Fair'. Playing on commonplace perceptions in this era of the unattractiveness of those categorised as black, the paradox brings to the surface the tradition's implied criticism of beautiful women in its direct address to 'a Lady exceeding fair'.[55] 'Madam, you more properly appear to be, than are,' asserts the speaker, insisting that her looks, even if authentic, are ugly in comparison with the beauty visible elsewhere in nature: 'han't you, pray, great reason to be proud of what a Tulip enjoys in so much greater perfection[?]' If he were to examine her skin closely, he claims, he would find 'Deformity in 't': 'how Yellow and Tawny might it appear? What an odious Scurf upon it? How many Armies of Living Creatures might we there discover?' The paradox ultimately uncovers the repulsiveness of the female body, whatever its outward show: 'You are all Blacks as soon as the impartial Night has drawn her Veil over the World... and who knows whether you are not so by day, too.'[56] Far from exonerating the 'imperfect' body, the work, like many others in the tradition, reveals the true ugliness of womankind, an ugliness which, once exposed, is anything but celebrated.

Through revealing female ugliness and then appropriating the right to define its meanings, the speakers of the paradoxes wrest control from the painted lady, she who can fashion herself and deceive men, displacing her problematic agency with their own authoritative rhetorical constructions of her body. Apparently emphasising the subjectivity of constructions of beauty and ugliness ('each wrinckle is a smile/(Had they my eyes to see)'),[57] the deformed mistress tradition more precisely betrays the extent to which beauty exists solely in the eye (and through the pen) of the male beholder. As Donne so memorably states in one of his contributions to the genre, 'She hath yet an Anagram of a good face/If we might put the letters but one way/In the leane dearth of words, what could wee say?' The ugly woman is passive and incoherent matter: her beauty, if it is to exist, depends on the intervention of a male agent. She is a 'Gamut', or a musical scale: any harmony that is to be attributed to her must come from the 'Musitions' who transform her into a 'perfect song.'[58]

Emphasising masculine constructions of the female body, the deformed mistress tradition perpetuates the displacement of the female body by (male) art that Cropper analyses in relation to portraits of female beauty in this era. While the beautiful woman is 'necessarily absent' from discourses that claim to portray her but in fact operate in a self-referential manner, we might have assumed that the ugly woman would fare differently.[59] The depiction of ugliness seems to require a rejection of clichéd, non-mimetic metaphors in favour of lifelike, individual portraits. Far from drawing on life rather than art for their inspiration, however, mock celebrations of female ugliness in early modern English texts consciously parody Petrarchan conventions, further illustrating the extent to which early modern portraits of women, whether depicting beautiful or ugly subjects, are generated within self-referential masculine schemes of representation rather than in relation to the female body.[60] Snot, for example, is likened to a 'pearl' in Suckling's 'The Deformed Mistress', as are drops of sweat in Donne's 'The Comparison', while spots become rubies and yellow skin is likened to gold in other examples of the genre.[61] Wittily inverting and reordering conventional literary metaphors of beauty, the authors of these works place even sharper focus on their own art than do artists depicting beauty.

Displacing the ugly woman from the texts in which she is supposedly praised, these works have the effect of subjecting ugliness to the disciplinary regime of male-defined discourses of beauty. The repulsive figures are characterised by leaking, unregulated, necrotic, contagious flesh. Their bodies thus accord with Cousins's model of ugliness as that which is marked by excess, perpetually transgressing the boundaries between the self and the other.[62] As we have seen, the ugly body in its insistent and uncontrolled corporeality is a particular threat to emerging early modern forms of identity, premised as they are on principles of self-regulation and the transcendence of the body. One means of countering the anxieties generated by ugliness, argues Cousins, is the construction of particular canons of beauty. Beauty, aligned with symmetry, wholeness and coherence, is not simply the norm from which ugliness deviates, then, but is a 'defence against the precariousness of the subject if exposed to the ugly object'.[63] According to Bakhtin, the grotesque is 'the epitome of incompleteness', a mode highlighting the openness and interconnectedness of the body and the world. The beautiful body as it came to be defined in the Renaissance, conversely, was

> first of all a strictly completed, finished product. All signs of its unfinished character, of its growth and proliferation were eliminated, its protuberances and offshoots were removed, its convexities ... smoothed out, its apertures closed. ... The accent was placed on the completed, self-sufficient individual of the given body.[64]

Models of beauty are inextricable from wider constructs of identity: the beautiful in its self-sufficiency and wholeness represents and helps to shape the rational, self-controlled and discrete individual as he began to be understood in this era. Bakhtin's depiction of the beautiful body as one in which the 'unfinished character' of the grotesque body is 'eliminated' suggests that canons of beauty emerging in this period are indeed a reaction against, a means of suppressing and denying, the disturbingly incomplete grotesque body in order to formulate an alternative model of the self. The largely inorganic nature of Petrarchan metaphors for female bodily parts dehumanises and commodifies the female body while evoking the hard, bounded nature of the classical Renaissance canon of beauty. The smooth, closed, marble-like appearance of the Petrarchan mistress is thus a particular example of the 'narcissistic turning away from ugliness' involved in early modern ideals of beauty, a means of establishing and preserving an emerging model of a discrete, bounded, coherent self.[65]

On the surface, mock encomia of ugly women, by contrast, draw attention to the grotesque body that the canon of beauty identifies as hideous and formless.[66] Snot drips from the repulsive woman's nose, spots erupt on her neck: her body is transgressive, excessive, incomplete. The anti-Petrarchan nature of this writing nevertheless works to relocate the ugly body within the literary parameters of beauty, if in inverted form.[67] Insisting on the repulsiveness of the female body, these works reveal that the terms in which the beautiful female body has been fragmented and dismembered through masculine description can equally be applied to the ugly woman.⁶⁸ As Donne's 'The Anagram' states, 'shee/Hath all things, whereby others beauteous bee', merely in the wrong order.⁶⁹ Depicting the ugly body through an inverted form of the literary discourse of beauty counters its threatening tendency to 'spread itself about', bringing it within the confines of the known and the controlled.⁷⁰ While critics have argued that portraits of ugliness in this era reveal the artist's desire to escape the rigid conventions governing representations of beauty, assuming that ugliness, unlike beauty, allows idiosyncratic, naturalistic depiction, paradoxical encomia therefore betray precisely the opposite impulse.⁷¹ Far from seeking freedom from the literary stereotypes shaping beautiful portraits, they insistently bring the ugly body within the scope of these rigid models, in parodied form.

Emerging from a very different context, Antonio Tempesta's *The Twelve Principal Roman Heroes and Heroines, Drawn in a Grotesque Manner* (c. 1597) provides a visual illustration of some of the principles at work in the texts that I have been discussing in this chapter. Depicting hideously deformed women and men, Tempesta's drawings (e.g. Figures 7 and 20) frame and categorise the physical ugliness they delineate with the visual and linguistic vocabulary of beauty. Identified as Roman heroes and heroines, the figures are dressed in elaborate clothes, framed with intricate ornamentation and labelled 'beautiful' or 'lovely'. The disparity between the celebratory setting and the ugly faces in this series is the root of the startling, comic impact of the works, a comic effect that defuses the horrific, unsettling impact of such extreme forms of physical unattractiveness. Whether primarily visual or linguistic in approach, mock encomia seek to regulate and control the (ugly) female body that they expose, bringing it within the discursive framework of beauty and thus ensuring that it no longer poses a threat to the male subject.

Located as the inverse of canons of beauty rather than as a transgressive, unknown quality, ugliness within this tradition is defused of much of its power to disrupt. The ugly woman, repositioned as an object of desire, becomes newly silent and passive. Implicitly identified as the authentic feminine condition, deformity, presented in these terms, is a stable, fixed, and knowable property. Somewhat ironically, given the fact that ugliness is ostensibly being redefined as beauty, the unattractive female body is repeatedly celebrated in this mode of writing for its resistance to transformation, its immutability. Sickness and age will 'ruine many a good face', observes the speaker in 'Madam Gabrina', but 'Thy choice cannot impair; no cunning curse/Can mend that night-peece, that is, make her worse.'⁷² "'Tis less griefe to be foule, then to have been faire,' agrees Donne in 'The Anagram', constructing the temporality of beauty in contrast to the stable permanence of a deformed female body. 'Women are all like Angels,' he posits: 'the faire be/Like those which fell to worse; but such as shee/Like to good Angels nothing can impaire.'⁷³ Blackness, in particular, is equated with authenticity and changelessness in these texts. Fair Petrarchan mistresses, those whose beauty aligns with their whiteness, alter with the 'seasons, they but bud and blow/And then expire for ever', notes Thomas Jordan's 'A Paradox on his Mistresse, who is cole Blacke, Blinde, Wrinckled, Crooked and Dumbe'

(1637). The 'changeless Hue' of his black mistress, on the other hand, is a fixed sign: '[A]ll mens eyes/May trust thy face, for it brookes no disguise,' he insists.[74] Unable to hide her shameful physicality, the ugly woman, in these works, is devoid of agency. Constructed by the male gaze, divorced from any possibility of self-fashioning, she becomes 'an easie booke/Written in plain language for the meaner wit'.[75]

The 'plain language' of an ugly woman's body is only an 'easie booke' for an authoritative reader, however. Uncoupled from the self-evident moral frameworks within which it had previously been interpreted, the ugly body does not readily display its own meaning, and nor can the unattractive woman shape the significance of her own appearance. Physical ugliness has instead become a blank space whose meanings are determined by the privileged (male) beholder. '[T]hy blackness is a spark/Of light inaccessible,' claims the 'Sonnet of Black Beauty' (1665), 'and alone/ Our darkness which can make us think it dark,' emphasising the subjective judgements, the artful projections, involved in categorisations of the beautiful and the ugly.[76] Despite the fact that the mistress in Jordan's 'A Paradox' is 'constant' in her 'changelesse Hue', her face supposedly a 'fit Emblem to [her] mind', the speaker subsequently likens her face to a 'Vaile', withholding its meanings. Various male viewers insist on very different constructions of 'Negra', some apparently more nuanced and sophisticated than others:

> Some call thee Wrinkled (Negra) and are bold
> To tell me that my Mistresse is as old
> As twice my age (thus all seeke to beguile
> Thy pretious worth) each wrinkle is a smile,
> (Had they my eyes to see) Then, they would know
> (If they be smiles) why they continue so;
> I answer'd that those smiles are always shewne,
> To tell thou still art friends with every one.
> So art thou termed crooked, cause they see
> Thee (like the figure of Humility)
> Still bending to the earth; but thou art wise
> And wilt salute all creatures (since thy eyes
> Deny thee to make choyse) twere better be
> Alwayes so bent, then lose humility.

Rather than the transparent sign that it initially appeared to be, the mistress's ugly body is a mysterious, cryptic code for which the speaker alone possesses the key: 'These were Enigmaes to them, till I told/The meaning, and the Riddle did unfould … onely I,/Retaine the knowledge of that mystery.'[77] Contesting the terms in which her body is described, he nevertheless confirms her physical deformity, displaying her wrinkled, crooked, blind body even as he ostensibly seeks to redefine its worth. As Dubrow observes, works which on one level praise or celebrate ugliness are perpetually haunted by the possibility that they could revert to more conventional abuse and denigration of the unattractive female form.[78] The negative perspectives

Figure 20 Antonio Tempesta, 'The neat Marfisa' and 'The beautiful Bradamante', *The Twelve Principal Roman Heroes and Heroines Drawn in a Grotesque Manner*, c. 1597

imputed to other men here create a parallel poem in which the mistress's features are mocked rather than celebrated. Displaced onto the opinions of others, the speaker reminds 'Negra' of less celebratory perspectives even as he ostensibly refutes them, drawing attention to the fact that her worth resides solely in his perverse decision to take the opposite view.

Instead of celebrating the ugly woman, then, this group of texts works to shore up masculine agency and power, insisting on the male speaker's authority to construct the female body in his own terms.[79] Beauty is in his gift, not her possession. 'So art thou none but mine,' insists the speaker of Jordan's 'A Paradox'; 'I made thee gold, tis I can make thee brasse,' threatens the speaker of Collop's 'To Aureola'.[80] Edmund Prestwich's 'To Almanna, Why she should marry me' (1651) also draws attention to the fact that the ugly woman's newly defined worth rests entirely in the hands of the poet. 'Thou wert most excellently fayr/But now, I grieve to say 't, thou 'rt nothing so,' he instructs the object of his desire, explaining that it is his perception of her relative physical and spiritual charms that has altered. 'Reading thy body o'r and o'r', the speaker appropriates the power to interpret and inscribe the woman he addresses as either beautiful or ugly according to his own explicitly subjective perceptions. If she agrees to marry him, her beauty ('Both in thy Mortall and Immortall part') will be eternally secured through his verse. If not, however, 'Beleeve it others shal thee prize/Not as the wonder of thy sex but shame.'[81] The beauty of the woman resides only in male constructions: she can be returned to her natural ugliness at any time. Thomas Carew's 'Ingrateful Beauty Threatened' (1640) agrees, drawing attention to the fact that Petrarchan forms of beauty are a masculine construct:

> That killing power is none of thine,
> I gave it to thy voice, and eyes;
> Thy sweets, thy graces, are all mine;
> Thou art my star, shin'st in my skies[.]

Unless she complies with his wishes, he will 'uncreate' what he has 'made', returning her to her implicitly ugly 'mortal state'.[82]

Arrogating the power to define and redefine the objects of his desire, the male speaker, not the ugly woman, is the true subject being inscribed in mock encomia. On the most basic level, the libertarian amorality expressed in some versions of the convention constructs a Cavalier persona:[83] 'What I fancy, I approve,' opens Herrick's 'No Loathsomnesse in Love', 'No Dislike there is in Love:/Be my Mistresse short or tall,/And distorted there-withall.'[84] 'Each man his humour hath, and faith tis mine/To love that woman which I now define,' states Suckling's 'The Deformed Mistress', a poem exploring his 'humour' rather than the woman who is explicitly constructed according to his own desires.[85] James Shirley entitles one example of the genre 'One that loved none but deformed women' (1646), again drawing attention to the lover rather than the beloved, while in Henry King's 'The Defence' (1664) the focus is so entirely on the subjective position of the speaker that the implicitly ugly mistress is never actually described. Her physical appearance is irrelevant: 'Nor canst thou discern where her form lyes,/Unless thou saw'st her with my eyes.'[86] Materialising in his eyes only, he alone determines her aesthetic value: 'If lik't by me, tis I alone/Can make a beauty where was none;/For rated in my fancie, she/Is so as she appears to me.' Casting himself in the position of a sovereign deity, the speaker likens his mistress to a Calvinist subject, that is, to one defined by total depravity: "tis not feature, or a face/That does my free election grace,' he jokes. Wittily playing on the doctrine of predestination, which states that salvation is the arbitrary gift of God rather than a consequence of the innate worth or personal decision of the individual, the speaker insists that his desire for his mistress originates in his own will rather than in her qualities. 'Had'st thou a perspective so cleere/Thou could'st behold my object there,' he instructs his male readers. Proving himself a Platonic lover, that is, one who loves 'by judgement not by sense', he establishes his own moral worth while also displaying his wit in front of a male audience.[87] 'The Defence' is a defence and celebration not of an unattractive woman, but of the speaker as lover, drawing attention to the masculine self-promotion by which the deformed mistress tradition is characterised.[88] The desire for the unattractive woman articulated in this tradition, then, emerges as a desire to define and control the (ugly) female body in order to preserve particular constructions of the male self. Located within specific literary discourses of beauty even as she inverts them, the 'desirable' ugly woman, perhaps surprisingly, is disempowered even more effectively than is her counterpart in abusive depictions where she is overtly loathed and feared.

The limits of transformation: smallpox writing

Another group of texts where male authors attempt to contain the threat of an amorphous, feminised ugliness through discourses of beauty is smallpox poetry. As this body of writing reveals, much of the horror of smallpox lies in its power to unravel recognisable categories of identity. The disease obliterates physical features, and this material erasure of the self is matched by its disregard for class distinctions, its obscene collapsing of social divisions. The disease, moreover, is imagined in feminine terms in the era and threatens to undermine gender divisions alongside those of social rank.[89] Those disfigured by smallpox consequently illustrate in particularly acute form the ability of ugliness to undo acceptable or knowable forms of identity. '[A]n ugly Face reduces a Woman into a kind of Non-existence,' states Scott's *Agreeable Ugliness*, and smallpox writing suggests that this unhappy fate is shared by early modern victims of the disease, both male and female.[90] Confronted with the physical and social horror of this new condition, authors seek to relocate its victims within recognisable categories of selfhood, gender and social status by describing them with the vocabulary of beauty. The result, however, is a series of lurid and often incongruous images of 'beautiful' disease-ravaged features which enhance, rather than distract from, the visual impact of scarred features. Attempting through the at times absurd imposition of discourses of beauty to bring unattractive feminised matter within the bounds of the known and the safe, the authors of smallpox poems ultimately fail to counter the unsettling power of the ugly body to elude normative categories of the self.

Smallpox was a relatively new disease in England in the seventeenth century, but it spread rampantly during the period.[91] Margaret Cavendish's *Wits Cabal*, Part 1 (1662) conveys its grimly commonplace prevalence: on being told that a widow has smallpox, Faction replies, 'That's no newes': 'all mankind/In these parts of the World have that disease at one time or other, if they/live to "t".[92] The mortality rate was lower than it was for the plague, but those who were lucky enough to survive were likely to be left disfigured. '[T]he mealy scales' of the disease are 'of a very corrosive nature', observes the physician Thomas Sydenham, 'which leave Pits behind them, and oftentimes scars. Sometimes the Skin of the Shoulders and Back comes off.'[93] Later estimates state that 12–16 per cent of the population of seventeenth-century London were disfigured by the disease.[94] The deformity caused by smallpox dominates its literary representation, indicating the levels of distress and anxiety generated by the disease's ability to 'nullifie a face'.[95] 'O thou deformed unwoman-like disgrace,' apostrophises the speaker of Richard Corbett's 'Upon the Death of the Lady Haddington dying of the Small Pox' (1647), 'thou plowst up flesh and blood . . . /And leaves such print on beauty if thou come,/ As clouted shoes doe on a floore of loome'. The marring of Lady Haddington's beauty seems as much if not more of a scandal than the fact of her death in the poem, as the poet articulates the horror of a disease 'that of faces hony combes dost make'.[96] The speaker is particularly outraged by the fact that a member of the aristocracy has been overcome by a condition whose deformities, the imprint of 'clouted shoes . . . on a floore of loome', seem better suited to the labouring classes. Lady Haddington's beauty and virtue are inextricable from her class position in the poem, while the lower orders are aligned with both ugliness and sin. 'Goe where thou art invoked every houre;/Amongst the gamesters,' the speaker instructs the disease, suggesting that it 'shouldst have chosen out some homely face,/Where thy ill favoured kindnesse might adde grace'.[97] The poem's insistence on appropriate class boundaries for smallpox seeks to counter one of the disease's most unsettling characteristics, its lack of social discrimination. Smallpox was in fact believed to attack those from the higher echelons of society with particular ferocity. Transgressing social divides, it was experienced as a threat on levels beyond the simply physical. John Dunton described it as an 'envious Jade' that 'invade[s]/Fair Bodies'.[98] Explicitly feminised, smallpox is repeatedly depicted as an insubordinate, impudent entity whose ability to eradicate beauty mirrors its terrifying propensity to erase social divisions and the identities dependent upon them. Dryden's elegy 'Upon the Death of the Lord Hastings' notoriously depicts the progress of the disease through images of class war: each 'little Pimple had a Tear in it,/To wail the fault its rising did commit:/Who, Rebel-like, with their own Lord at strife,/Thus made an Insurrection 'gainst his Life'.[99] Thomas Shipman's 'Beauty's Enemy: Upon the Death of M. Princess of Orange, by the Small Pox' (1660) likewise complains that the 'spite' of the disease is 'sent/Like Sequestrators, on the Eminent'.[100]

To Alexander Brome, like Corbett, the disease would have been much easier to interpret if it had remained in its rightful place among the lower orders. 'Were it your Butlers face,' he postulates in 'To a Gentleman that fell Sick of the Small Pox. When he should be Married' (1664), 'A Man would think/They had but been new boylings of the drink;/Or had his nose been such, one would have swore/'Twere red with anger, 'cause he'd drink no more.'[101] Disfigurement among the lower classes is thus readily aligned with sinful, unbalanced living. Had smallpox respected social hierarchies, it could have taken its place alongside syphilis as a disease whose visible outworkings could be equated with the moral condition of its victim. Smallpox had been represented in similarly moral terms to maladies such as syphilis earlier in the century: in Thomas Dekker's *The Whore of Babylon* (1607), for instance, the marks of smallpox on a 'freckled face queane' are taken as signs of deceit and depravity.[102] John Lamport's medical treatise *A Direct Method of Ordering and Curing People of that Loathsome Disease, the Small-pox* (1685) insists that digestive and humoural imbalances (often equated with reckless, indulgent living) render subjects susceptible to the disease: 'as the stomach is more or less loaded with ill humors', he states, 'so is this disease more or less violent'. If smallpox thrives on particular diets, though, it favours those of the rich: 'Country people conjecture, as people that are fat and corpulent to be full of the small-pox,' he observes, while 'the spare lean people' escape unscathed.[103] While Lamport attempts to place some distance between the 'conjecture' of the ignorant and his own more informed manual (which recommends strong beer as a remedy for the condition), others confront the puzzling social pattern of the disease more directly. 'How is it,' questions Sydenham simply, 'that so few of the common people die of this disease compared with the number that perish by it among the rich?'[104]

Failing to provide an answer to this conundrum, literary representations of smallpox in this era exhibit the anxiety caused by a condition whose ability to 'nullifie a face' is matched by its propensity to unfix social and moral moorings. The deformed features of the great and the good victims of smallpox render disfigurement illegible to the authors of smallpox poems, who struggle to make sense of a physically repulsive appearance that they cannot regard simply as evidence of immorality.[105] 'You are not spotless though you're innocent,' states Brome, generating wit out of the ugly body's resistance to a simple or transparent moral reading. Fascinated by the visible effects of the disease, he observes that the ugly body cannot determine its own meanings: 'These things I guess not by your face,' he states. 'I find/Your front is not the Index of your mind.'[106] In the absence of a readily interpretable framework for scarred features, their meaning must be constructed and imposed by the viewer or the poet.

Exhibited in the skin, the marks of smallpox become the occasion for a wider exploration of the superficiality of physical ugliness. The unprecedented literary concern with disease exhibited in smallpox writing is generated at least in part by the fact that this condition brings the modern dislocation of the body and the self into sharp focus.[107] Drawing on class-specific imagery as he compares a gentlewoman's body to a 'rich Palace' that has been besieged by 'some sulphurous spirit', Owen Felltham's 'On a Gentlewoman, whose Nose was pitted with the Small Pox' (1661) attempts to resist the transgressions of the disease through insisting that the 'Guest within, her purer soul' is unaffected by the invasion.[108] William Hammond also seeks to mitigate the terrifying ability of the disease to blur both physical and social boundaries through establishing a clear-cut difference between outer and inner identity: 'What though she pit thy skin? She onely can/Deface the woman in thee, not the Man.'[109] Body and self are assigned different genders as the poet insists that corporeal disfigurement is ultimately irrelevant to the (masculine) self, that which is located out of physical reach, within.

The unexpected metaphors deployed for pockmarked faces in these poems similarly register the perception that the ugly face no longer possesses stable meanings. To John Oldham, lamenting the death of his friend, deformity becomes a mark of consecration:

> Those marks of Death which did its surface stain
> Now hallow, not profane.
> Each spot does to a Ruby turn;
> What soil'd but now, would now adorn ...
> Those Asterisks plac'd in the margin of thy skin
> Point out the nobler Soul that dwelt within[.][110]

Reinterpreted as a sign of virtue, facial disfigurement is depicted through the language of beauty, which ostensibly becomes a means of imposing acceptable order and form on to horrifically meaningless matter. Oldham's elegy draws on the concept of beauty as the interplay of opposites: ''Twas here thy Picture look'd most neat,' claims the speaker, 'when deep'st in Shades 'twas set./Thy Vertues only thus could fairer be/Advantag'd by the Foil of Misery.' The familiar Neoplatonic model of man as a microcosm is reinterpreted to startling effect in the poem as the speaker likens Morwent's disfigured body to the cosmos: 'Thy lesser, like the greater World appears/All over bright, all over stuck with stars.' His pockmarks also become pearls of 'Indian luxury'.[111] Other poets join Oldham in deploying Petrarchan images to describe the faces of smallpox victims. Describing the hideous scarring caused by smallpox, Brome's 'To a Gentleman that fell Sick of the Small Pox' draws on the conflict of red and white definitive of beauty in Petrarchan poetry. The florid facial colour characteristic of the disease becomes the gentleman's 'red-rose', as the ravages of the condition are presented as a battle 'to try which is more lovely Red, or White'.[112] The pockmarks left by the virus are also described as stars and as red letters marking holy days, as Brome repeatedly reinterprets ugly features as marks of beauty. The scars are 'but Love-letters written on your brow', he asserts: the disease 'went to write foul, but Cupid made it prove/Spite of his spite, the alphabet of love'.[113] 'Thou were Enammel'd rather than Defil'd,' concludes the speaker of William Cartwright's 'On the Lady Newburgh, who dyed of the Small Pox' (1651), while Edmund Elys's 'To Mrs K.G. having been lately Sick of the Small Pox' (1655) compares facial spots to 'venus mole[s]' and the flushed complexion of smallpox victims to the 'rose'. Thomas Jordan's 'On the Death of the most worthily honour'd Mr. John Sidney' (1643) meanwhile describes a pitted face as 'sprinkled about with stars'.[114] Despite apparently transforming the deformed body into an object of beauty, Petrarchan imagery such as pearls, stars, rubies and roses in fact provides a startlingly visual register for the physical manifestations of the disease, as Anselment notes.[115] Dryden's depiction of Hastings, whose 'blisters with pride swelled, which through's flesh did sprout/Like rosebuds, stuck i' the lily-skin about' is one of many nauseatingly graphic depictions presented by writers who are ostensibly redefining the victims as beautiful.[116] Perhaps seeking to transform the horrible into the ridiculous, as Anselment argues, the poems expose the deformed body of the victim to public view.[117] 'From the detestable and loathsome Sight/We turn our Eyes,' proclaims one poet, yet the imagery through which poets ostensibly divert our attention from the 'Holes and Pits' of the disease achieves precisely the opposite effect.[118] Once again, then, writing 'praising' ugliness reveals and betrays the repulsiveness of the body whose meanings it contests and seeks to control. Neither poet nor reader, in the end, can look away.

Faced with an ugly body that 'resists imaginative transformation',[119] and in the absence of clear moral or social frameworks through which to interpret such deformity, all that is left is incongruous and superficial word play. The conscious manipulation of conventional poetic discourses taking place in this body of writing once again draws attention to the witty, ingenious imagination of the poet, who is playing with multiple possible interpretations of a face that cannot be ignored but at the same time no longer tells its own story. The macabre material reality of smallpox nevertheless means that the poetic ingenuity celebrated in other forms of 'ugly beauty' writing rings hollow: it is not easy to 'relish Torment, and enjoy a Misery' in the face of a terrifying viral epidemic.[120] Shipman's 'Beauty's Enemy', written on the death of the Princess of Orange from smallpox, criticises the poet who would be 'a witty praiser of Misery/Like those hard Wits, who name the Scars/Upon her Face, Enammel, and bright Stars'. As Anselment observes, however, the speaker then goes on to compare 'each spot upon her face' to 'a Comet', her 'fatal Mask' to an 'Angel's Veil'.[121] Ostensibly addressing the subject of the Princess's death, Shipman's poem more directly tackles the question of representing ugliness, inviting the reader to observe the limitations of artful constructions of apparently meaningless instances of death and deformity. Far from redeeming fallen nature, art is here exposed as that which spectacularly fails

Figure 21 Mummy of a two-year-old child who died of smallpox in Naples in the mid-sixteenth century

to compensate for or to transform physical horror. Brome's poem also ends on a note of defeat, with the speaker finally conceding the impossibility of constructing a beautiful piece of art out of the ugly face before him. Beauty is often seen to exceed the limits of representation, but it is now ugliness that defies linguistic framing: 'if these verses go at halting pace,/They stumble in the vallies of your face', he concludes.[122] Having failed either to redeem the ugly body or to locate it in relation to stable moral or social co-ordinates, all that the poem displays, in the end, is the ugly physical fact of a pockmarked face.[123]

Failing to penetrate the mysteries of the disfigured face, then, smallpox poetry remains frozen at the level of the scarred skin, ultimately drawing attention to the marred features whose value it attempts to invert but whose meaninglessness it fails to counter. On one level the moral opacity of the body disfigured by smallpox enables the poet to transform the significance of feminised, amorphous deformity, reinterpreting marks of disease as signs of virtue, ugliness as beauty. Racing frantically through a series of consciously lurid images, the poems emphasise the cleverness of the poet while ostensibly resisting the inexorable march of the disease through insisting on the worth and identity of the victims it has obliterated. At the same time, however, the poems highlight their speakers' inability to transform skin-deep deformity into something more transcendent and thus the impossibility of getting beyond the material fact of the ugly face. Imagery that attempts to contain and transform ultimately exposes to view, as poetic language 'stumble[s] in the vallies' of this chilling form of modern deformity.

6

Sacrificing beauty: defeatured women

Representations of ugliness in early modern texts have so far largely been shown to shore up dominant identities at the expense of the female body and models of female subjectivity. In this final chapter, I ask whether ugliness can work to the opposite effect in early modern texts. Can an ugly face be turned to female advantage? Female agency is repeatedly aligned with ugliness in early modern culture, an equation that usually works to condemn the destructive effects of female self-assertion and art, as is apparent in anti-cosmetic statements from the era.[1] 'Some people handsome by nature have wilfully deformed themselves,' laments an incredulous Thomas Fuller in *The Holy State*: 'should God survey [their] faces ... he would not own and acknowledge them for those he created'.[2] Miso-Spilus echoes Fuller's anger and disbelief at what he sees as the self-disfigurement involved in Restoration cosmetic fashions. The use of black patches on the face is the 'adulterating and counterfeiting of God's Image in [women's] visages', he insists.[3] Any attempt to interfere with 'God's Image' is questionable, but the fact that women 'speckle [their] fair faces with foul spots' beggars belief:

> It is a wonder that any creature should presume to correct the work of his Creator; but that any Christian should delight to deform the lively Image of his Creator written in his forehead, as you do ... it may properly be styled a Wonder of Wonders.[4]

Beauty, these anti-cosmetic treatises suggest, belongs to divinely ordained nature alone. Impudent efforts to alter one's appearance result in ugliness. The beautiful, implicitly, passively submit to the created order, while the ugly have wilfully and deplorably departed from it. Ugliness, in other words, is that which perverts God's natural order and is linked to female attempts to construct an autonomous, self-fashioned identity.

Taking a different view of the 'impudence' involved in rejecting beauty, some twentieth-century feminists celebrate displays of physical ugliness as a means of resisting dominant gender ideologies. Welcoming rather than condemning the wilfulness involved in the desire to shape one's own identity, such critics also establish a connection between ugliness and female self-determination. Mary Russo, for instance, discusses 'freakish' self-display as a potentially liberating avenue of self-construction for women. Despite its potential pitfalls, she argues, the female grotesque 'as public spectacle is still powerfully resonant, and the possibilities of redeploying this representation as a demystifying or utopian model have not been exhausted'.[5] The association of ugliness with female agency thus spans the early modern era to the present day. Whether viewed negatively or positively, the rejection of beauty, it seems, is a gendered act of rebellion, linked to the formation of a dissenting subjectivity that refuses to be cowed by dominant ('natural') models of identity.

Aphra Behn's novella *The Dumb Virgin: or The Force of Imagination* (1700), a rare example of a female author representing female ugliness in an early modern English text, begins to explore the subversive potential of the ugly heroine. The monstrosity concomitant with female agency is the premise of the story's action, which tells of the deformed daughter resulting from a mother's wilful pursuit of a dangerous voyage. Having lost her perfect male child in the course of the fraught journey, the mother subsequently gives birth to a child who in every respect, including, implicitly, her gender, falls short of her elder sibling:

> upon its appearance their sorrows were redoubled, 'twas a Daughter, its limbs were distorted, its back bent, and tho the face was the freest from deformity, yet had it no beauty to recompence the dis-symetry of the other parts: Physicians being consulted in this affair, derived the cause from the frights and dismal apprehensions of the Mother, at her being taken by the Pyrates[.][6]

Maternal 'apprehensions' generate ugliness and deformity, reflecting seventeenth-century understandings of the potentially damaging role of female agency in reproduction.[7] The ugly daughter, Belvideera, perpetuates the story's association of female agency with ugliness as she fails to conform to the passive feminine ideals embodied by her attractive yet dumb sister, Maria.[8] Belvideera is 'indefatigably addicted to study', and possesses 'a piercing wit, and depth of understanding peculiar to herself'.[9] The singularity of her appearance is matched by, and is ultimately indistinguishable from, her unique ability to articulate herself. Her confident intelligence implicitly transgresses feminine boundaries: when she is in disguise, a listener is unable to judge from her speech whether she is male or female. Belvideera's articulate ugliness, as Felicity Nussbaum observes, aligns her with the late seventeenth- and early eighteenth-century female writers who were frequently depicted in the wider culture as 'monstrous, mutilated and compromised'.[10]

While on one level conforming to conventional gendered discourses in its depiction of female self-assertion as ugliness, *The Dumb Virgin* nevertheless unsettles the binaries around which it initially revolves. The beautiful, silent Maria ultimately secures the attentions of the hero, but Belvideera is also the object of desire in the narrative, as Behn celebrates the appeal of witty intelligence alongside Maria's more conventional charms. Although thwarted in love, the ugly heroine escapes the incestuous and ultimately fatal consequences of romance which befall her sister, suggesting that ugliness, for all its social humiliations, potentially has more to offer a woman than does beauty. Ugliness, in this narrative, is certainly no longer the sign of a morally depraved character, even if it originates in maternal flaws. Behn's heroine thus anticipates the ugly heroines of the eighteenth-century novel, figures whose 'unsightliness', as Nussbaum argues, 'becomes a legible rendering of a highly valued interior state and a virtuous femininity'.[11] Despite its association of female intelligence with physical unattractiveness, then, *The Dumb Virgin* suggests that an ugly face potentially opens up opportunities for women, releasing them from the stifling constraints of the role of romantic heroine and enabling them to pursue an independent existence dedicated to the pursuit of knowledge and witty self-expression.

Earlier in the seventeenth century, however, in texts largely authored by men, the possibility that ugliness may represent a positive alternative for female characters, while at times considered, tends to be swiftly undermined. Early modern texts contain several instances of female characters either wishing themselves ugly or resorting to self-disfigurement. Florinda in William Painter's *The Palace of Pleasure* (1566) and Margaret in George Chapman's *The Gentleman Usher* (1606) both mutilate their own faces, expressing disgust at the effects of their beauty as they turn on their features. Celia in Jonson's *Volpone* (1606), meanwhile, prays for 'dire lightning' to strike 'this my offending face' in order to avert Volpone's lust, identifying that 'Which you miscall my beauty' as an 'unhappy crime of nature': 'flay my face/Or poison it with ointments ... any thing/That may disfavor me'.[12] Lady Anne in Shakespeare's *Richard III* threatens to 'rend [her] beauty from [her] cheeks' with her own fingernails rather than remain the object of Richard's desire, while the rebellious Vittoria of Webster's *The White Devil* (1612) wishes that her eyes 'were not matches' and imagines biting off her own lip, savagely rejecting her own sexually appealing features.[13] Several female characters in early modern drama also use make-up to create the impression of black skin, a colour widely associated with ugliness in England in this period.[14] These examples, alongside a group of texts from the early seventeenth century depicting the mutilation of women by men, illuminate the relationship between acquired ugliness and female identity. Whether self-inflicted or imposed by others, the disfigurement of these characters is linked to their refusal to submit to sexual objectification, suggesting a desire for self-fashioning which seems to reinforce the link between ugliness, autonomy and agency. Cautioning against a celebratory reading of self-mutilation as self-determination, however, the material that I explore in this chapter suggests that representations of the desire to escape beauty are largely generated within a framework of culpable female physicality rather than in relation to the construction of alternative female identities. Representations of deformity in this context ultimately confirm rather than contest dominant gender discourses. The ugliness of mutilated women is repeatedly presented in terms of a nullifying amorphousness. Ugliness is not identity in these texts, but is that which erases identity: '[t]his [u]gly thing is now no more a face', exclaims Margaret following her self-mutilation in *The Gentleman Usher*.[15] Figured through images of disease and decomposition, the mutilated features of the female characters do not forge alternative boundaries for the self but instead mark the disfigured as abject, inhabiting a space beyond meaningful subjectivity.

The fact that an ugly face repeatedly seems preferable to an attractive one to female characters in early modern texts gives some indication of the constraints experienced by women whose (beautiful) bodies are seen to threaten their virtue and their honour. As numerous early modern texts imply, beautiful women are pervasively judged to be complicit in the transgressive desire provoked by their appearance, leading to the misogynist commonplace that the only virtuous woman is an ugly one. Those that nature 'makes fair she scarce makes honest', states Celia in *As You Like It* (c. 1599–1600), 'and those that she makes honest she makes very ill-favouredly'.[16] Aemilia Lanyer's savage critique of beauty in *Salve Deus Rex Judaeorum* (1611) is a more sympathetic reading of the problematic position of the beautiful woman than is found in most texts from the era. Lanyer's work nevertheless continues to assume that a woman is morally accountable for the desire that she provokes, making it almost impossible to reconcile chaste purity with attractive female features. Casting women as the objects of male desire while simultaneously holding them responsible for the sinful transgression that ensues, beauty guarantees women 'sorrow and discontent':

> As for those matchlesse colours Red and White,
> Or perfit features in a fading face
> Or due proportion pleasing to the sight;
> All these doe draw but dangers and disgrace[.][17]

Beauty is not only transient ('That outward Beautie which the world commends,/... Whose date expir'd, that tyrant Time soone ends' (ll. 185–7)), but makes women miserable:

> That pride of Nature which adornes the faire,
> Like blasing Comets to allure all eies,
> Is but the thred, that weaves their web of Care[.]
>
> (ll. 201–3)

Beautiful women are the passive objects of unwanted and threatening male attention: 'greatest perills do attend the faire/When men do seeke, attempt, plot and devise,/How they may overthrow the chastest Dame,/Whose Beautie is the White whereat they aime' (ll. 205–8). Yet the alluring female body, at the same time, generates its own violation: it was Helen of Troy's beauty that 'bred in Troy the ten yeares strife,/And carried Hellen from her lawfull Lord', while "Twas Beautie made chaste Lucrece loose her life' (ll. 209–11). It was 'Great Cleopatraes Beautie and defects', moreover, not Mark Antony's actions, that 'Did work Octavias wrongs' (ll. 215–16).

Crucially, however, Lanyer's poem opens up a gap between women and their beautiful bodies: beauty is the agent of its owner's downfall, whilst women themselves have no control over this fate (except, perhaps, in the case of Cleopatra, whose 'defects' co-operate with her beauty to wreak her fall, although her 'defects' do not appear to be entirely distinct from her beauty). A beautiful woman's body is locked in deadly combat with her soul, a fate women can escape only if they are fortunate enough to have escaped the curse of 'perfit features' (l. 194). Beauty works against women's spiritual interests and is to be shunned in favour of the inner virtue which defines 'true grace' (l. 198). 'A mind enrich'd with Virtue,' not a temporarily beautiful face, 'frames an immortal Goddesse on the earth,/Who though she dies, yet Fame gives her new birth' (ll. 197, 199–200). Lanyer's 'Holy Matilda' exemplifies the fatal struggle between external and internal female properties that the poem establishes. '[I]n a haplesse houre' Matilda's 'noble minde' is born within a beautiful body. Her body becomes the battleground for the opposing interests that result: 'Beauty the cause that turn'd her Sweet to Sowre,/While Chastity sought Folly to prevent' (ll. 233, 243, 235–6). Matilda's only means of escape from the 'base subjection' inextricable from her beauty is suicide, 'to die with Honour, not to live in Shame' (ll. 237, 246). Beautiful bodies must be destroyed in order for virtue to remain unspotted, a lesson clearly not learned by 'Fair Rosamund', who 'had been much fairer, had shee bin not faire'. Her '[b]eautie betraid her' and '[d]id worke her fall' (ll. 225–7, 230). It is women's tragedy, then, that they possess sexually alluring, and thus dangerous, corrupting bodies, yet Lanyer refuses to equate women fully with such bodies. Women can fashion an acceptable identity within the terms of Christian discourses of virtue by cultivating the 'rare perfection' of internal grace that alone can make them 'pleasing in [their] Makers sight' (l. 250). But only, it seems, in the absence of a beautiful face. Lanyer's poem implicitly conflates beauty with the female body so that physical ugliness, as well as death, seems to release women from corrupting carnal influences.

Lanyer is not the first author to recognise the constraints that beauty places on women. Ovid's *Metamorphoses* repeatedly draws attention to the relationship between physical attractiveness and the abuse suffered by so many of its female characters. Daphne, for example, pleads to be allowed to maintain her 'maidenhead', only to be told by her father that her wishes (as well as his own) are irrelevant: 'thy beauty and thy form impugn thy chaste desire,/So that thy will and [my] consent are nothing in this case/By reason of the beauty bright that shineth in thy face'. Beauty opposes and resists 'chaste desire', as Daphne's 'form' is afforded an agency that overrides her socially constructed desire to preserve her virginity. Pursued by Apollo, she believes that she will control her own destiny only if she becomes ugly: 'O let the earth devour me quick on which I seem too fair,/Or else this shape which is my harm by changing straight appair.'[18] In Shakespeare's *The Rape of Lucrece*, Tarquin insists that Lucrece's attractive features hold the responsibility for his assault: 'Thy beauty hath ensnared thee to this night.'[19] Sarah Scott's *Millenium Hall* (1762) later again registers the impasse created by female beauty. Louisa Mancel's physical charms, for instance, are a 'great obstacle', preventing her from living the life that she desires.[20] In order to flourish within a virtuous and autonomous female community, the novel suggests, the scars of smallpox or the marks of age are a prerequisite.

In all of these examples, then, a beautiful body aligns a woman with a carnal destiny that prevents her from constructing or maintaining a virtuous identity. Within the terms of the texts, beauty prevents a woman from pursuing her own desires, even though these desires are clearly generated by wider discourses of female honour. Ugliness, on the other hand, seems to offer a means of escape from corrupt feminine embodiment. To mar one's face is not simply to become ugly, but is, in theory, to escape association with feminine corporeality itself. Margaret, in *The Gentleman Usher*, states that her self-disfigurement is the first step in a process of '[feeling] death by degrees'.[21] The deformity of the female characters in the group of texts I discuss in this chapter is repeatedly described in terms of rotting, decomposing flesh, reinforcing the sense in which the pursuit of ugliness is inextricable from a desire to eradicate the female body. The goal, however, is not simply self-annihilation. Flaying their own skin, and thus stripping away the (beautiful) physicality that they experience as an alien, and alienable, aspect of the self, self-mutilating female characters seek to peel away an ostensibly corrupt exterior in order to reveal an inner, authentic core, a self, 'all soul', 'severed from all concretion', and thus the site of virtuous personal agency.[22] Tragically, however, female characters who pursue such a goal within early modern texts ultimately achieve the opposite effect. Far from transcending the overdetermined meanings of their flesh, mutilation parades their gross corporeality. The excoriated female body brings to light not an alternative, spiritual and virtuous self, and certainly not a self-determining one, but repulsive and corrupt flesh, that which denies and undermines rational, self-regulated identity. As Titian disturbingly suggests in his painting of the flaying of Marsyas (Figure 22), if we peel away the skin we may not find a 'precious, metaphysically charged interior', the inner recess of the Silenus privileged in the Renaissance as the location of truth, but may instead be confronted with a horrifically undifferentiated, opaque materiality.[23] The decorticated body promises to divest what is concealed but in the case of these female characters exposes only deformity, 'the sheer matter, the meaningless stuff, of the inside'.[24] 'This [u]gly thing is now no more a face,' as Margaret recognises: far from carving out new forms of identity, disfigured women on the early seventeenth-century stage and in texts from this era are instead 'defeatured'.

The term 'defeature', deployed for the first time in the 1590s, links the disfigurement of the face to an overthrow or undoing, often moral in nature.[25] The heroine of Daniel's *Complaint of Rosamond* (1592) speaks of the 'Night of [her] Defeature'.[26] 'Impure defeature', as Venus instructs Adonis in Shakespeare's *Venus and Adonis* (1593), perpetually threatens to ruin 'pure perfection', '[bringing] beauty under/... on the sudden wasted, thawed and done'.[27] Through this term, ugliness, linked to both moral and physical degeneration, is imagined in terms of an erasure of identity, its loss rather than its renegotiation. Egeon in Shakespeare's *The Comedy of Errors* states that 'careful hours with time's deformed hand,/Have written

Figure 22 Titian, *The Flaying of Marsyas*, c. 1570–75

strange defeatures in my face'.[28] The original script of his face has been displaced by characters written in a 'deformed hand' whose 'strange', unknown, unaccountable meanings are not readily open to interpretation. Rather than inscribing an alternative, intelligible script of the self, then, acquired ugliness erases a natural beauty suffused with decipherable divine signatures only to leave in its place, in the words of Jeamson's *Artificiall Embellishments*, a 'discolourable blank'. Jeamson's cosmetic manual agrees with Egeon that 'Grief is the moth of Beauty':

> it frets out the characters of natures fairest Orthography; wearing off those ruddie and carnation flourishes which her skilfull pencil drew, it makes the face a discolourable blank; and renders those who over much indulge it, so wannish and pale, that they seem but walking shrouds to carry themselves to their own shadie sepulchres.[29]

The unattractive appearance resulting from suffering unravels the identity previously inscribed in the features, generating abject figures whose 'blank' faces are suggestive of the ultimate loss of identity embodied in the corpse.[30] Like the subjects whose features are '[fretted] out' by grief, disfigured female characters in early modern texts represent the polar opposite of emerging modern forms of identity. Far from marking out, or becoming a means of constructing, a distinct character, the rotten, corrupt flesh exposed in these texts is opposed in its essence to discourses of individuality. While female ugliness in Behn's novellas and later in the eighteenth century potentially operates as a marker of singularity, of difference, and even of virtue, the loss of beauty suffered by these earlier female characters establishes only their abject status as 'discolourable blank[s]'.

Female characters' efforts to fashion their own identities through marring their bodies ultimately reveal the extent to which female subjectivity continues to depend on the visible, corporeal presence whose tyranny these characters are so anxious to escape. Attempting to open up a gap between their bodies and their selves, they demonstrate the resistance of early modern paradigms of female subjectivity to such an enterprise. Female characters' struggles to escape beauty in early modern texts thus highlight the awkward position of the female subject within emerging models of modern identity, betraying the constraints attendant upon her continuing association with a body which stubbornly refuses to be silenced and yet which cannot be made to speak in her own terms.

'Flay my face':[31] self-mutilation

Jonson's Celia, who prays for 'dire lightning' to strike her 'offending face', is one of several female characters in early modern English drama and literature to long to be ugly. Celia identifies her physical appearance as the cause of Volpone's adulterous lust and therefore believes that she will be able to preserve her virtue only if her body is disfigured:

> punish that unhappy crime of nature,
> Which you miscall my beauty; flay my face,
> Or poison it with ointments, for seducing
> Your blood to this rebellion. Rub these hands
> With what may cause an eating leprosy,
> ... any thing,
> That may disfavor me, save in my honour.[32]

Celia describes her beauty as a 'crime of nature', representing her attractive face as a prodigious oddity, a freakish entity loaded with ominous meaning. The protection of her honour nevertheless requires more than a simple loss of beauty: praying for 'eating leprosy' to consume her flesh, she fantasises not merely about self-mutilation but about physical dissolution.

Celia edges close to recognition that beauty is a rhetorical construct rather than a physical quality ('beauty', she insists, is a misnomer) yet she ultimately fails to extract herself from wider gendered constructions in which her body is inherently tainted. Lady Anne in Shakespeare's *Richard III* is similarly disempowered by the corrupt agency attributed to her (beautiful) physicality. In the shocking scene where Richard seduces Anne over the corpse of her husband, his insistence on her beauty is a sophisticated strategy designed to undermine Anne's ability to define herself and thus to place her under his control. Richard shirks responsibility for the murder of Anne's husband through declaring that her 'beauty was the cause of that effect'. 'If I thought that,' responds Anne, 'I tell thee, homicide,/These nails should rend that beauty from my cheeks.' Richard nevertheless refuses her the right to define (even negatively) her own appearance, retorting, 'These eyes could not endure sweet beauty's wrack;/You should not blemish it if I stood by.'[33] The violently contested and contestable meaning of the body, particularly in relation to its aesthetic value, is key to this scene, and indeed to *Richard III* as a whole. Power resides with those who rhetorically claim the right to define the meaning of physical appearances, most notably Richard, whose own apparent helplessness in the face of his deformity is countered by his ability to manipulate the significance of his appearance.[34]

Anne initially resists Richard through labelling him ugly ('fouler than heart can think thee'). Her strategy is rhetorically matched by his equally violent insistence on her beauty ('fairer than tongue can name thee'). Her depiction of Richard as a 'lump of foul deformity' points to his moral culpability, yet he imposes a reading of her beauty which similarly makes her appearance a sign of her moral lack, establishing her responsibility for his transgressive desire. Richard's descriptions of the power of Anne's beauty are ironically accompanied by her increasingly desperate articulation of her own powerlessness: he identifies her as a god, since her beauty controls his 'day' and 'life', leading her to state helplessly, 'I would I were, to be reveng'd on thee.' Anne labels Richard a foul 'toad' who 'dost infect mine eyes', but Richard again inverts the moral status of ugliness and beauty so that her beauty becomes the cause of the contagion: 'thine eyes, sweet lady, have infected mine'. He thus again ascribes agency to her physical attributes, whose meaning he alone determines. Anne wishes that her eyes were 'basilisks, to strike thee dead', but Richard's reply that 'they kill me with a living death' again insists on his right to redefine her body, identifying her with the monstrous creature from whose power she is excluded. Richard's control of the discourses of ugliness and beauty comes to a rhetorical climax as he again insists ''twas thy beauty that provoked me ... 'twas thy heavenly face that set me on'.[35] It is at this moment that Anne is finally silenced and succumbs to his will. The extreme implausibility of Richard's successful 'wooing' in this scene highlights the power of discourses of beauty to place and control women. It is not that Anne is merely flattered by Richard's attentions, in the weak and inconstant way mocked by both Richard and some critics. Instead, her desire to construct her own identity in opposition to the meanings given to her body by Richard is undermined by the fact that her body is afforded an agency of its own and is seen to work against her own desires and interests to the extent of causing the death of her husband. For both Celia and Anne, then, a beautiful body, whose meanings are already fixed, is anything but silent. Tragically, they cannot in the end see beyond its pre-inscribed script.

The disruptive Vittoria in Webster's *The White Devil*, by contrast, refuses to be equated with her physical appearance, incisively criticising the unjust double standard on which discourses of beauty are premised. On trial for her complicity in the murders of her husband and her adulterous lover's wife, Vittoria is well aware not only that female beauty is perceived to be a crime, but that it is one for which women are unfairly held responsible:

> Sum up my faults I pray, and you shall find
> That beauty and gay clothes, a merry heart,
> And a good stomach to a feast, are all,
> All the poor crimes that you can charge me with.

Vittoria vigorously denies that women's beauty is the agent behind transgressive male desire:

> Condemn you me for that the Duke did love me?
> So may you blame some fair and crystal river
> For that some melancholic distracted man
> Hath drown'd himself in 't.

The responsibility for male desire, Vittoria insists, lies with men. Her representation of herself in passive terms as a 'fair and crystal river', unexpectedly, is a subversive gesture.

Vittoria's angry insight into the misogyny governing discourses of beauty is not shared by other characters in the play, however. While she exonerates her beauty from moral responsibility, the court does not, and she is incarcerated while her more culpable lover walks free. Later in the play, Vittoria articulates a desire for the autonomy that only ugliness, it seems, enables. Her beauty objectifies her as a male possession, as Bracciano makes clear when he itemises her features as his acquisitions:

> BRACCIANO. Are not those matchless eyes mine?
> VITTORIA. I had rather
> They were not matches.
> BRACCIANO. Is not this lip mine?
> VITTORIA. Yes: thus to bite it off, rather than give it thee.

Flamineo, so often the voice of cynical wisdom in the play, clarifies Vittoria's implicit equation of female agency with repulsive physicality when he likens 'a woman's will' to 'a damned imposthume', or a festering abscess, identifying feminine self-assertion with a lack of sexual appeal: 'How scurvily this frowardness becomes you!'[36] Katherine's closing speech in Shakespeare's *The Taming of the Shrew* (*c.* 1592) echoes the sentiment, warning the 'froward, peevish, sullen, sour' women who refuse to subordinate themselves to their husbands that their 'scornful' glances '[blot their] beauty as frosts do bite the meads': 'A woman mov'd is like a fountain troubled,/Muddy, ill-seeming, thick, bereft of beauty.'[37] The self-determination apparently offered by revolting disfigurement, it seems to Vittoria, Celia and Anne, may nevertheless have more to offer than the 'fair looks' that align them with bodies whose meanings they are not free to shape.[38] In making this assumption, however, they overlook the equally constrained meanings of the ugly female body.

Rather than merely fantasising about the supposed moral and practical benefits of an unattractive face, Margaret, the heroine of Chapman's *The Gentleman Usher*, goes one step further. The Duke's illicit desire for her has led, she believes, to the death of her lover, the Duke's son, leading her to deface herself with depilatory ointment:

> I'll feele death by degrees; and first deforme
> This my accursed face with uglie wounds,
> That was the first cause of my deare loves death.

Margaret's self-disfigurement expresses self-loathing, locating the responsibility for the Duke's incestuous desire in her own features, but is also an act of resistance, destroying that which the Duke hoped to possess and aiming to repulse him: 'that feare of me may shiver him to dust,/That eate his owne childe with the jawes of lust'.[39]

Margaret's name recalls that of a well known virgin saint, said in medieval accounts to have cut off her hair and lived as a monk in order to avoid marriage.[40] The heroine of Chapman's play is encouraged to self-mutilate by her aunt's anecdote of 'Adelasia', who 'with such a knife as this/Cut off her cheeks, and nose, and was commended/More then all the Dames that kept their faces whole'.[41] *The Gentleman Usher* thus explicitly links Margaret's act of self-mutilation to the medieval hagiographic tradition of female saints disfiguring themselves in order to prevent either sexual assault or unwanted marriage.[42] St Ebba, daughter of Ethelfred, King of Northumbria, for instance, led her fellow nuns in an act of heroic self-defence against a threatened attack of Danish invaders by cutting off her own nose and upper lip.[43] On its own terms, self-mutilation in this tradition is a successful tactic, enabling women to escape rape. While it may not prevent a virgin's death, a disfigured face allows her to enter heaven untainted. Self-disfigurement (including the deformity that results from prayer) in hagiographic accounts also usually succeeds in thwarting unwanted marriages: the narratives largely work from the assumption that it is inconceivable for a man to desire, still less to desire to marry, an ugly woman. A statement in the *Lombard Codes* gives legal expression to this sentiment:

> If it happens that after a girl or woman has been betrothed she becomes leprous or mad or blind in both eyes, then her betrothed husband shall receive back his property and he shall not be required to take her to wife against his will.[44]

The impossibility of representing male desire for a deformed woman is further apparent in the narrative of the seventh-century St Licinius, Bishop of Angers. Diverging interestingly from the pattern of a woman's chastity being preserved through her disfigurement, in this instance it is the bishop's virginity that is miraculously protected. It is not his face that becomes deformed however, but that of his bride-to-be, who contracts leprosy, allowing him to escape the marriage. A disfigured male face, implicitly, may not preclude desire or marriage as self-evidently as does an ugly female one.[45]

In her reading of medieval accounts of self-mutilation, Jane Tibbetts Schulenburg interprets self-inflicted violence as a strategy of female self-assertion: it is 'an effective vehicle to manipulate [women's] family or society; it provide[s] a means to achieve ends which they could not readily attain directly'. Mutilation is thus a tactic that can be 'used by women to their advantage'.[46] Corinne Saunders similarly highlights the female agency celebrated in these accounts, while Claire Marshall states that 'the humiliations and extreme physical tortures endured by the female Saint facilitate her empowerment and entry into language'. The broken body of Christ, she observes, provided a model for religious women, whose self-disfigurement became 'an *imitatio Christi* which gave them authority to speak from the body'.[47] These readings of self-mutilation as an expression of agency to some extent align with present-day interpretations of self-harm, described as a means of articulating the self when alternative avenues of self-expression are inaccessible. One twentieth-century critic describes self-inflicted violence as 'the creation of a voice on the skin'.[48] Self-harm can work to construct a unified sense of self and of personal agency in the wake of abusive breaches to personal autonomy: it 'helps the self-injurer restore firm boundaries between self and other. . . . Self-directed violence preempts, or tries to preempt, injuries from others. For although self-mutilation causes harm, that harm is not caused by others.'[49] Self-mutilation has therefore been understood by critics and theorists in relation to a broad span of historical periods as an attempt to construct ownership of the self. In the wake of threats to a woman's autonomy, the practice can seem to insist that 'her life and her body are her own; possession of it is literally carved on her skin.'[50] Reiterating this interpretation of self-inflicted wounds as a form of text, Marshall speaks of 'the enclosed female religious' in the medieval period '[authorising] the inscription of her own body with the instruments of pain'.[51] The deformed body thus 'speaks' the self, its mutilation potentially enabling a woman to control and articulate her identity.

Medieval hagiographic narratives are rarely able to imagine a virtuous virgin remaining ugly for all eternity: mutilated saints tend to regain their physical charms at the end of the account, symbolising their triumphant vindication while simultaneously revealing the role of beauty as a marker of virtue in these narratives.[52] The physical deformities inflicted on the female body in these narratives nevertheless also work as visual symbols of holiness. The account of St Margaret, also known as Pelagien, in the popular medieval text *The Golden Legend* (*c.* 1275) highlights the complexities characterising the materialisation of holiness in the female body in these accounts. Margaret disguises herself as a monk in order to preserve her virginity. As her death approaches, however, she reveals her sex in order to clear her name following accusations that she has impregnated a woman:

> [I] was called Margaret in the world, but for I would eschew the temptations of the world, I called myself Pelagien. I am a man. I have not lived for to deceive, but I have showed that I have the virtue of a man.

Virtue is gendered masculine, located in the part of Margaret's identity labelled 'Pelagien' that opposes itself to the feminine corporeality signified by 'Margaret'. The 'masculine' part of the saint's identity demands the rejection of her sensuous feminine appearance, limited in this account to the removal of Margaret's hair. Virtue is not simply predicated on the absence of the female body, however, since it is the revelation of Margaret's virginal body which ultimately secures her saintly identity. Her 'masculine virtue', paradoxically, is exhibited and guaranteed through the display of her 'hymen', intact because of her repudiation of feminine beauty: 'the women then had knowledge that she was a woman, and virgin without touching of man.'[53] The narrative of St Agatha in *The Golden Legend* likewise exhibits the virgin's deformed body as proof of her virtue. 'My soul may not enter into the realm of heaven but if thou wilt torment my body,' Agatha assures her persecutor as both her breasts are cut off. The integrity of her soul not only survives the loss of her physical integrity but appears to require it: 'I have my paps whole in my soul,' she insists, following the assault, 'of which I nourish all my wits.'[54] She refuses medical help to restore her breasts, insisting on the holiness embodied in her mutilated flesh. Medieval accounts of virgin martyrs in which beauty symbolises purity thus also present the disfigured body of the female saint both as a vehicle for the attainment of holiness and as a visual manifestation of this holiness.

Following the Reformation, however, it became more difficult for the body, especially the deformed body, to be presented as a visible emblem of virtue, or, indeed, as a site of self-inscription. As Greenblatt observes, the self-mutilated bodies that had once signified 'somatic holiness' came in Protestant England to represent 'fraud, credulity, vain superstition, and, worst of all, a fall into pagan or demonic worship'.[55] 'Christians, whom it concerns to worship God in spirit and truth, and not with wrie faces and antic Gestures, do not think it necessary to maim any part of the body which Nature has made perfect,' declares J. Philips in his English translation of Guillaume-Joseph Grelot's *A Late Voyage to Constantinople* (1683), contrasting the internal, spiritual nature of Christian holiness with heretical 'Turkish' practices of circumcision.[56] The 'unresolved tensions' of Foxe's *Actes and Monuments*, where visual and textual depictions of tortured bodies bear witness to a form of truth that ostensibly rejects the ability of the body to resonate with this truth, nevertheless betrays the ambivalent role of the body, particularly the mutilated body, following the Reformation.[57] Whatever his theoretical uneasiness with the tactic, Foxe finds the impact of the deformed body, its power to generate pathos, irresistible in his quest to build a Protestant nation.

If the body is a problematic category in accounts of Protestant martyrdom, the female body is particularly so. As Frances E. Dolan argues, virtue is not usually signified through women's bodies in early modern narratives of suffering but is instead 'registered by means of [women's] disembodiment'.[58] Cynthia's lauded self-starvation in Chapman's *The Widow's Tears* (c. 1605) suggests that female spiritual development requires the erasure of the body:

> thou disdain'st
> (Severed from all concretion) to feed
> Upon the base food of gross elements.
> Thou art all soul; all immortality.
> Thou fast'st for nectar and ambrosia,
> Which till thou find'st and eat'st above the stars,
> To all food here thou bidd'st celestial war.[59]

Food refusal does not necessarily signal a disregard for the power of the body to validate holiness, however. Displays of the starving yet miraculously sustained body are a key means by which radical religious women in the mid-seventeenth century authorise their spiritual status and thus their public, political voices. The Fifth Monarchist prophetess Anna Trapnel, for instance, performs public trances in which her fasting yet supernaturally nourished body takes centre stage, as it does in her graphic published accounts of these episodes. Trapnel illustrates the extent to which seventeenth-century radical religious women parade what Diane Purkiss describes as 'the uncanny return of what had been forgotten or repressed by orthodox Protestant culture', that is, 'the believer's body as the site of [supernatural] power'.[60] While Trapnel's narratives attempt to reconcile the display of a suffering female body with the projection of a powerful prophetic voice, however, the suffering or mutilated female body is an awkward vehicle for self-inscription within more orthodox contexts in which the body, as well as being divested of its potential to inscribe holiness, is increasingly set against reason, voice and subjectivity itself.

Elaine Scarry's analysis of 'the body in pain' emphasises the extent to which, within an order in which body is set against voice, mutilation entails powerless embodiment. The torturer's power is constructed through his or her distance from the body: 'to have no body, to have only a voice ... is to be the wounder but not oneself woundable.' The victim is conversely rendered powerless through his or her 'emphatic' embodiment:

> to have a body, a body made emphatic by being continually altered ... is to have one's sphere of extension contracted down to the small circle of one's immediate presence. Consequently, to be intensely embodied is the equivalent of being unrepresented and ... is almost always the condition of those without power.

Self-directed violence complicates the terms of Scarry's argument: through casting the self as torturer, self-mutilating women are seeking to establish their distance from their bodies, casting themselves as creator (which, as Scarry establishes, is closely related to wounder, or alterer), rather than created.[61] Women's cultural position is so 'intensely embodied' that the creation of an authoritative voice, premised on the mastery of the body, appears to demand the wounding of their own bodies rather than the torture of another's. In a context in which bodies cannot speak virtue, however, where if they speak at all it is to confirm the subject's failure to construct a rational or self-regulated identity, a mutilated body cannot easily become a vehicle for self-determination. In the emerging modern order, self-determination requires the silence of the body, not its violent, articulate, inscription. The script of physical beauty may have been written so as to condemn the female subject, but the self-inscription of ugliness ironically aligns the subject further with morally depraved, irrational corporeality, failing to offer any escape route for female characters from the constraints of their flawed bodies. Violently rejecting models of beauty and thus trying to distance themselves from the sinful 'inordinate desires', the 'gross elements', of feminine corporeality, mutilated characters remain helplessly, tragically, embodied.[62] Partly inhabiting a past order in which their ugliness is a heroic choice, figuring holiness, they are also caught in a present in which their acquired deformity resonates problematically in ways beyond their control. Self-mutilation in early modern texts therefore operates in futile, self-defeating circles, generated by a desire to escape a corporeality that it at once reinforces.[63]

Turning on their own bodies in an attempt to escape the cultural implications of a female body, these disfigured characters in fact confirm specific constructions of the female body as a site of dangerous pollution. Adulterous women in the early Middle Ages were liable to have their noses amputated.[64] While female sexual transgressors were not routinely publicly disfigured in this way in the sixteenth and seventeenth centuries, the physical branding of 'whores' remained potent both in the cultural imagination and, more disturbingly, as a violent private practice.[65] Adriana in *The Comedy of Errors* believes that if her husband suspects that her body is contaminated by 'ruffian lust', he will 'tear the stain'd skin off [her] harlot brow'.[66] Phillip Stubbes, meanwhile, laments the fact that sexual sinners are not visibly marked by the state. The immoral and their 'bastard' offspring should be 'cauterized and seared with a hote iron on the cheeke, forehead, or some other part of their bodye that they might be seene', he declares.[67] Marking the body in response to transgression visibly inscribes that transgression, the body becoming the site and emblem of the crime as well as a testament to attempts to limit and eradicate that crime.[68] The mutilated features of female characters on the early modern stage and in the literature of the era likewise emblematise the corrupt, excessive, transgressive feminine carnality which their disfigurement attempts to eliminate.[69]

The moral ambivalence of representations of self-inflicted ugliness in this era, demonstrating in some ways a commitment to virtue while at the same time confirming morally flawed feminine embodiment, is brought to the fore in the tale of Amadour and Florinda, translated from Marguerite de Navarre's *The Heptameron* (1558) by William Painter in *The Palace of Pleasure* (1566). Originating from France, yet written by an author with reformist sympathies whose morals are held by Painter to chime with English Protestant sensibilities, the narrative straddles pre- and post-Reformation accounts of female self-mutilation.[70] The story relates the tragic experiences of the beautiful and chaste Florinda and the military hero Amadour. Recognising that he cannot marry Florinda because of his lowly status, Amadour resolves to become her devoted and honourable servant, in line with traditions of courtly love. Overcome by passion, he nevertheless ultimately attempts to rape her. Faced later with the prospect of another assault, Florinda takes a stone and gives 'her selfe suche a great blowe on the face, that her mouth, eyes and nose [are] altogether deformed'.[71] Narrowly avoiding the threatened rape (although not because of her disfigurement), Florinda finally enters a monastery, while Amadour dies a heroic death in battle.

The English translators of the *The Heptameron* held the work to be an edifying piece of literature. The reading public of sixteenth-century England were familiar with the fusion of the romantic with the religious: following medieval traditions, the genre of saints' lives dovetailed with that of romance in this era.[72] Female readers were the particular targets of such texts, and it is 'the Ladye' or 'Gentlewoman' who wishes to 'behold a mirrour of chastitie' whom Painter imagines benefiting from the story of Florinda. The moral dimensions of the work are not, to Painter, undermined by its value as entertainment: he claims that his volume is 'bothe profitable and pleasaunte', refreshing 'weried mindes' even as it sets forth examples that are 'right commodious and profitable to them that wil vouchsafe to read them'.

Florinda's exemplary status is highlighted by Painter from the outset of his translation (which does not diverge significantly from the original account), where he promises to relate the 'renowmed chastitie of the saide Florinda'.[73] The narrative is shaped by medieval hagiographic models, most obviously in Florinda's self-disfigurement within a chapel in order to avoid rape. It nevertheless constitutes a more nuanced reading of the dynamics of sexual assault, and particularly of the problematic role of beauty in such abuse, than is typically found in earlier virgin martyr accounts. Despite Painter's insistence on the transparent moral worth of his translation, the account of Florinda and Amadour in fact creates an ambivalent moral climate within which the identity of the 'martyr' is open to question, exemplifying the 'fundamental ambiguity' that critics have identified in *The Heptameron* as a whole.[74] Amadour's assaults are condemned in the account, contravening as they do his commitment to ideals of chivalric devotion, but they are also treated with a degree of sympathy as the blind passion of a long-suffering, hopeless man. His martyr status is enhanced through his noble death, after which he is 'lamented as his vertues did deserve'.[75] The tale provokes contradictory responses among its audience within *The Heptameron*: some insist that Amadour remains a model of virtue, some criticise him for being 'put off' too easily, while others hold the moral of the tale to be the virtuous endurance of its heroine.[76] Even the narrator seems unsure how to judge the heroine. Elevating Florinda as a model for other women, she simultaneously uses her to warn against the dangers of women being 'harsh' and naive in their dealings with men.[77]

Florinda's body thus emerges as a morally questionable entity in the narrative. Her face, in particular, is subject to contradictory readings. Florinda believes that her beauty is to blame for Amadour's transgressive desire. She remembers

> howe often Amadour had praysed her beautie.... Wherfore thinking it better to doe injurie to her beautie by defacing it, than to suffer the heart of so honeste a personage by meanes thereof wickedly to be inflamed....

She assumes that her ruptured features will lead Amadour to 'forget the pleasure which once [he] receyved in [her]', so that he will no longer 'forcibly approche'. Diverging from earlier narrative models, however, her self-mutilation fails to repel her attacker. Amadour betrays the fact that power, not lust, motivates his assault, so that beauty or ugliness are irrelevant: 'the deformitie of your face (which I thinke was done by you of set purpose) shall not let me to accomplishe my will'.[78] His act aims to deny Florinda the self-determination she attempts to achieve through her self-disfigurement: he wants to control her body rather than enjoy her beauty. As a result, Florinda's dramatic act of self-mutilation has surprisingly little impact on the plot. Basing its heroine on a medieval virgin saint, the sixteenth-century text can no longer provide a meaningful interpretation of her deformed features, which do not secure her identity.

The narrative is fraught with contradictory depictions of the body, betraying an anxiety around its meanings and interpretability.[79] On one level, faces openly betray emotions. Amadour 'coulde not staye the blushing colour of his face' in Florinda's presence, while Florinda hides herself in a dark staircase as Amadour approaches, so 'that none coulde perceyve if she chaunged colour'. As the 'motif' of the tale promises, though, this is a story of 'many sleightes and dissimulations', and both lovers in fact manage to cover the visible evidence of their true feelings. Florinda, in particular, is so inscrutable that even her mother 'could never perceive by her countenaunce, any cause of certayne suspicion'. She repeatedly attempts to control both her appearance and the meanings attached to this appearance, most notably in her act of self-disfigurement, which she disguises as an accident. After her mutilation, which on one level visibly marks her as a threatened, chaste virgin, the narrative continues to insist that she possesses a 'dissembling countenance'.[80] Her beauty was problematic; her ugliness is hardly less so. Stemming from the heroine's 'set purpose', it is unclear whether such wilfulness is to be praised or condemned. Her act emphasises her physical presence, in itself casting her in a potentially negative moral light. The meanings of Florinda's mutilated features thus remain uncertain in the account. Contrary to Painter's stated intention in translating the work, her body is less a clear 'mirror of chastitie' than a potentially dangerous and unreadable entity.

The contradictions of self-imposed ugliness for a female character in this era are further played out on the early seventeenth-century English stage, notably, as we have seen, in Chapman's *The Gentleman Usher*. Shocking the court with her disfigured features, Margaret appears momentarily powerful. Through destroying her own beauty, she has 'robbed' the Duke of that which he was seeking to claim as his possession. Rather than allowing the meanings of her body to be inscribed by others, she insists on her own interpretation of her features, which she identifies as a visual demonstration of the Duke's inadequacy:

> Tyrant! behold how thou hast usde thy love,
> See, theefe to Nature, thou hast kil'd and rob'd,
> Kil'd what my selfe kill'd, rob'd what makes thee poore.
> Beautie (a Lovers treasure) thou hast lost
> Where none can find it; all a poore Maides dowres
> Thou hast forc'd from me: all my joy and hope.
> No man will love me more; all Dames excell me.
> This ougly thing is now no more a face,
> Nor any vile forme in all Earth resembled,
> But thy fowle tyrannie.

Margaret presents her ruined face as sign of the Duke's corruption, identifying him, rather than herself, as the source of moral ugliness in the court. For this instant, at least, she forces her body to speak a narrative of her own making.

The play does not maintain a consistent perspective on the meanings of Margaret's body, however. She intends to 'leave [her] beautie like a wildernesse,/ That never mans eie more may dare t'invade', seemingly echoing the self-protecting cries of threatened medieval virgin martyrs. The victims for whom she fears are nevertheless the men who will be seduced by her looks: it is her 'accursed face', after all, that she identifies as the 'first cause of [her] deare loves death'. Women's physical appeal, she laments, is a worthless, transitory veneer, covering moral weakness: 'Unworthy women, why doe men adore/Our fading Beauties, when their worthiest lives,/Being lost for us, we dare not die for them?' Beauty is ephemeral and artificial, covering feminine lack and corruption, properties made visible in her scarred features. Margaret's deformed face, like Florinda's, is ultimately an enigma. At one point inscribing the heroine's anger at male appropriation of the female body, it elsewhere draws attention to culpable female physicality. Marking her body as site and emblem of moral taint, Margaret briefly attempts to identify the court as the source of that corruption, but ultimately only indicts herself: her ability to redeem the court through her 'beauty's sacrifice' locates the source of social disarray in her own attractiveness.[81] Although her self-mutilation brings the Duke to his senses, it does not ultimately grant the heroine the means of shaping her identity outside of dominant gender discourses.

The contradictions surrounding female self-disfigurement on the early seventeenth-century English stage are further apparent in Jolenta's adoption of 'black face' in Webster's *The Devil's Law-Case* (*c.* 1619). The depiction of an aristocratic white woman disguising herself as a black 'Moor' in order to escape (or, sometimes, to revenge) abusive male behaviour was to become increasingly familiar to the audiences of plays in the 1620s and 1630s.[82] Such characters are often objectified in sexual terms by the white male characters who interpret their blackness, as Virginia Mason Vaughan notes, as a 'sign of their sexual availability'.[83] Despite such objectification, however, blackness is taken to be a mark of ugliness as well as one of social inferiority and moral depravity. ''Tis the hansomest/I ere saw of her cuntry,' Bellisant remarks of the disguised 'Moor' Calista in Philip Massinger's *The Parliament of Love* (1624). 'She hath neither/Thick lips nor rough curld haire.'[84] While the 'fair' features of the white woman are here perceived to transcend the repulsiveness of her black skin, blackness is elsewhere depicted as a 'cloud' eclipsing beauty. Margaret in *The Gentleman Usher* longs to possess 'the ugliest face/That ever Aethiop, or affrigtfull fiend/Shew'd in th'amazed eye of prophan'd light'.[85] Phormio's desire for the apparently Egyptian 'Moore' Acanthe in William Berkeley's *The Lost Lady*, meanwhile, is a 'strange capriccio of love': he is possessed by an unfathomable impulse to 'court that shade'.[86] 'Capriccio', referring to a sudden impulse or a prank, is a term used interchangeably with 'freak' from the late sixteenth century and with 'grotesque' in later eras.[87] When Acanthe's make-up begins to dissolve at the end of the play, revealing the 'purer forme' of the white Milesia, the opposition of (freakish) blackness to (natural) white beauty is confirmed: 'she is white as Lillies, as the snowe/that falls upon Pernassus', rhapsodises Lysicles. 'Egipt never saw/a beauty like to this.'[88] Disguising oneself as a black character in this context is therefore an act of self-disfigurement born of a desire to escape the meanings attached to a 'fair' face and body. For Jolenta, in *The Devil's Law-Case*, these meanings are both specific and damning: her brother has impregnated a nun but plans to escape censure through claiming that the child is Jolenta's illegitimate offspring. Rather than be identified as a fallen woman, Jolenta colours her face 'like a Moore', making a dramatic entrance as a 'strange Fowle' at the conclusion of the play in order to clear her name. 'Like or dislike me,' she states,

> choose you whether.
> The down upon the raven's feather
> Is as gentle and as sleek
> As the Mole on Venus' cheek.
> Hence vain show! I only care
> To preserve my soul most fair;
> Never mind the outward skin,
> But the jewel that's within;
> And though I want the crimson blood,
> Angels boast my sisterhood.
> Which of us now judge you whiter:
> Her whose credit proves the lighter,

> Or this black and ebon hue
> That, unstained, keeps fresh and true?
> For I proclaim't without control,
> There's no true beauty but i' th' soul.[89]

Drawing on the assumption that her black 'outward skin' is the opposite pole from her virtuous 'soul most fair', Jolenta, like other literary and dramatic 'self-disfiguring' women, attempts to dissociate herself from the body which men have appropriated for their own purposes. She insists that her identity, the site of her 'true beauty' is located elsewhere: a 'jewel that's within'.

Instead of repudiating the body, however, Jolenta paradoxically attempts to deploy her 'disfigured' body as a sign of her virtue. She sets her soul against her skin while simultaneously pointing to this skin as a sign of her 'unstained', 'fresh and true' nature. Jolenta concedes that she 'want[s] the crimson blood', referring to the perceived failure of black skin to blush, a property seen in this era to indicate that black people are shameless.[90] Paradoxically, however, blackness is also praised for its ostensible resistance to transformation, its fixed, stable authenticity standing against the artificiality and mutability of white beauty. Jolenta thus deploys her 'black and ebon hue' (despite the fact that it is a disguise) as evidence of her moral fixity. The attempt to present 'ugliness' as a mark of virtuous autonomy is once again mired in contradiction, however. Attempting to fashion her body into a sign of her virtue, Jolenta inevitably embroils herself in wider, less positive meanings ascribed to the 'ugly' black female body. Black women in early modern texts are repeatedly associated with sexual corruption, and Jolenta's 'self-disfigurement' visually confirms the very 'blackened' reputation that her brother has ascribed her.[91] She escapes the problematic associations of a 'fair' body only to become a visual emblem of moral taint. Her exoneration by the judges results from the revelation of her white interiority, not the display of her black body.

Self-disfiguring women in early modern texts thus either try to alienate themselves from the corruption that they recognise in their own beauty or seek to escape the extent to which beauty makes them vulnerable to the loss of virtue. Despite their attempts to differentiate themselves from their bodies, however, they continue to be identified with a corrupt femininity which is now visibly inscribed in their deformed (de)features. Cast in the mould of virgin martyrs but operating in new contexts in which the deformed body cannot easily be shaped into a symbol of holiness or deployed as a vehicle of self-inscription, the characters are the site of confusion rather than moral certainty. Self-disfiguring men are much rarer in early modern texts. Where they do appear, their ugly bodies are not characterised by the same degree of ambivalence that we see in depictions of female self-mutilation. Francisco, in Webster's *The White Devil*, for instance, disguises himself as a 'Moor' for strategic reasons. His '[goodly] personage' nevertheless remains visible, emphasising the extent to which male identity has the potential to transcend the body:

his 'personage', evidently, is not located in his skin.[92] The characters that I have discussed so far in this chapter conversely illustrate the extent to which women remain constrained by their appearances, trapped in relation to bodies whose beauty is corrupt and whose ugliness is obscene. They attempt to rework the significance of their physical appearance but cannot escape the cultural script of their bodies. To shape one's identity on the skin in the sixteenth or seventeenth centuries is an inevitably contradictory manoeuvre.

Alongside self-disfiguring characters, early seventeenth-century texts contain a surprising number of female figures mutilated by spurned suitors. Although the disfigurement of these characters is not self-inflicted, the works again evoke the tradition of self-mutilating virgin martyrs, implying that these characters willingly sacrifice their beauty in the name of chastity. Once more, however, blemished features are not easy to reconcile with virtuous or positive forms of identity. The manner in which these women are 'defeatured' aligns their acquired ugliness with the erasure of identity rather than its consolidation. Presenting a nauseating display of the necrotic flesh to be found beneath female skin, the texts establish an opposition between feminine corporeality and emergent models of early modern identity. Visibly marked in abject terms, excluded from idealised forms of subjectivity, the disfigured women in these texts further illuminate the role played by representations of the ugly woman in the formulation of dominant models of masculine identity.

'Eating poison':[93] Parthenia and her sisters

Increasingly awkward as a model of virtue, the self-mutilating virgin martyr gradually disappears from the stage and from literature in the early modern era. Taking her place is a new prototype of the disfigured heroine, instantiated in Sidney's *The Countess of Pembroke's Arcadia* in the character of Parthenia. An exemplar of virtuous beauty, Parthenia is assaulted by a spurned suitor, who '[rubs] all over her face a most horrible poison, the effect whereof was such that never leper looked more ugly than she did'.[94] *The History of the Tryall of Chevalry* (c. 1601), attributed to Henry Chettle, subsequently dramatises the disfigurement of Bellamira, whose face is also poisoned by a rejected suitor until it resembles 'A broyld herring, or a tortur'de/Image made of playster worke'.[95] John Marston's *Jack Drum's Entertainment* (1601), which has been interpreted as a burlesque version of both the *Arcadia* and *The Tryall of Chevalry*, meanwhile depicts the ugly usurer Mamon disfiguring Katherine's face with 'the eating poison' of 'venomde' toads because she has rejected his advances.[96] The ugliness of the mutilated characters in these texts is associated with images of disease, specifically leprosy, involving the loss and decomposition of the flesh.

In each of these instances, the heroine's loss of beauty is intimately related to her chastity, understood in these post-Reformation texts primarily in terms of faithfulness to a (prospective) husband. Echoes of earlier virgin martyrs are strong: despite the fact that the female characters are disfigured by others, the plays present them as willingly sacrificing their beauty in order to preserve their virtue.[97] In *The History of the Tryall of Chevalry*, Bellamira is depicted as heroically complicit in her own disfigurement, which exhibits her chaste fidelity: 'For Philips sake I have bin martyred thus,' she declares. Katherine's loss of beauty in *Jack Drum's Entertainment*, meanwhile, follows swiftly upon her prayer to be detested by heaven rather than be forced to love the hideous Mamon. Earlier in the play, Katherine is on the point of suicide because she mistakenly believes that her lover Pasquill is dead. Her threatened act of self-harm wins her the accolades 'thou miracle of constancie' and 'Renown of Virgins, whose name shal ne're fleet'.[98] Momentarily, at least, Katherine's deformity becomes the emblem of an exemplary chastity which has already been confirmed through her willingness to destroy her own body.

Seventeenth-century texts nevertheless depart from medieval models of the virgin martyr in the fact that the heroine's disfigurement no longer necessarily prohibits male desire. Insisting that their love was not based upon superficial appearances, the prospective bridegrooms declare the ugliness of their brides to be no impediment to their devotion. Sidney's narrative celebrates the 'rare example' of Parthenia's betrothed Argalus, who 'unfeignedly shewed himself no less cheerfully earnest than if she had never been disinherited of that goodly portion which nature had so liberally bequeathed upon her'. '[B]y an affection sprung from excessive beauty' he comes to 'delight in horrible foulness'.[99] While Argalus claims that he sees in Parthenia's scars 'the loveliness of her love towards him',[100] Philip in *The Tryall of Chevalry* goes as far as to argue that Bellamira's disfigured face is a more 'perfect beauty':

> She was too bright before, till being hid
> Under that envious cloud, it tooke the place
> Of a darke ground, to show a lovelyer face.
> That Leprosie in her seemd perfect beauty:
> And she did gild her imperfections o're
> With virtue, which no foul calumnious breath
> Could ever soyle, true vertues dye is such,
> That malice cannot stayne, nor envy tuch.
> Then say not but her worth surmounts these woes.

Illustrating the era's love of contrasts, he claims that ugliness is an apt foil for virtue. Like the 'loveliness' of Parthenia's mutilated face, however, Bellamira's deformed features can be constructed as a 'lovelyer face' only because of her lover's ability to perceive this virtue: it is only in the eyes of a man that the disfigured heroine's 'worth surmounts [her] woes'. As we shall see, the heroine takes a very different perspective.

The focus of these texts, as in other forms of ugly mistress writing, is displaced from the suffering virgin to her male lover: rather than manifesting female virtue, a scarred female face is the occasion for a male character to display his moral fibre. As Samuel Schoenbaum observes, early seventeenth-century accounts of the deformed mistress explore, and to some extent prefigure, the cult of Platonic love that would become increasingly fashionable in the Caroline court under Henrietta Maria's influence.[101] A letter of 1634 draws attention to this later fashion:

> The Court offers little News at present, but there is a love call'd Platonic love, which much sways there of late; it is a Love abstracted from all corporeal gross Impressions and sensual Appetite, but consists in Contemplations and Ideas of the Mind, not in any carnal Fruition.[102]

In its more extreme manifestations, the cult made a virtue of a man loving an ugly woman as proof of his interest in her soul, not her body.[103] Shirley, who for a time gained Henrietta Maria's patronage, gently satirises courtly idealisations of the Platonic lover through the character of Horatio in *The Dukes Mistris*. Rejecting the 'false and perjur'd natures' of beautiful women, Horatio believes that he will find 'more faith in those that looke all ore like Devills'. 'Mine's a Platonicke love', he declares, 'give me the soule, /I care not what course flesh, and blood inshrine it'.[104] Within Neoplatonic thought, the lover's worth depends on the worthiness of the object of his love.[105] An ugly body, however, as *The Dukes Mistris* ultimately reveals, is no guarantee of this worthiness. 'You that are han[d]some Ladies, I doe aske/Forgivenesse, and beleeve it possible/You may be lesse vexations to men,' concludes Horatio after being hounded by competitive ugly mistresses. The play ultimately vindicates more orthodox binaries of beauty and ugliness, setting the beautiful and virtuous wife of the Duke, Euphemia, against the socially inferior 'beldams' and 'devills' whose ugly faces, after all, align with 'unseene deformity'.[106]

Plato claimed that love inspired the soul's progress from the 'carnal world to moral beauty and ultimately to the contemplation of eternal, unchanging Beauty.'[107] Plotinus emphasised the positive role that physical beauty could play in initiating this process but insisted that the lover's quest must move beyond physical desire:

> He that has the strength, let him arise and withdraw into himself, foregoing all that is known by the eyes, turning away for ever from the material beauty that once made his joy. When he perceives those shapes of grace that show in body, let him not pursue: he must know them for copies, vestiges, shadows, and hasten away towards That they tell of ... one that is held by material beauty and will not break free shall be precipitated, not in body but in Soul, down to the dark depths loathed of the Intellective-Being, where, blind even in the Lower-World, he shall have commerce only with shadows, there as here.[108]

Early seventeenth-century plays featuring disfigured heroines enable the hero to progress along the desired path of the Neoplatonic lover: attracted initially by physical charms, he is led to a deeper appreciation of inner virtue, his prioritisation of which is proved through his continued devotion after beauty has vanished. Echoing the statements of Argalus to Parthenia, Philip, in *The Tryall of Chevalry*, identifies himself as a Platonic lover:

> Thy face to me was but a Marshall,
> To lodge the sacred person in my mind,
> Which long agoe is surely chambered there:
> And now what needs an outward Harbinger?
> I doe affect, not superficially:
> My love extendeth further then the skin.
> The inward Bellamira tis I seeke,
> And unto her will Philip be espousde.

Vincentio in *The Gentleman Usher* likewise claims that beauty is important only as an initial sign: 'I wooed your beautie first/But as a lover: now as a deare husband/That title and your vertues binde me ever.'[109] An ugly female face in these texts is therefore primarily a vehicle for exhibiting male, not female, virtue.

Far from celebrating female moral integrity, in fact, plays with deformed female characters insist on the hypocrisy of female beauty. Pembroke, in *The Tryall of Chevalry*, blames social disorder on 'the force/of [women's] resistlesse and controwling beauty'. Planet, the voice of reason in Marston's *Jack Drum's Entertainment*, also attacks the dangerous external appeal of women, at the same time lampooning the men foolish enough to fall victim to it:

> o that the soules of men
> Were temperate like mine, then Natures painte
> Should not triumph o're our infirmities.
> I do adore with infinite respect,
> Weomen whose merit issues from their worth
> Of inward graces, but these rotten poasts
> That are but guilt with outward garnishment,
> O how my soule abhorres them.[110]

To Brabant Jr, in *The Tryall of Chevalry*, female beauty is 'Natures witchcraft', which '[enchants] our soules/So infinitely unrecoverable,/That Hell, death, shame, eternall infamy/Cannot reclaime our desperate resolves'. Given such pervasive cynicism regarding beauty, ugliness initially appears to offer some reassurance. For Horatio, in *The Dukes Mistris*, 'There was some dealing with an Elvish female,/That had but a course face, or say but halfe a one':

> A nose of many fashions, and as many
> Water-workes in 'em, lips of honest hide,
> And made to last, teeth of a Moore's complexion,
> A chinne, without all controversie, good
> To goe a fishing with, a witches beard on 't
> With twentie other commendations, such a thing

> Were no mischiefe, and a man might trust
> Her with no scruple in his Conscience.[111]

Rather than suggesting that a woman with a 'course face' possesses more moral backbone than a handsome 'fiend', however, Horatio merely suggests that an ugly woman lacks the opportunity to stray. The idea that ugly women are 'no mischiefe' is resoundingly disproved by the play, in which Fiametta and Scolopendra turn out to be just as unpleasant as the beautiful 'goblins' loathed by Horatio. Instead of materialising virtue, the scars on the faces of mutilated women in texts depicting deformed heroines ultimately resonate problematically as visual emblems of the 'Nature's witchcraft' at the heart of femininity. Disfiguring a woman's body in this era, as Nancy A. Gutierrez demonstrates, potentially identifies this woman with the witches whose bodies bore telling marks of deformity and whose faces were scratched 'above the breath' (higher than the mouth) in order to break the spells that they had cast.[112] While beauty suggests hypocrisy, then, ugliness patently does not exonerate women from the suspicion of moral taint, and may even work to confirm it.

Evoking carnal corruption more readily than holiness, the disfigured features of female characters on the early seventeenth-century stage are repeatedly described through images of contagious disease. Philip's initial reaction to Bellamira's deformed face in *The Tryall of Chevalry* identifies her as leprous:

> What's here, a Leper amongst Noble men?
> What creatures this? Why stayes she in this place?
> O, tis no marvell though she hide her face:
> For tis infectious: let her leave the presence
> Or Leprosie will cleave unto us all.

The decomposition of Bellamira's face unnerves and terrifies the men who view it: the excoriated face, in which the internal has leaked on to the surface, is an intensely threatening sight. The flesh-rotting ugliness depicted in these texts is a very different condition from the unattractive physique of the male Silenus. While for the Silenus figure ugliness works to shore up desirable forms of identity, the deformed mistress possesses an incoherent, contagious ugliness in which is found 'the end of distinctions; the end of difference; the end of space; the end of time; the end of everything'.[113] The terms in which mutilation is depicted in this group of texts emphasise the abject status of the female body, identifying its failure to maintain its boundaries and consequently its threat to dominant forms of identity. The fantasy of mutilating the female body played out in these works is implicitly related to the anxiety provoked by the model of female corporeality in which they are grounded. 'Leakiness is contagion,' as Hutchinson observes, and must therefore be violently occluded if the self is to be preserved as discrete and whole: 'let her leave the presence / Or Leprosie will cleave unto us all'.

Texts depicting mutilated women draw specifically on images of the 'pocky' or syphilitic body to depict their heroines.[114] The Clown refers to Bellamira's 'bald face', for instance, playing on the hair loss characterising syphilitic infection. Marston's *Jack Drum's Entertainment* also presents a society contaminated with the pox. Morally corrupt characters in the play are described through images of putrefying flesh, playing on early modern imaginings of syphilitic bodies, in which moral and physical degeneration are seen to be inextricable.[115] Imitating the signs of the pox, Mamon's 'nose will rot off with grief' at the loss of his possessions, while Planet refers to the 'leprosie' of Camelia's fickle 'judgement', again tainting her through association with syphilis, which, as we have seen, was often described in relation to leprosy in this era.[116] These metaphors of rotting and disfigurement anticipate and frame Katherine's fate, as her face is subsequently marred by 'the eating poison', in itself suggestive of the slowly rotting syphilitic body. *The Gentleman Usher*, meanwhile, draws on the physical, moral and social associations of syphilis in its representation of Margaret's loss of beauty. She scars her face with depilatory cream, again evoking the hair loss caused by syphilis, while she describes the workings of the poison in terms which suggest the disease:

Sweate thy envenom'd furie, make my eyes
Burne with thy sulphre like the lakes of hell.[117]

Early descriptions of syphilis emphasised the sensations of 'lyen in the fyre', while early treatments involved the use of hot tubs to induce excessive sweating.[118] Margaret mutilates her face, causing disfiguring blisters, in order to 'feele death by degrees', again evoking the living death of the pox, with its slow, inexorable consumption of its victim.[119] Despite the fact that the characters' deformities are not caused by syphilis, the echoes of the disease in their features associate them with the corrupt female sexuality inextricable from contemporary understandings of this disease.[120] Whatever the innocence of these characters, their blemished features emblazon the fallen nature of female physicality, becoming at once emblem of and punishment for the original pollution of the female sex.

The female characters mutilated by men, like rape victims in this era, bear the shame of male crimes in their own bodies, which become figures of sin and contagion.[121] As in contemporary models of rape, the assault of the female characters in these plays is understood primarily in terms of the robbery of the men who 'possess' them: 'Leave the revenge to me whom it concerns,' states Philip. ''Tis I am robd of a delicious looke,/A heavenly sparkling brow, a starry eye.' The symbolic parallels between rape and mutilation are explored in *The Tryall of Chevalry* through the pairing of Bellamira and Katherine. A false rumour spreads that Katherine has been raped, an act that is seen to have deformed her honour and reputation, echoing Bellamira's literal disfigurement. Lewes refers to

The marriage of thy stayned and leprous child
Whilst in our absence, Ferdinand unjust
Hath staind our daughters beautie with vile lust.

Both women are 'stained': beauty here is synonymous with virtue and chastity and is thus destroyed by rape, as the visible marks of mutilation figure the destruction of female honour. Bellamira's mutilation meanwhile is retrospectively justified by the fact that she is the 'sister of a ravisher', further connecting her deformity with the act of rape, while again exemplifying the manner in which the female body carries both the responsibility for and the consequences of male crimes. As Lucrece declaims from beyond the grave in Middleton's *The Ghost of Lucrece* (1600), her rapist 'writes himself the shamer, I the shame'.[122] Lucrece's putrid, noisome body in this poem, like the mutilated female characters in early seventeenth-century plays, testifies to the fact that a tragic lack of agency does not preclude moral responsibility for female victims of assault.

Drawing on discourses of disease, rape and pollution to depict mutilated features, plays containing deformed heroines cannot, therefore, be said either to celebrate or to rehabilitate ugliness. The disfigured features of the heroines are presented in ambivalent terms, at once representing the 'beauty's sacrifice' on which virtue is predicated and the corruption that demands this sacrifice in the first place. Elsewhere in the plays, ugliness retains more straightforwardly negative associations. Katherine's sister Camelia, in Marston's *Jacke Drums Entertainment*, for instance, displays her folly and sexual incontinence in her features:

> Harther lips looke like a dride
> Neats-tongue: her face as richly yeallow, as the skin of
> A cold custard, and her mind as settled as the feet of bald
> Pated time.

The contrast between the 'constant, vertuous' and 'debonayre' Katherine and the 'proud/Inconstant, fantasticke' and 'vain' Camelia is marked from the outset in conventional terms in the relative appeal of their features. The usurer and poisoner Mamon, meanwhile, exhibits his deviance in his 'yellow toothd/Suncke-eyde, gowtie shankt' body, as well as in his 'great nose', playing on stereotypes of Jewish features.[123]

While the male heroes demonstrate their nobility through their ostensible disregard for beauty, the deformed women confirm the overwhelmingly negative status of the ugly woman through uniformly refusing to inhabit the seemingly inconceivable role of ugly wife. Following Parthenia, Bellamira exemplifies the self-disgust of the mutilated female characters:

> Marry with me? Fetch me a looking glasse
> That I may see how sweet a Bride I am.
> Oh, I detest my selfe: Deare, hate me too:
> I am not to be maryed but to death.

Bellamira succinctly articulates the paradoxical convention governing these texts where a beauty ostensibly irrelevant to male love precludes any possibility of marriage:

>   should I suffer
> So brave a gentleman as Philip is,
> To wed himselfe to my unworthy selfe
> It would be counted vertue in the Prince
> But I were worthy a world of blame.
> No, Philip, no, thou shalt not wrong thine honour
> Nor be impeacht by Bellamireaes spots.

Margaret is more pragmatic still, undermining Neoplatonic ideals with an earthy realism: 'You first lov'd me/Closely for beautie; which being with'red thus/Your love must fade.' Only after death, she claims, can the ideal of a purely spiritual love be attained. In the meantime, 'Love must have outward objects to delight him,/... when wives want/Outward excitements, husbands loves grow skant.'[124] Whatever the aspirations of female characters or their male lovers, a woman, Margaret realises, can never be located 'all in the soule'.[125]

Removing themselves from society, the female characters internalise their own abjection. They are only permitted to return once the disruptive threat of their excessive, leaky bodies has been neutralised and contained through the reimposition of beauty. The restoration of beauty which characterises this group of texts is repeatedly depicted as an act of purification, the removal of a stain. Bellamira, in *The Tryall of Chevalry*, for instance, is healed by a Hermit 'whose skill in phisike warrants present cure/And pure refining of [her] poisoned blood'. This 'poisoned blood' is not limited to the disfigured body but is also implicitly present in the female body before the loss of beauty. Refined by male agents at the end of the texts, the heroines' features are presented as more attractive after they have been 'restored' than they were before they were assaulted. Parthenia's features, for example, are 'more pure and dainty' after Queen Helen's physician, 'the most excellent man in the world', has intervened than they were before she was disfigured.[126] *The Gentleman Usher* also depicts the restoration of its heroine's beauty in terms which imply that true beauty relies on a male art that redeems the fallen female body, a fallenness not limited to Margaret's disfigurement. Margaret is given a 'recureful Maske', which will be 'fix'd/With painelesse operation' to her face, until, after three days, 'Like a dissolved clowd it shall fall off/And [her] faire lookes regaine their freshest raies.' The line between her face and the mask is obfuscated: the mask is said to 'fall off', revealing Margaret's own 'lookes', but the cure is described in terms which more accurately suggest that the mask melts ('like a dissolved clowd') into her features, 'restoring' a beauty which is, in fact, the artificial creation of magico-medical technology. The mask is designed to 'hide this staine of Beauty'. Referring on one level to Margaret's disfigurement, the ambiguous phrasing suggests that the mask will also work to purify her beauty itself, a problematic entity that has been exposed as a moral 'staine' in the play. The doctor invokes the powers of 'Heaven, and Art', which will 'open' for him the 'little store-house of great Nature': masculine art, echoing the words of Sidney, is aligned with divine creativity, making 'new forms' rather than merely patching up old ones.¹²⁷ If male art is the origin of true beauty, the apparent beauty of the natural female form is 'brazen', not 'golden'.¹²⁸ Evidently the relationship between beauty and nature, as between ugliness and artifice, is more complicated than the anti-cosmetic polemicists led us to believe. The refining of the female body that takes place in the course of these texts, a refining of the 'staine' of female beauty as much as of the ugliness from which it is ultimately indistinguishable, identifies the female body as inherently transgressive at the same time as it contains its potentially disruptive nature.

Beauty, in the end, then, is once again revealed to be that which men impose on to the (ugly) female body in order to neutralise its threatening, excessive corporeality. The startling death scene of Parthenia in the *Arcadia* illustrates the extent to which the beauty of the female body is a male construct; one, moreover, that is projected on to a hideously disfigured female form. Fatally wounded after disguising herself as the 'Knight of the Tomb' in order to avenge Argalus's death, Parthenia's bleeding body, in the eyes of Amphilius, becomes the apotheosis of the Petrarchan fair: 'her neck, a neck indeed of alabaster, displaying the wound, which with most dainty blood laboured to drown his own beauties, so as here was a river of purest red, there an island of perfectest white, each giving lustre to the other'. Sidney's description reveals the violence that Nancy Vickers has identified at the heart of Petrarchan conventions of description.¹²⁹ Beauty, moreover, exists solely in the eye of the male beholder. '[H]e is the ground/Of my defeatures,' comments Adriana in *The Comedy of Errors*, 'my decayed fair/A sunny look of his would soon repair.'¹³⁰ It is only in the eyes of Amphilius that Parthenia's mutilated body becomes a type of perfect beauty: 'though these things to a grossly conceiving sense might seem disgraces, yet indeed were they but apparelling beauty in a new fashion which, all looked-upon through the spectacles of pity, did even increase the lines of her natural fairness.'¹³¹ Quarles's verse rendition of Sidney's narrative, *Argalus and Parthenia* (1629), further highlights the extent to which beauty is achieved through the refraction of certain 'spectacles': 'Beauty's but bare opinion,' insists Quarles's Argalus. 'White and Red/Have no more priviledge then what is bred/By humane fancie; which was ne're confinde/To certaine bounds, but varies like the winde.' The fact that beauty is in the eye of the beholder places the power to evaluate the (ugly) female body with the male viewer alone: 'Parthenia, in my eye/Out shines faire Hellen,' continues Argalus, insisting that the female body is a text whose meanings are fixed by the male 'reader':

> a letter's but a blot
> To such as cannot reade; but, who have skill,
> Can know the faire impression of a Quill
> From grosse and heedlesse blurres; and such can thinke
> No paper foule, that's fairely writ with Inke:
> What others hold a blemish in thy face,
> My skilfull eyes reade Characters of grace[.]¹³²

The meaning of signs, including the female body, are not self-evident, but require 'skilfull' interpretation, indicating the hierarchical structures governing visual cultures in this era as well as contemporary anxieties surrounding the transparency of visual signs. The ugliness of the female body is visible to all, however: it is its beauty that the 'skilfull' must bestow on this unpromising form. Ugliness is not, in the end, imposed on to the female characters in these texts. It is instead revealed as the truth of the female body, a body whose beauty is finally pure and refined only when artificially projected on to it by the male viewer. Beauty defined in these terms is associated with the silence and compliance of the female figures. Margaret is silenced by the unsolicited imposition of attractive features, as is Bellamira, despite being begged to 'speak, speak'. Parthenia, meanwhile, dutifully submits to her husband following the restoration of her 'more pure' complexion, becoming an exemplar of meek wifely obedience.[133]

The representation of disfigured female bodies in these texts therefore participates in a wider movement to neutralise the threat posed by the female body and to authorise specific forms of gendered identity. The mutilated female face provides an opportunity for male characters to display their ability to transcend the corporeal order, not only through their continuing professions of desire, but also through their ability to control and define the abject body. At the same time, the disfigured features of the female characters reveal not only the fact that women continue to be defined by their bodies, but that this association with the body is constructed in increasingly negative terms in the early modern era. Disfigured female faces reveal not virtue but the disruptive, polluting nature of femininity, tied to a disorderly body. Mutilated female bodies are transgressive entities, their violently flayed boundaries undermining concepts of a stable, discrete self. Their threat lies in their meaninglessness, however, rather than in the autonomy or self-determination that they inscribe. Their liquefied, necrotic flesh tragically confirms rather than renegotiates dominant narratives of amorphous, abject feminine corporeality. Confronted with obscene, mouldering female flesh, male viewers are quick to project their own interpretive frameworks on to its horrific incoherence. While the ugly female body holds subversive potential, then, in these texts it is framed, displayed and contained in terms that confirm dominant narratives of gendered identity. In the end, acquired ugliness suggests the same moral flaws that were less visible yet equally present in the beautiful female body. Only through a violent fantasy of its destruction and displacement by explicitly male constructions can the female body be imagined in positive terms, its recalcitrant and problematic materiality finally erased.

Mutilated female characters in early modern texts provide an extreme illustration of some of the key features characterising the representation of unattractive bodies in early modern English texts. Ugliness in early modern culture, time and again, is aligned with female matter. Ugly femininity, moreover, is linked with a breach of form, with the transgression of the boundaries of the self. Constructed in such terms, ugliness is the truth of the female subject, whatever her outward veneer.

Disturbingly, the ugly woman makes 'contradictions meet', collapsing binaries of beauty and ugliness just as she threatens to transgress other categories of the self on which early modern identity depends.[134] For the masculine subject, on the other hand, the unattractive body potentially illustrates the growing gap between the body and the ideal self. Into the eighteenth century, the gender divisions characterising depictions of ugliness begin to close. In *Agreeable Ugliness*, for example, as we have seen, the ugly heroine is able to transcend the limitations of her unsightly body through her rational self-cultivation. In the seventeenth century, however, ugliness is not so readily turned to positive effect for the female subject, for whom neither beauty nor ugliness spells escape from a restrictive alignment with the body.

Representations of ugliness thus illuminate wider constructions of identity in early modern England. Bringing into focus the relationship of the body and the self, they reveal the complicated and uneven negotiations between the two entities that help to shape subjectivity in this period. The dualistic Cartesian self, while increasingly prominent in writing from the era, is by no means universally visible or applicable as a model. Rather than simply displacing earlier paradigms of the self in which body and self were inextricable from each other, moreover, the ideal modern subject depends for his self-differentiation on the presence of his 'other', the diabolically repulsive hag, whose chaotic, incomplete and polluting body continues to manifest her corrupt soul. Seemingly an antiquated relic, this repellent figure consequently haunts early modern literary and visual texts, refusing to be suppressed. Ugliness, evidently, cannot be reduced to a physically quantifiable property but is a designation infused with power dynamics which helps to police wider categories of gender, social class, race and subjectivity itself. The manner in which it operates in early modern culture, moreover, resonates in many ways with its continuing significance today.

Notes

Introduction

1. William Shakespeare, *Hamlet*, ed. G. R. Hibbard (Oxford: Oxford University Press, 1987), 2.2.301–5, 306, 300–1.
2. Roy Porter, *Flesh in the Age of Reason* (London: Allen Lane, 2003), 25. See also Emily Cockayne, *Hubbub: Filth, Noise, and Stench in England* (New Haven, CT, and London: Yale University Press, 2007), 22–37.
3. See Michael W. Kwakkelstein, 'Leonardo da Vinci's Grotesque Heads and the Breaking of the Physiognomic Mould', *Journal of the Warburg and Courtauld Institutes* 54 (1991), 127–36.
4. Post-Reformation England has often been seen to be isolated from the visual cultures developed elsewhere in Renaissance Europe. Recent work on the interaction between visual, textual and dramatic cultures in early modern England has nevertheless begun to reveal a more complex picture in which English culture is informed by and negotiates with visual discourses and experiences derived from wider European contexts. See for example Chlöe Porter, 'Interactions between English Drama and Visual Culture, 1576–1642', unpublished Ph.D. thesis, University of Manchester, 2007; Edward Chaney (ed.), *The Evolution of English Collecting: Receptions of Italian Art in the Tudor and Stuart Periods* (New Haven, CT, and London: Yale University Press, 2003); Tara Hamling and Richard L. Williams (eds), *Art Re-formed: Reassessing the Impact of the Reformation on the Visual Arts* (Cambridge: Cambridge Scholars Publishing, 2007).
5. See Mikhail Bakhtin, *Rabelais and his World*, trans. Hélène Iswolsky (Bloomington, IN, and Indianapolis: Indiana University Press, 1984), 320–2.
6. See Mark Cousins, 'The Ugly' (2 pts), *AA Files* 28 (1994), 61–4 and 29 (1995), 3–6.
7. Thomas Jeamson, *Artificiall Embellishments, or Arts Best Directions How to Preserve Beauty or Procure it* (Oxford, 1665), 21. EEBO. 12 March 2006. http://eebo.chadwyck.com.
8. Sarah Scott, *Agreeable Ugliness: or The Triumph of the Graces* (1754), 25. Eighteenth Century Collections Online. 13 December 2007. http://galenet.galegroup.com.
9. See Michael C. Schoenfeldt, *Bodies and Selves in Early Modern England: Physiology and Inwardness in Spenser, Shakespeare, Herbert, and Milton* (Cambridge: Cambridge University Press, 1999), 11.
10. René Descartes, *Discourse on Method* (1637), *René Descartes: Philosophical Essays and Correspondence*, ed. Roger Ariew (Indianapolis, IN, and Cambridge: Hackett, 2000), 61.

11. Charles Taylor, *Sources of the Self: The Making of the Modern Identity* (Cambridge: Cambridge University Press, 1989), 146. For a discussion of the 'mechanical' physical order in the seventeenth century see also Jonathan Sawday, '"Forms Such as Never Were in Nature": the Renaissance Cyborg', *At the Borders of the Human: Beasts, Bodies and Natural Philosophy in the Early Modern Period*, eds Erica Fudge, Ruth Gilbert and Susan Wiseman (London: Macmillan, 1999), 171–95. See also Schoenfeldt, *Bodies and Selves*, 11.
12. Jonathan Sawday, *The Body Emblazoned: Dissection and the Human Body in Renaissance Culture* (London and New York: Routledge, 1995), 28–30, 37.
13. For observations on the role of ugliness in medieval literature see Henrik Specht, 'The Beautiful, the Handsome and the Ugly: Some Aspects of the Art of Character Portrayal in Medieval Literature', *Studia Neophilologia* 56:2 (1984), 129–46; Jan Ziolkowski, 'Avatars of Ugliness in Medieval Literature', *Modern Language Review* 79:1 (1984), 1–20.
14. On the medical diagnosis of the old man see for instance John E. Wolf, MD, 'Acne and Rosacea: Differential Diagnosis and Treatment in the Primary Care Setting', *Medscape Today* (September 2002). 25 October 2007. http://medscape.com/viewprogram/2032.
15. Robert Burton, *The Anatomy of Melancholy* (1621), intro. William H. Gass, ed. and intro. Holbrook Jackson (New York: *New York Review of Books*, 2001), 2.3.2.
16. Stephen Pender, '"No Monsters at the Resurrection": Inside some Conjoined Twins', *Monster Theory: Reading Culture*, ed. Jeffrey Jerome Cohen (Minneapolis, MN, and London: University of Minnesota Press, 1996), 143–67, 146. Pender counters simplistic historical narratives of the monstrous body in relation to this era, arguing that 'contrary to the notion that they were emptied of political or theological resonance at a certain point in history, monsters continued to exert a specific gravity on the imaginations of men and women'. He insists on the 'complex, often conflictual status of the monstrous in the early modern period'. 147, 145.
17. Martin Porter discusses the prevalence of physiognomy in *Windows of the Soul: The Art of Physiognomy in European Culture, 1470–1780* (Oxford: Clarendon Press, 2005), 79–119.
18. Pender discusses the manner in which the deformed body continued to be seen by many in the era as a sign of a deformed soul, '"No Monsters at the Resurrection"', 150–5.
19. Thomas Dekker, John Ford and William Rowley, *The Witch of Edmonton* (performed 1621, publ. 1658), *Three Jacobean Witchcraft Plays*, eds Peter Corbin and Douglas Sedge, Revels Plays Companion Library (Manchester and New York: Manchester University Press, 1986), 4.1.121, 2.1.100–1.
20. For a discussion of 'dominant', 'residual' and 'emergent' cultures, see Raymond Williams, 'Base and Superstructure in Marxist Cultural Theory', *The Raymond Williams Reader*, ed. John Higgins (Oxford: Blackwell, 2001), 158–78.
21. William Shakespeare, *Macbeth*, ed. Kenneth Muir (London: Arden Shakespeare, 1962, repr. 2002), 1.5.62, 1.4.11–12.
22. Sir Francis Bacon, 'Of Deformity' (1612), *The Essays* (1668), 191.
23. Helen Deutsch, 'The Body's Moments: Visible Disability, the Essay and the Limits of

Sympathy', *Prose Studies* 27:1–2 (April–August 2005), 11–26, 15. Michael Torrey also discusses the irresolution of Bacon's discussion of appearances in '"The plain devil and dissembling looks": Ambivalent Physiognomy and Shakespeare's *Richard III*', *ELR* 30:2 (2000), 123–53. See also Brian Vickers, 'Introduction', *Occult and Scientific Mentalities in the Renaissance*, ed. Brian Vickers (Cambridge: Cambridge University Press, 1984), 19–20.

24. Robert Herrick, 'Upon some Women' (H-195), *Hesperides* (1648), *The Complete Poetry of Robert Herrick*, ed. J. Max Patrick (New York: New York University Press, 1963), ll. 7–8, 6.
25. Herrick, 'Upon Jone and Jane' (H-659), ll. 1, 3–5, 6–7, 2, 9.
26. Bakhtin, *Rabelais and his World*, 320.
27. Julia Kristeva, *Powers of Horror: An Essay on Abjection*, trans. Leon S. Roudiez (New York: Columbia University Press, 1982), 4, 15, 13, 85, 102, 67, 5.
28. For an instance of an ugly woman being told to 'Go!' see Burton, *Anatomy*, 3.2.5.3.
29. William Shakespeare, Sonnet 130, *The Norton Shakespeare*, eds Stephen Greenblatt *et. al.* (New York and London: Norton, 1997), ll. 1, 3, 5–6.
30. Patrizia Bettella discusses the 'male agenda of narcissistic aggrandizement' in Italian baroque poetry in praise of unconventional beauty in *The Ugly Woman: Transgressive Aesthetic Models in Italian Poetry from the Middle Ages to the Baroque* (Toronto and London: University of Toronto Press, 2005), 128–64.

1 Theorising ugliness

1. *OED*.
2. John Donne, 'That Women ought to Paint', *Paradoxes and Problemes* (1633) (London: Nonesuch Press, 1923), 6; Burton, *Anatomy*, 3.2.2.2.
3. See Claire Colebrook, 'Introduction', *Feminist Theory* 7:2 (August 2006), 131–42, 133.
4. William of Auvergne (d. 1245), *De bono et malo* (MS. Balliol, 207); cited in Wladyslaw Tatarkiewicz, *History of Aesthetics*, ed. D. Petsch, Vol. 3 of 3 (The Hague: Mouton, 1974), 223.
5. John Foxe, *Actes and Monuments of Matters most Speciall and Memorable happenyng in the Church* (1563), 1632.
6. John Milton, *Paradise Lost*, ed. Alastair Fowler (London and New York: Longman, 1968), Bk 11, ll. 463–5.
7. Thomas Bowes (trans.), *De La Primaudaye's French Academie* (1594); cited in *OED*, 'ugly' 4a.
8. Agnolo Firenzuola, *On the Beauty of Women*, trans. and ed. Konrad Eisenbichler and Jacqueline Murray (Philadelphia: University of Pennsylvania Press, 1992), 34, 14.
9. See Lorraine Daston and Katherine Park, *Wonders and the Order of Nature, 1150–1750* (New York: Zone Books, 1998), 201–14.
10. The *OED* cites Thomas Overbury's *A Wife* (1613) as the first text to use the term.
11. Augustine (354–430), *De vera religione*, XXXII, 59; cited in Tatarkiewicz, *History of Aesthetics*, 59.
12. Aquinas (1225–74) notes that 'beauty relates to a cognitive power, for those things are

said to be beautiful which please when seen', *Summa Theologica, Basic Writings of Saint Thomas Aquinas*, ed. and trans. Anton C. Pegis (New York: Random House, 1945), Vol. 1 of 2, 47.
13. Francis Hutcheson, *An Inquiry concerning Beauty, Order, Harmony, Design*, ed. Peter Kivy (The Hague: Nijhoff, 1973), 34, 40, 77, 45.
14. David Hume, 'Of the Standard of Taste', *Four Dissertations*, Pt 4 (1757), 209, 214. Eighteenth Century Collections Online. 26 September 2007. http://galenet.galegroup.com.
15. Henry King, 'The Defence', *Poems, Elegies, Paradoxes and Sonets* (1664), ll. 3–4, 7–10.
16. Firenzuola, *On the Beauty of Women*, 10.
17. Thomas Hobbes, *Leviathan* (1651), ed. C. B. Macpherson (London: Penguin, 1968), 120.
18. Thomasso Buoni, *Problemes of Beautie and all Humane Affections* (1606), trans. Sampson Lennard, 26, 14, 26–7. EEBO. 12 April 2006. http://eebo.chadwyck.com. Lennard, translator and antiquary, accompanied Philip Sidney to The Netherlands and was present at the battle of Zutphen in 1586, when Sidney was fatally injured. See *ODNB* and Mary Augusta Scott, 'Elizabethan Translations from the Italian', *PMLA* 14:4 (1899), 465–571, 548.
19. Manuel de Faria e Sousa, *The Portugues Ásia*, trans. John Stevens (1695), 463. EEBO. 23 August 2007. http://eebo.chadwyck.com.
20. Sir Thomas Browne, *Pseudodoxia Epidemica* (1646), ed. Robin Robbins (Oxford: Clarendon Press, 1981), 522.
21. John Bulwer, *Anthropometamorphosis: Man Transform'd: or The Artificiall Changling Historically Presented in the Mad and Cruell Gallantry, Foolish Bravery, Ridiculous Beauty, Filthy Finenesse, and Loathsome Loveliness of most Nations, fashioning and altering their Bodies from the Mould intended by Nature . . . To which artificiall and affected Deformations are added, all the Native and Nationall Monstrosities that have appeared to disfigure the Humane Fabrick. With a Vindication of the Regular Beauty and Honesty of Nature* (1650, this edn 1653), fol. B1v, 118, 124, 127. For a discussion of Bulwer's tract, see Mary Baine Campbell, '*Anthropometamorphosis:* John Bulwer's Monsters of Cosmetology and the Science of Culture', *Monster Theory*, 202–24.
22. Michel de Montaigne (1533–92), 'An Apology for Raymond Sebond', *The Complete Essays*, trans. and ed. M. A. Screech (London: Penguin, 1991), 537–8, 673.
23. Montaigne, 'On the Lame', *Complete Essays*, 1170–1.
24. Sir Thomas Browne, *Religio Medici, Sir Thomas Browne: The Major Works*, ed. C. A. Patrides (London: Penguin, 1977), 81.
25. William of Auvergne, *De bono et malo*, 206; cited in Taratkiewicz, *History of Aesthetics*, 222.
26. See Cousins, 'The Ugly' (1994), 61–4.
27. William Sanderson, *Graphice: The Use of the Pen and Pensil, or The Most Excellent Art of Painting: in Two Parts* (1658), 46.
28. Firenzuola, *On the Beauty of Women*, 53.
29. George Puttenham, *The Arte of English Poesie* (1589), eds Alice Walker and Gladys Willcock (Cambridge: 1936), 261; cited in Neil Rhodes, *Elizabethan Grotesque* (London: Routledge & Kegan Paul, 1980), 11.

30. Plotinus (204/5–270), *The Enneads*, trans. Stephen Mackenna, 4th edn (London: Faber, 1969), I.6.6.
31. Mark Hutchinson, *Nausea: Encounters with Ugliness* (Nottingham: Djanogly Art Gallery, 2002), 11.
32. George Chapman, *The Gentleman Usher* (1606), fol. I2v, unlineated. EEBO. 7 July 2007. http://eebo.chadwyck.com.
33. Browne, *Religio Medici*, 80–1. *Religio Medici* circulated in manuscript until an unauthorised edition was printed in 1642. An authorised version was published in 1643.
34. Augustine, *De vera religione*, XXXII, 60; cited in Tatarkiewicz, *History of Aesthetics*, 64.
35. Augustine, *De natura boni*, 14–17; cited in Tatarkiewicz, *History of Aesthetics*, 63–4.
36. See Daston and Park, *Wonders*, 215–20.
37. Thomas Bedford, *A True and Certaine Relation of a Strange-birth which was born at Stonehouse in the Parish of Plimmouth, the 20. of October 1635* (1635), 12.
38. Augustine, *The City of God*, trans. John Healy, ed. R. V. G. Tasker, intro. Sir Ernest Barker, Vol. 2 of 2 (London: Dent, 1945), 107.
39. Thomas Fuller, *The Holy State* (1642), 190–1. EEBO. 21 January 2006. http://eebo.chadwyck.com.
40. Augustine, *City of God*, 107.
41. Montaigne, 'On a Monster-child', *Complete Essays*, 808.
42. Leonardo da Vinci (1452–1519), *Treatise on Painting*, trans. A. Philip McMahon, intro. Ludwig H. Heydenreich, Vol. 1 of 2 (Princeton, NJ: Princeton University Press, 1956), 112. On the role of *contrapposto* in Renaissance art, see David Summers, *Michelangelo and the Language of Art* (Princeton, NJ: Princeton University Press, 1981), 76.
43. Herrick, 'Upon his Gray Haires' (H-527), ll. 5–7.
44. John Lyly, 'To the right honourable my very good Lord and Master Sir William West, etc.', *Euphues: The Anatomy of Wit* (1579), *Euphues: The Anatomy of Wit and Euphues and his England*, ed. Leah Scragg, The Revels Plays Companion Library (Manchester and New York: Manchester University Press, 2003), 29.
45. James Shirley, *The Dukes Mistris* (1636, publ. 1638), fol. D2, unlineated. EEBO. 12 September 2007. http://eebo.chadwyck.com.
46. Bulwer, *Anthropometamorphosis*, 262.
47. Richard Lovelace, 'A Paradox', *Lucasta* (1649), ll. 8–10. Literature Online. 1 November 2007. http://lion.chadwyck.co.uk.
48. Bulwer, *Anthropometamorphosis*, 241–2.
49. Edward Ward, *Satyrical Reflections on Clubs: in XXIX Chapters* (1710), Vol. 5, 83–4. Eighteenth Century Collections Online. 1 November 2007. http://galenet.galegoup.com.
50. See Daston and Park, *Wonders*, 355–61.
51. Thomas Middleton and William Rowley, *The Changeling*, ed. N. W. Bawcutt, The Revels Plays (Manchester and New York: Manchester University Press, 1998), 3.3.262.
52. See Stephen Pender, 'In the Bodyshop: Human Exhibition in Early Modern England', *'Defects': Engendering the Modern Body*, eds Helen Deutsch and Felicity Nussbaum (Ann Arbor, MI: University of Michigan Press, 2000), 95–126.

53. Paula Findlen, 'Jokes of Nature and Jokes of Knowledge: The Playfulness of Scientific Discourse in Early Modern Europe', *Renaissance Quarterly* 43:2 (Summer 1990), 292–331.
54. John Spencer, *A Discourse Concerning Prodigies* (1663), 2. EEBO. 1 November 2007. http://eebo.chadwyck.com. See William E. Burns, '"A proverb of versatile mutability": Proteus and Natural Knowledge in Early Modern Britain', *Sixteenth-Century Journal* 32:4 (2001), 969–80.
55. See *OED*, 'freak' 4a.
56. See Pender, 'In the Bodyshop', 95–126.
57. Samuel Pepys, *The Diary of Samuel Pepys: A Selection*, ed. Robert Latham (London: Penguin, 1985, reissue 2003), 973. For a discussion of female facial hair in the period, see Mark Albert Johnston, 'Bearded Women in Early Modern England', *Studies in English Literature, 1500–1900* 47:1 (Winter 2007), 1–28.
58. Daston and Park, *Wonders*, 190–201.
59. Edward Reynolds, *A Treatise of the Passions and Faculties of the Soule of Man* (1640, this edn 1647), 173.
60. Marquis de Sade, *The 120 Days of Sodom and other Writings*, trans. Austryn Wainhouse and Richard Seaver (New York: Grove Press, 1966), 233.
61. Edmund Burke, *A Philosophical Enquiry into the Origin of our Ideas of the Sublime and the Beautiful*, 2nd edn (1759), 191, 226. Eighteenth Century Collections Online. 1 November 2007. http://galenet.galegroup.com. Ugliness in itself is not a 'sublime idea', qualifies Burke, 'unless united with such qualities as excite a strong terror', *Philosophical Enquiry*, 226.
62. Ward, *Satyrical Reflections*, 36, 38, 81, 82.
63. Leonardo da Vinci, *Treatise on Painting*, Vol. 1 of 2, 24.
64. Donne, *Paradoxes and Problemes*, 7.
65. Aristotle (384–22 BC), *Poetics*, ed. and trans. Stephen Halliwell (Cambridge, MA: Harvard University Press, 1995), 37–9.
66. Aquinas, *Summa Theologica*, 378. Scott's *Agreeable Ugliness* also depicts a painter creating an 'agreeable' portrait out of an exact resemblance of the unattractive narrator, 116–20.
67. St Bonaventure (1221–74) *Commentary on the Book of Sentences* I, 32, 2; cited in Umberto Eco (ed.), *On Beauty: A History of a Western Idea*, trans. Alastair McEwen (London: Secker & Warburg, 2004), 132.
68. Leonardo da Vinci, *Treatise on Painting*, Vol. 1 of 2, 161.
69. See Kwakkelstein, 'Leonardo da Vinci's Grotesque Heads', 127–36; Martin Clayton, *Leonardo da Vinci: The Divine and the Grotesque* (London: Royal Collection Enterprises, 2002).
70. Horace Walpole, *Anecdotes of Painting in England*, 2nd edn, Vol. 3 of 4 (1765). Eighteenth Century Collections Online. 17 October 2007. http://galenet.galegroup.com.
71. Lyly, 'To the right honourable my very good Lord and Master Sir William West Knight, etc.', *Euphues: The Anatomy of Wit*, 27–8.
72. See Tatarkiewicz, *History of Aesthetics*, 151–9. See also Bettella, *The Ugly Woman*, 128–9.

73. See Jurgis Baltrušaitis, *Anamorphic Art*, trans. W. J. Strachan (Cambridge: Chadwyck-Healey, 1977).
74. Roland Barthes, 'Arcimboldo, or Magician and Rhétoriqueur', *The Responsibility of Forms: Critical Essays on Music, Art, and Representation*, trans. Richard Howard (Berkeley and Los Angeles, CA: University of California Press, 1985), 145, 146-7; Bakhtin, *Rabelais and his World*, 19-27.
75. Tatarkiewicz, *History of Aesthetics*, 255.
76. See Tatarkiewicz, *History of Aesthetics*, 254; Wolfgang Kayser, *The Grotesque in Art and Literature*, trans. Ulrich Weisstein (Bloomington, IN: Indiana University Press, 1963).
77. Philip Thomson, *The Grotesque* (London: Methuen, 1972), 12.
78. Cited in John Peacock, *The Stage Designs of Inigo Jones: The European Context* (Cambridge: Cambridge University Press, 1995), 219.
79. Vasari for instance celebrates Michelangelo's championing of 'new fantasies' which 'exhibit more of the grotesque than reason or rules in their decorations', Giorgio Vasari, *The Lives of the Artists*, trans. and eds Julia Conaway Bondanella and Peter Bondanella (Oxford: Oxford University Press, 1991), 454. On Inigo Jones, see Peacock, *Stage Designs*, 227-35.
80. John Florio's Italian-English dictionary, for example, defined *grottesca* in derisive terms as 'a kinde of rugged unpolished painters worke, anticke worke', John Florio, *A Worlde of Wordes, or Most copious, and exact Dictionarie in Italian and English* (1598), 157.
81. Browne, *Religio Medici*, 77.
82. Cited in Peacock, *Stage Designs*, 219.
83. Cited in Peacock, *Stage Designs*, 139.
84. See Thomson, *Grotesque*, 25; Kayser, *Grotesque*, 37.
85. Bernard of Clairvaux (1090-1153), cited in G. G. Coulton (selected, trans. and annotated), *A Medieval Garner: Human Documents from the Four Centuries preceding the Reformation* (London: Constable, 1910), 72. See Willard Farnham, *The Shakespearean Grotesque: Its Genesis and Transformations* (Oxford: Clarendon Press, 1971), 1-46.
86. James Shirley, 'To a Beautiful Lady', *Poems* (1646), ll. 1-2. Literature Online. 26 October 2007. http://lion.chadwyck.co.uk.
87. James H. Marrow, *Passion Iconography in Northern European Art of the Late Middle Ages and Early Renaissance: A Study of the Transformation of Sacred Metaphor into Descriptive Narrative* (Kortrijk: Van Ghemmert, 1979), 33-43.
88. Marrow, *Passion Iconography*, 57.
89. Harald Hendrix, 'The Repulsive Body: Images of Torture in Seventeenth-Century Naples', *Bodily Extremities: Preoccupations with the Human Body in Early Modern European Culture*, eds Florike Egmond and Robert Zwijnenberg (Aldershot: Ashgate, 2003), 68-91, 81, 83, 90.
90. George Lauder (trans.), Lelio Capilupi and Francesco Petrarca (orig.), *The Anatomie of the Romane Clergie: or A Discoverie of the Abuses thereof. Written in Latine by Sundrie Authors of their own Profession* (1623), ll. 97-100. Literature Online. 1 November 2007. http://lion.chadwyck.co.uk.
91. See Stephen Greenblatt, 'Mutilation and Meaning', *The Body in Parts: Fantasies of Corporeality in Early Modern Europe*, eds David Hillman and Carlo Mazzio (New York and London: Routledge, 1997), 221-42; John R. Knott, *Discourses of Martyrdom*

in English Literature, 1563–1694 (Cambridge: Cambridge University Press, 1993), 38–46.
92. Fuller, *Holy State*, 191.
93. N.H., *The Ladies Dictionary: Being a General Entertainment for the Fair Sex* (1694), 163. EEBO. 3 October 2007. http://eebo.chadwyck.com.
94. John Donne, 'What if this present were the worlds last night?' *The Complete English Poems of John Donne*, ed. C. A. Patrides (London: Dent, 1985), l. 14.
95. Bedford, *A True and Certaine Relation of a Strange-birth*, 15.
96. Paul Semonin argues that the 'monsters' put on display in early modern England were greeted at a popular level simply with delight, rather than being interpreted as morally or spiritually significant. See his 'Monsters in the Marketplace: The Exhibition of Human Oddities in Early Modern England', *Freakery: Cultural Spectacles of the Exraordinary Body*, ed. Rosemarie Garland Thomson (New York and London: New York University Press, 1996), 69–81, 79.
97. See Sebastian Buffa (ed.), *Antonio Tempesta, The Illustrated Bartsch*, Vol. 37, ser. ed. Walter L. Strauss (New York: Abaris Books, 1984), 198–203.
98. See Mark J. Zunker, 'Homeliness and Humor in Renaissance Italy: Tales of Ugly (and Witty) Artists and other Paragons of Ugliness', *Explorations in Renaissance Culture* 30:2 (Winter 2004), 231–59; Roger Lund, 'Laughing at Cripples: Ridicule, Deformity and the Argument from Design', *Eighteenth Century Studies* 39:1 (2005), 91–114.
99. Samuel Johnson, *A Dictionary of the English Language*, 2nd edn (1755), Vol. 1 of 2, 'Deformity', 2. Eighteenth Century Collections Online. 6 June 2008. http://galenet.galegroup.com.
100. Ben Jonson, *Timber, or Discoveries* (1640), 130. Literature Online. 26 November 2007. http://lion.chadwyck.co.uk.
101. Aristotle, *Poetics*, 45.
102. Laurent Joubert, *Traite du Ris (Treatise on Laughter)* (1579), trans. Gregory David de Rocher (Tuscaloosa, AL: University of Alabama Press, 1980), 23, 39.
103. Sir Philip Sidney, *An Apology for Poetry*, ed. Geoffrey Shepherd (Manchester: Manchester University Press, 1973), 136–7.
104. Bakhtin, *Rabelais and his World*, 88–96.
105. N.H., *The Ladies Dictionary*, 410.
106. John Dryden, 'Preface', C. A. Du Fresnoy, *De Arte Graphica: The Art of Painting* (1695), xvii; 'An Account of the ensuing poem, in a Letter to the Honorable Sir Robert Howard', *Annus Mirabilis: The Year of Wonders, 1666* (1667), n.p. EEBO. 1 December 2006. http://eebo.chadwyck.com.
107. See John O'Connor, 'Physical Deformity and Chivalric Laughter in Renaissance England', *New York Literary Forum* 1 (1978), 59–71.
108. Julie Crawford, *Marvelous Protestantism: Monstrous Births in Post-Reformation England* (Baltimore, MD, and London: Johns Hopkins University Press, 2005), 18. See also Pender, '"No Monsters at the Resurrection"', 143–67; Margrit Shildrick, *Embodying the Monster: Encounters with the Vulnerable Self* (London: Sage, 2002), 13–19.
109. John Sadler, *The Sick Womans Private Looking-glasse* (1636), 136. EEBO. 15 November 2007. http://eebo.chadwyck.com. This passage is cited in Crawford, *Marvelous*

Protestantism, 20. Sadler is nevertheless careful to state that 'there are many borne depraved which ought not to bee ascribed unto the infirmity of the parents', 136.
110. Bedford, *A True and Certaine Relation of a Strange-birth*, 17.
111. Anthony Wood, *Athenae Oxonienses* (1692), Vol. 2 of 2, 260. EEBO. 27 November 2007. http://eebo.chadwyck.com. Wood's reference to Shirley is cited in the *ODNB*. For the biblical basis of the argument that the deformed should not become priests, see Leviticus 21.16–21. Wood relates that Shirley nevertheless did take holy orders in St Albans, but then 'changed his Religion for that of Rome' and became a grammar school teacher, before leaving for London to 'set up for a play-maker', ultimately gaining the patronage of Queen Henrietta Maria. Wood, *Athenae Oxonienses*, Vol. 2 of 2, 260–1.
112. Bedford, *A True and Certaine Relation of a Strange-birth*, 9–10, 20, 13–14, 21, 18. Semonin argues that the display of early modern 'monsters' '[bears] witness to a long tradition of popular folk humour' in which the monstrous is devoid of wider spiritual significance. See his 'Monsters in the Marketplace', 79.
113. Bedford, *A True and Certaine Relation of a Strange-birth*, 20–1, 14.
114. Spencer, *Discourse Concerning Prodigies*, 42.
115. Robert Boyle, *A Free Enquiry into the Vulgarly Receiv'd Notion of Nature* (1686), 58, 81, 79, 11–12.
116. See Daston and Park, *Wonders*, 355–61. Rosemarie Garland Thomson summarises the process by which the 'freak' was recast in the early modern era 'from astonishing corporeal extravagance into the pathological specimen of the terata' in her 'Introduction. From Wonder to Error: A Genealogy of Freak Discourse in Modernity', *Freakery*, 1–19, especially 3–4.
117. Boyle, *Free Enquiry*, 150, 152–3, 154–5.
118. Margaret Cavendish, *The Worlds Olio* (1655), 137–8. EEBO. 26 March 2006. http://eebo.chadwyck.com.
119. Boyle, *Free Enquiry*, 167, 164, 288–9, 170.
120. Deutsch and Nussbaum comment that 'the moment when attempts are made to define difference as natural fact – no longer as a sign for divine or preternatural agency – it is revealed as the norm's inverse reflection', 'Introduction', 'Defects', 13.
121. Boyle, *Free Enquiry*, 176, 264, 323–4.
122. Spencer, *Discourse Concerning Prodigies*, 42, 3, 10.
123. Hutcheson, *An Inquiry*, 73, 77, 45.
124. Boyle, *Free Enquiry*, 403.
125. Spencer, *Discourse Concerning Prodigies*, 44.
126. Francis Bacon, *The Novum Organum of Sir Francis Bacon* (1620, this edn 1676), 31. EEBO. 12 October 2006. http://eebo.chadwyck.com. For a discussion of the manner in which the 'deformed is controlled by being assimilated to the known' in the early modern era, see David Williams, *Deformed Discourse: The Function of the Monster in Medieval Thought and Literature* (Exeter: University of Exeter Press, 1996), 323–30.
127. Spencer, *Discourse Concerning Prodigies*, 103, 102, 10, 27, 87, 6.
128. Francis Bacon, 'The Masculine Birth of Time' (c. 1602), *The Philosophy of Francis Bacon: An Essay on its Development from 1603 to 1609, with New Translations of*

Fundamental Texts, trans. Benjamin Farrington (Liverpool: Liverpool University Press, 1970), 66.
129. Spencer, *Discourse Concerning Prodigies*, 72.
130. Spencer's text is partly a response to Thomas Jackson's *Diverse Sermons, with a Short Treatise befitting these Times* (1637). EEBO. 27 November 2007. http://eebo.chadwyck.com. Jackson (1579–1640) was a former president of Spencer's college, Corpus Christi, Cambridge. For more on the historical and political contexts of Spencer's arguments, see William E. Burns, *An Age of Wonders: Prodigies, Politics and Providence in England, 1657–1727* (Manchester and New York: Manchester University Press, 2002), esp. 58–68.
131. Thomas Knagg, *A Sermon Preach'd at the Cathedral Church of St Paul* (1716), 9. On the persistence of 'credulous' beliefs supposedly supplanted by the new science, see Shildrick, *Embodying the Monster*, 23–5; Pender, '"No Monsters at the Resurrection"', 145–56.
132. For a discussion of the coexistence of contradictory models of nature in this era, see Vickers, 'Introduction', *Occult and Scientific Mentalities*, 13–17.

2 'Charactered in my brow'

1. William Shakespeare, *The Rape of Lucrece* (1594), *The Norton Shakespeare*, l. 807.
2. *OED*, 'character' 10.
3. Christopher Marlowe, *Tamburlaine the Great, Part One, Christopher Marlowe: The Complete Plays*, ed. J. B. Steane (London: Penguin, 1969), 1.2.169–71. This example is cited by the *OED*, 'character' 1b.
4. *OED*, 'character' 11, 12.
5. David Jenner, *Cain's Mark. And Murder. K. Charles the I his Martyrdom. Delivered in a Sermon on January the Thirtieth* (1680), 6. EEBO. 4 May 2007. http://eebo.chadwyck.com.
6. Jeremy Collier, *Miscellanies upon Moral Subjects* (1695), Part 2 of 2, 119. EEBO. 4 May 2007. http://eebo.chadwyck.com.
7. Plotinus, *Enneads*, II.9.17.
8. The philosophy of Aquinas, grounded in Aristotelian paradigms and emphasising material over spiritual beauty, is a notable exception.
9. Bernard of Clairvaux (1090–1153), *Sermones in Cantica* LXXV, 11; cited in Umberto Eco, *Art and Beauty in the Middle Ages*, trans. Hugh Bredin (New Haven, CT, and London: Yale University Press, 1986), 10.
10. Alain, Bishop of Auxerre (d. 1185), *Medieval Garner*, 59.
11. Edmund Spenser, 'An Hymne in Honour of Beautie', *Fowre Hymnes* (1596), 17, unlineated. EEBO. 2 November 2007. http://eebo.chadwyck.com.
12. Plotinus, *Enneads*, I.6.1.
13. Spenser, 'An Hymne in Honour of Beautie', 18.
14. See Plotinus, *Enneads*, I.6.5.
15. Genesis 1.27, 1 Corinthians 6.19.
16. John Calvin, *The Institution of Christian Religion* (1559, this edn 1562), trans. Thomas Norton, 1.15.4.

17. N.H., *The Ladies Dictionary*, 56.
18. Sanderson, *Graphice*, 46.
19. John Donne, *Donne's Sermons*, ed. Logan Pearsall Smith (Oxford: Clarendon Press, 1919), 92.
20. Kristeva, *Powers of Horror*, 109.
21. Donne, *Sermons*, 241.
22. See Bettella, *Ugly Woman*, 15–16.
23. Specht, 'The Beautiful, the Handsome and the Ugly', 134. Ziolkowski also argues that medieval literary descriptions are governed by the 'unshakeable conviction that the beautiful and the good, like the ugly and the bad, were merely different names for the same qualities', 'Avatars of Ugliness in Medieval Literature', 19. See also Denis Donoghue, *Speaking of Beauty* (New Haven, CT, and London: Yale University Press, 2003), 65–6.
24. *Wisdom, The Macro Plays*, ed. Mark Eccles (Oxford: Early English Text Society, 1969), ll. 900–2; cited in Annette Drew-Bear, *Painted Faces on the Renaissance Stage: The Moral Significance of Face-painting Conventions* (Lewisburg, PA: Bucknell University Press, 1994), 37–8.
25. Gregory the Great (540–604), *Pastoral Care* (Baltimore, MD: Newman Press, 1958), 41–2; cited in Jonathan Sinclair Carey, 'The Quasimodo Complex: Deformity Reconsidered', *The Tyranny of the Normal: An Anthology*, eds Carol Donley and Sheryl Buckley (Kent, OH: Kent State University Press, 1996), 27–52, 31.
26. Susanne Fendler, 'The Emancipation of the Sign: The Changing Significance of Beauty in some English Renaissance Romances', *Critical Studies: Nominalism and Literary Discourse: New Perspectives*, eds Hugo Keiper, Christoph Bode and Richard J. Utz (Amsterdam: Rodopi, 1997), 269–82, 269–70.
27. Jonson, *Timber, or Discoveries*, 95.
28. Donne, *Paradoxes and Problemes*, 27.
29. William Shakespeare, *King John*, ed. E. A. J. Honigmann, The Arden Shakespeare (London: Methuen, 1954, repr. 1959), 2.2.43–52.
30. See Pat Thane, *Old Age in English History: Past Experiences, Present Issues* (Oxford: Oxford University Press, 2000), 38.
31. John Webster, *The Duchess of Malfi, John Webster: The Duchess of Malfi and other plays*, ed. René Weis (Oxford: Oxford University Press, 1996), 2.1.24, 37, 39–40.
32. See pp. 107–15 for a more detailed discussion of ageing bodies in early modern texts.
33. Nancy Selleck, 'Donne's Body', *SEL* 41:1 (Winter 2001), 149–74. See also Nancy G. Siraisi, *Medieval and Early Renaissance Medicine: An Introduction to Knowledge and Practice* (Chicago: University of Chicago Press, 1990), 106; cited in Gail Kern Paster, *The Body Embarrassed: Drama and the Disciplines of Shame in Early Modern England* (Ithaca, NY: Cornell University Press, 1993), 7.
34. See Joubert, *Treatise on Laughter*, 55; Thomas Bartholin, *Bartholinus Anatomy, made from the Precepts of his Father, and from the Observations of all Modern Anatomists, together with his own*, publ. Nicholas Culpeper and Abdiah Cole (1668), 7. EEBO. 3 June 2007. http://eebo.chadwyck.com.
35. William Shakespeare, *1 Henry IV*, ed. David Bevington (Oxford: Oxford University Press, 1987), 2.4.313–14.

36. Piers D. G. Britton, 'The Signs of Faces: Leonardo on Physiognomic Science and the "Four Universal States of Man"', *Renaissance Studies* 16:2 (2002), 143–62.
37. Henry Peacham, *The Compleat Gentleman: Fashioning him Absolut, in the most Necessary and Commendable Qualities concerning Minde or Bodie, that may be Required in a Noble Gentleman* (1622, this edn 1634), 215. The latter part of this quotation is cited in Schoenfeldt, *Bodies and Selves*, 12.
38. Schoenfeldt, *Bodies and Selves*, 7. See also Margaret Healy, *Fictions of Disease in Early Modern England: Bodies, Plagues and Politics* (Basingstoke: Palgrave, 2002), 21.
39. Firenzuola, *On the Beauty of Women*, 40.
40. Anon., 'That a Black-a-moor Woman is the greatest Beauty; in a Letter to a Lady exceeding Fair', *Athenian Sport: or Two Thousand Paradoxes Merrily Argued, To Amuse and Divert the Age*, [ed. John Dunton] (1707), 104.
41. Francis Bacon, 'Dionysus, or Passions', *The Wisdome of the Ancients* (1609), *The Essays*, 85.
42. Joubert, *Treatise on Laughter*, 6–7.
43. See Selleck, 'Donne's Body', 151–3. See also Paster, *The Body Embarrassed*, 8.
44. William Shakespeare, *The Comedy of Errors*, ed. R. A. Foakes, The Arden Shakespeare (London: Methuen, 1962), 5.1.298–300.
45. Selleck, 'Donne's Body', 170 n. 20.
46. Porter, *Windows of the Soul*, 119, 319.
47. Richard Saunders, *Physiognomie and Chiromancie* (1653, this edn 1671), 270.
48. Thomas Wright, *The Passions of the Minde* (1598, publ. 1601), 2. EEBO. 3 February 2006. http://eebo.chadwyck.com.
49. Wright, *Passions of the Mind*, 266.
50. See Schoenfeldt, *Bodies and Selves*, 11; Sawday, *Body Emblazoned*, 28–30; Taylor, *Sources of the Self*, 146.
51. René Descartes, *The Passions of the Soul* (1649), trans. Stephen Voss (Indianapolis, IN. and Cambridge: Hackett, 1989), 46, 49.
52. William Shakespeare, *Othello*, ed. E. A. J. Honigmann (London: Arden Shakespeare, 1999), 1.3.320–3.
53. Milton, *Paradise Lost*, Bk 12, ll. 82, 87–8.
54. John Martin comments on the 'explicitly layered quaility' of 'Renaissance notions of the self', noting the 'sense not only of inwardness or interiority but also of mystery about what Renaissance writers ... imagined as their inner selves', 'Inventing Sincerity, Refashioning Prudence: The Discovery of the Individual in Renaissance Europe', *American Historical Review* 102:5 (December 1995), 1309–42, 1321.
55. Katherine Eisaman Maus, *Inwardness and Theater in the English Renaissance* (Chicago and London: University of Chicago Press, 1995), 16, 24, 26.
56. Calvin, *Institution*, 3.14.4, 2.3.4, 2.3.2. John Stachniewski discusses Calvin's emphasis on hidden depravity in 'Calvinist Psychology in Middleton's Tragedies', *Three Jacobean Revenge Tragedies: A Casebook*, ed. R. V. Holdsworth (Basingstoke: Macmillan, 1990), 226–47.
57. Donne, *Sermons*, 89–92.
58. See Romans 7.23.
59. See Torrey, '"The plain devil and dissembling looks"', 123–53.

60. Bartholomew Cocles, *A Brief and most Pleasant Epitomye of the whole Art of Physiognomie*, trans. Thomas Hill (1556), 'Preface', n.p. For a discussion of the physiognomical reading of Socrates, see K. J. H. Berland, 'Reading Character in the Face: Lavater, Socrates and Physiognomy', *Word and Image* 9:1 (January–March 1993), 252–69.
61. See Porter, *Windows of the Soul*, 168–71.
62. Marin Cureau de la Chambre, *The Art How to Know Men*, trans. John Davies (1665), fol. B3v. EEBO. 3 February 2006. http://eebo.chadwyck.com.
63. William Berkeley, *The Lost Lady* (performed c. 1637, publ. 1638), ed. D. F. Rowan and G. R. Proudfoot, Malone Society Reprints (Oxford: Oxford University Press, 1987), 2.3.633, 690, 782–3.
64. Peacham, *Compleat Gentleman*, 215.
65. Bacon, 'Of Deformity', 191.
66. Wright, *Passions of the Minde*, 27, 56.
67. Porter, *Windows of the Soul*, 312. Charles B. Schmitt notes that between 1550 and 1650 Jesuits 'were at the vanguard of observational and computational astronomy', *Aristotle and the Renaissance* (Cambridge, MA: Harvard University Press, 1983), 104.
68. Webster, *The Duchess of Malfi*, 1.1.226–9.
69. Thomas Nashe, *The Terrors of the Night, or A Discourse of Apparitions* (1594), *The Works of Thomas Nashe*, Vol. 1 of 5, ed. Ronald B. McKerrow and F. P. Wilson (Oxford: Blackwell, 1966), 370–1.
70. Rhodes discusses Nashe's grotesque style, including the 'vivid physicality' of his writing, in *Elizabethan Grotesque*, 3–62, 34.
71. Nashe, *Terrors of the Night*, 349.
72. Spencer, *Discourse Concerning Prodigies*, 44, 91, 93.
73. John Evelyn, *Numismata: A Discourse of Medals . . . to which is added a Digression concerning Physiognomy* (1697), 294, 305, 302, 309, 306, 310.
74. George Chapman, *Bussy D'Ambois*, ed. Nicholas Brooke, The Revels Plays (Manchester and New York: Manchester University Press, 1964, repr. 1999), 3.2.18.
75. See Ruth Mellinkoff, *Outcasts: Signs of Otherness* (Berkeley, CA: University of California Press, 1993), Vol. 1 of 2, 150–9.
76. Genesis 4.12, 15.
77. See Henry Glover, *Cain and Abel Parallel'd with King Charles and his Murderers in a Sermon Preached in S. Thomas Church in Salisbury, January 30 1663* (1664), 23–4; Jenner, *Cain's Mark*, 4–12.
78. See Ruth Mellinkoff, *The Mark of Cain* (Berkeley, CA: University of California Press, 1981), 76–80.
79. *The Creation of the World*, transcr. William Jordan (1611), ll. 1508, 1589–90, *Transactions of the Philological Society*, ed. Whitley Stokes (1864), 118–19, 124–5; cited in Mellinkoff, *Mark of Cain*, 70–1.
80. Mellinkoff, *Mark of Cain*, 44.
81. Arthur Jackson, *A Help for the Understanding of the Holy Scripture* (1643), 15. EEBO. 4 May 2007. http://eebo.chadwyck.com.
82. Glover, *Cain and Abel Parallel'd*, 24.
83. Jenner, *Cain's Mark*, 3. See 1 Samuel 16.7.
84. Jenner, *Cain's Mark*, 6.

85. Genesis 4.6.
86. See *OED*, 'wroth' 2.
87. Jenner, *Cain's Mark*, 6–7.
88. For a brief discussion of the symbolism of animals in medieval and Renaissance visual art, see Carl Nordenfalk, 'The Five Senses in Late Medieval and Renaissance Art', *Journal of the Warburg and Courtauld Institutes* 48 (1985), 1–22, 4.
89. Berland discusses the pseudo-Aristotelian tradition of linking human and animal features in 'Reading Character', 252–3.
90. Jenner, *Cain's Mark*, 8, 12.
91. Mellinkoff cites the Ezekiel passage in *Mark of Cain*, 24–5.
92. Jenner, *Cain's Mark*, 18, 10.
93. Mary Douglas, *Purity and Danger: An Analysis of Concepts of Pollution and Taboo* (London and Henley: Routledge & Kegan Paul, 1966).
94. Jenner, *Cain's Mark*, 15.
95. See *ODNB*.
96. Collier, *Miscellanies*, 120, 114, 117–20. EEBO. 4 May 2007. http://eebo.chadwyck.com.
97. Chapman, *Bussy D'Ambois*, 5.3.48. Further references will be marked in the main body of the text.
98. Jane Melbourne, 'The Inverted World of Bussy D'Ambois', *SEL* 25:2 (Spring 1985), 381–95, 395.
99. Melbourne discusses the play in the context of contemporary optics in 'The Inverted World', 381–95. Deborah Montuori discusses Bussy's 'posture of naturalness' in 'The Confusion of Self and Role in Chapman's *Bussy D'Ambois*', *SEL* 28:2 (Spring 1988), 287–99, 292.
100. See for instance 1.2.138. Montuori notes Chapman's use of sea imagery, 'The Confusion of Self and Role', 295.
101. Sarah Eaton argues that mutilated women in early modern drama, particularly Tamyra and Lavinia, 'reveal in their mutilations their presence as "alphabets" in a patriarchal script. Written on by violence, they write and are read,' 'Defacing the Feminine in Renaissance Tragedy', *The Matter of Difference: Materialist Feminist Criticism of Shakespeare*, ed. Valerie Wayne (New York: Harvester Wheatsheaf, 1991), 185. I discuss representations of mutilation in early modern texts in Chapter 6.
102. Melbourne, 'The Inverted World', 389.
103. Melbourne notes that Monsieur is the 'spokesman for the new knowledge' in which 'Nature has no purpose', 'The Inverted World', 384, 392.

3 Opening the Silenus

1. Taylor, *Sources of the Self*, 159.
2. Stachniewski, 'Calvinist Psychology', 241.
3. Bulwer, *Anthropometamorphosis*, title page.
4. Cocles, *A Brief and Most Pleasant Epitomye*, 'Preface'.
5. Wright, *Passions of the Minde*, 30.
6. Saunders, *Physiognomie*, 'To the deserving-Ladies Satyrically', n.p.

7. Thomas Hill, *The Contemplation of Mankinde, containing a Singular Discourse after the Art of Phisiognomie* (1571), fols. 1v, 126r.
8. Wright, *Passions of the Minde*, 29.
9. Boethius (c. 475–c. 526), *The Consolation of Philosophy*, trans. V. E. Watts (London: Penguin, 1969), 92; cited in Anthony Synnott, 'Truth and Goodness, Mirrors and Masks: A Sociology of Beauty and the Face', Pt 1, *British Journal of Sociology* 40:4 (December 1989), 607–36, 619.
10. Marsilio Ficino (1433–99), *Commentary on Plato's Symposium on Love*, trans. Sears Jayne (Woodstock, CT: Spring Publications, 1985), V.v, 92. See Erwin Panofsky, *Idea: A Concept in Art Theory*, trans. Joseph J. S. Peake (Columbia, SC: University of South Carolina Press, 1968), 135–6.
11. Ficino, *Commentary*, V.vi, 95.
12. Buoni, *Problemes of Beautie*, 16, 76–7, 73, 31, 19, 12.
13. See Erica Veevers, *Images of Love and Religion: Queen Henrietta Maria and Court Entertainments* (Cambridge: Cambridge University Press, 1989), 16–17.
14. Inigo Jones, *Tempe Restored: A Masque* (1631), fol. C3r, unlineated. EEBO. 14 November 2007. http://eebo.chadwyck.com. Veevers cites this masque, *Images of Love*, 174.
15. See Veevers, *Images of Love*, 172–9.
16. John Calvin, *Commentaries on the Catholic Epistles*, trans. and ed. John Owen (Grand Rapids, MI: Christian Classics Ethereal Library), n.p. 9 October 2006. www.ccel.org.
17. Revelation describes a 'great Whore', sitting on a seven-headed beast, 'arayed in purple and scarlet colour, and decked with gold, and precious stones and pearles, having her golden cup in her hand, full of abominations and filthinesse of her fornication'. She will ultimately be made 'desolate, and naked', her flesh eaten and burned. See Revelation 17.1–4, 16. For a discussion of competing visual and textual representations of the 'Whore of Babylon' in this era, see Laura Lunger Knoppers, '"The Antichrist, the Babilon, the Great Dragon": Oliver Cromwell, Andrew Marvell, and the Apocalyptic Monstrous', *Monstrous Bodies/Political Monstrosities in Early Modern Europe* (Ithaca, NY, and London: Cornell University Press, 2004), 93–123.
18. Calvin, *Institution*, 3.10.3.
19. Edmund Spenser, *The Faerie Queene*, ed. A. C. Hamilton (London and New York: Longman, 1997), 2.12.42–87. See Stephen Greenblatt, *Renaissance Self-fashioning: From More to Shakespeare* (Chicago and London: University of Chicago Press, 1980), 170–89.
20. Phillip Stubbes, *Anatomy of the Abuses in England in Shakespeare's Youth* (1583), ed. Frederick J. Furnival (London: Trubner, 1877–79), Pt 1, 66.
21. Stubbes, *Anatomy of the Abuses*, 79–80.
22. Francis Lenton, 'Queene Esters Haliluiahs and Hamans Madrigalls Expressed and Illustrated in a Sacred Poem' (1638), BL Add MS 34805. See Veevers, *Images of Love*, 82.
23. Francis Quarles, *Hadassa, or The History of Queene Ester* (1621), fols E3v–E4r, unlineated.
24. Jo Carruthers discusses Quarles's sexualised representation of Esther, including his misogynist representation of her beauty as a sign of sin, in *Esther through the Centuries* (Oxford: Blackwell, 2008), 113–14.

25. Thomas Cooper, *The Churches Deliverance, containing Meditations and Short Notes uppon the Booke of Hester* (1609), 68–9. EEBO. 12 April 2006. http://eebo.chadwyck.com.
26. Thomas Hall, *Comarum Akosmia: The Loathsomenesse of Long Haire* (1654), 71.
27. Hall, *The Loathsomenesse of Long Haire*, 40. Richard Moore describes Hall as wearing his hair 'very short, scarce to cover his ears; his Face pale, and somewhat long', *Ho thesaurus en ostrakinois: A Pearl in an Oyster-shel* (1675), 44. EEBO. 19 April 2006. http://eebo.chadwyck.com. See entry for Hall in *ODNB*.
28. Felicity A. Nussbaum argues in relation to the eighteenth century that femaleness 'aligns itself with disfigurement', *The Limits of the Human: Fictions of Anomaly, Race, and Gender in the long Eighteenth Century* (Cambridge: Cambridge University Press, 2003), 25.
29. Aristotle, *Generation of Animals*, trans. A. L. Peck (Cambridge, MA: Harvard University Press; London: Heinemann, 1953), 175.
30. Anon., *The Female Monster, or The Second Part of The World turn'd Topsy Turvey: A Satyr* (1705), 7, 10. Eighteenth Century Collections Online. 13 June 2007. http://galenet.galegroup.com.
31. Gideon Harvey, *Morbus Anglicus: or The Anatomy of Consumptions* (1666), 54–6. EEBO. 14 November 2006. http://eebo.chadwyck.com.
32. M.R., *The Mothers Counsell, or Live within Compasse* (1631), 32, 27. EEBO. 13 April 2006. http://eebo.chadwyck.com. Many thanks to Jacqueline Pearson for drawing my attention to this work.
33. Anon., *The Wonders of the Female World, or A General History of Women* (1682), 13, 11, 12. EEBO. 6 March 2006. http://eebo.chadwyck.com.
34. John Hagthorpe, 'Malum et finis rerum: or Sinne and Vertue', *Visiones rerum* (1623), ll. 29–42. Literature Online. 15 October 2004. http://lion.chadwyck.co.uk.
35. Montaigne, 'On Physiognomy', *Complete Essays*, 1199.
36. Francis Barker states that 'The woman is allotted to the place of the body outside discourse, and therefore also outside the pertinent domain of legitimate subjecthood,' *The Tremulous Private Body: Essays on Subjection* (London: Methuen, 1984), 100. Schoenfeldt notes that women were believed in this era to be less capable of self-discipline than were men, *Bodies and Selves*, 36.
37. Margaret Cavendish, *The Publick Wooing* (1662), 3.25. Literature Online. 19 April 2007. http://lion.chadwyck.co.uk.
38. Evelyn, *Numismata*, 308–9.
39. Montaigne, 'On Physiognomy', *Complete Essays*, 1198–9.
40. François Rabelais, *Gargantua and Pantagruel*, trans. Sir Thomas Urquhart and Pierre le Motteux, intro. Terence Cave (London: David Campbell, 1994), 19.
41. Plato, *Symposium*, *The Collected Dialogues*, eds Edith Hamilton and Huntington Carins, trans. Michael Joyce (Princeton, NJ: Princeton University Press, 1961), 566.
42. Rabelais, *Gargantua and Pantagruel*, 19.
43. Desiderius Erasmus, 'The *Sileni* of Alcibiades', *Thomas More: Utopia, with Erasmus's 'The Sileni of Alcibiades'* ed. and trans. David Wooton (Indianapolis, IN: Hackett, 1999), 177–8, 181, 175, 185.
44. Desiderius Erasmus, *The Praise of Folly*, ed. Clarence H. Miller (New Haven, CT: Yale University Press, 1979), 29.
45. Rabelais, *Gargantua and Pantagruel*, 19.

46. Fuller, *Holy State*, 192.
47. Shakespeare, *Othello*, 1.2.70, 1.3.290–1, 3.3.267, 3.3.389–91, 3.3.456, 4.1.266, 4.1.275.
48. Caliban, 'not honoured with/A human shape', is also seen by Prospero and Miranda as being incapable of 'any print of goodness' because of his 'vile race', a position which *The Tempest* at least partially questions, for instance in its inclusion of his poetic celebration of the island. William Shakespeare, *The Tempest*, ed. Frank Kermode, The Arden Shakespeare (London and New York: Routledge, 1954), 1.2.283–4, 354, 360, 3.2.133–41. Mark Thornton Burnett explores the play's gradual 'dismantling of Caliban's "monstrosity"', arguing that *The Tempest* reveals that '"monsters" are inevitably socially and culturally determined', *Constructing 'Monsters' in Shakespearean Drama and Early Modern Culture* (Basingstoke and New York: Palgrave Macmillan, 2002), 148–53.
49. Middleton and Rowley, *The Changeling*, 5.3.196.
50. William Shakespeare, *The Tragedy of King Richard III*, ed. John Jowett (Oxford: Oxford University Press, 2000), 1.2.48, 55. Further references will be marked in the main text.
51. See, for example, Linda Charnes, *Notorious Identity: Materializing the Subject in Shakespeare* (Cambridge, MA: Harvard University Press, 1993), 28–69; Michael Torrey, '"The plain devil and dissembling looks"', 139–53. Burnett notes that Richard manipulates 'physical difference . . . making "monstrosity" a quality that is performed rather than inherently possessed'. He observes Richard's 'improvization of a range of identities. . . . Richard revels in propagating varieties of a shifting self,' *Constructing 'Monsters'*, 84–6.
52. Hamlet observes the manner in which a natural blemish is associated at a popular level with evil: 'oft it chances in particular men/That for some vicious mole of nature in them,/As in their birth, wherein they are not guilty/. . . Carrying, I say, the stamp of defect,/Being Nature's livery or Fortune's star,/His virtues else, be they as pure as grace,/As infinite as man may undergo,/Shall in the general censure take corruption/From that particular fault,' *Hamlet*, 1.4.23–36.
53. Charnes, *Notorious Identity*, 32.
54. Taylor, *Sources of the Self*, 155.
55. Torrey, '"The plain devil and dissembling looks"', 126.
56. See Porter, *Windows of the Soul*, 168–71.
57. Buoni, *Problemes of Beautie*, 53.
58. M.R., *The Mothers Counsell*, 18–19.
59. See Burnett, *Constructing 'Monsters'*, 66, 86.
60. See Marjorie Garber, *Shakespeare's Ghost Writers: Literature as Uncanny Causality* (New York and London: Methuen, 1987), 39; Charnes, *Notorious Identity*, 51–2; Torrey, '"The plain devil and dissembling looks"', 146–7; Burnett, *Constructing 'Monsters'*, 73–4.
61. Descartes, *Meditations on First Philosophy* (1641), *Philosophical Essays and Correspondence*, 112. This passage is cited in Taylor, *Sources of the Self*, 145.
62. Modern subjectivity, argues Taylor, is grounded in the 'disengaged reason', where 'we demystify the cosmos as a setter of ends by grasping it mechanistically and functionally as a domain of possible means', *Sources of the Self*, 149.

63. Middleton and Rowley, *The Changeling*, 1.1.77, 5.3.196. All further references will be marked in the main text.
64. Montaigne, 'On Physiognomy', *Complete Essays*, 1198.
65. See for example Deborah B. Burks, '"I'll want my will else": *The Changeling* and Women's Complicity with their Rapists', *ELH* 62:4 (1995), 759–90; Karen Armstrong, 'Possets, Pills and Poisons: Physicking the Female Body in Early Seventeenth-Century Drama', *Cahiers Elisabethains: Late Medieval and Renaissance Studies* 61 (2002), 43–56.
66. Bruce Boehrer, '"Alsemero's closet": Privacy and Interiority in *The Changeling*', *Journal of English and Germanic Philology* 96:3 (1997), n.p. 8 October 2007. http://galenet.galegroup.com.
67. Montaigne, 'On Physiognomy', *Complete Essays*, 1198.
68. See Sarah Eaton, 'Beatrice-Joanna and the Rhetoric of Love', *Staging the Renaissance: Reinterpretations of Elizabethan and Jacobean Drama*, eds David Scott Kastan and Peter Stallybrass (New York: Routledge, 1991), 275–89.
69. Burks, '"I'll want my will else"', 759–90, 779.
70. Burks, '"I'll want my will else"', 779.
71. Armstrong, 'Possets, Pills and Poisons', 43–56, 44.
72. Arthur L. Little, '"Transshaped" Women: Virginity and Hysteria in *The Changeling*', *Madness in Drama*, ed. James Redmond (Cambridge: Cambridge University Press, 1993), 19–42, 22.
73. Little, '"Transshaped" Women', 34.
74. The *OED* cites 1575 as the earliest use of 'visor' in the sense of 'a face or countenance; an outward aspect or appearance', 'visor' 4.
75. Eaton, 'Beatrice-Joanna and the Rhetoric of Love', 281.
76. See Eaton, 'Beatrice-Joanna and the Rhetoric of Love', 282.
77. Little, '"Transshaped" Women', 23; Eaton, 'Beatrice-Joanna and the Rhetoric of Love', 277.
78. Boehrer, '"Alsemero's closet"', n.p.
79. Maurizio Calbi notes the 'intimate connection' between De Flores's appearance and his social fall, stating that 'De Flores's deformed "looks" are anything but "natural",' *Approximate Bodies: Gender and Power in Early Modern Drama and Anatomy* (London: Routledge, 2005), 41.
80. Montaigne, 'On Physiognomy', *Complete Essays*, 1198.
81. Fuller, *Holy State*, 191–2.
82. Felicity Rosslyn, 'Villainy, Virtue and Projection', *Cambridge Quarterly* 30:1 (2001), 1–17, 7.
83. Roberta Barker and David Nicol, 'Does Beatrice-Joanna have a Subtext? *The Changeling* on the London stage', *EMLS* 10:1 (2004), 1–43.
84. Bacon, 'Of Deformity', 191.
85. Calbi, *Approximate Bodies*, 46–7, 34.
86. Stachniewski discusses the Calvinist context of the play in 'Calvinist Psychology', *Three Jacobean Revenge Tragedies*, 226–47.
87. See Andrew Stott, 'Tiresias and the Basilisk: Vision and Madness in Middleton and Rowley's *The Changeling*', *Revista alicantina de estudios ingleses* 12 (1999), 165–79.

88. William Hay, *Deformity: An Essay* (1754), 3, 4. Eighteenth Century Collections Online. 7 July 2006. http://galenet.galegroup.com. Further references will be given in the main text.
89. Pender, 'In the Bodyshop', 95–126, 115. Felicity Nussbaum states that Hay 'conceptualises disability as an identity for the first time', 'Feminotopias: The Pleasures of "Deformity" in Mid-Eighteenth-Century England', *The Body and Physical Difference: Discourses of Disability*, eds David T. Mitchell and Sharon L. Snyder (Ann Arbor, MI: University of Michigan Press, 1997), 161–73, 168. Deutsch also argues that Hay is 'arguably the first writer in the history of English literature to conceptualise and articulate physical disability as a personal identity'. 'The Body's Moments', 11–25, 11.
90. See Kathleen James-Cavan, '"[A]ll in me is nature": The Values of Deformity in William Hay's *Deformity: An Essay*', *Prose Studies* 27: 1–2 (April–August 2005), 27–38, 27.
91. Deutsch, 'The Body's Moments', 14.
92. James-Cavan, '"[A]ll in me is nature"', 33.
93. Scott, *Agreeable Ugliness*, 126. Robert W. Jones discusses the relationship between ugliness and virtue in *Agreeable Ugliness* in 'Obedient Faces: The Virtue of Deformity in Sarah Scott's Fiction', *'Defects'*, 280–302.
94. See William Hogarth, *The Analysis of Beauty* (1753), ed. Ronald Paulson (New Haven, CT: Yale University Press, 1997), 50–9. James-Cavan comments that Hay's 'rhetorical strategies of undermining such binaries as "great" and "small", "crooked" and "upright", and associating beauty with curvature combine to fracture the connections between body and character', '"[A]ll in me is nature"', 29.
95. Deutsch, 'The Body's Moments', 17.
96. James-Cavan notes that Hay '[reduces] the body to an artifact', '"[A]ll in me is nature"', 28.

4 'Sight of her is a vomit'

1. Aphra Behn, *The Luckey Chance, or An Alderman's bargain* (1687), unlineated. EEBO. 12 April 2006. http://eebo.chadwyck.com.
2. Mary Russo argues that 'subjectivity as it has been understood in the West requires the image of the grotesque body', noting that 'the category of the female grotesque is crucial to identity formation for both men and women as a space of risk and abjection', *The Female Grotesque: Risk, Excess and Modernity* (London and New York: Routledge, 1994), 12.
3. Kristeva, *Powers of Horror*, 4, 102, 3, 210.
4. Judith Butler, *Bodies that Matter: On the Discursive Limits of 'Sex'* (London: Routledge, 1993), 3. Peter Stallybrass and Allon White discuss similar processes in relation to the 'high/low opposition' that they identify as a fundamental structuring principle in European cultures. See *The Politics and Poetics of Transgression* (Ithaca, NY: Cornell University Press, 1986), 3–5.
5. Kristeva discusses the masculine insecurity displayed in the identification of women as 'defiling witches': 'the masculine, apparently victorious, confesses through its very

relentlessness against the other, the feminine, that it is threatened by an asymmetrical, irrational, wily, uncontrollable power', *Powers of Horror*, 70.
6. R. Grant Williams, 'Disfiguring the Body of Knowledge: Anatomical Discourse and Robert Burton's *The Anatomy of Melancholy*', *ELH* 68:3 (2001), 593–613.
7. Webster, *The Duchess of Malfi*, 2.2.9–10.
8. See Bettella, *Ugly Woman*, 17–18.
9. Matthew of Vendome, *Ars versificatoria*, trans. Aubrey E. Galyon (Ames, IA: Iowa State University Press, 1980), 57, 44.
10. Bakhtin, *Rabelais and his World*, 320.
11. Matthew of Vendome, *Ars versificatoria*, 44.
12. Spenser, *The Faerie Queene*, 1.8.49, 46.
13. See Clayton, *Leonardo da Vinci*, 90–3.
14. Samuel Wesley, 'On a Discourteous Damsel that call'd the Right Worshipful Author – (an 't please ye!) Sawcy Puppy' (1685), *Maggots, or Poems on Several Subjects, never before Handled by a Schollar* (1685), ll. 1–2. EEBO. 26 October 2007. http://eebo.chadwyck.com.
15. See *OED*, 'slut' 1a, 2a.
16. George Villiers, second Duke of Buckingham, *A Character of an Ugly Woman* (1678), *Miscellaneous Works, Written by his Grace, George, late Duke of Buckingham* (1704), 24–8. Eighteenth Century Collections Online. 26 October 2007. http://galenet.galegroup.com.
17. See Heather Dubrow, *Echoes of Desire: English Petrarchanism and its Counterdiscourses* (Ithaca, NY, and London: Cornell University Press, 1995), 175–6; Bettella, *Ugly Woman*, 114–23.
18. Donne, 'The Comparison', ll. 7–8, 6.
19. See Dubrow, *Echoes of Desire*, 238, 242–3.
20. Donne, 'The Comparison', l. 54. See Dubrow, *Echoes of Desire*, 243.
21. Arthur Hildersam, *CLII Lectures on Psalm LI* (1635), 659. EEBO. 15 November 2007. http://eebo.chadwyck.com.
22. Chapman, *Gentleman Usher*, fol. I2v.
23. Donne, 'The Comparison', ll. 19–21.
24. Edmund Prestwich, 'On an old ill-favoured Woman, become a young Lover', *Hippolitus, translated out of Seneca* (1651), 61–3, unlineated. EEBO. 26 October 2007. http://eebo.chadwyck.com.
25. James Shirley, 'To the Proud M.', *Poems* (1646), l. 3.
26. Hugh Crompton, 'Deformity', 'Poems' (1657), l. 15. Literature Online. 26 October 2007. http://lion.chadwyck.co.uk.
27. Peter Stallybrass, 'Patriarchal Territories: The Body Enclosed', *Rewriting the Renaissance: The Discourses of Sexual Difference in Early Modern Europe*, eds Margaret W. Ferguson, Maureen Quilligan and Nancy J. Vickers (Chicago and London: University of Chicago Press, 1986), 123–42, 125. See also Norbert Elias, *The Civilizing Process: The History of Manners*, trans. Edmund Jephcott (publ. as *Über den Prozess der Zivilisation*, 1939; this edn Oxford: Blackwell, 1978), Vol. 1, 138–9.
28. Paster, *The Body Embarrassed*, 23–63.

29. John Johnstone, *An History of the Wonderful Things of Nature* (1657), anonymously translated from Latin, 328. EEBO. 26 October 2007. http://eebo.chadwyck.com. The *ODNB* entry for Johnstone notes the esteem in which his works were held in seventeenth-century England.
30. Villiers, *Character of an Ugly Woman*, 26.
31. Anon., *The Olde Bride, or The Gilded Beauty* (c. 1635), unlineated. EEBO. 26 October 2007. http://eebo.chadwyck.com.
32. Anon., *The Merry Dutch Miller: And New Invented Windmill* (1672), n.p. EEBO. 12 March 2006. http://eebo.chadwyck.com.
33. John Skelton, *Elynour Rummynge* (c. 1517), *John Skelton: The Complete English Poems*, ed. John Scattergood (Harmondsworth: Penguin, 1983), ll. 22–3, 29–30, 351, 370, 373–4.
34. Herrick, 'Upon a cheap Laundresse' (H-474), ll. 1–2; 'Upon Dol' (H-1078), ll. 1–2; 'Upon Shopter' (H-1107), ll. 1–2.
35. See Mark Breitenberg, *Anxious Masculinity in Early Modern England* (Cambridge: Cambridge University Press, 1996), 38.
36. Hall, *The Loathsomenesse of Long Haire*, fol. A3v.
37. Helkiah Crooke, *Mikrokosmographia: A Description of the Body of Man* (1615), 70. EEBO. 13 December 2006. http://eebo.chadwyck.com.
38. Donne, 'The Comparison', ll. 43–4; Villiers, *Character of an Ugly Woman*, 25.
39. See Bettella, *Ugly Woman*, 158–64; Elias, *Civilizing Process*, 57–9. For a discussion of the class-specific nature of medieval descriptions of ugliness in relation to scabies see Specht, 'The Beautiful, the Handsome and the Ugly', 129–46.
40. Skelton, *Elynour Rummynge*, ll. 14–16, 139–41.
41. See Herrick's 'Upon Glasco' (H-129), 'Upon Bridget' (H-419), 'Upon One who said She was always Young' (H-462), 'Upon Ursley' (H-543), 'Of Horne a Comb-maker' (H-595), 'Upon Franck' (H-728), 'To Women, to hide their Teeth, if they be Rotten or Rusty' (H-738), 'Upon Mudge' (H-965) and 'Upon Gorgonius' (H-1066). Cockayne notes the widespread tooth decay in early modern England, *Hubbub*, 23.
42. Francis Lenton, *Lentons Leisures Described, in Divers Moderne Characters* (1636), fols. C3r–v, C4v. EEBO. 12 November 2007. http://eebo.chadwyck.com.
43. Samuel Sheppard, 'An old Woman Letcherous', *Epigrams Theological, Philosophical, and Romantick* (1651), ll. 5–6. Literature Online. 21 July 2006. http://lion.chadwyck.co.uk; Prestwich, 'On an old Ill-favoured Woman', 64.
44. Ben Jonson, *Volpone* (1606, publ. 1607), *Ben Jonson's Plays and Masques*, ed. Richard Harp (New York and London: Norton, 2001), 1.5.105, 3.4.8–9, 64; Prestwich, 'On an old Ill-favoured Woman', 64–5.
45. Wesley, 'On a Discourteous Damsel', ll. 6–7. See also Donne, 'The Comparison', l. 51.
46. Johnstone, *An History of the Wonderful Things of Nature*, 328.
47. Crooke, *Mikrokosmographia*, 260, 291.
48. Herrick, 'To Women, to hide their Teeth, if they be Rotten or Rusty' (H-738), ll. 1–4.
49. Prestwich, 'On an old Ill-favoured Woman', 63.
50. Thomas Jordan, 'To a Black-moor that had married a Deformed Spanish Woman, and was jealous of an English Gentleman', *The Muses Melody* (c. 1680), n.p., unlineated. EEBO. 1 February 2006. http://eebo.chadwyck.com.

51. See Healy, *Fictions of Disease*, 130–2, 149.
52. Numbers 12.1–10; 2 Chronicles 26.19–20.
53. Hildersam, *CLII Lectures*, 670.
54. Hobbes, *Leviathan*, 519. Miles Hogarde, *The Displaying of the Protestantes* (1556), 61; cited in Knott, *Discourses of Martyrdom*, 79.
55. Calvin, *Institution*, 1.1.3. See Healy, *Fictions of Disease*, 135.
56. Kristeva, *Powers of Horror*, 101.
57. Hildersam, *CLII Lectures*, 659.
58. Katherine Sutton, *A Christian Womans Experiences of the Glorious Working of Gods Free Grace* (1663), 33. EEBO. 12 December 2007. http://eebo.chadwyck.com. Many thanks to Jacqueline Pearson for drawing my attention to this reference.
59. William Cowper, *Pathmos: or A Commentary on the Revelation of Saint John* (1619), 317. EEBO. 26 October 2007 http://eebo.chadwyck.com.
60. Robert Bolton, *Certaine Devout Prayers of Mr. Bolton upon Solemne Occasions* (1638), 107. EEBO. 13 December 2006. http://eebo.chadwyck.com.
61. Robert Heath, 'To Megaera', *Clarastella* (1650), ll. 1–2. Literature Online. 1 March 2006. http://lion.chadwyck.co.uk.
62. Crompton, 'Deformity', ll. 21–2, 16.
63. Calbi argues that anxiety induced by the destabilising effect of the abject activates violence, *Approximate Bodies*, 81.
64. John Ford, *Tis Pity She's a Whore* (c. 1629–33), *English Renaissance Drama: A Norton Anthology*, eds David Bevington et al. (New York and London: Norton, 2002), 4.3.229, 234–6.
65. Thomas Randolph, 'Upon a very Deformed Gentlewoman, but of a Voice Incomparable Sweet', *Poems* (1652), ll. 69, 75. Literature Online. 26 July 2006. http://lion.chadwyck.co.uk.
66. Thomas Freeman, 'In Miluum', *Rubbe and A Great Cast* (1614), ll. 2, 8. Literature Online. 5 April 2006. http://lion.chadwyck.co.uk.
67. Shirley, 'To the proud M.', ll. 14–15, 17, 21–2.
68. See Georges Minois, *History of Old Age: From Antiquity to the Renaissance*, trans. Sarah Hanbury Tenison (Cambridge: Polity Press, 1989), 272–3; Thane, *Old Age in English History*, 38; Alice Trobiner, 'Old Age in Tudor–Stuart Broadside Ballads', *Folklore* 102:2 (1991), 149–74, 152.
69. Dekker, Ford and Rowley, *The Witch of Edmonton*, 2.1.100–1, 4.1.121, 2.1.111.
70. N.H., *The Ladies Dictionary*, 57.
71. Herrick, 'To a Gentlewoman, objecting to him his Gray Haires' (H-164A), l.1. See also 'Upon his Gray Haires' (H-527), in which Herrick concedes that his ageing body is ugly.
72. See for instance N.H., *The Ladies Dictionary*, 49.
73. *The Oxford Dictionary of English Proverbs*, 3rd edn, revised F. P. Wilson (Oxford: 1970); cited in Thane, *Old Age in English History*, 44, see also 57–8; Trobiner, 'Old Age in Tudor–Stuart Broadside Ballads', 154. In *Volpone*, Mosca comments of Corbaccio: 'Bountiful bones! What horrid strange offense/Did he commit 'gainst nature, in his youth,/Worthy this age?' (4.6.89–91).
74. William Harrison and Raphael Holinshed, *The First and Second Volumes of Chronicles*

(1587), 115. EEBO. 26 March 2006. http://eebo.chadwyck.com. Cockayne cites this reference in *Hubbub*, 33. Erin J. Campbell discusses the manner in which early modern women were seen to age more quickly than men in '"Unenduring" Beauty: Gender and Old Age in Early Modern Art and Aesthetics', *Growing Old in Early Modern Europe: Cultural Representations*, ed. Erin J. Campbell (Aldershot: Ashgate 2006), 157–9.

75. Minois, *History of Old Age*, 249. See also Trobiner, 'Old Age in Tudor–Stuart Broadside Ballads', 149–74.
76. Ford, *Tis Pity*, 4.3.233–4.
77. Minois, *History of Old Age*, 293.
78. Leonardo da Vinci, *Treatise on Painting*, Vol. 1, 106. Old men, on the other hand, 'should be represented with languid, slow movements', *Treatise on Painting*, Vol. 1, 106.
79. Middleton and Rowley, *The Changeling*, 4.2.54–5.
80. Shakespeare, *The Tempest*, 1.2.258–9. Richard Head and Francis Kirkman, *The English Rogue*, Pt 4 (1671), 223. Literature Online. 3 January 2006. http://lion.chadwyck.co.uk. To be old in early modern England, particularly for a woman, usually meant to be poor. See Lynn Botelho and Pat Thane (eds), *Women and Ageing in British Society since 1500* (Harlow: Longman, 2001), 14, 23.
81. John Hall, 'To an Old Wife talking to him', *Poems* (1646–47), l. 1. Literature Online. 26 October 2007. http://lion.chadwyck.co.uk.
82. *OED*, 'beldam' 3.
83. Campbell discusses this painting in '"Unenduring" Beauty', 153–67.
84. See Allison Levy (ed.), *Widowhood and Visual Culture in Early Modern Europe* (Aldershot: Ashgate, 2003), 1–5.
85. See Sandra Cavallo and Lyndan Warner (eds), *Widowhood in Medieval and Early Modern Europe* (London: Longman, 1999), 1–15. Cavallo and Warner nevertheless emphasise the constraints as well as the opportunities afforded by the status of widow.
86. Kristeva, *Powers of Horror*, 4.
87. George Wither, 'Looke well, I pray, upon this Beldame here', *A Collection of Emblems, Ancient and Moderne* (1635), Bk 4, 229. EEBO. 7 November 2006. http://eebo.chadwyck.com.
88. Webster, *The Duchess of Malfi*, 2.1.24–7.
89. Richard Leigh, 'On an old Beldame, washing her Face', *Poems upon Several Occasions* (1675), 119, unlineated. EEBO. 7 November 2006. http://eebo.chadwyck.com.
90. Minois, *History of Old Age*, 272–3.
91. Anon., *The Olde Bride*, unlineated.
92. Kristeva describes the corpse as 'the utmost of abjection. It is death infecting life. Abject,' *Powers of Horror*, 4.
93. Prestwich, 'On an old Ill-favoured Woman', 63.
94. See Nussbaum, *Limits of the Human*, 32.
95. Anon., *The Olde Bride*, unlineated.
96. John Cleveland, 'A Young Man to an Old Woman courting him', *The Character of a London-Diurnall* (1647), 21–3, unlineated. EEBO. 7 November 2006. http://eebo.chadwyck.com.

97. See Dubrow, *Echoes of Desire*, 174–5, 234. As Dubrow notes, 'these poems are also concerned to elide those distinctions', 175.
98. John Donne, 'The Autumnall', ll. 11–12, 3, 22, 25.
99. Dubrow discusses the 'unsettling' nature of Donne's 'ugly beauty' poems, including 'The Autumnall', *Echoes of Desire*, 233–44.
100. Donne, 'The Autumnall', ll. 31–2, 9–10, 37–42.
101. Donne, 'The Autumnall', ll. 13–14, 43. See Dubrow, *Echoes of Desire*, 234–5.
102. Thomas Middleton, *Women beware Women* (c. 1620–24), *English Renaissance Drama*, 4.1.247–51.
103. Donne, 'The Comparison', ll. 25–6.
104. John Collop, 'The Vanity of Courtship devotion to Relicks asserted and confuted', *The Poems of John Collop*, ed. Conrad Hilberry (Madison, WI: University of Wisconsin Press, 1962), ll. 121–4.
105. Calbi discusses the failure of 'the Other' to be 'at a safe distance' in *Approximate Bodies*, 80.
106. Burton, *Anatomy*, 3.2.3.
107. Ben Jonson, 'Epistle: To my Lady Covell', *The Workes* (1640), ll. 7–11. Literature Online. 1 October 2007. http://lion.chadwyck.co.uk.
108. Ben Jonson, 'My Picture left in Scotland' (1619), ll. 16–17, *Ben Jonson and the Cavalier Poets*, ed. Hugh Maclean (New York and London: Norton, 1974), 57.
109. Elena Levy-Navarro presents a polemical reading of Jonson's work in relation to obesity, insisting that he 'resists the bodily aesthetic that privileged the thin body over the fat one', *The Culture of Obesity in Early and Late Modernity: Body Image in Shakespeare, Jonson, Middleton, and Skelton* (New York and Basingstoke: Palgrave Macmillan, 2008), 175.
110. N.H., *The Ladies Dictionary*, 62.
111. See Porter, *Flesh in the Age of Reason*, 234.
112. John Fletcher, *Bonduca, or The British Heroine, A Tragedy* (1696), 2.1, unlineated. EEBO. 7 November 2007. http://eebo.chadwyck.com.
113. See *OED*, 'fat' *a* and *n* 2, 3a, 10a.
114. Sanderson, *Graphice*, 37.
115. Bartholin, *Bartholinus Anatomy*, 7; George Keith, *The Arguments of the Quakers* (1698), 52–3.
116. Bartholin, *Bartholinus Anatomy*, 7.
117. Jeamson, *Artificiall Embellishments*, 65–6.
118. N.H., *The Ladies Dictionary*, 61.
119. William Shakespeare, *Romeo and Juliet*, ed. Brian Gibbons, The Arden Shakespeare (London and New York: Methuen, 1980), 5.1.40–1, 69–70.
120. Bartholin, *Bartholinus Anatomy*, 14.
121. Burton, *Anatomy*, 3.2.3.
122. Firenzuola, *On the Beauty of Women*, 40.
123. Herrick, 'The Definition of Beauty' (H-102), ll. 1–2.
124. Laurence Twyne, *The Patterne of Painefull Adventures* (c. 1594), 40. EEBO. 7 November 2007. http://eebo.chadwyck.com.

125. Firenzuola, *On the Beauty of Women*, 49.
126. See John Lamport, *A Direct Method of Ordering and Curing People of that Loathsome Disease, the Small-pox* (1685), 5. EEBO. 6 November 2005. http://eebo.chadwyck.com.
127. Richard Baxter, *A Christian Directory, or A Summ of Practical Theology and Cases of Conscience directing Christians how to use their Knowledge and Faith, how to improve all Helps and Means, and to perform all Duties, how to overcome Temptations, and to escape or mortify every Sin* (1673), 373. EEBO. 7 November 2007. http://eebo.chadwyck.com.
128. See Rhodes, *Elizabethan Grotesque*, 117–20.
129. William Shakespeare, *The Second Part of King Henry IV*, ed. A. R. Humphreys, The Arden Shakespeare (London: Methuen, 1966), 4.1.54–7, 65–6.
130. Healy, *Fictions of Disease*, 188–228. See also Schoenfeldt, *Bodies and Selves*, 15.
131. N.H., *The Ladies Dictionary*, 63.
132. Samuel Rowlands, 'The Devil's Health-drinker', *The Knave of Clubbs* (1611), ll. 37–41. Literature Online. 20 August 2007. http://lion.chadwyck.co.uk.
133. Shakespeare, *1 Henry IV*, 2.4.433–5, 2.4.237, 1.2.2. The *OED* refers to 'slow-witted' and 'indolent' as potential meanings for 'fat' *a* and *n* 2, 11.
134. N.H., *The Ladies Dictionary*, 62.
135. John Norden, *The Labyrinth of Man's Life* (1614), ll. 1580–3, 1614, 1605. Literature Online. 20 August 2007. http://lion.chadwyck.co.uk.
136. John Reynolds, *The Triumph of God's Revenge*, Bk 2 (1622, this edn 1635), 106, 112, 121, 123, 125.
137. Anon., 'Aldobrandino, a fat Cardinal' (1656), *Choyce Drollery: Songs and Sonnets*, eds Robert Pollard and John Sweeting (1656), 17. EEBO. 26 March 2007. http://eebo.chadwyck.com.
138. Wright, *Passions of the Minde*, 129.
139. Shakespeare, *1 Henry IV*, 3.3.148–50, 160–1.
140. *2 Henry IV*, 5.5.52.
141. Milton, *Paradise Lost*, Bk 6, ll. 551–2. Healy discusses Milton's 'politics of dietery regimen(t)' in *Fictions of Disease*, 219–23. See also Schoenfeldt, *Bodies and Selves*, 35. The term 'gross' denotes 'vices, errors, faults' (*OED* 4a), potentially referring to that which is opposed to the spiritual or ethereal (*OED* 8c) as well as to the bulky and the coarse (*OED* 1, 13a).
142. Ben Jonson, *Bartholomew Fair* (first performed 1614), *English Renaissance Drama*, 2.5.108–9, 2.2.74, 3.6.32–5. See Patricia Parker, *Literary Fat Ladies: Rhetoric, Gender, Property* (London and New York: Methuen, 1987), 24–6; Margaret Tudeau-Clayton, '"I do not know my selfe": the Topography and Politics of Self-knowledge in Ben Jonson's *Bartholomew Fair*', *Textures of Renaissance Knowledge*, eds Philippa Berry and Margaret Tudeau-Clayton (Manchester and New York: Manchester University Press, 2003), 177–98, 184–5.
143. George Herbert, 'The Size', *The Temple* (1633), *George Herbert: The Complete English Poems*, ed. John Tobin (London: Penguin, 1991), ll. 31–6.
144. Shakespeare, *1 Henry IV*, 2.2.102–3.
145. Shakespeare, *Comedy of Errors*, 3.2.101–2.

146. Jonson, *Bartholomew Fair*, 2.5.77–9, 2.3.121–2, 2.2.52–5.
147. Levy-Navarro notes the tendency of fat bodies in early modern texts to transgress bodily boundaries, *Culture of Obesity*, 84.
148. Bartholin, *Bartholinus Anatomy*, 4.
149. Joubert, *Treatise on Laughter*, 55, 125, 57–60. Rhodes alludes to Joubert's alignment of laughter and obesity in *Elizabethan Grotesque*, 107.
150. Shakespeare, *1 Henry IV*, 2.4.433; *2 Henry IV*, 4.3.20–3. See Parker, *Literary Fat Ladies*, 21–2.
151. Johnstone, *An History of the Wonderful Things of Nature*, 328.
152. N.H., *The Ladies Dictionary*, 62.
153. Shakespeare, *Comedy of Errors*, 3.2.86–154.
154. Breitenberg, *Anxious Masculinity*, 38.
155. See Breitenberg, *Anxious Masculinity*, 47–8.
156. See Juliana Schiesari, *The Gendering of Melancholia: Feminism, Psychoanalysis, and the Symbolics of Loss in Renaissance Literature* (Ithaca, NY, and London: Cornell University Press, 1992), 3–32.
157. Breitenberg, *Anxious Masculinity*, 57, 40, 39.
158. Christopher Tilmouth, 'Burton's "Turning Picture": Argument and Anxiety in *The Anatomy of Melancholy*', *RES* 56:226 (2005), 524–49, 542.
159. Williams, 'Disfiguring the Body of Knowledge', 593–613.
160. Burton, 'Democritus Junior to the Reader', *Anatomy*, 26, 31, 30, 27.
161. Burton, *Anatomy*, 1.2.4.3.
162. Williams, 'Disfiguring the Body of Knowledge', 606.
163. See Breitenberg, *Anxious Masculinity*, 48–9.
164. Burton, *Anatomy*, 1.3.2.4.
165. Schiesari notes Burton's 'fearful identification' with women in this passage, but argues that the situation is 'recuperated, and the potential danger of confronting his own castration is averted' through his identification with Pallas, who turns away from 'feminine sexuality', *The Gendering of Melancholia*, 252. In my reading, however, the 'feminine' refuses to be exorcised in any final manner.
166. Burton, *Anatomy*, 3.2.3.
167. Burton, *Anatomy*, 3.2.3, 3.2.2.2.
168. Burton, *Anatomy*, 3.2.5.3.
169. Burton, *Anatomy*, 3.2.2.3.
170. Burton, *Anatomy*, 3.2.5.3. Harvey nevertheless relates a case of 'amorous consumption' where a lover 'could not master the passion he bore to a Gentlewoman' and refused to part with her corpse that 'stunk like a Carrion, yet scented to him like a Violet', *Morbus Anglicus*, 24.
171. Kristeva, *Powers of Horror*, 4.
172. Burton, *Anatomy*, 3.2.5.3.
173. Burton, *Anatomy*, 3.2.5.3.
174. Burton, *Anatomy*, 2.3.2.
175. Burton, *Anatomy*, 2.3.2.
176. See Schiesari, *The Gendering of Melancholia*, 3–32.
177. Aristotle, *Problems*, trans. W. S. Hett (Cambridge, MA: Harvard University Press;

London: Heinemann, 1937), Vol. 2 of 2, 155. Schiesari notes this passage in *The Gendering of Melancholia*, 6.
178. Burton, *Anatomy*, 1.3.1.2.

5 'To make love to a deformity'

1. Henry King, 'Madam Gabrina, or The Ill-favoured Choice', *Poems*, l. 31.
2. Burton, *Anatomy*, 3.2.2.3.
3. Sir Philip Sidney, *The Countess of Pembroke's Arcadia*, ed. Maurice Evans (London: Penguin, 1977), 77–8.
4. *OED*, 'counterfeit' 1a.
5. Bulwer, *Anthropometamorphosis*, title page.
6. For a discussion of beauty as dependent on nature in this era, see Edward William Tayler, *Nature and Art in Renaissance Literature* (New York: Columbia University Press, 1964), 2–7.
7. Calvin, *Institution*, 1.15.4.
8. Milton, *Paradise Lost*, Bk 2, ll. 650–2, 781–5.
9. Richard Taverner, *Proverbes of Adagies, with Newe Addicions gathered out of the Chiliades of Erasmus* (1539), fols. xliv–xlvr. Cited in Tayler, *Nature and Art*, 180 n.6.
10. Milton, 'Of Education' (1644), *John Milton: Complete English Poems*, ed. Gordon Campbell (London: Dent, 1980), 557.
11. Sidney, *Apology for Poetry*, 114.
12. Sidney, *Apology for Poetry*, 100.
13. See Plotinus, *Enneads*, V.8.1; Panofsky, *Idea*, 27.
14. Sidney, *Arcadia*, 104. I discuss the representation of Parthenia on pp. 178–87.
15. Sidney, *Apology for Poetry*, 110.
16. See Elizabeth Cropper, 'The Beauty of Woman: Problems in the Rhetoric of Renaissance Portraiture', *Rewriting the Renaissance*, 175–90, 176.
17. Cropper, 'The Beauty of Woman', 175–90.
18. Paul A. Welsby (ed.), *The Book of Homilies: Sermons and Society* (Harmondsworth: Penguin, 1970), 61, cited in Drew-Bear, *Painted Faces on the Renaissance Stage*, 18. For a discussion of the destructive female agency associated with the use of cosmetics, see Frances E. Dolan, 'Taking the Pencil out of God's Hand: Art, Nature and the Face-painting Debate in Early Modern England', *PMLA* 108:2 (1993), 224–39.
19. Miso-Spilus, *A Wonder of Wonders: or A Metamorphosis of Fair Faces voluntarily transform'd into Foul Visages, or An Invective against Black-spotted Faces: by a Well-willer to Modest Matrons and Virgins* (1662), 11. EEBO. 6 February 2006. http://eeebo.chadwyck.com.
20. N.H., *The Ladies Dictionary*, 411–12.
21. Jeamson, *Artificiall Embellishments*, 30, 5, 6, fols. A4v–A5r, A6r–v.
22. Dolan discusses Jeamson's text, noting how the author 'builds up his own authority as [women's] savior', leaving 'creativity and power in the hands of men', 'Taking the Pencil out of God's Hand', 235.
23. Jeamson, *Artificiall Embellishments*, iii–iv.
24. Anon., *The Merry Dutch Miller*, n.p.

25. Shakespeare, Sonnet 127, l. 6, *The Norton Shakespeare*, 1966.
26. Shirley, 'To a Beautiful Lady', ll. 1–2.
27. Peter Ure, 'The "Deformed Mistress" Theme and the Platonic Convention', *Notes and Queries* 193 (1948), 269–70, 269.
28. See Hilberry (ed.), *Poems of John Collop*; John Donne, 'Elegie II. The Anagram', l. 16; Shakespeare, Sonnet 130, l. 1. For a discussion of Italian anti-Petrarchanism, see Bettella, *Ugly Woman*, 114–23.
29. Bettella, *Ugly Woman*, 128.
30. Bacon, 'Of Beauty', *Essays*, 190.
31. Shakespeare, Sonnet 127, ll. 1–3, *The Norton Shakespeare*, 1966.
32. On the Renaissance paradox, see Bettella, *Ugly Woman*, 81–3; Rosalie L. Colie, *Paradoxia Epidemica: The Renaissance Tradition of Paradox* (Princeton, NJ: Princeton University Press, 1966); J. B. Leishman, *The Monarch of Wit: An Analytical and Comparative Study of the Poetry of John Donne* (London: Hutchinson University Library, 1951, this edn 1965), 77–90; A. E. Malloch, 'The Techniques and Function of the Renaissance Paradox', *Studies in Philology* 53 (1956), 191–203, and Henry Knight Miller, 'The Paradoxical Encomium, with Special Reference to its Vogue in England, 1600–1800', *Modern Philology* 53:3 (February 1956), 145–78. Dubrow outlines the classical origins of 'ugly beauty' poems in *Echoes of Desire*, 165. See also Maria Galli Stampino, 'Bodily Boundaries Represented: the Petrarchan, the Burlesque and Arcimboldo's Example', *Quaderni d'italianistica* 16:1 (Spring 1995), 61–79.
33. Henry King, 'Paradox: That Fruition destroyes Love' , *Poems*, ll. 1–2.
34. Evelyn M. Simpson, *A Study of the Prose Works of John Donne*, 2nd edn (Oxford: 1948), 316.
35. William Shakespeare, *Love's Labours Lost*, ed. H. R. Woudhuysen (London: Arden Shakespeare, 1998), 4.3.249–50.
36. Thomas Hobbes, *The Questions Concerning Liberty, Necessity, and Chance clearly Stated and Debated between Dr Bramhall, Bishop of Derry, and Thomas Hobbes of Malmesbury* (1656). EEBO. 25 March 2007. http://eebo.chadwyck.com. This reference is cited in *OED*, 'paradox' 1a.
37. Shakespeare, *Hamlet*, 3.1.114–15.
38. Dunton (ed.), *Athenian Sport*, 30.
39. John Suckling, 'The Deformed Mistress', *Last Remains* (1659), ll. 13–14, 42. Literature Online. 28 March 2007. http://lion.chadwyck.co.uk.
40. See Dubrow, *Echoes of Desire*, 164–201; Hilberry (ed.), *Poems of John Collop*, 21–3.
41. Herbert of Cherbury, 'Another Sonnet to Black itself', *Occasional Verses* (1665), 39, unlineated. EEBO. 28 March 2007. http://eebo.chadwyck.com.
42. Suckling, 'The Deformed Mistress', ll. 15–16, 24.
43. John Lyly, *Endymion*, ed. David Bevington, The Revels Plays (Manchester and New York: Manchester University Press, 1996), 3.3.55–64.
44. Suckling, 'The Deformed Mistress', ll. 18–20.
45. Sidney, *Arcadia*, 645, 223.
46. Anon., 'In Praise of a Deformed Woman', *Choyce Drollery*, ll. 49–52.
47. King, 'Madam Gabrina', ll. 3–4, 6, 13, 26.

48. Anthony Munday (trans.), 'That it is better to be fowle than fair', *The Defence of Contraries* (1593), 20. EEBO. 12 April 2007. http://eebo.chadwyck.com.
49. Abraham Fleming (trans.), *A Paradoxe, Proving by Reason and Example, that Baldnesse is much better than Bushie Haire, etc., written by that Excellent Philosopher Synesius, Bishop of Thebes* (1579), n.p. EEBO. 3 April 2007. http://eebo.chadwyck.com.
50. Thomas Nashe, *Nashes Lenten Stuffe* (1599), *Works*, Vol. 3, 151–12. This passage is cited in Miller, 'The Paradoxical Encomium', 146–7. See also Stampino, 'Bodily Boundaries Represented', 63.
51. King, 'Madam Gabrina', ll. 31–4.
52. Munday, *Defence of Contraries*, 21–3, 18.
53. Shirley, 'To a Beautiful Lady', l. 8.
54. Munday, *Defence of Contraries*, 22.
55. Kim F. Hall discusses the 'infinitely malleable' application of the term 'black' in the early modern era in *Things of Darkness: Economies of Race and Gender in Early Modern England* (Ithaca, NY, and London: Cornell University Press, 1995), 4–7.
56. Anon., 'That a Black-a-moor Woman is the greatest Beauty; in a Letter to a Lady exceeding Fair' (n.d.), *Athenian Sport*, 103–5.
57. Thomas Jordan, 'A Paradox on his Mistresse, who is Cole Blacke, Blinde, Wrinckled, Crooked and Dumbe', *Poeticall Varieties* (1637), 11, unlineated. EEBO. 28 March 2007. http://eebo.chadwyck.com.
58. Donne, 'The Anagram', ll. 16–18, 19–21.
59. Cropper, 'The Beauty of Woman', 175–90.
60. Dubrow notes that 'ugly beauty' poems 'do not so much ignore or reject Petrarchan rhetoric as appropriate and reinterpret it', *Echoes of Desire*, 172–3. See also Bettella, *Ugly Woman*, 129.
61. Suckling, 'The Deformed Mistress', l. 15; Donne, 'The Comparison', l. 6; Shakespeare, *Comedy of Errors*, 3.2.132–3; John Collop, 'The Praise of a Yellow Skin', *Poems of John Collop*, 112–13.
62. Cousins, 'The Ugly', (1995), 3–6, 5.
63. Cousins, 'The Ugly', (1995), 6.
64. Bakhtin, *Rabelais and his World*, 25–6, 29.
65. Cousins, 'The Ugly', (1995), 6.
66. See Bakhtin, *Rabelais and his World*, 25.
67. Bakhtin mentions the possibility of interaction between classical and grotesque canons in *Rabelais and his World*, 30.
68. For a discussion of the blazon in relation to violence against women, see Nancy Vickers, '"The blazon of sweet beauty's best": Shakespeare's *Lucrece*', *Shakespeare and the Question of Theory*, eds Patricia Parker and Geoffrey Hartman (New York and London: Methuen, 1985), 95–115. See also Bettella, *Ugly Woman*, 91.
69. Donne, 'The Anagram', ll. 1–2.
70. Cousins discusses the manner in which ugliness seems to be 'spreading itself about', 'The Ugly' (1995), 4.
71. See for example Miller, 'The Paradoxical Encomium', 167. Bettella also counters this reading in *Ugly Woman*, 129.
72. King, 'Madam Gabrina', ll. 41–4.

73. Donne, 'The Anagram', ll. 32, 29–31.
74. Jordan, 'A Paradox', 10–11.
75. Anon., 'Upon his Constant Mistresse', *Choyce Drollery*, 99. The poem is an altered version of Aurelian Townshend, *fl.* 1601–43, 'La Boiuinette'.
76. Herbert of Cherbury, 'Sonnet of Black Beauty', *Occasional Verses*, 38, unlineated. 28 March 2007. http://lion.chadwyck.co.uk.
77. Jordan, 'A Paradox', 11–12.
78. See Dubrow, *Echoes of Desire*, 176–7.
79. Dubrow notes that 'ugly beauty' poetry affords the male speaker far greater power and agency than he possesses in conventional Petrarchan descriptions, *Echoes of Desire*, 198. See also Bettella, *Ugly Woman*, 164.
80. Jordan, 'A Paradox', 12; John Collop, 'To Aureola, or the Yellow Skin'd Lady; asking who could love a Fancy' (1656), l. 21, *Poems of John Collop*, 114–15.
81. Edmund Prestwich, 'To Almanna, Why she should marry me', *Hippolitus*, 115–18.
82. Thomas Carew, 'Ingrateful Beauty Threatened' (1640), ll. 7–10, 14, 16, *Ben Jonson and the Cavalier Poets*, 161–2.
83. Dubrow notes the 'Cavalier' tone of some examples of the tradition, *Echoes of Desire*, 164.
84. Herrick, 'No Loathsomnesse in Love' (H-21), ll. 1–4. See also Herrick's 'Love dislikes Nothing' (H-750).
85. Suckling, 'The Deformed Mistress', ll. 7–8.
86. James Shirley, 'One that loved none but deformed Women' (1646). Literature Online. 28 March 2007. http://lion.chadwyck.co.uk; King, 'The Defence', ll. 3–4.
87. King, 'The Defence', ll. 7–10, 11–12, 23–4, 28.
88. Bettella discusses the 'male agenda of narcissistic aggrandizement' in Italian baroque poetry written in praise of unconventional beauty, *Ugly Woman*, 164, 128–64.
89. Raymond A. Anselment notes the feminisation of smallpox in the poetry of this era in *The Realms of Apollo: Literature and Healing in Seventeenth-Century England* (Newark, NJ: University of Delaware Press, London: Associated University Presses, 1994), 199.
90. Scott, *Agreeable Ugliness*, 3.
91. See Raymond A. Anselment, 'Smallpox in Seventeenth-Century English Literature: Reality and the Metamorphosis of Wit', *Medical History* 33 (1989), 72–95, especially 72–86. See also Anselment, *The Realms of Apollo*, 172–212.
92. Margaret Cavendish, *Wits Cabal* Pt 1 (1662), 5.35, unlineated. Literature Online. 5 November 2005. http://lion.chadwyck.co.uk.
93. Thomas Sydenham, *The Compleat Method of Curing almost all Diseases, to which is added an Exact Description of their Several Symptoms. Written in Latin by Dr Thomas Sydenham, and now faithfully Englished* (1694), 32–3. EEBO. 5 November 2005. http://eebo.chadwyck.com.
94. Charles Creighton, *A History of Epidemics in Britain* (1891–94) (repr. New York: Barnes & Noble, 1965), Vol. 2, 453–6. Cited in Anselment, 'Smallpox in Seventeenth-Century Literature', 81.
95. Ben Jonson, 'An Epigram. To the Small Poxe', *The Workes*, l. 14.
96. Richard Corbett, 'Upon the Death of the Lady Haddington dying of the Small Pox', *Certain Elegant Poems* (1647), ll. 59–62, 63. Literature Online. 5 November 2005.

http://lion.chadwyck.co.uk. Sydenham describes the manner in which the pocks 'cast forth a Yellowish Juice, in colour not unlike a Honeycomb'. He is particularly horrified by the fact that the disfigurement caused by the disease continues after death, when the pocks remain 'red and high', *Compleat Method*, 30, 31.

97. Corbett, 'Upon the Death of the Lady Haddington', ll. 67–8, 78–9.
98. John Dunton, *A Voyage round the World*, Vol. 2 (1691), 44. EEBO. 5 November 2005. http://eebo.chadwyck.com.
99. John Dryden, 'Upon the Death of the Lord Hastings', ll. 59–62, *Lachrymae musarum: The tears of the Muses, exprest in Elegies written by Divers Persons of Nobility and Worth upon the Death of the most hopefull, Henry Lord Hastings*, ed. Richard Brome (1649), 90. EEBO. 12 November 2005. http://eebo.chadwyck.com.
100. Thomas Shipman, 'Beauty's Enemy: Upon the Death of M. Princess of Orange, by the Small Pox' (1660), *Carolina: or Loyal Poems* (1683), 78, unlineated. EEBO. 5 November 2005. http://eebo.chadwyck.com.
101. Alexander Brome, 'To a Gentleman that fell sick of the Small Pox. When he should be married', *Songs and other Poems*, 2nd edn (1664), 232, unlineated. EEBO. 5 November 2006. http://eebo.chadwyck.com.
102. Thomas Dekker, *The Whore of Babylon* (1607), ed. Marianne Gateson Riely (New York and London: Garland, 1980), 4.1.64. See Healy, *Fictions of Disease*, 158–72.
103. Lamport, *A Direct Method*, 5.
104. Cited in F. M. Sandwith, 'Smallpox and its Early History', *Clinical Journal* 36 (1910), 294–302, 301; see Donald R. Hopkins, *Princes and Peasants: Smallpox in History* (Chicago: University of Chicago Press, 1983), 33.
105. See Anselment, 'Smallpox in Seventeenth-Century English Literature', 83.
106. Brome, 'To a Gentleman', 233.
107. Anselment argues that smallpox poetry is unique in its direct confrontation of disease in this era, 'Smallpox in Seventeenth-Century English Literature', 87.
108. Owen Felltham, 'On a Gentlewoman, whose Nose was pitted with the Small Pox', *Lusoria*, (1661), ll. 11, 9, 16. Literature Online. 5 November 2005. http://lion.chadwyck.co.uk.
109. Willliam Hammond, 'To the Same, Recovered of the Small Pox', *Poems* (1655), 34, unlineated. EEBO. 5 November 2005. http://eebo.chadwyck.com.
110. John Oldham, 'To the Memory of my Dear Friend, Mr. Charles Morwent', *The Works of John Oldham, together with his Remains* (1684), 89–92, unlineated. EEBO. 13 November 2005. http://www.eebo.co.uk.
111. Oldham, 'To the Memory of my Dear Friend', 85, 92.
112. Brome, 'To a Gentleman', 231. Sydenham describes the progress of the 'pimples' of smallpox from a white to a red appearance in *Compleat Method*, 30.
113. Brome, 'To a Gentleman', 231–2.
114. William Cartwright, 'On the Lady Newburgh, who dyed of the Small Pox', *Poems* (1651), l. 76. Literature Online. 5 November 2005. http://lion.chadwyck.co.uk.; Edmund Elys, 'To Mrs K.G. having been lately sick of the Small Pox', *Dia poemata, Poetick Feet standing upon Holy Ground* (1655), 44, unlineated. EEBO. 5 November 2005. http://eebo.chadwyck.com.; Thomas Jordan, 'On the Death of the most

worthily honour'd Mr. John Sidney who dyed full of the Small Pox', *Piety, and Poesy* (1643), D2v, unlineated. EEBO. 5 November 2005. http://eebo.chadwyck.com.
115. Anselment comments that such images '[call] attention to the smallpox by envisioning their actual nature in order to reenvision them poetically', *Realms of Apollo*, 207.
116. Dryden, 'Upon the Death of the Lord Hastings', ll. 57–8.
117. Anselment, 'Smallpox in Seventeenth-Century English Literature', 90–1.
118. Robert Gould, *A Poem most humbly offered to the Memory of Her late Sacred Majesty, Queen Mary* (1695), ll. 278–9. Literature Online. 5 November 2005. http://lion.chadwyck.co.uk.; Sydenham, *Compleat Method*, 31. See Anselment, *Realms of Apollo*, 207.
119. Anselment, 'Smallpox in Seventeenth-Century English Literature', 92.
120. Oldham, 'To the Memory of my Dear Friend', 87.
121. Shipman, 'Beauty's Enemy', 78–9. See Anselment, *Realms of Apollo*, 207–8.
122. Brome, 'To a Gentleman', ll. 83–4.
123. Anselment notes of this poem that 'the gentleman invited to use his wit to find consolation is faced in the end with a crudely witty reminder of the truth. [...] The poem is] an intentionally ironic, albeit grotesque, comment on the metamorphoses of wit in smallpox poetry', *Realms of Apollo*, 211.

6 Sacrificing beauty

1. See Dolan, 'Taking the Pencil out of God's Hand', 224–39.
2. Fuller, *Holy State*, 191.
3. Miso-Spilus, *Wonder of Wonders*, 'To the Young Ladies and Gentlewomen of the Society of Black-spotted Faces'.
4. Miso-Spilus, *Wonder of Wonders*, 31, 'To the Young Ladies'.
5. Russo, *The Female Grotesque*, 61.
6. Aphra Behn, *The Dumb Virgin: or The Force of Imagination* (1700), *The Works of Aphra Behn*, ed. Janet Todd, Vol. 3 (London: Pickering, 1995), 335–60, 344.
7. See Marie-Hélène Huet, *Monstrous Imagination* (Cambridge, MA: Harvard University Press, 1993). The tradition of seeing the female role in reproduction as essentially passive goes back to Aristotle, who stated that 'The female always provides the material, the male provides that which fashions the material into shape; this, in our view, is the specific characteristic of each of the sexes: that is what it means to be male or to be female,' *Generation of Animals*, 185. Maternal imagination potentially disrupts the natural order, resulting in deformity. Sadler relates the story of a 'worthy gentlewoman of Suffolk', for instance, who believed that a drop of blood spurted on to her face by a butcher when she was pregnant would result in her child's deformity, 'and at the birth it was found marked with a red spot', *Sicke Womans Private Looking Glasse*, 139–40.
8. See Susannah B. Mintz, 'Freak Space: Aphra Behn's Strange Bodies', *Restoration* 30:2 (Fall 2006), 1–19.
9. Behn, *The Dumb Virgin*, 344.
10. Nussbaum, *'Defects'*, 39.
11. Nussbaum, *Limits of the Human*, 116. See also Jones, 'Obedient Faces', 280–302.
12. Jonson, *Volpone*, 3.7.183, 250–6.

13. Shakespeare, *Richard III*, 1.2.124; John Webster, *The White Devil* (1612), *John Webster: The Duchess of Malfi and other Plays*, 4.2.131.
14. See Jolenta in Webster's *The Devil's Law-Case* (1623); Beaupre in Philip Massinger's *The Parliament of Love* (1624); Milesia in William Berkeley's *The Lost Lady* (performed c. 1637, publ. 1638) and Chrotilda in William Heming's *The Fatal Contract* (1638–39).
15. Chapman, *Gentleman Usher*, fol. I2v.
16. William Shakespeare, *As You Like It*, ed. Alan Brissenden (Oxford: Clarendon Press, 1993), 1.2.35–7. See also *Hamlet* 3.1.111–14, 'the power of beauty will sooner transform honesty from what it is to a bawd than the force of honesty can translate beauty into his likeness'; and Herrick, 'Another upon her' (H-511).
17. Aemilia Lanyer, *Salve Deus Rex Judaeorum* (1611), ll. 193–6, *Isabella Whitney, Mary Sidney and Aemilia Lanyer: Renaissance Women Poets*, ed. Danielle Clarke (London: Penguin, 2000), 229–80. Further line references will be given in the main body of the text.
18. Ovid, *Metamorphoses*, trans. Arthur Golding, ed. Madeleine Forey (London: Penguin, 2002), ll. 588, 591–3, 669–70.
19. Shakespeare, *Rape of Lucrece*, l. 485. See also ll. 482–3: 'The fault is thine,/For those thine eyes betray thee unto mine.'
20. Sarah Scott, *A Description of Millenium Hall* (1762), ed. Gary Kelly (Peterborough, Ont.: Broadview, 1995), 136.
21. Chapman, *Gentleman Usher*, fol. I1v.
22. See George Chapman, *The Widow's Tears*, ed. Akihiro Yamada (Manchester and New York: Manchester University Press, 1975), 4.2.181–8. The *OED* states that the meanings of 'flay' include the stripping of the skin, and also the 'stripping' of clothing, or the 'stripping' of an exterior ornament or covering, *OED* 2a, 2b, 2d.
23. Daniela Bohde, 'Skin and the Search for the Interior: The Representation of Flaying in the Art and Anatomy of the Cinquecento', *Bodily Extremities*, 10–47, 19. Bohde describes the difficulty of distinguishing between 'skinned flesh and intact skin' in Titian's painting, observing that it undermines Renaissance models of a 'hidden interior', 16–17.
24. Hutchinson, *Nausea*, 11.
25. See *OED*, 'defeature', 1.
26. Samuel Daniel, *The Complaint of Rosamond*, *The Poeticall Essayes of Sam. Danyel* (1599), fol. D1v. EEBO. 23 October 2007. http://eebo.chadwyck.com.
27. William Shakespeare, *Venus and Adonis* (1593), *The Norton Shakespeare*, ll. 736, 746, 749–50.
28. Shakespeare, *Comedy of Errors*, 5.1.299–300.
29. Jeamson, *Artificiall Embellishments*, 21.
30. See Kristeva, *Powers of Horror*, 4.
31. Jonson, *Volpone*, 3.7.251.
32. Jonson, *Volpone*, 3.7.183–4, 250–6.
33. Shakespeare, *Richard III*, 1.2.119, 123–4, 125–6.
34. See above, pp. 80–3.
35. Shakespeare, *Richard III*, 1.2.81, 79, 55, 131, 145–50, 166, 168.
36. Webster, *The White Devil*, 3.2.207–10, 203–6, 4.2.129–32, 146, 155.

37. William Shakespeare, *The Taming of the Shrew*, ed. Brian Morris, The Arden Shakespeare (London and New York: Methuen, 1981), 5.2.158, 137–44.
38. Shakespeare, *Taming of the Shrew*, 5.2.154.
39. Chapman, *Gentleman Usher*, fols. I1v, I2r.
40. See Jacobus de Voragine, *The Golden Legend of Lives of the Saints* (c. 1275), trans. William Caxton (1800), Vol. 5 of 7, 238–9.
41. Chapman, *Gentleman Usher*, fol. I1v. T. M. Parrott describes Cortezza's allusion as 'a tissue of confusions'. T. M. Parrott (ed.), *Comedies of George Chapman* (London: Routledge, 1912), 768–9. He nevertheless outlines the tradition to which she may be referring in his introduction to the play.
42. Drew-Bear states that early modern examples of women disfiguring themselves in order to avoid sexual assault should be understood within the 'medieval tradition of self-disfigurement as virginal defense', *Painted Faces on the Renaissance Stage*, 63.
43. See Jane Tibbets Schulenburg, 'The Heroics of Virginity: Brides of Christ and Sacrificial Mutilation', *Women in the Middle Ages and the Renaissance: Literary and Historical Perspectives*, ed. Mary Beth Rose (Syracuse, NY: Syracuse University Press, 1986), 29–72; Corinne Saunders, *Rape and Ravishment in the Literature of Medieval England* (Cambridge: Brewer, 2001), 140–1.
44. 'Rothair's Edict' No. 180 in *The Lombard Laws*, trans. Katherine Fischer Drew (Philadelphia: University of Pennsylvania Press, 1973), 84–5; cited in Schulenburg, 'Heroics of Virginity', 53.
45. See Schulenburg, 'Heroics of Virginity', 53.
46. Schulenburg, 'Heroics of Virginity', 53.
47. Saunders, *Rape and Ravishment*, 141–7; Claire Marshall, 'The Politics of Self-mutilation: Forms of Female Devotion in the Late Middle Ages', *The Body in Late Medieval and Early Modern Culture*, eds Darryl Grantley and Nina Taunton (Aldershot: Ashgate, 2000), 11–22, 12–13.
48. Janice McLane, 'The Voice on the Skin: Self-mutilation and Merleau-Ponty's Theory of Language', *Hypatia* 11:4 (Fall 1996), n.p. Literature Online. 3 May 2005. http://lion.chadwyck.co.uk. Nancy A. Gutierriz also interprets some acts of female self-starvation as acts of self-assertion and resistance to patriarchy. See her *Shall She Famish, Then? Female Food Refusal in Early Modern England* (Aldershot: Ashgate, 2003), 53–78. Wioleta Polinska draws parallels between medieval women's self-harming practices and those of modern-day anorexics: 'just as medieval women found their voice within the culturally acceptable ways of expression, so do contemporary anorexics', 'Bodies under Siege: Eating Disorders and Self-mutilation among Women', *Journal of the American Academy of Religion* 68:3 (September 2000), 569–89, 10.
49. McLane, 'Voice on the Skin', n.p.
50. McLane, 'Voice on the Skin', n.p.
51. Marshall, 'Politics of Self-mutilation', 15.
52. See for instance the case of St Brigid, who escapes marriage as a result of her eye bursting but whose features are healed as soon as she takes the veil. *Vita I S Brigidae*, *Acta Sanctorum*, Joannes Bollandus et al., edit. novissima (Paris: Palme, 1845–1940), Februaris, I: 120 (1 February); cited in Schulenburg, 'Heroics of Virginity', 51. Agatha's breasts are also miraculously restored. See de Voragine, *The Golden Legend*,

Vol. 3, 37. Many thanks to Anke Bernau for her comments in relation to medieval hagiography.
53. de Voragine, *The Golden Legend*, Vol. 5, 240.
54. de Voragine, *The Golden Legend*, Vol. 3, 35.
55. Greenblatt, 'Mutilation and Meaning', *The Body in Parts*, 230.
56. Guillaume-Joseph Grelot, *A Late Voyage to Constantinople* (1683), 173. EEBO. 23 October 2007. http://eebo.chadwyck.com.
57. See Knott, *Discourses of Martyrdom*, 3.
58. Frances E. Dolan, '"Gentlemen, I have one thing more to say": Women on Scaffolds in England, 1563–1680', *Modern Philology* 92:2 (November 1994), 157–78, 162. See also Lucinda Becker, 'The Absent Body: Representations of dying early modern women in a selection of seventeenth-century diaries', *Women's Writing* 8:2 (2001), 251–62.
59. Chapman, *Widow's Tears*, 4.2.181–8. See Becker, 'The Absent Body', 251–62; Gutierrez, *Shall She Famish Then?*, 15.
60. Diane Purkiss, 'Producing the Voice, Consuming the Body: Women Prophets of the Seventeenth Century', *Women, Writing, History, 1640–1740*, eds Isobel Grundy and Susan Wiseman (Athens, GA: University of Georgia Press, 1992), 145. Nigel Smith comments on the use of medieval and sixteenth-century Catholic and mystical writings by radical Puritans in the seventeenth century in *Perfection Proclaimed: Language and Literature in English Radical Religion, 1640–1660* (Oxford: Clarendon Press, 1989), 17. For a discussion of Anna Trapnel's representations of her suffering body see Naomi Baker, '"Break down the walls of flesh": Anna Trapnel, John James and Fifth Monarchist Self-representation', *Women, Gender and Radical Religion in Early Modern Europe*, ed. Sylvia Brown (Leiden and Boston, MA: Brill, 2007), 117–38.
61. Elaine Scarry, *The Body in Pain: The Making and Unmaking of the World* (New York and Oxford: Oxford University Press, 1985), 34, 206, 207, 184.
62. Chapman, *Widow's Tears*, 4.2.183.
63. Eaton discusses in 'Defacing the Feminine', 181–98, the manner in which mutilation works to emphasise the materiality of female physicality.
64. See Jane Tibbets Schulenberg, *Forgetful of their Sex: Female Sanctity and Society ca. 500–1100* (Chicago: University of Chicago Press, 1998), 149.
65. Pieter Spierenburg demonstrates that between 1550 and 1650 public feeling increasingly turned against the mutilation of criminals. See his *The Spectacle of Suffering: Executions and the Evolution of Repression from a Preindustrial Metropolis to the European Experience* (Cambridge: Cambridge University Press, 1984). Standish Henning also argues that, despite literary references to the practice, women accused of sexual crimes were not branded on the face in the early modern era, 'Branding Harlots on the Brow', *Shakespeare Quarterly* 51:1 (Spring 2000), 86–9. Nancy A. Gutierrez states that 'the brutal treatment' of female adulteresses on the Renaissance stage 'has no correspondence with the actual, rather mild, treatment of adulteresses by the English law', 'Philomela Strikes Back: Adultery and Mutilation as Female Self-assertion', *Women's Studies* 16:3–4 (1989), 429–43, 436. Eaton nevertheless argues that 'what social changes had rendered private, the theatric space publicised', 'Defacing the Feminine', 181–98, 193. See also Crawford, *Marvelous Protestantism*, 66–72.
66. Shakespeare, *Comedy of Errors*, 2.2.133, 136.

67. Stubbes, *Anatomie of the Abuses*, 99; cited in Crawford, *Marvelous Protestantism*, 24.
68. Crawford discusses the manner in which the punishment for a crime illustrated that crime in this era in *Marvelous Protestantism*, 24.
69. Leonard Tennenhouse argues that the disfigurement of female characters on the Jacobean stage was driven by the identification of the female body as a source of pollution to the aristocratic body. See his *Power on Display: The Politics of Shakespeare's Genres* (London and New York: Methuen, 1986), 117.
70. See P. A. Chilton (ed.), *Marguerite de Navarre: The Heptameron* (London: Penguin, 1984), 21–3.
71. William Painter, *The Palace of Pleasure* (1566, this edn 1569), fol. 247v.
72. See Helen C. White, *Tudor Books of Saints and Martyrs* (Madison, WI: University of Wisconsin Press, 1963), 281–9.
73. Painter, *Palace of Pleasure*, 'To the Reader', fol. 233v.
74. See André Tournon, 'Rules of the Game', *Critical Tales: New Studies of* The Heptameron *and Early Modern Culture*, eds John D. Lyons and Mary B. McKinley (Philadelphia: University of Pennsylvania Press, 1993), 188–99, 195.
75. Painter, *Palace of Pleasure*, fol. 251r.
76. *Heptameron*, 153–4. Tournon notes that the opinion of Hircan and Saffredent regarding Amadour 'can be discounted since it comes from characters whose bias is both known and criticised'. He nevertheless observes that the judgement of the anonymous second narrator 'is used in order to muddle or to oppose the different criteria by which the story will be judged'. See 'Rules of the Game', 194.
77. *Heptameron*, 152. Tom Conley notes the ambivalence of the tale of 'Floride and Amadour' in *The Heptameron*, commenting that 'forms are mirrored into infinity without resolution', 'The Graphics of Dissimulation: Between *Heptameron* 10 and *l'histoire tragique*', *Critical Tales*, 65–82, 76. Tournon concurs that 'acts and motives' within this tale 'no longer offer the transparency expected of supposedly exemplary deeds, but instead acquire the disconcerting irregularity of real actions', 'Rules of the Game', 194.
78. Painter, *Palace of Pleasure*, fols. 247v, 248v.
79. Conley similarly observes that 'deception emerges everywhere the text underscores its traits of visibility. Ocularity seems to betray the play of shimmering appearance,' 'The Graphics of Dissimulation', 77.
80. Painter, *Palace of Pleasure*, fols. 237r, 243r, 233v, 242r, 250r.
81. Chapman, *Gentleman Usher*, fols. I2v, I1v, I3v.
82. See Virginia Mason Vaughan, *Performing Blackness on English Stages, 1500–1800* (Cambridge: Cambridge University Press, 2005), 107–29.
83. Vaughan, *Performing Blackness*, 112.
84. Massinger, *The Parliament of Love* (1624), Act 1, unlineated. Literature Online. 16 September 2006. http://lion.chadwyck.co.uk. Cited in Vaughan, *Performing Blackness*, 112.
85. Chapman, *Gentleman Usher*, fol. I2r.
86. Berkeley, *Lost Lady*, 3.2.1620–1.
87. See Kayser, *Grotesque*, 178.
88. Berkeley, *Lost Lady*, 5.2.2303–8.

89. John Webster, *The Devil's Law-Case* (c. 1619), *John Webster: The Duchess of Malfi and other plays*, 5.6.34–49.
90. See Vaughan, *Performing Blackness*, 8.
91. See for example the representation of Zanche in Webster's *The White Devil*.
92. Webster, *The White Devil*, 5.1.6.
93. John Marston, *Jack Drums Entertainment, or The Comedie of Pasquill and Katherine* (1601), fol. F2v, unlineated. EEBO. 23 October 2007. http://eebo.chadwyck.com.
94. Sidney, *Arcadia*, 90.
95. *The History of the Tryall of Chevalry* (c. 1601, publ. 1605), unlineated. EEBO. 23 October 2007. http://eebo.chadwyck.com. Fred L. Jones attributes the play to Chettle in 'The Trial of Chivalry, a Chettle Play', *PMLA* 41:2 (June 1926), 304–24. See also Frederic L. Jones, 'Another Source for The Trial of Chivalry', *PMLA* 47:3 (September 1932), 668–70.
96. Marston, *Jack Drums Entertainment*, fol. F2v. See Michael C. Andrews, 'Jack Drum's Entertainment as Burlesque', *Renaissance Quarterly* 24:2 (Summer 1971), 226–31.
97. While death for Protestant martyrs comes at the hands of others rather being undertaken by the self, the willingness of martyrs to die is emphasised in Foxe's accounts and other Protestant accounts of martyrdom to the extent that they are almost seen to initiate their own demise. For example, Massinger and Dekker's *The Virgin Martyr* (c. 1620, publ. 1622) has its titular heroine asking for the hangman to be recalled, saying 'here's on[e] prisoner left/To be the subject of his knife', 3.1, unlineated. EEBO. 15 November 2007. http://eebo.chadwyck.com. Elizabeth A. Castelli discusses the self-sacrificial nature of Protestant martyrdom in *Martyrdom and Memory: Early Christian Culture Making* (New York: Columbia University Press, 2004), 53.
98. Marston, *Jack Drums Entertainment*, fol. F1r–v.
99. Sidney, *Arcadia*, 91, 92.
100. Sidney, *Arcadia*, 92.
101. Samuel Schoenbaum, 'The "Deformed Mistress" Theme and Chapman's *Gentleman Usher*', *Notes and Queries* 205 (1960), 22–4. For an earlier discussion of the 'theme', see Ure, 'The "Deformed Mistress" Theme', 269–70.
102. James Howell (1634), in *Epistolae Ho-Elianae: The Familiar Letters of James Howell*, ed. J. Jacobs, Vol. 1 of 2 (London: David Nutt, 1892), 317; cited in Alfred Harbage, *Cavalier Drama* (New York: MLA; London: Oxford University Press, 1936), 36.
103. See Schoenbaum, 'Deformed Mistress', 23.
104. Shirley, *Dukes Mistris*, fols. D4v, F1r.
105. See C. Bigg, *Neoplatonism* (London: E. & J. B. Young, 1895), 277; Thomas Gould, *Platonic Love* (London: Routledge & Kegan Paul, 1963), 17.
106. Shirley, *Dukes Mistris*, fol. I4r–v.
107. Anne Sheppard, 'Plato and the Neoplatonists', eds Anna Baldwin and Sarah Hutton, *Platonism and the English Imagination* (Cambridge: Cambridge University Press, 1994), 10. See also Gould, *Platonic Love*, 9.

108. Plotinus, *Enneads*, I.6.8. See Laura Westra, 'Love and Beauty in Ficino and Plotinus', *Ficino and Renaissance Neoplatonism*, ed. Konrad Eisenblicher and Olga Zorzi Pugliese (Ottawa: Dovehouse, 1986), 175–87, 179.
109. Chapman, *Gentleman Usher*, fols. I3v–I4r.
110. Marson, *Jack Drums Entertainment*, fols. G4v–H1r.
111. Shirley, *Dukes Mistris*, fol. C3v. Tophas also proclaims of Dipsas, an ugly woman in Lyly's *Endymion*, 'how virtuous is she like to be, over whom no man can be jealous!', 3.3.63–4.
112. Gutierrez, 'Philomela Strikes Back', 438–9.
113. Hutchinson, *Nausea*, 12.
114. As I discuss in Chapter 4, leprosy and syphilis are often aligned in early modern descriptions of disease.
115. See Healy, *Fictions of Disease*, 134, 140.
116. Marson, *Jack Drums Entertainment*, fols. F3r, E4r.
117. Chapman, *Gentleman Usher*, fol. I2r.
118. See Ulrich Von Hutten, *De Morbo Gallico*, trans. Thomas Paynell (1533), fol. 2v; cited in Healy, *Fictions of Disease*, 125. For a discussion of early treatments of syphilis, see Healy, *Fictions of Disease*, 129.
119. Chapman, *Gentleman Usher*, fol. I1v.
120. See Healy, *Fictions of Disease*, 128.
121. Tennenhouse distinguishes between dramatic representations of mutilation in the Elizabethan and Jacobean eras, arguing that in the former the body of an aristocratic woman represents the state, so that rape aligns with the dismemberment of the state, while in the latter the mutilation of female characters becomes a means of purifying the state. See *Power on Display*, 107–18. Spanning the end of the Elizabethan era and the beginning of the Jacobean, these plays complicate this distinction. For analysis of early modern representations of rape see Robin L. Bott, '"O, keep me from their worse than killing lust": Ideologies of Rape and Mutilation in Chaucer's "Physician's Tale" and Shakespeare's *Titus Andronicus*', *Representing Rape in Medieval and Early Modern Literature*, eds Elizabeth Robertson and Christine M. Rose (New York: Palgrave, 2001), 189–211, 190–2; Sharon Beehler and Linda Woodbridge (eds), *Women, Violence, and English Renaissance Literature: Essays Honoring Paul Jorgensen* (Tempe, AZ: Arizona Center for Medieval and Renaissance Studies, 2003).
122. Thomas Middleton, *The Ghost of Lucrece* (1600), unlineated. EEBO. 19 November 2007. http://eebo.chadwyck.com.
123. Marston, *Jack Drums Entertainment*, fols. B3v, D1v, A2v.
124. Chapman, *Gentleman Usher*, fols. I3v–I4r.
125. Chapman, *Widow's Tears*, 4.2.184.
126. Sidney, *Arcadia*, 106, 104.
127. Chapman, *Gentleman Usher*, fol. I4r.
128. Sidney, *Apology for Poetry*, 100.
129. Vickers, '"The blazon of sweet beauty's best"', 95–115.
130. Shakespeare, *Comedy of Errors*, 2.1.97–9.
131. Sidney, *Arcadia*, 528.

132. Francis Quarles, *Argalus and Parthenia* (1629), ed. David Freeman, Renaissance English Text Society (Washington, DC, London and Toronto: Associated University Presses, 1986), Bk 2, ll. 535–8, 544–5, 550–6.
133. See Sidney, *Arcadia*, 501.
134. Cleveland, 'A Young Man to an Old Woman courting him', l. 55.

Bibliography

Primary texts

Anon., *The Creation of the World*, transcr. William Jordan (1611), *Transactions of the Philological Society*, ed. Whitley Stokes (1864), 118–19.

Anon., *The Female Monster, or The Second Part of the World Turn'd Topsy Turvey: A Satyr* (1705). Eighteenth Century Collections Online. 13 June 2007.

Anon., *The Merry Dutch Miller: And New Invented Windmill* (1672). EEBO. 12 March 2006.

Anon., *The Olde Bride, or The Gilded Beauty* (c. 1635). EEBO. 26 October 2007.

Anon., *Wisdom, The Macro Plays*, ed. Mark Eccles (Oxford: Early English Text Society, 1969).

Anon., *The Wonders of the Female World, or A General History of Women* (1682). EEBO. 6 March 2006.

Aquinas, Thomas, *Basic Writings of Saint Thomas Aquinas*, ed. Anton C. Pegis (New York: Random House, 1945).

Aristotle, *Generation of Animals*, trans. A. L. Peck (Cambridge, MA: Harvard University Press; London: Heinemann, 1953).

Aristotle, *Poetics*, ed. and trans. Stephen Halliwell (Cambridge, MA: Harvard University Press, 1995).

Aristotle, *Problems*, trans. W. S. Hett, 2 vols (Cambridge, MA: Harvard University Press; London: Heinemann, 1937).

Augustine, *The City of God*, trans. John Healy, ed. R. V. G. Tasker, intro. Sir Ernest Barker, 2 vols (London: Dent, 1945).

Bacon, Sir Francis, *The Essays* (1668).

Bacon, Sir Francis, *The Novum Organum of Sir Francis Bacon* (1620, this edn 1676). EEBO. 12 October 2006.

Bacon, Sir Francis, *The Philosophy of Francis Bacon: An Essay on its Development from 1603 to 1609 with New Translations of Fundamental Texts*, trans. Benjamin Farrington (Liverpool: Liverpool University Press, 1970).

Bartholin, Thomas, *Bartholinus Anatomy made from the Precepts of his Father, and from the Observations of all modern Anatomists, together with his own*, publ. Nicholas Culpeper and Abdiah Cole (1668). EEBO. 3 June 2007.

Baxter, Richard, *A Christian Directory, or A Summ of Practical Theology and Cases of Conscience directing Christians how to use their Knowledge and Faith, how to improve all Helps and*

Means, and to perform all Duties, how to overcome Temptations, and to escape or mortify every Sin (1673). EEBO. 7 November 2007.

Bedford, Thomas, *A True and Certaine Relation of a Strange-birth which was born at Stonehouse in the Parish of Plimmouth, the 20. of October 1635. Together with the Notes of a Sermon, preached Octob. 23 1635 ... at the interring of the sayd Birth* (1635).

Behn, Aphra, *The Luckey Chance, or An Alderman's Bargain* (1687). EEBO. 12 April 2006.

Behn, Aphra, *The Works of Aphra Behn*, ed. Janet Todd, 7 vols (London: Pickering & Chatto; Columbus, OH: Ohio State University Press, 1992–96).

Berkeley, William, *The Lost Lady* (performed c. 1637, publ. 1638), ed. D. F. Rowan and G. R. Proudfoot, Malone Society Reprints (Oxford: Oxford University Press, 1987).

Boethius, *The Consolation of Philosophy*, trans. V. E. Watts (London: Penguin, 1969).

Bolton, Robert, *Certaine Devout Prayers of Mr. Bolton upon Solemne Occasions* (1638). EEBO. 13 December 2006.

Bowes, Thomas (trans.), *De La Primaudaye's French Academie* (1594).

Boyle, Robert, *A Free Enquiry into the Vulgarly Receiv'd Notion of Nature* (1686).

Brome, Alexander, 'To a Gentleman that fell Sick of the Small Pox. When he should be married', *Songs and other Poems*, 2nd edn (1664). EEBO. 5 November 2006.

Browne, Sir Thomas, *Pseudodoxia Epidemica* (1646), ed. Robin Robbins (Oxford: Clarendon Press, 1981).

Browne, Sir Thomas, *Sir Thomas Browne: The Major Works*, ed. C. A. Patrides (London: Penguin, 1977).

Bulwer, John, *Anthropometamorphosis: Man Transform'd: or The Artificiall Changeling historically presented in the Mad and Cruell Gallantry, Foolish Bravery, Ridiculous Beauty, Filthy Finenesse, and Loathsome Lovelinesse of most Nations, fashioning and altering their Bodies from the Mould intended by Nature [...] To which artificiall and affected Deformations are added, all the Native and Nationall Monstrosities that have appeared to disfigure the Humane Fabrick. With a Vindication of the regular Beauty and Honesty of Nature* (1650, this edn 1653).

Buoni, Thomasso, *Problemes of Beautie and all Humane Affections*, trans. Sampson Lennard (1606). EEBO. 12 April 2006.

Burke, Edmund, *A Philosophical Enquiry into the Origin of our Ideas of the Sublime and the Beautiful*, 2nd edn (1759). Eighteenth Century Collections Online. 1 November 2007.

Burton, Robert, *The Anatomy of Melancholy* (1621), intro. William H. Gass, ed. and intro. Holbrook Jackson (New York: *New York Review of Books*, 2001).

Calvin, John, *Commentaries on the Catholic Epistles* (1621), trans. and ed. John Owen. Christian Classics Ethereal Library. 9 October 2006. www.ccel.org.

Calvin, John, *The Institution of Christian Religion*, trans. Thomas Norton (1559, this edn 1562).

Cartwright, William, *Poems* (1651). Literature Online. 5 November 2005.

Cavendish, Margaret, *The Publick Wooing* (1662). Literature Online. 19 April 2007.

Cavendish, Margaret, *Wits Cabal*, Pt 1 (1662). Literature Online. 5 November 2005.

Cavendish, Margaret, *The Worlds Olio* (1655). EEBO. 26 March 2006.

Chapman, George, *Bussy D'Ambois* (c. 1603–04, publ. 1607), ed. Nicholas Brooke, The Revels Plays (Manchester and New York: Manchester University Press, 1964, repr. 1999).

Chapman, George, *Comedies of George Chapman*, ed. T. M. Parrott (London: 1912).
Chapman, George, *The Gentleman Usher* (1606). EEBO. 7 July 2007.
Chapman, George, *The Widow's Tears* (c. 1605), ed. Akihiro Yamada, The Revels Plays (Manchester and New York: Manchester University Press, 1975).
Cleveland, John, *The Character of a London-Diurnall* (1647). EEBO. 7 November 2006.
Cocles, Bartholomew, *A Brief and most Pleasant Epitomye of the whole Art of Phisiognomie, gathered ... by that learned Chyrurgian Cocles, and Englished by Thomas Hyll* (1556). EEBO. 3 February 2006.
Collier, Jeremy, *Miscellanies upon Moral Subjects* (1695), 2 parts. EEBO. 4 May 2007.
Collop, John, *The Poems of John Collop*, ed. Conrad Hilberry (Madison, WI: University of Wisconsin Press, 1962).
Cooper, Thomas, *The Churches Deliverance, containing Meditations and Short Notes upon the Booke of Hester* (1609). EEBO. 12 April 2006.
Corbett, Richard, *Certain Elegant Poems* (1647). Literature Online. 5 November 2005.
Coulton, G. G. (selected, trans. and annotated), *A Medieval Garner: Human Documents from the Four Centuries preceding the Reformation* (London: Constable, 1910).
Cowper, William, *Pathmos: or A Commentary on the Revelation of Saint John* (1619). EEBO. 26 October 2007.
Crompton, Hugh, *Poems* (1657). Literature Online. 26 October 2007.
Crooke, Helkiah, *Mikrokosmographia: A Description of the Body of Man* (1615). EEBO. 13 December 2006.
Cureau de la Chambre, Marin, *The Art how to Know Men*, trans. John Davies (1665). EEBO. 3 February 2006.
Daniel, Samuel, *The Complaint of Rosamond, The Poeticall Essayes of Sam. Danyel* (1599). EEBO. 23 October 2007.
Dekker, Thomas, *The Whore of Babylon* (1607), ed. Marianne Gateson Riely (New York and London: Garland, 1980).
Dekker, Thomas, and Philip Massinger, *The Virgin Martyr* (c. 1620, publ. 1622). EEBO. 15 November 2007.
Dekker, Thomas, John Ford and William Rowley, *The Witch of Edmonton* (performed 1621, publ. 1658), *Three Jacobean Witchcraft Plays*, eds Peter Corbin and Douglas Sedge, Revels Plays Companion Library (Manchester and New York: Manchester University Press, 1986).
Descartes, René, *The Passions of the Soul* (1649), trans. Stephen Voss (Indianapolis, IN, and Cambridge: Hackett, 1989).
Descartes, René, *Philosophical Essays and Correspondence*, ed. Roger Ariew (Indianapolis, IN, and Cambridge: Hackett, 2000).
Donne, John, *The Complete English Poems of John Donne*, ed. C. A. Patrides (London: Dent, 1985).
Donne, John, *Donne's Sermons*, ed. Logan Pearsall Smith (Oxford: Clarendon Press, 1919).
Donne, John, *Paradoxes and Problems* (1633) (London: Nonesuch Press, 1923).
Drew, Katherine Fischer (trans.), *The Lombard Laws* (Philadelphia: University of Pennsylvania Press, 1973).
Dryden, John, *Annus Mirabilis, the Year of Wonders, 1666* (1667). EEBO. 1 December 2006.

Dryden, John, 'Preface', C. A. Du Fresnoy, *De arte graphica: The Art of Painting* (1695), EEBO. 1 December 2006.
Dryden, John, 'Upon the Death of the Lord Hastings', *Lachrymae musarum, The Tears of the Muses: exprest in Elegies written by divers Persons of Nobility and Worth upon the Death of the most hopefull, Henry Lord Hastings*, ed. Richard Brome (1649). EEBO. 12 November 2005.
[Dunton, John (ed.),] *Athenian Sport: or Two Thousand Paradoxes merrily Argued, to Amuse and Divert the Age* (1707).
Dunton, John, *A Voyage round the World* (1691), Vol. 2. EEBO. 5 November 2005.
Elys, Edmund, *Dia poemata, Poetick Feet standing upon Holy Ground* (1655). EEBO. 5 November 2005.
Erasmus, Desiderius, *The Praise of Folly*, ed. Clarence H. Miller (New Haven, CT: Yale University Press, 1979).
Erasmus, Desiderius, *The Sileni of Alcibiades, Thomas More: 'Utopia', with Erasmus's 'The Sileni of Alcibiades'*, ed. and trans. David Wooton (Indianapolis, IN: Hackett, 1999).
Evelyn, John, *Numismata: A Discourse of Medals . . . to which is added a Digression concerning Physiognomy* (1697).
de Faria e Sousa, Manuel, *The Portugues Ásia*, trans. John Stevens (1695). EEBO. 23 August 2007.
Felltham, Owen, *Lusoria* (1661). Literature Online. 5 November 2005.
Ficino, Marsilio, *Commentary on Plato's Symposium on Love*, trans. Sears Jayne (Woodstock, CT: Spring Publications, 1985).
Firenzuola, Agnolo, *On the Beauty of Women* (1541, publ. 1548), trans. and ed. Konrad Eisenbichler and Jacqueline Murray (Philadelphia: University of Pennsylvania Press, 1992).
Fleming, Abraham (trans.), *A Paradoxe, Proving by Reason and Example, that Baldnesse is much better than Bushie Haire, etc., written by that excellent Philosopher Synesius, Bishop of Thebes* (1579). EEBO. 3 April 2007.
Fletcher, John, *Bonduca, or The British Heroine: A Tragedy* (1696). EEBO. 7 November 2007.
Florio, John, *A Worlde of Wordes, or Most Copious, and Exact Dictionarie in Italian and English* (1598).
Ford, John, *Tis Pity She's a Whore, English Renaissance Drama: A Norton Anthology*, eds David Bevington et al. (New York and London: Norton, 2002).
Foxe, John, *Actes and Monuments of Matters most Speciall and Memorable happenying in the Church* (1563).
Freeman, Thomas, *Rubbe and A Great Cast* (1614). Literature Online. 5 April 2006.
Fuller, Thomas, *The Holy State* (1642). EEBO. 21 January 2006.
Glover, Henry, *Cain and Abel parallel'd with King Charles and his Murderers in a Sermon preached in S. Thomas Church in Salisbury, Jan. 30 1663* (1664). EEBO. 4 May 2007.
Gould, Robert, *A Poem most humbly Offered to the Memory of Her late Sacred Majesty, Queen Mary* (1695). Literature Online. 5 November 2005.
Gregory the Great, *Pastoral Care* (Baltimore, MD: Newman Press, 1958).
Grelot, Guillaume-Joseph, *A Late Voyage to Constantinople* (1683). EEBO. 23 October 2007.
H., N., *The Ladies Dictionary: Being a General Entertainment for the Fair Sex* (1694). EEBO. 3 October 2007.

Hagthorpe, John, *Visiones rerum* (1623). Literature Online. 15 October 2004.
Hall, John, *Poems* (1646–47). Literature Online. 26 October 2007.
Hall, Thomas, *Comarum Akosmia: The Loathsomenesse of Long Haire* (1654).
Hammond, Willliam, *Poems* (1655). EEBO. 5 November 2005.
Harrison, William, and Raphael Holinshed, *The First and Second Volumes of Chronicles* (1587). EEBO. 26 March 2006.
Harvey, Gideon, *Morbus Anglicus: or The Anatomy of Consumptions* (1666). EEBO. 14 November 2006.
Hay, William, *Deformity: An Essay* (1754). Eighteenth Century Collections Online. 7 July 2006.
Head, Richard, and Francis Kirkman, *The English Rogue* (1671), Pt 4. Literature Online. 3 January 2006.
Heath, Robert, *Clarastella* (1650). Literature Online. 1 March 2006.
Herbert, George, *The Complete English Poems of George Herbert*, ed. John Tobin (London: Penguin, 1991).
Herbert of Cherbury, *Occasional Verses* (1665). EEBO. 28 March 2007.
Herrick, Robert, *The Complete Poetry of Robert Herrick*, ed. J. Max Patrick (New York: New York University Press, 1963).
Hildersam, Arthur, *CLII Lectures on Psalm LI* (1635). EEBO. 15 November 2007.
Hill, Thomas, *The Contemplation of Mankinde, containing a Singular Discourse after the Art of Phisiognomie* (1571).
Hobbes, Thomas, *Leviathan* (1651), ed. C. B. Macpherson (London: Penguin, 1968).
Hobbes, Thomas, *The Questions concerning Liberty, Necessity, and Chance clearly Stated and Debated between Dr Bramhall, Bishop of Derry, and Thomas Hobbes of Malmesbury* (1656). EEBO. 25 March 2007.
Hogarde, Miles, *The Displaying of the Protestantes* (1556).
Hogarth, William, *The Analysis of Beauty* (1753), ed. Ronald Paulson (New Haven, CT: Yale University Press, 1997).
Howell, James, *Epistolae Ho-Elianae: The Familiar Letters of James Howell*, ed. J. Jacobs (London: David Nutt, 1892).
Hume, David, *Four Dissertations* (1757), Pt 4. Eighteenth Century Collections Online. 26 September 2007.
Hutcheson, Francis, *An Inquiry concerning Beauty, Order, Harmony, Design* (1725), ed. Peter Kivy (The Hague: Nijhoff, 1973).
Jackson, Arthur, *A Help for the Understanding of the Holy Scripture* (1643). EEBO. 4 May 2007.
Jackson, Thomas, *Diverse Sermons, with a Short Treatise befitting these Times* (1637). EEBO. 27 November 2007.
Jeamson, Thomas, *Artificiall Embellishments, or, Arts best Directions how to Preserve Beauty or Procure it* (1665). EEBO. 12 March 2006.
Jenner, David, *Cain's Mark, and Murder: K. Charles the I his Martyrdom. Delivered in a Sermon on January the Thirtieth* (1680). EEBO. 4 May 2007.
Johnson, Samuel, *A Dictionary of the English Language*, 2nd edn (1755), Vol. 1 of 2. Eighteenth Century Collections Online. 6 June 2008.
Johnstone, John, *An History of the Wonderful Things of Nature* (1657). EEBO. 26 October 2007.

Jones, Inigo, *Tempe Restored: A Masque* (1631). EEBO. 14 November 2007.
Jonson, Ben, *Ben Jonson's Plays and Masques*, ed. Richard Harp (New York and London: Norton, 2001).
Jonson, Ben, *Timber, or Discoveries* (1640). Literature Online. 26 November 2007.
Jonson, Ben, *The Workes* (this edn 1640). Literature Online. 1 October 2007.
Jordan, Thomas, *The Muses Melody* (c. 1680). EEBO. 1 February 2006.
Jordan, Thomas, *Piety, and Poesy* (1643). EEBO. 5 November 2005.
Jordan, Thomas, *Poeticall Varieties* (1637). EEBO. 28 March 2007.
Joubert, Laurent, *Traite du Ris (Treatise on Laughter)* (1579), trans. Gregory David de Rocher (Tuscaloosa, AL: University of Alabama Press, 1980).
Keith, George, *The Arguments of the Quakers* (1698).
King, Henry, *Poems, Elegies, Paradoxes and Sonets* (1664).
Knagg, Thomas, *A Sermon Preach'd at the Cathedral Church of St Paul* (1716).
Lamport, John, *A Direct Method of Ordering and Curing People of that Loathsome Disease, the Small-pox* (1685). EEBO. 6 November 2005.
Lanyer, Aemilia, *Salve Deus Rex Judaeorum* (1611), *Isabella Whitney, Mary Sidney and Aemilia Lanyer: Renaissance Women Poets*, ed. Danielle Clarke (London: Penguin, 2000).
Lauder, George (trans.), Lelio Capilupi and Francesco Petrarca (orig.), *The Anatomie of the Romane Clergie* (1623). Literature Online. 1 November 2007.
Leigh, Richard, *Poems upon Several Occasions* (1675). EEBO. 7 November 2006.
Lenton, Francis, *Lentons Leisures Described, in Divers Moderne Characters* (1636). EEBO. 12 November 2007.
Lenton, Francis, 'Queene Esters Haliluiahs and Hamans Madrigalls Expressed and Illustrated in a Sacred Poem' (1638). BL Add MS 34805.
Leonardo da Vinci, *Treatise on Painting*, trans. A. Philip McMahon, intro. Ludwig H. Heydenreich, 2 vols (Princeton, NJ: Princeton University Press, 1956).
Lovelace, Richard, 'A Paradox', *Lucasta* (1649). Literature Online. 1 November 2007.
Lyly, John, *Endymion* (1591), ed. David Bevington, The Revels Plays (Manchester and New York: Manchester University Press, 1996).
Lyly, John, *Euphues: The Anatomy of Wit and Euphues and his England*, ed. Leah Scragg, The Revels Plays Companion Library (Manchester and New York: Manchester University Press, 2003).
Maclean, Hugh (ed.), *Ben Jonson and the Cavalier Poets* (New York and London: Norton, 1974).
Marlowe, Christopher, *The Complete Plays*, ed. J. B. Steane (London: Penguin, 1969).
Massinger, Philip, *The Parliament of Love* (1624). Literature Online. 16 September 2006.
Matthew of Vendome, *Ars versificatoria* (c. 1175), trans. Aubrey E. Galyon (Ames, IA: Iowa State University Press, 1980).
Middleton, Thomas, *The Ghost of Lucrece* (1600). EEBO. 19 November 2007.
Middleton, Thomas, and William Rowley, *The Changeling* (1622), ed. N. W. Bawcutt, The Revels Plays (Manchester: Manchester University Press, 1998).
Milton, John, *Complete English Poems*, ed. Gordon Campbell (London: Dent, 1980).
Milton, John, *Paradise Lost* (1667), ed. Alastair Fowler (London and New York: Longman, 1968).
Miso-Spilus, *A Wonder of Wonders: or A Metamorphosis of Fair Faces voluntarily transformed*

into Foul Visages, or An Invective against Black-spotted Faces: by a Well-willer to Modest Matrons and Virgins (1662). EEBO. 6 February 2006.

de Montaigne, Michel, *Michel de Montaigne: The Complete Essays*, ed. and trans. M. A. Screech (London: Penguin, 1991).

Moore, Richard, *Ho thesaurus en ostrakinois: A Pearl in an Oyster-shel* (1675). EEBO. 19 April 2006.

Munday, Anthony (trans.), *The Defence of Contraries* (1593). EEBO. 12 April 2007.

Nashe, Thomas, *The Works of Thomas Nashe*, eds Ronald B. McKerrow and F. P. Wilson, 5 vols (Oxford: Blackwell, 1966).

de Navarre, Marguerite, *The Heptameron*, ed. P. A. Chilton (London: Penguin, 1984).

Norden, John, *The Labyrinth of Man's Life* (1614). Literature Online. 20 August 2007.

Oldham, John, *The Works of John Oldham, together with his Remains* (1684). EEBO. 13 November 2005.

Overbury, Sir Thomas, *A Wife, now the Widow of Sir Thomas Overbury, being a most Exquisite and Singular Poem of the Choice of a Wife*, 2nd edn (London, 1614). EEBO. 19 April 2007.

Ovid, *Metamorphoses*, trans. Arthur Golding, ed. Madeleine Forey (London: Penguin, 2002).

Painter, William, *The Palace of Pleasure* (1566, this edn 1569).

Peacham, Henry, *The Compleat Gentleman: Fashioning him Absolut, in the most Necessary and Commendable Qualities concerning Minde or Bodie that may be required in a Noble Gentleman* (1622, this edn 1634).

Pepys, Samuel, *The Diary of Samuel Pepys: A Selection*, ed. Robert Latham (London: Penguin, 1985, repr. 2003).

Plato, *Symposium, The Collected Dialogues*, eds Edith Hamilton and Huntington Carins, trans. Michael Joyce (Princeton, NJ: Princeton University Press, 1961).

Plotinus, *The Enneads*, trans. Stephen Mackenna, 4th edn (London: Faber, 1969).

Pollard, Robert, and John Sweeting (eds), *Choyce Drollery: Songs and Sonnets* (1656). EEBO. 7 November 2007.

Prestwich, Edmund, *Hippolitus, translated out of Seneca* (1651). EEBO. 26 October 2007.

Puttenham, George, *The Arte of English Poesie* (1589), eds Alice Walker and Gladys Willcock (Cambridge: Cambridge University Press, 1936).

Quarles, Francis, *Argalus and Parthenia* (1629), ed. David Freeman, Renaissance English Text Society (Washington, DC, London and Toronto: Associated University Presses, 1986).

Quarles, Francis, *Hadassa, or The History of Queene Ester* (1621).

R., M., *The Mothers Counsell, or Live within Compasse* (1631). EEBO. 13 April 2006.

Rabelais, François, *Gargantua and Pantagruel*, trans. Sir Thomas Urquhart and Pierre Le Motteux, intro. Terence Cave (London: David Campbell, 1994).

Randolph, Thomas, *Poems* (1652). Literature Online. 26 July 2006.

Reynolds, Edward, *A Treatise of the Passions and Faculties of the Soule of Man* (1640, this edn 1647).

Reynolds, John, *The Triumph of God's Revenge* (1622, this edn 1635).

Rowlands, Samuel, *The Knave of Clubbs* (1611). Literature Online. 20 August 2007.

de Sade, Marquis, *The 120 Days of Sodom and other Writings*, trans. Austryn Wainhouse and Richard Seaver (New York: Grove Press, 1966).

Sadler, John, *The Sick Womans Private Looking-glasse* (1636). EEBO. 15 November 2007.

Sanderson, Sir William, *Graphice: The Use of Pen and Pensil, or The Most Excellent Art of Painting: in Two Parts* (1658).
Saunders, Richard, *Physiognomie and Chiromancie* (1653, this edn 1671).
Scott, Sarah, *Agreeable Ugliness: or The Triumph of the Graces* (1754). Eighteenth Century Collections Online. 13 December 2007.
Scott, Sarah, *A Description of Millenium Hall* (1762), ed. Gary Kelly (Peterborough, Ont.: Broadview Press, 1995).
Shakespeare, William, *As You Like It*, ed. Alan Brissenden (Oxford: Clarendon Press, 1993).
Shakespeare, William, *The Comedy of Errors*, ed. R. A. Foakes, The Arden Shakespeare (London: Methuen, 1962).
Shakespeare, William, *Hamlet*, ed. G. R. Hibbard (Oxford: Oxford University Press, 1987).
Shakespeare, William, *I Henry IV*, ed. David Bevington (Oxford: Oxford University Press, 1987).
Shakespeare, William, *The Second Part of King Henry IV*, ed. A. R. Humphreys, The Arden Shakespeare (London: Methuen, 1966).
Shakespeare, William, *King John*, ed. E. A. J. Honigmann, The Arden Shakespeare (London: Methuen, 1954, repr. 1959).
Shakespeare, William, *Love's Labours Lost*, ed. H. R. Woudhuysen (London: Arden Shakespeare, 1998).
Shakespeare, William, *Macbeth*, ed. Kenneth Muir (London: Arden Shakespeare, 1962, repr. 2002).
Shakespeare, William, *Othello*, ed. E. A. J. Honigmann (London: Arden Shakespeare, 1999).
Shakespeare, William, *The Rape of Lucrece*, *The Norton Shakespeare*, eds Stephen Greenblatt *et al.* (New York and London: Norton, 1997).
Shakespeare, William, *Romeo and Juliet*, ed. Brian Gibbons, The Arden Shakespeare (London and New York: Methuen, 1980).
Shakespeare, William, *Sonnets*, *The Norton Shakespeare*, eds Stephen Greenblatt *et al.* (New York and London: Norton, 1997).
Shakespeare, William, *The Taming of the Shrew*, ed. Brian Morris, The Arden Shakespeare (London and New York: Methuen, 1981).
Shakespeare, William, *The Tempest*, ed. Frank Kermode, The Arden Shakespeare (London and New York: Routledge, 1954).
Shakespeare, William, *The Tragedy of King Richard III*, ed. John Jowett (Oxford: Oxford University Press, 2000).
Shakespeare, William, *Venus and Adonis*, *The Norton Shakespeare*, eds Stephen Greenblatt *et al.* (New York and London: Norton, 1997).
Sheppard, Samuel, *Epigrams Theological, Philosophical, and Romantick* (1651). Literature Online. 21 July 2006.
Shipman, Thomas, *Carolina: or Loyal Poems* (1683). EEBO. 5 November 2005.
Shirley, James, *The Dukes Mistris* (1636, publ. 1638). EEBO. 12 September 2007.
Shirley, James, *Poems* (1646). Literature Online. 26 October 2007.
Sidney, Sir Philip, *An Apology for Poetry*, ed. Geoffrey Shepherd (Manchester: Manchester University Press, 1973).
Sidney, Sir Philip, *The Countess of Pembroke's Arcadia*, ed. Maurice Evans (London: Penguin, 1977).

Skelton, John, *The Complete English Poems*, ed. John Scattergood (Harmondsworth: Penguin, 1983).
Spencer, John, *A Discourse Concerning Prodigies* (1663). EEBO. 1 November 2007.
Spenser, Edmund, *The Faerie Queene* (1590–96), ed. A. C. Hamilton (London and New York: Longman, 1997).
Spenser, Edmund, *Fowre Hymnes* (1596). EEBO. 2 November 2007.
Stubbes, Phillip, *Anatomy of the Abuses in England, in Shakespeare's Youth* (1583), Pt 1, ed. Frederick J. Furnival (London: Trubner, 1877).
Suckling, John, 'The Deformed Mistress', *Last Remains* (1659). Literature Online. 28 March 2007.
Sutton, Katherine, *A Christian Womans Experiences of the Glorious Working of Gods Free Grace* (1663). EEBO. 12 December 2007.
Sydenham, Thomas, *The Compleat Method of Curing almost all Diseases, to which is added an Exact Description of their Several Symptoms. Written in Latin by Dr Thomas Sydenham, And now faithfully Englished* (1694). EEBO. 5 November 2005.
Taverner, Richard, *Proverbes of Adagies with Newe Addicions gathered out of the Chiliades of Erasmus* (1539).
Twyne, Laurence, *The Patterne of Painefull Adventures* (c. 1594). EEBO. 7 November 2007.
Villiers, George, second Duke of Buckingham, *Miscellaneous Works, written by his Grace, George, late Duke of Buckingham* (1704). Eighteenth Century Collections Online. 26 October 2007.
Von Hutten, Ulrich, *De Morbo Gallico*, trans. Thomas Paynell (1533).
de Voragine, Jacobus, *The Golden Legend of Lives of the Saints* (c. 1275), trans. William Caxton, 7 vols (London: Dent, 1900).
Walpole, Horace, *Anecdotes of Painting in England*, 2nd edn (1765), Vol. 3 of 4. Eighteenth Century Collections Online. 17 October 2007.
Ward, Edward, *Satyrical Reflections on Clubs: in XXIX Chapters* (1710), Vol. 5. Eighteenth Century Collections Online. 1 November 2007.
Webster, John, *The Duchess of Malfi and other Plays*, ed. René Weis (Oxford: Oxford University Press, 1996).
Welsby, Paul A. (ed.), *The Book of Homilies, Sermons and Society* (Harmondsworth: Penguin, 1970).
Wesley, Samuel, *Maggots, or Poems on Several Subjects, never before Handled by a Schollar* (1685). EEBO. 26 October 2007.
William of Auvergne, *De bono et malo* (MS. Balliol 207).
Wither, George, *A Collection of Emblems, Ancient and Moderne* (1635). EEBO. 7 November 2006.
Wood, Anthony, *Athenae Oxonienses* (1692), 2 vols. EEBO. 27 November 2007.
Wright, Thomas, *The Passions of the Minde* (1598, publ. 1601). 3 February. 2006.

Electronic databases

Christian Classics Ethereal Library: www.ccel.org.
EEBO (Early English Books Online): http://eebo.chadwyck.com.
Eighteenth Century Collections Online: http://galenet.galegroup.com.
Literature Online: http://lion.chadwyck.co.uk.

Secondary texts

Ames-Lewis, Francis, and Mary Rogers (eds), *Concepts of Beauty in Renaissance Art* (Aldershot: Ashgate, 1998).
Andrews, Michael C., '*Jack Drum's Entertainment* as Burlesque', *Renaissance Quarterly* 24:2 (Summer 1971), 226–31.
Anselment, Raymond A., *The Realms of Apollo: Literature and Healing in Seventeenth-Century England* (Newark, NJ: University of Delaware Press; London: Associated University Presses, 1994).
Anselment, Raymond A., 'Smallpox in Seventeenth-Century English Literature: Reality and the Metamorphosis of Wit', *Medical History* 33 (1989), 72–95.
Armstrong, Karen, 'Possets, Pills and Poisons: Physicking the Female Body in Early Seventeenth-Century Drama', *Cahiers Elisabethains: Late Medieval and Renaissance Studies* 61 (2002), 43–56.
Baker, Moira P., 'The Uncanny Stranger on Display: The Female Body in Sixteenth- and Seventeenth-Century Love Poetry', *South Atlantic Review* 56:2 (May 1991), 7–25.
Baker, Naomi, '"Break down the walls of flesh": Anna Trapnel, John James and Fifth Monarchist Self-representation', *Women, Gender and Radical Religion in Early Modern Europe*, ed. Sylvia Brown (Leiden and Boston, MA: Brill, 2007), 117–38.
Bakhtin, Mikhail, *Rabelais and his World*, trans. Hélène Iswolsky (Bloomington and Indianapolis, IN: Indiana University Press, 1984).
Baldwin, Anna, and Sarah Hutton (eds), *Platonism and the English Imagination* (Cambridge: Cambridge University Press, 1994).
Baltrušaitis, Jurgis, *Anamorphic Art*, trans. W. J. Strachan (Cambridge: Chadwyck-Healey, 1977).
Banks, Carol, '"You are Pictures out of Doores . . . Saints in your Iniuries": picturing the female body in Shakespeare's plays', *Women's Writing* 8:2 (2001), 295–311.
Barasch, Frances K., *The Grotesque: A Study in Meanings* (The Hague and Paris: Mouton, 1971).
Barker, Francis, *The Tremulous Private Body: Essays on Subjection* (London: Methuen, 1984).
Barker, Roberta, and David Nicol, 'Does Beatrice-Joanna have a Subtext? *The Changeling* on the London Stage', *EMLS* 10:1 (2004), 1–43.
Barthes, Roland, 'Arcimboldo, or Magician and Rhétoriqueur', *The Responsibility of Forms: Critical Essays on Music, Art, and Representation*, trans. Richard Howard (Berkeley and Los Angeles: University of California Press, 1985), 129–48.
Becker, Lucinda, 'The Absent Body: Representations of dying early modern women in a selection of seventeenth-century diaries', *Women's Writing* 8:2 (2001), 251–62.
Beehler, Sharon, and Linda Woodbridge (eds), *Women, Violence, and English Renaissance Literature: Essays Honoring Paul Jorgensen* (Tempe, AZ: Arizona Center for Medieval and Renaissance Studies, 2003).
Benedict, Barbara M., *Curiosity: A Cultural History of Early Modern Inquiry* (Chicago and London: University of Chicago Press, 2001).
Berland, K. J. H., 'The Marks of Character: Physiology and Physiognomy in *Absalom and Achitophel*', *Philological Quarterly* 76:2 (Spring 1997), 193–218.
Berland, K. J. H., 'Reading Character in the Face: Lavater, Socrates and Physiognomy', *Word and Image* 9:1 (January–March 1993), 252–69.

Berry, Philippa, and Margaret Tudeau-Clayton (eds), *Textures of Renaissance Knowledge* (Manchester and New York: Manchester University Press, 2003)

Bettella, Patrizia, *The Ugly Woman: Transgressive Aesthetic Models in Italian Poetry from the Middle Ages to the Baroque* (Toronto: Toronto University Press, 2005).

Bigg, C., *Neoplatonism* (London: E. & J. B. Young, 1895).

Boehrer, Bruce, "'Alsemero's Closet": Privacy and Interiority in *The Changeling*', *Journal of English and Germanic Philology*. 96:3 (1997), n.p. 8 October 2007. http://galenet.galegroup.com.

Bohde, Daniela, 'Skin and the Search for the Interior: The Representation of Flaying in the Art and Anatomy of the Cinquecento', *Bodily Extremities: Preoccupations with the Human Body in Early Modern European Culture*, eds Florike Egmond and Robert Zwijnenberg (Aldershot: Ashgate, 2003), 10–47.

Botelho, Lynn, and Pat Thane (eds), *Women and Ageing in British Society since 1500* (Harlow: Longman, 2001).

Bott, Robin L., "'O, keep me from their worse than killing lust": Ideologies of Rape and Mutilation in Chaucer's "Physician's Tale" and Shakespeare's *Titus Andronicus*', *Representing Rape in Medieval and Early Modern Literature*, eds Elizabeth Robertson and Christine M. Rose (New York: Palgrave, 2001), 189–211.

Breitenberg, Mark, *Anxious Masculinity in Early Modern England* (Cambridge: Cambridge University Press, 1996).

Britton, Piers D. G., 'The Signs of Faces: Leonardo on Physiognomic Science and the "Four Universal States of Man"', *Renaissance Studies* 16:2 (2002), 143–62.

Brown, Frank Burch, 'The Beauty of Hell: Anselm on God's Eternal Design', *Journal of Religion* 73:3 (July 1993), 329–56.

Buffa, Sebastian (ed.), *Antonio Tempesta, The Illustrated Bartsch*, ser. ed. Walter L. Strauss (New York: Abaris Books, 1984), Vol. 37.

Burks, Deborah B., "'I'll want my will else": *The Changeling* and Women's Complicity with their Rapists', *ELH* 62:4 (1995), 759–90.

Burnett, Mark Thornton, *Constructing 'Monsters' in Shakespearean Drama and Early Modern Culture* (Basingstoke and New York: Palgrave Macmillan, 2002).

Burns, William E., *An Age of Wonders: Prodigies, Politics and Providence in England, 1657–1727* (Manchester and New York: Manchester University Press, 2002).

Burns, William E., "'A proverb of versatile mutability": Proteus and Natural Knowledge in Early Modern Britain', *Sixteenth-Century Journal* 32:4 (2001), 969–80.

Butler, Judith, *Bodies that Matter: On the Discursive Limits of 'Sex'* (London: Routledge, 1993).

Calbi, Maurizio, *Approximate Bodies: Gender and Power in Early Modern Drama and Anatomy* (London: Routledge, 2005).

Camden, Carrol, 'The Mind's Construction in the Face', *Renaissance Studies in Honor of Hardin Craig*, eds Baldwin Maxwell *et al*. (Stanford, CA: Stanford University Press, 1972), 208–20.

Carey, Jonathan Sinclair, 'The Quasimodo Complex: Deformity Reconsidered', *The Tyranny of the Normal: An Anthology*, eds Carol Donley and Sheryl Buckley (Kent, OH: Kent State University Press, 1996), 27–52.

Carmichael, Peter A., 'The Sense of Ugliness', *Journal of Aesthetics and Art Criticism* 30 (1972), 495–8.

Campbell, Erin J., '"Unenduring" Beauty: Gender and Old Age in Early Modern Art and Aesthetics', *Growing Old in Early Modern Europe: Cultural Representations*, ed. Erin J. Campbell (Aldershot: Ashgate, 2006).
Campbell, Mary Baine, '*Anthropometamorphosis*: John Bulwer's Monsters of Cosmetology and the Science of Culture', *Monster Theory: Reading Culture*, ed. Jeffrey Jerome Cohen (Minneapolis, MN: University of Minnesota Press, 1996), 202–24.
Campbell, Stephen J., and Sandra Seekins, *The Body Unveiled: Boundaries of the Figure in Early Modern Europe* (Ann Arbor, MI: University of Michigan Press, 1997).
Carruthers, Jo, *Esther through the Centuries* (Oxford: Blackwell, 2008).
Castelli, Elizabeth A., *Martyrdom and Memory: Early Christian Culture Making* (New York: Columbia University Press, 2004).
Cavallo, Sandra, and Lyndan Warner (eds), *Widowhood in Medieval and Early Modern Europe* (London: Longman, 1999).
Chaney, Edward (ed.), *The Evolution of English Collecting: Receptions of Italian Art in the Tudor and Stuart Periods* (New Haven, CT, and London: Yale University Press, 2003).
Charnes, Linda, *Notorious Identity: Materializing the Subject in Shakespeare* (Cambridge, MA: Harvard University Press, 1993).
Clayton, Martin, *Leonardo da Vinci: The Divine and the Grotesque* (London: Royal Collection Enterprises, 2002).
Cockayne, Emily, *Hubbub: Filth, Noise and Stench in England* (New Haven, CT, and London: Yale University Press, 2007).
Cohen, Jeffrey Jerome, *Monster Theory: Reading Culture* (London and Minneapolis, MN: University of Minnesota Press, 1996).
Colebrook, Claire, 'Introduction', *Feminist Theory* 7:2 (August 2006), 131–42.
Colie, Rosalie L., *Paradoxia Epidemica: The Renaissance Tradition of Paradox* (Princeton, NJ: Princeton University Press, 1966).
Conley, Tom, 'The Graphics of Dissimulation: Between *Heptameron* 10 and *l'histoire tragique*', *Critical Tales: New Studies of the* Heptameron *and Early Modern Culture*, eds John D. Lyons and Mary B. McKinley (Philadelphia: University of Pennsylvania Press, 1993), 65–82.
Cousins, Mark, 'The Ugly', 2 parts, *AA Files* 28 (1994), 61–4 and 29 (1995), 3–6.
Crawford, Julie, *Marvelous Protestantism: Monstrous Births in Post-Reformation England* (Baltimore, MD, and London: Johns Hopkins University Press, 2005).
Creighton, Charles, *A History of Epidemics in Britain* (1891–94), Vol. 2 (repr. New York: Barnes and Noble, 1965).
Cressy, David, *Agnes Bowker's Cat: Travesties and Transgressions in Tudor and Stuart England* (Oxford: Oxford University Press, 2000).
Cropper, Elizabeth, 'On Beautiful Women, Parmigianino, Petrarchismo, and the Vernacular Style', *Art Bulletin* 58:3 (September 1976), 374–94.
Cropper, Elizabeth, 'The Beauty of Woman: Problems in the Rhetoric of Renaissance Portraiture', *Rewriting the Renaissance: The Discourses of Sexual Difference in Early Modern Europe*, eds Margaret W. Ferguson, Maureen Quilligan and Nancy J. Vickers (Chicago and London: University of Chicago Press, 1986), 175–90.
Curran, Andrew, and Patrick Graille, 'The Faces of Eighteenth-Century Monstrosity', *Eighteenth-Century Life* 21:2 (1997), 1–15.

Daston, Lorraine, and Katherine Park, *Wonders and the Order of Nature, 1150–1750* (New York: Zone Books, 1998).

Deutsch, Helen, 'The Body's Moments: Visible Disability, the Essay and the Limits of Sympathy', *Prose Studies* 27: 1–2 (April–August 2005), 11–26.

Deutsch, Helen, and Felicity Nussbaum (eds), *'Defects': Engendering the Modern Body* (Ann Arbor, MI: University of Michigan Press, 2000).

Dolan, Frances E., '"Gentleman, I have one thing more to say": Women on Scaffolds in England, 1563–1680', *Modern Philology* 92:2 (November 1994), 157–78.

Dolan, Frances E., 'Taking the Pencil out of God's Hand: Art, Nature and the Face-painting Debate in Early Modern England', *PMLA* 108:2 (1993), 224–39.

Donley, Carol, and Sheryl Buckley (eds), *The Tyranny of the Normal: An Anthology* (Kent, OH: Kent State University Press, 1996).

Donoghue, Denis, *Speaking of Beauty* (New Haven, CT, and London: Yale University Press, 2003).

Douglas, Mary, *Purity and Danger: An Analysis of Concepts of Pollution and Taboo* (London and Henley: Routledge & Kegan Paul, 1966).

Drew-Bear, Annette, *Painted Faces on the Renaissance Stage: The Moral Significance of Face-painting Conventions* (Lewisburg, PA: Bucknell University Press, 1994).

Dubrow, Heather, *Echoes of Desire: English Petrarchanism and its Counterdiscourses* (Ithaca, NY, and London: Cornell University Press, 1995).

Eaton, Sarah, 'Beatrice-Joanna and the Rhetoric of Love', *Staging the Renaissance: Reinterpretations of Elizabethan and Jacobean Drama*, eds David Scott Kastan and Peter Stallybrass (New York: Routledge, 1991), 275–89.

Eaton, Sarah, 'Defacing the Feminine in Renaissance Tragedy', *The Matter of Difference: Materialist Feminist Criticism of Shakespeare*, ed. Valerie Wayne (New York: Harvester Wheatsheaf, 1991), 181–98.

Eco, Umberto, *Art and Beauty in the Middle Ages*, trans. Hugh Bredin (New Haven, CT, and London: Yale University Press, 1986).

Eco, Umberto (ed.), *On Beauty: A History of a Western Idea*, trans. Alastair McEwen (London: Secker & Warburg, 2004).

Eco, Umberto (ed.), *On Ugliness*, trans. Alastair McEwen (London: Harvill Secker, 2007).

Egmond, Florike, and Robert Zwijnenberg (eds), *Bodily Extremities: Preoccupations with the Human Body in Early Modern European Culture* (Aldershot: Ashgate, 2003).

Elias, Norbert, *The Civilizing Process: The History of Manners*, Vol. 1, trans. Edmund Jephcott (publ. as *Über den Prozess der Zivilisation*, 1939; this edn Oxford: Blackwell, 1978).

Enterline, Lynn, *The Rhetoric of the Body from Ovid to Shakespeare* (Cambridge: Cambridge University Press, 2000).

Estok, Simon, 'Environmental Implications of the Writing and Policing of the Early Modern Body: Dismemberment and Monstrosity in Shakespearean Drama', *Shakespeare Review* 33 (1998), 107–42.

Everett, Barbara, 'The Fatness of Falstaff: Shakespeare and Character', *Proceedings of the British Academy* 76 (1991), 109–28.

Farley, Edward, *Faith and Beauty: A Theological Aesthetic* (Aldershot: Ashgate, 2001).

Farnham, Willard, *The Shakespearean Grotesque: Its Genesis and Transformations* (Oxford: Clarendon Press, 1971).

Fendler, Susanne, 'The Emancipation of the Sign: The Changing Significance of Beauty in some English Renaissance Romances', *Critical Studies: Nominalism and Literary Discourse: New Perspectives*, eds Hugo Keiper, Christoph Bode and Richard J. Utz (Amsterdam: Rodopi, 1997), 269–82.

Ferguson, Margaret W., Maureen Quilligan and Nancy J. Vickers (eds), *Rewriting the Renaissance: The Discourses of Sexual Difference in Early Modern Europe* (Chicago and London: University of Chicago Press, 1986).

Fernie, Ewan, *Shame in Shakespeare* (London and New York: Routledge, 2002).

Findlen, Paula, 'Jokes of Nature and Jokes of Knowledge: The Playfulness of Scientific Discourse in Early Modern Europe', *Renaissance Quarterly* 43:2 (Summer 1990), 292–331.

Fudge, Erica, Ruth Gilbert and Susan Wiseman (eds), *At the Borders of the Human: Beasts, Bodies and Natural Philosophy in the Early Modern Period* (London: Macmillan, 1999).

Garber, Marjorie, *Shakespeare's Ghost Writers: Literature as Uncanny Causality* (New York and London: Methuen, 1987).

Garland, Madge, *The Changing Face of Beauty: Four Thousand Years of Beautiful Women* (London: Weidenfeld & Nicolson, 1957).

Gent, Lucy, and Nigel Llewellyn (eds), *Renaissance Bodies: The Human Figure in English Culture, c. 1540–1660* (London: Reaktion Books, 1990).

Gilbert, Ruth, *Early Modern Hermaphrodites: Sex and other Stories* (Basingstoke: Palgrave, 2002).

Gould, Thomas, *Platonic Love* (London: Routledge & Kegan Paul, 1963).

Gowing, Laura, *Common Bodies: Women, Touch and Power in Seventeenth-Century England* (New Haven, CT, and London: Yale University Press, 2003).

Grantley, Darryl, and Nina Taunton (eds), *The Body in Late Medieval and Early Modern Culture* (Aldershot: Ashgate, 2000).

Greenblatt, Stephen, 'Mutilation and Meaning', *The Body in Parts: Fantasies of Corporeality in Early Modern Europe*, eds David Hillman and Carlo Mazzio (New York and London: Routledge, 1997), 221–42.

Greenblatt, Stephen, *Renaissance Self-fashioning: From More to Shakespeare* (Chicago and London: University of Chicago Press, 1980).

Grundy, Isobel, and Susan Wiseman (eds), *Women, Writing, History, 1640–1740* (Athens, GA: University of Georgia Press, 1992).

Gutierrez, Nancy A., 'Philomela strikes back: Adultery and Mutilation as Female Self-assertion', *Women's Studies* 16:3–4 (1989), 429–43.

Gutierrez, Nancy A., *Shall She Famish Then? Female Food Refusal in Early Modern England* (Aldershot: Ashgate, 2003).

Hall, Kim F., *Things of Darkness: Economies of Race and Gender in Early Modern England* (Ithaca, NY, and London: Cornell University Press, 1995).

Hamling, Tara, and Richard L. Williams (eds), *Art Re-formed: Reassessing the Impact of the Reformation on the Visual Arts* (Cambridge: Cambridge Scholars Publishing, 2007).

Harbage, Alfred, *Cavalier Drama* (New York: MLA; London: Oxford University Press, 1936).

Harpham, Geoffrey Galt, *On the Grotesque: Strategies of Contradiction in Art and Literature* (Princeton, NJ: Princeton University Press, 1982).

Hays, Peter L., *The Limping Hero: Grotesques in Literature* (New York: New York University Press, 1971).
Healy, Margaret, *Fictions of Disease in Early Modern England: Bodies, Plagues and Politics* (Basingstoke: Palgrave, 2002).
Hendricks, Margo, and Patricia Parker (eds), *Women, 'Race', and Writing in the Early Modern Period* (London and New York: Routledge, 1994).
Hendrix, Harald, 'The Repulsive Body: Images of Torture in Seventeenth-Century Naples', *Bodily Extremities: Preoccupations with the Human Body in Early Modern European Culture*, eds Florike Egmond and Robert Zwijnenberg (Aldershot: Ashgate, 2003), 68–91.
Henein, Elgal, 'Male and Female Ugliness through the Ages', *Merveilles et Contes* 3:1 (May 1989), 45–56.
Henning, Standish, 'Branding Harlots on the Brow', *Shakespeare Quarterly* 51:1 (Spring 2000), 86–9.
Hillman, David, and Carlo Mazzio (eds), *The Body in Parts: Fantasies of Corporeality in Early Modern Europe* (New York and London: Routledge, 1997).
Holdsworth, R. V. (ed.), *Three Jacobean Revenge Tragedies: A Casebook* (Basingstoke: Macmillan, 1990).
Hopkins, Donald R., *Princes and Peasants: Smallpox in History* (Chicago: University of Chicago Press, 1983).
Huet, Marie-Hélène, *Monstrous Imagination* (Cambridge, MA: Harvard University Press, 1993).
Hutchinson, Mark, *Nausea: Encounters with Ugliness* (Nottingham: Djangoly Art Gallery, 2002).
Iyengar, Sujata, *Shades of Difference: Mythologies of Skin Color in Early Modern England* (Philadelphia: University of Pennsylvania Press, 2005).
James-Cavan, Kathleen, '"[A]ll in me is nature": The Values of Deformity in William Hay's *Deformity: An Essay*', *Prose Studies* 27:1–2 (April–August 2005), 27–38.
Johnston, Mark Albert, 'Bearded Women in Early Modern England', *SEL* 47:1 (Winter 2007), 1–28.
Jones, Frederic L. 'Another Source for *The Trial of Chivalry*', *PMLA* 47:3 (September 1932), 668–70.
Jones, Fred L., '*The Trial of Chivalry*, a Chettle Play', *PMLA* 41:2 (June 1926), 304–24.
Jones, Robert W., 'Obedient Faces: The Virtue of Deformity in Sarah Scott's Fiction', *'Defects': Engendering the Modern Body*, eds Helen Deutsch and Felicity Nussbaum (Ann Arbor, MI: University of Michigan Press, 2000), 280–302.
Jones-Davies, M. T., 'Monsters in the Literature and Spectacles of the English Renaissance: An Expression of Insecurity', *French Essays on Shakespeare and his Contemporaries*, eds Jean-Marie Maguin and Michele Willems (Newark, NJ: University of Delaware Press; London: Associated University Presses, 1995), 289–304.
Kayser, Wolfgang, *The Grotesque in Art and Literature*, trans. Ulrich Weisstein (Bloomington, IN: Indiana University Press, 1963).
Kirwan, James, *Beauty* (Manchester and New York: Manchester University Press, 1999).
Knoppers, Laura Lunger, '"The Antichrist, the Babilon, the Great Dragon": Oliver Cromwell, Andrew Marvell, and the Apocalyptic Monstrous', *Monstrous Bodies/Political Monstrosities in Early Modern Europe* (Ithaca, NY, and London: Cornell University Press, 2004), 93–123.

Knoppers, Laura Lunger, and Joan B. Landes (eds), *Monstrous Bodies/Political Monstrosities in Early Modern Europe* (Ithaca, NY, and London: Cornell University Press, 2004).

Knott, John R., *Discourses of Martyrdom in English Literature, 1563-1694* (Cambridge: Cambridge University Press, 1993).

Kristeva, Julia, *Powers of Horror: An Essay on Abjection*, trans. Leon S. Roudiez (New York: Columbia University Press, 1982).

Kwakkelstein, Michael W., 'Leonardo da Vinci's Grotesque Heads and the Breaking of the Physiognomic Mould', *Journal of the Warburg and Courtauld Institutes* 54 (1991), 127-36.

Leishman, J. B., *The Monarch of Wit: An Analytical and Comparative Study of the Poetry of John Donne* (London: Hutchinson, 1951, this edn 1965).

Levy, Allison (ed.), *Widowhood and Visual Culture in Early Modern Europe* (Aldershot: Ashgate, 2003).

Levy-Navarro, Elena, *The Culture of Obesity in Early and Late Modernity: Body Image in Shakespeare, Jonson, Middleton, and Skelton* (New York and Basingstoke: Palgrave Macmillan, 2008).

Little, Arthur L, '"Transshaped" Women: Virginity and Hysteria in *The Changeling*', *Madness in Drama*, ed. James Redmond (Cambridge: Cambridge University Press, 1993), 19-42.

Loomba, Ania, *Gender, Race, Renaissance Drama* (Manchester and New York: Manchester University Press, 1989).

Lund, Roger, 'Laughing at Cripples: Ridicule, Deformity and the Argument from Design', *Eighteenth Century Studies* 39:1 (2005), 91-114.

Lynch, Kathleen M., *The Social Mode of Restoration Comedy* (New York and London: Macmillan, 1926).

McAvoy, Liz Herbert, and Teresa Walters (eds), *Consuming Narratives: Gender and Monstrous Appetite in the Middle Ages and the Renaissance* (Cardiff: University of Wales Press, 2002).

Macdonald, Joyce Green, *Women and Race in Early Modern Texts* (Cambridge: Cambridge University Press, 2002).

McLane, Janice, 'The Voice on the Skin: Self-mutilation and Merleau-Ponty's Theory of Language', *Hypatia* 11:4 (Fall 1996), n.p. Literature Online. 3 May 2005.

Malloch, A. E., 'The Techniques and Function of the Renaissance Paradox', *Studies in Philology* 53 (1956), 191-203.

Marienstras, Richard, 'Of a Monstrous Body', *French Essays on Shakespeare and his Contemporaries*, eds Jean-Marie Maguin and Michele Willems (Newark, NJ: University of Delaware Press; London: Associated University Presses, 1995), 153-74.

Marrow, James H., *Passion Iconography in Northern European Art of the Late Middle Ages and Early Renaissance: A Study of the Transformation of Sacred Metaphor into Descriptive Narrative* (Kortrijk: Van Ghemmert, 1979).

Marsh, Derick R. C., '"Why should not old men be mad?" Old Age in Shakespeare's Plays', *Imperfect Apprehensions: Essays in English Literature in Honour of G. A. Wilkes*, ed. Geoffrey Little (Sydney: Challis Press, 1996), 44-55.

Marshall, Claire, 'The Politics of Self-mutilation: Forms of Female Devotion in the Late Middle Ages', *The Body in Late Medieval and Early Modern Culture*, eds Darryl Grantley and Nina Taunton (Aldershot: Ashgate, 2000), 11-22.

Marshall, Cynthia, *The Shattering of the Self: Violence, Subjectivity and Early Modern Texts* (Baltimore, MD, and London: Johns Hopkins University Press, 2002).

Martin, John, 'Inventing Sincerity, Refashioning Prudence: The Discovery of the Individual in Renaissance Europe', *American Historical Review* 102:5 (December 1995), 1309–42.

Marwick, Arthur, *Beauty in History: Society, Politics and Personal Appearance* (London: Thames & Hudson, 1988).

Marwick, Arthur, *It: A History of Human Beauty* (London and New York: Hambledon & London, 2004).

Maus, Katherine Eisaman, *Inwardness and Theater in the English Renaissance* (Chicago and London: University of Chicago Press, 1995).

Melbourne, Jane, 'The Inverted World of Bussy D'Ambois', *SEL* 25:2 (Spring 1985), 381–95.

Mellinkoff, Ruth, *The Mark of Cain* (Berkeley, CA: University of California Press, 1981).

Mellinkoff, Ruth, *Outcasts: Signs of Otherness*, 2 vols (Berkeley, CA: University of California Press, 1993).

Miller, Henry Knight, 'The Paradoxical Encomium, with Special Reference to its Vogue in England, 1600–1800', *Modern Philology* 53:3 (February 1956), 145–78.

Minois, Georges, *History of Old Age: From Antiquity to the Renaissance*, trans. Sarah Hanbury Tenison (Cambridge: Polity Press, 1989).

Mintz, Susannah B., 'Freak Space: Aphra Behn's Strange Bodies', *Restoration* 30:2 (Fall 2006), 1–19.

Mitchell, David T., and Sharon L. Snyder (eds), *The Body and Physical Difference: Discourses of Disability* (Ann Arbor, MI: University of Michigan Press, 1997).

Montuori, Deborah, 'The Confusion of Self and Role in Chapman's *Bussy D'Ambois*', *SEL* 28:2 (Spring 1988), 287–99.

Nordenfalk, Carl, 'The Five Senses in Late Medieval and Renaissance Art', *Journal of the Warburg and Courtauld Institutes* 48 (1985), 1–22.

Nussbaum, Felicity, 'Feminotopias: The Pleasures of "Deformity" in Mid-Eighteenth-Century England', *The Body and Physical Difference: Discourses of Disability*, eds David T. Mitchell and Sharon L. Snyder (Ann Arbor, MI: University of Michigan Press, 1997), 161–73.

Nussbaum, Felicity A., *The Limits of the Human: Fictions of Anomaly, Race, and Gender in the Long Eighteenth Century* (Cambridge: Cambridge University Press, 2003).

O'Connor, John, 'Physical Deformity and Chivalric Laughter in Renaissance England', *New York Literary Forum* 1 (1978), 59–71.

Osmond, Rosalie, *Mutual Accusation: Seventeenth-Century Body and Soul Dialogues in their Literary and Theological Context* (Toronto, Buffalo, NY, and London: University of Toronto Press, 1990).

Panofsky, Erwin, *Idea: A Concept in Art Theory*, trans. Joseph J. S. Peake (Columbia, SC: University of South Carolina Press, 1968).

Parker, Patricia, *Literary Fat Ladies: Rhetoric, Gender, Property* (London and New York: Methuen, 1987).

Paster, Gail Kern, *The Body Embarrassed: Drama and the Disciplines of Shame in Early Modern England* (Ithaca, NY: Cornell University Press, 1993).

Peacock, John, *The Stage Designs of Inigo Jones: The European Context* (Cambridge: Cambridge University Press, 1995).

Pender, Stephen, 'In the Bodyshop: Human Exhibition in Early Modern England', *"Defects"*:

Engendering the Modern Body, eds Helen Deutsch and Felicity Nussbaum (Ann Arbor, MI: University of Michigan Press, 2000).

Pender, Stephen, '"No Monsters at the Resurrection": Inside some Conjoined Twins', *Monster Theory: Reading Culture*, ed. Jeffrey Jerome Cohen (London Minneapolis, MN: University of Minnesota Press, 1996), 143–67.

Pino, Melissa, 'Devilish Appetites, Doubtful Beauty, and Dull Satisfaction: Rochester's *scorn of ugly ladies (which are very near all)*', *Restoration* 27:1 (Spring 2003), 1–21.

Platt, Peter G. (ed.), *Wonders, Marvels, and Monsters in Early Modern Culture* (Newark and London: University of Delaware Press and Associated University Presses, 1999).

Polinska, Wioleta, 'Bodies under Siege: Eating Disorders and Self-mutilation among Women', *Journal of the American Academy of Religion* 68:3 (September 2000), 569–89.

Porter, Chlöe, 'Interactions between English Drama and Visual Culture, 1576–1642', unpublished Ph.D. thesis, University of Manchester, 2007.

Porter, Martin, *Windows of the Soul: The Art of Physiognomy in European Culture, 1470–1780* (Oxford: Clarendon Press, 2005).

Porter, Roy, *Flesh in the Age of Reason* (London: Allen Lane, 2003).

Purkiss, Diane, 'Producing the Voice, Consuming the Body: Women Prophets of the Seventeenth Century', *Women, Writing, History, 1640–1740*, eds Isobel Grundy and Susan Wiseman (Athens, GA: University of Georgia Press, 1992).

Rhodes, Neil, *Eizabethan Grotesque* (London: Routledge & Kegan Paul, 1980).

Roberts, Marie Mulvey, and Roy Porter (eds), *Literature and Medicine during the Eighteenth Century* (London: Routledge, 1993).

Rosslyn, Felicity, 'Villainy, Virtue and Projection', *Cambridge Quarterly* 30:1 (2001), 1–17.

Rowe, Katherine, '"God's handy worke": Divine Complicity and the Anatomist's Touch', *The Body in Parts: Fantasies of Corporeality in Early Modern Europe*, eds David Hillman and Carlo Mazzio (New York and London: Routledge, 1997), 285–309.

Russo, Mary, *The Female Grotesque: Risk, Excess and Modernity* (London and New York: Routledge, 1994).

Sandwith, F. M., 'Smallpox and its Early History', *Clinical Journal* 36 (1910), 294–302.

Saunders, Corinne, *Rape and Ravishment in the Literature of Medieval England* (Cambridge: Brewer, 2001).

Sawday, Jonathan, *The Body Emblazoned: Dissection and the Human Body in Renaissance Culture* (London and New York: Routledge, 1995).

Sawday, Jonathan, '"Forms such as never were in Nature": The Renaissance Cyborg', *At the Borders of the Human: Beasts, Bodies and Natural Philosophy in the Early Modern Period*, eds Erica Fudge, Ruth Gilbert and Susan Wiseman (London: Macmillan, 1999).

Scarry, Elaine, *The Body in Pain: The Making and Unmaking of the World* (New York and Oxford: Oxford University Press, 1985).

Schiesari, Juliana, *The Gendering of Melancholia: Feminism, Psychoanalysis, and the Symbolics of Loss in Renaissance Literature* (Ithaca, NY, and London: Cornell University Press, 1992).

Schmitt, Charles B., *Aristotle and the Renaissance* (Cambridge, MA: Harvard University Press, 1983).

Schoenbaum, Samuel, 'The "Deformed Mistress" Theme and Chapman's *Gentleman Usher*', *Notes and Queries* 205 (1960), 22–4.

Schoenfeldt, Michael C., *Bodies and Selves in Early Modern England: Physiology and*

Inwardness in Spenser, Shakespeare, Herbert, and Milton (Cambridge: Cambridge University Press, 1999).

Schulenburg, Jane Tibbets, *Forgetful of their Sex: Female Sanctity and Society ca. 500–1100* (Chicago: University of Chicago Press, 1998).

Schulenburg, Jane Tibbets, 'The Heroics of Virginity: Brides of Christ and Sacrificial Mutilation', *Women in the Middle Ages and the Renaissance: Literary and Historical Perspectives*, ed. Mary Beth Rose (Syracuse, NY: Syracuse University Press, 1986), 29–72.

Scott, Mary Augusta, 'Elizabethan Translations from the Italian', *PMLA* 14:4 (1899), 465–571.

Selleck, Nancy, 'Donne's Body', *SEL* 41:1 (Winter 2001), 149–74.

Semonin, Paul, 'Monsters in the Marketplace: The Exhibition of Human Oddities in Early Modern England', *Freakery: Cultural Spectacles of the Extraordinary Body*, ed. Rosemarie Garland Thomson (New York and London: New York University Press, 1996), 69–81.

Shildrick, Margrit, *Embodying the Monster: Encounters with the Vulnerable Self* (London: Sage, 2002).

Simpson, Evelyn M., *A Study of the Prose Works of John Donne*, 2nd edn (Oxford, 1948).

Siraisi, Nancy, *Medieval and Early Renaissance Medicine: An Introduction to Knowledge and Practice* (Chicago: University of Chicago Press, 1990).

Smith, Nigel, *Perfection Proclaimed: Language and Literature in English Radical Religion, 1640–1660* (Oxford: Clarendon Press, 1989),

Specht, Henrik, 'The Beautiful, the Handsome and the Ugly: Some Aspects of the Art of Character Portrayal in Medieval Literature', *Studia Neophilologica* 56:2 (1984), 129–46.

Spierenburg, Pieter, *The Spectacle of Suffering: Executions and the Evolution of Repression from a Preindustrial Metropolis to the European Experience* (Cambridge: Cambridge University Press, 1984).

Stachniewski, John, 'Calvinist Psychology in Middleton's Tragedies', *Three Jacobean Revenge Tragedies: A Casebook*, ed. R. V. Holdsworth (Basingstoke: Macmillan, 1990), 226–47.

Stallybrass, Peter, 'Patriarchal Territories: The Body Enclosed', *Rewriting the Renaissance: The Discourses of Sexual Difference in Early Modern Europe*, eds Margaret W. Ferguson, Maureen Quilligan and Nancy J. Vickers (Chicago and London: University of Chicago Press, 1986), 123–42.

Stallybrass, Peter, and Allon White, *The Politics and Poetics of Transgression* (Ithaca, NY: Cornell University Press, 1986).

Stampino, Maria Galli, 'Bodily Boundaries Represented: the Petrarchan, the Burlesque and Arcimboldo's Example', *Quaderni d'Italianistica* 16:1 (Spring 1995), 61–79.

Stanivukovic, Goran V. (ed.), *Ovid and the Renaissance Body* (Toronto, Buffalo, NY, and London: University of Toronto Press, 2001).

Stott, Andrew, 'Tiresias and the Basilisk: Vision and Madness in Middleton and Rowley's *The Changeling*', *Revista alicantina de estudios ingleses* 12 (1999), 165–79.

Sugg, Richard, *Murder after Death: Literature and Anatomy in Early Modern England* (Ithaca, NY, and London: Cornell University Press, 2007).

Summers, Claude, and Ted-Larry Pebworth (eds), *Renaissance Discourses of Desire* (Columbia, MO: University of Missouri Press, 1993).

Summers, David, *Michelangelo and the Language of Art* (Princeton, NJ: Princeton University Press, 1981).

Suzuki, Mihoko, *Subordinate Subjects: Gender, the Political Nation, and Literary Form in England, 1588–1688* (Aldershot: Ashgate, 2003).
Synnott, Anthony, 'Truth and Goodness, Mirrors and Masks: A Sociology of Beauty and the Face', *British Journal of Sociology*, Part 1, 40:4 (December 1989), 607–36; Part 2, 41:1 (March 1990), 55–76.
Tatarkiewicz, Wladyslaw, *History of Aesthetics*, ed. D. Petsch, Vol. 3 (The Hague: Mouton, 1974).
Taylor, Charles, *Sources of the Self: The Making of the Modern Identity* (Cambridge: Cambridge University Press, 1989).
Tayler, Edward William, *Nature and Art in Renaissance Literature* (New York: Columbia University Press, 1964).
Tennenhouse, Leonard, *Power on Display: The Politics of Shakespeare's Genres* (New York and London: Methuen, 1986).
Thane, Pat, *Old Age in English History: Past Experiences, Present Issues* (Oxford: Oxford University Press, 2000).
Thomson, Philip, *The Grotesque* (London: Methuen, 1972).
Thomson, Rosemarie Garland (ed.), *Freakery: Cultural Spectacles of the Extraordinary Body* (New York and London: New York University Press, 1996).
Tilmouth, Christopher, 'Burton's "Turning Picture": Argument and Anxiety in *The Anatomy of Melancholy*', *RES* 56:226 (2005), 524–49.
Todd, Dennis, *Imagining Monsters: Miscreations of the Self in Eighteenth-Century England* (Chicago and London: University of Chicago Press, 1995).
Torrey, Michael, '"The plain devil and dissembling looks": Ambivalent Physiognomy and Shakespeare's *Richard III*', *ELR* 30:2 (2000), 123–53.
Tournon, André, 'Rules of the Game', *Critical Tales: New Studies of the* Heptameron *and Early Modern Culture*, eds John D. Lyons and Mary B. McKinley (Philadelphia: University of Pennsylvania Press, 1993), 188–99.
Trobiner, Alice, 'Old Age in Tudor–Stuart Broadside Ballads', *Folklore* 102:2 (1991), 149–74.
Tudeau-Clayton, Margaret, '"I do not know my selfe": the Topography and Politics of Self-knowledge in Ben Jonson's *Bartholomew Fair*', *Textures of Renaissance Knowledge*, eds Philippa Berry and Margaret Tudeau-Clayton (Manchester and New York: Manchester University Press, 2003), 177–98.
Ure, Peter, 'The "Deformed Mistress" Theme and the Platonic Convention', *Notes and Queries* 193 (1948), 269–70.
Vasari, Giorgio, *The Lives of the Artists*, trans. and eds Julia Conaway Bondanella and Peter Bondanella (Oxford: Oxford University Press, 1991).
Vaughan, Virginia Mason, *Performing Blackness on English Stages, 1500–1800* (Cambridge: Cambridge University Press, 2005).
Veevers, Erica, *Images of Love and Religion: Queen Henrietta Maria and Court Entertainments* (Cambridge: Cambridge University Press, 1989).
Vickers, Brian (ed.), *Occult and Scientific Mentalities in the Renaissance* (Cambridge: Cambridge University Press, 1984).
Vickers, Nancy, '"The blazon of sweet beauty's best": Shakespeare's *Lucrece*', *Shakespeare and the Question of Theory*, eds Patricia Parker and Geoffrey Harman (New York and London: Methuen, 1985).

Vickers, Nancy, 'Diana Described: Scattered Women and Scattered Rhyme', *Critical Inquiry* 8 (1981), 265–79.
Vickers, Nancy, 'This Heraldry in Lucrece's Face', *Poetics Today* 6:1–2 (1985), 171–84.
Walker, Julia M. (ed), *Dissing Elizabeth: Negative Representations of Gloriana* (Durham, NC, and London: Duke University Press, 1998).
Westra, Laura, 'Love and Beauty in Ficino and Plotinus', *Ficino and Renaissance Neoplatonism*, eds Konrad Eisenblicher and Olga Zorzi Pugliese (Ottawa: Dovehouse Editions, 1986), 175–87.
White, Helen C., *Tudor Books of Saints and Martyrs* (Madison, WI: University of Wisconsin Press, 1963).
Wilks, Stephen, *Medusa: Solving the Mystery of the Gorgon* (Oxford: Oxford University Press, 2000).
Williams, Andrew P. (ed.), *The Image of Manhood in Early Modern Literature: Viewing the Male* (Westport, CT, and London: Greenwood Press, 1999).
Williams, David, *Deformed Discourse: The Function of the Monster in Medieval Thought and Literature* (Exeter: University of Exeter Press, 1996).
Williams, R. Grant, 'Disfiguring the Body of Knowledge: Anatomical Discourse and Robert Burton's *The Anatomy of Melancholy*', *ELH* 68:3 (2001), 593–613.
Williams, Raymond, 'Base and Superstructure in Marxist Cultural Theory', *The Raymond Williams Reader*, ed. John Higgins (Oxford: Blackwell, 2001).
Wilson, F. P. (ed.), *The Oxford Dictionary of English Proverbs*, 3rd edn (Oxford: 1970).
Wind, Barry, *'A Foul and Pestilent Congregation': Images of 'Freaks' in Baroque Art* (Aldershot: Ashgate, 1998).
Wolf, John E., 'Acne and Rosacea: Differential Diagnosis and Treatment in the Primary Care Setting', *Medscape Today* (September 2002). 25 October 2007. http://medscape.com.
Wright, Thomas, *A History of Caricature and Grotesque in Literature and Art* (London: Virtue Brothers, 1865).
Ziolkowski, Jan, 'Avatars of Ugliness in Medieval Literature', *Modern Language Review* 79:1 (1984), 1–20.
Zunker, Mark J., 'Homeliness and Humor in Renaissance Italy: Tales of Ugly (and Witty) Artists and other Paragons of Ugliness', *Explorations in Renaissance Culture* 30:2 (Winter 2004), 231–59.

Index

abject 6, 44, 58, 92, 97–130, 161, 165, 178, 182, 185, 187, 207n.2, 210n.63, 211n.92
adultery 67, 223n.65
aesthetics 11, 17, 24–5, 35, 140
agency 2, 46, 79, 84, 94, 137, 144, 147, 150, 158–87, 215n.18, 218n.79
Alcibiades 71, 78
America 121
anamorphic art 25
anatomy 3, 20, 29, 49, 52, 93, 97–8, 107, 116, 117, 121, 122–30, 131
anger 48–9, 58–9, 60, 74, 153, 158, 175
  'wroth' 58–9
anorexic 222n.48
Anselment, Raymond A. 155, 218n.89, 219n.107, 220n.115 and n.123
ape 19
Aquinas, Thomas 13, 23, 191n.12, 198n.8
Arcimboldo, Giuseppe
  Autumn 25
  Winter 25, 26
Aristotle 23, 31, 71, 75, 117, 130, 133, 198n.8, 220n.7
  pseudo-Aristotle 59, 202n.89
Armstrong, Karen 206n.65 and n.71
art, visual 1–2, 3–4, 6, 11, 19, 23–30, 31–3, 46–7, 49–50, 57, 59–60, 72–3, 97, 99–100, 107–8, 111–12, 130, 134–5, 137–9, 146–9, 163–4, 170, 187, 188
Augustine 13, 18, 19–20

Bacon, Francis
  The Essays 5, 53, 92, 94, 140, 190–1n.23
  The Novum Organum 38–9
  'The Masculine Birth of Time' 39
  The Wisdom of the Ancients 48
Baker, Naomi 223n.60
Bakhtin, Mikhail 2, 6, 25, 31, 99, 145, 217n.67
baldness 54, 57, 125, 127, 142–3, 183, 184
Baldung, Hans
  The Three Ages of Man and Death 111, *112*
Baltrušaitis, Jurgis 195n.73
Barker, Francis 204n.36
Barker, Roberta 92
Baroque 25, 140
Barthes, Roland 25
Bartholin, Thomas
  Bartholinus Anatomy 116–17, 120
Baxter, Richard
  A Christian Directory 117
bear 18, 59, 121, 123
beard 57
bearded woman 21–2, 125, 181, 194n.57
beauty *see* fair
Bedford, Thomas
  A True and Certaine Relation 31, 34
Behn, Aphra
  The Dumb Virgin 159–60, 165
  The Luckey Chance 97
beldame 5, 6, 107, 108, *110*, 111, 130, 180
belly 95, 116, 118, 119, 121

Berkeley, William
 The Lost Lady 52–3, 176
Berland, K. J. H. 201n.60, 202n.89
Bernard of Clairvaux 27, 42
Bettella, Patrizia 191n.30, 218n.88
Bible, The 27, 29, 58, 105, 197n.111
 Adam 6, 11, 43, 111, 132
 Eve 6
 Ezekiel 61
 Job 105
 Revelation 203n.17
 see also Cain; Devil, The; Esther; Fall, The; hell; whore
black body 2, 5, 7, 14, 15–16, 34, 57, 77, 79–80, 87, 101, 105, 118, 125, 127, 140–1, 143–4, 146–7, 160, 175–8, 217n.55
 'Moor' 15, 53, 105, 143, 176–8, 181
 see also race
blindness 12, 36, 38, 76, 83–6, 129, 137, 146–7, 168, 180
blood 6, 25, 46, 51, 61, 66, 67, 80, 87–90, 92, 98, 117, 118, 119, 120, 125, 152, 165, 176–7, 180, 185, 186
 see also menstruation
Boehrer, Bruce 88
Boethius 71
Bohde, Daniela 221n.23
boil 101, 105
Bolton, Robert
 Certaine Devout Prayers 106
Bosch, Hieronymus
 Christ Carrying the Cross 27, 28
Botelho, Lynn 211n.80
Bott, Robin L. 226n.121
Bowes, Thomas 11
Boyle, Robert
 A Free Enquiry 35–40
branded 61, 63, 82, 172, 223n.65
breasts 7, 75, 98, 116, 142, 170, 222n.52
 bosom 75, 79, 104, 119, 126
 dugs 125, 142
breath, sour 103–4, 125, 142, 179
Breitenberg, Mark 122
Britton, Piers D. G. 200n.36

Brome, Alexander
 'To a Gentleman that fell sick of the Small Pox' 153–6
brow *see* forehead
Browne, Sir Thomas
 Pseudodoxia Epidemica 15
 Religio Medici 18, 27, 193n.33
Bulwer, John
 Anthropometamorphosis 15–16, 20, 132
Buoni, Thomasso
 Problemes of Beautie 14–15, 71–2, 81–2
Burke, Edmund 22, 194n.61
Burks, Deborah B. 206n.65, n.69 and n.70
burlesque 2, 31, 139, 178
Burnett, Mark Thornton 205n.48, n.51, n.59 and n.60
Burns, William E. 194n.54, 198n.130
Burton, Robert
 The Anatomy of Melancholy 3–4, 11, 98, 117, 122–30, 131, 132, 191n.28
Butler, Judith 97–8

Cain, mark of 41, 57–64
Calbi, Maurizio 92, 206n.79, 210n.63, 212n.105
Calvin, John 43, 51–2, 73, 105, 132, 200n.56
Calvinism 69, 83, 93, 151, 206n.86
Campbell, Erin J. 211n.74 and n.83
Campbell, Mary Baine 192n.21
cancer 25, 75
Carew, Thomas 27
 'Ingrateful Beauty Threatened' 150
Carey, Jonathan Sinclair 199n.25
carrion 76, 214n.170
Carruthers, Jo 74, 203n.24
Cartwright, William
 'On the Lady Newburgh' 155
Castelli, Elizabeth A. 225n.97
Cavallo, Sandra 211n.85
Cavendish, Margaret
 The Publick Wooing 77
 Wits Cabal 152
 The Worlds Olio 36
Chaney, Edward 189n.4

Chapman, George
  Bussy D'Ambois 41, 57, 64–8
  The Gentleman Usher 18, 101, 160, 163, 168, 175–6, 183–7
  The Widow's Tears 171
Charnes, Linda 81
cheek 7, 13, 17, 25, 34, 47, 76, 86, 98, 117, 118, 128, 131, 134, 142, 160, 166, 168, 172, 176
children 3, 34, 49–51, 66, 79, 95, 105, 121, 156, 159, 168, 176, 183, 220n.7
chin 17, 50, 86, 89, 108, 125, 142, 181
China 15, 125
Christ, body of 11, 27–9, 31, 63, 78–9, 169
Church of England *see* Protestantism
Clayton, Martin 194n.69, 208n.13
Cleveland, John
  'A Young Man to an Old Woman courting him' 113
clothing 43, 73, 93, 96, 103, 111, 115, 126–7, 146, 167, 221n.22
  tailor 82, 95
Cockayne, Emily 209n.41, 211n.74
Cocles, Bartholomew
  A Brief and most Pleasant Epitomye 50, 70
Colebrook, Claire 191n.3
Collier, Jeremy
  Miscellanies upon Moral Subjects 63–4
Collop, John
  The Poems 27, 115, 140, 150
complexion 14–15, 46, 66, 75, 101, 111, 116, 118, 125, 133, 136, 142, 155, 181, 187
conjoined twins 31, 34, 190n.16
Conley, Tom 224n.77 and n.79
consumption, disease of 104, 116, 117, 127, 214n.170
Cooper, Thomas
  The Churches Deliverance 74
Corbett, Richard
  'Upon the Death of Lady Haddington' 152–3
corpse *see* death

cosmetics 73, 76, 110, 134–7, 158, 160, 186, 215n.18
  painted face 6, 66, 76–7, 110–11, 134–6, 144, 181
  patch 45, 65, 101, 158
court, royal 16, 20, 21, 25, 65, 72–4, 139, 167, 175, 180
courtly love 84, 173
Cousins, Mark 145, 217n.70
Cowper, William
  Pathmos 106
Cranach, Lucas
  The Fountain of Youth 137–9, *138*
Crawford, Julie 34, 224n.68
Crompton, Hugh
  'Deformity' 102, 106
Cromwell, Oliver 24
Cropper, Elizabeth 134, 144
creation, divine 12, 17–20, 43, 133–4
The Creation of the World 57–8
Crooke, Helkiah
  Mikrokosmographia 103–5
crooked 16–17, 36, 45, 48, 49, *50*, 70, 75, 83, 93–5
  see also hunchback
Cureau de la Chambre, Marin
  The Art how to Know Men 52

Daniel, Samuel
  The Complaint of Rosamund 163
Daston, Lorraine 22
death 1, 2, 6, 11, 43–4, 57, 58, 67, 99, 104, 107, 111–15, *112*, 119, 120, 127, 136, 139, 151–6, 162, 163, 166–8, 170, 173, 175, 181, 183, 184–6
  corpse 6, 23, 44, 45, 97, 99, 111, 113, 115, 127, 165, 166, 211n.92, 214n.170
defeature 48, 163–5, 178, 186
deformed mistress 131–2, 139–51, 180, 182
  see also ugly beauty
Dekker, Thomas
  The Virgin Martyr (with Philip Massinger) 225n.97

Dekker, Thomas (*cont.*)
    The Witch of Edmonton (with John Ford and William Rowley) 5, 107
    The Whore of Babylon 153
Descartes, René
    Cartesian 3, 188
    Discourse on Method 2–3
    Meditations on First Philosophy 83
    The Passions of the Soul 51
Deutsch, Helen 5, 93–5, 197n.120, 207n.89
Devil, The 23, 73, 118, 120
    devils 54, 76, 81, 84, 86, 180
    Lucifer 44, 54
dirt 99, 103, 111, 126, 127
dissection 3, 66, 84, 107, 142
divine signatures 2, 39, 57–64, 164
dog 22, 57, 88, 104, 121
Dolan, Frances E. 137, 171, 215n.18 and n.22
Donne, John 27, 140
    'The Autumnall' 113–15
    'The Comparison' 101–3, 115, 144
    'Elegie II. The Anagram' 140, 144, 146
    Paradoxes and Problems 11, 23, 45
    Sermons 43–4, 52
    'What if this present were the worlds last night?' 31
Douglas, Mary 62
Drew-Bear, Annette 222n.42
Dryden, John 31, 34, 152, 155
Dubrow, Heather 114, 147, 212n.97 and n.99, 216n.32, 217n.60, 218n.79 and n.83
dunghill *see* excrement
Dunton, John
    Athenian Sport 48, 141, 144
    A Voyage round the World 152

ears 16, 48, 102, 104
Eaton, Sarah 86, 202n.101, 223n.63 and n.65
Eco, Umberto 194n.67, 198n.9
Egypt 176
elephant 18, 65
Elias, Norbert 208n.27, 209n.39

Elys, Edmund
    'To Mrs K.G. having been lately Sick of the Small Pox' 155
Erasmus, Desiderius 133
    The Praise of Folly 79
    The Sileni of Alcibiades 78–9
d'Este, Isabella 134, *135*
Esther 73–4, 203n.24
Ethiopia 77, 176
Evelyn, John
    Numismata 55–7, 77–8
excrement 101, 103–4, 117, 123, 128, 130
    dunghill 39, 44, 73, 104, 123, 127
    see also snot
eye 3, 7, 13, 17, 29, 47–8, 54, 59, 71, 85, 87–8, 90, 98, 101, 102, 103, 107, 110, 113, 114, 117, 118, 125, 127, 128, 131, 140, 142, 150, 160, 166, 167, 168, 173, 183, 221n.19, 222n.52
eye of the beholder 13–17, 31, 43, 144–51, 179, 186–7
eyesight 22, 23, 31, 43, 45, 51, 65, 70, 71, 74, 77, 78, 79, 83, 84, 87–8, 89, 93, 118, 119, 126, 129, 147, 155, 166, 176, 180
    squint 50, 125, 128
    see also blindness
eyebrow 48, 71
eyelashes 17

fair 2, 11, 14, 17, 20, 21, 25, 31, 36, 42, 45, 46, 48, 63, 71, 72, 74, 75, 76, 80, 81, 84, 86, 93, 101, 110, 113, 116, 117, 118, 126–8, 131, 132, 136, 139, 140, 143, 146, 152, 154, 158, 161, 162, 164, 166, 167, 168, 176–7, 185, 186
Fall, The 43–4, 132–4, 139, 155
de Faria e Sousa, Manuel
    The Portugues Ásia 15
Farnham, Willard 195n.85
fat *see* obesity
feet 48, 57, 59, 77, 125, 184
Feltham, Owen
    'On a Gentlewoman, whose Nose was pitted with the Small Pox' 154

The Female Monster 75
Fendler, Susanne 45
fever 104, 113, 117, 127, 143
Ficino, Marsilio *see* Platonism
Findlen, Paula 21
fingernails 125, 142, 160, 166
Firenzuola, Agnolo
   On the Beauty of Women 12, 14, 17–18, 46–7, 117
flayed body 163, 165–87
Fleming, Abraham
   A Paradoxe 142–3
Fletcher, John
   Bonduca 116
Florio, John
   A Worlde of Wordes 195n.80
flushed face 134
Ford, John
   Tis Pity She's a Whore 107, 108
   The Witch of Edmonton see Dekker, Thomas
forehead 16, 22, 25, 37, 57, 59, 61, 63, 82, 84, 98, 105, 131, 142, 158, 172
   brow 41, 59, 67, 77, 86, 101, 107, 125, 155, 172, 183
Foxe, John
   Actes and Monuments 11, 29, 170–1, 225n.97
freak 21, 158, 165, 176, 197n.116
   freak show 21
Freeman, Thomas
   'In Miluum' 107
Fuller, Thomas
   The Holy State 19, 29, 31, 79, 91, 158
Fury 108, 133, 183

gait 125
Galenic model of body 46, 102, 122
   see also humoural model of body
Galle, Philips
   Cain leaving the presence of God 62
gesture 34, 48, 71, 78, 94, 108, 125, 167, 170
Ghirlandaio, Domenico
   Old Man with a Young Boy 3, 4

gild 19, 102, 111, 113, 179
Giorgione
   La Vecchia 108, *109*
Glover, Henry
   Cain and Abel parallel'd 57–8
Goltzius, Conrad
   Pride 6, 8–9
Goltzius, Henrik
   Anger 59, *60*
Gould, Robert
   A Poem most humbly Offered 155
Greenblatt, Stephen 73, 170
Gregory the Great
   Pastoral Care 44–5
Grelot, Guillaume-Joseph
   A Late Voyage to Constantinople 170
grief 2, 48, 146, 164–5, 183
grotesque 1, 2, 6, 23, 24, 25–7, 31, 32–3, 46, 47, 54, 86, 99, 107, 125, 145, 146, 148–9, 159, 176, 195n.79 and 80, 207n.2, 220n.123
Grünewald, Matthias
   Isenheim altarpiece 30
guilt 34, 59, 61, 65, 88, 181, 205n.52
   see also shame
Gutierrez, Nancy A. 182, 223n.65

H., N.
   The Ladies Dictionary 29–31, 43, 116–18, 121, 134
hag 5, 6, 10, 99, 107, 108, 115, 118, 130, 137, 188
Hagthorpe, John
   'Sinne and Vertue' 77
hair 48, 54, 57–8, 74–5, 89, 98, 103, 106, 128, 131, 142, 168, 170, 176, 183, 194n.57, 204n.27
   black 7, 20, 25
   blonde 98
   depilatory cream 168, 183
   dyed 73
   grey 107, 210n.71
   red 57
   white 20
   see also baldness; beard

Hall, John
  'To an Old Wife talking to him' 108
Hall, Kim F. 217n.55
Hall, Thomas
  Comarum Akosmia: The Loathsomenesse of Long Haire 74–5
Hammond, William
  'To the Same' 154
Harrison, William
  The First and Second Volumes (with Raphael Holinshed) 108
Harvey, Gideon
  Morbus Anglicus 75
Hay, William
  Deformity: An Essay 70, 93–6, 207n.89, n.94 and n.96
Head, Richard
  The English Rogue (with Francis Kirkham) 108
Healy, Margaret 105, 117, 213n.141, 226n.118
Heath, Robert
  'To Megaera' 106
hell 44, 59, 76, 140, 181, 183
  infernal 101, 108
Hendrix, Harald 29
Henning, Standish 223n.65
Henrietta Maria 72–3, 180, 197n.111
Herbert, George
  'The Size' 120
Herbert of Cherbury
  'Another Sonnet to Black itself' 141
  'Sonnet of Black Beauty' 147
Herrick, Robert
  Hesperides 5, 20, 103, 105, 107, 117, 150, 210n.71
Hildersam, Arthur
  CLII Lectures on Psalm LI 105–6
Hill, Thomas
  The Contemplation of Mankinde 50, 70
Hillman, David 195n.91
Hobbes, Thomas
  Leviathan 14, 105
  The Questions Concerning Liberty 140

Hogarde, Miles
  The Displaying of the Protestantes 105
Hogarth, William
  The Analysis of Beauty 95
Hopkins, Donald R. 219n.104
Howell, James 180
Huet, Marie-Hélène 220n.7
Hume, David
  'Of the Standard of Taste' 13
humour *see* laughter
humoural body 46–8, 59, 66, 80, 102–6, 111, 117–22, 126, 129, 137, 150, 153
  see also complexion; passions
hunchback 81–3, 93–6
Hutcheson, Francis
  An Inquiry 13, 38
Hutchinson, Mark 18, 182

Indian 154
  Indies 16, 121
Italy 1–2, 12, 14, 16, 25, 27, 31, 139–40

Jackson, Arthur
  A Help for the Understanding 58
Jackson, Thomas
  Diverse Sermons 198n.130
James-Cavan, Kathleen 94, 207n.94 and n.96
Jeamson, Thomas
  Artificiall Embellishments 2, 116, 136–7, 164, 215n.22
Jenner, David
  Cain's Mark 58–63
jet 104, 142
Jews 57, 73, 184
Johnson, Samuel
  Dictionary 31
Johnston, Mark Albert 194n.57
Johnstone, John
  An History of the Wonderful Things of Nature 102, 104, 121, 209n.29
Jones, Fred L. 225n.95
Jones, Inigo 26
  Tempe Restor'd 72
Jones, Robert W. 207n.93

Jonson, Ben 27, 212n.109
  Bartholomew Fair 119–20
  'An Epigram. To the Small Poxe' 152
  'Epistle: To my Lady Covell' 115
  'My Picture left in Scotland' 116
  Timber, or Discoveries 31, 45
  Volpone 104, 160, 165–6, 210n.73
Jordan, Thomas
  'On the Death of the most worthily honour'd Mr. John Sidney' 155
  'A Paradox on his Mistresse' 146–7, 150
  'To a Black Moor' 105
Joubert, Laurent
  Traite du Ris (Treatise on Laughter) 31, 48, 120–1, 214n.149

Keith, George
  The Arguments of the Quakers 116
King, Henry
  'The Defence' 13, 150–1
  'Madam Gabrina' 142–3, 146
  'Paradox' 140
Knagg, Thomas 40
Knoppers, Laura Lunger 203n.17
Knott, John R. 195n.91, 210n.54, 223n.57
Kristeva, Julia 6–7, 44, 97–8, 106, 109, 123, 207n.5, 211n.92
Kwakkelstein, Michael W. 189n.3, 194n.69

lame 3, 16, 45, 125, 129, 137
Lamport, John
  A Direct Method 153
Lanyer, Aemilia
  Salve Deus Rex Judaeorum 161–2
Laud, William 34, 72
Lauder, George
  The Anatomie of the Romane Clergie 29
laughter 31, 34, 48, 72, 76, 78, 120–1, 214n.149
  humour 23, 124, 197n.112
leaky body 2, 101–6, 115, 121, 127, 137, 145, 182, 185
lean 5, 76, 107, 116–17, 119, 120, 125, 128, 144, 153
  see also anorexic; starvation

Leigh, Richard
  'On an old Beldame' 111
Lenton, Francis
  Lentons Leisures Described 103
  'Queene Esters Halliluiahs' 73
Leonardo da Vinci 1, 20, 23–4, 24, 31, 46, 47, 99, 108, 211n.78
leprosy 29, 103, 105–6, 165, 169, 178, 182–3, 226n.114
Levy, Allison 211n.84
Levy-Navarro, Elena 212n.109, 214n.147
lice 103, 125
lion 59, 65
lips 16, 25, 71, 98, 104, 105, 131, 142, 176, 181, 184
  see also mouth
Little, Arthur L. 85–6
Lovelace, Richard
  'A Paradox' 20
Lucifer *see* Devil, The
Lund, Roger 196n.98
Lyly, John
  Endymion 142, 226n.111
  Euphues: The Anatomy 20, 24–5

McLane, Janice 222n.48, n.49 and n.50
Mannerism 25, 140
Marlowe, Christopher
  Tamburlaine the Great, Pt 1 41
marriage 85, 113, 121, 168–9, 183, 184, 222n.52
Marrow, James H. 27–9
Marshall, Claire 169
Martin, John 200n.54
martyr 11, 29, 58, 63, 95, 130, 171, 173
  virgin martyr 168–79, 222n.42, 222n.52
masculinity 7, 14, 69, 70, 73, 77–96, 98, 103, 122–30, 131–57, 170, 178, 185–6, 188
mask 31, 39, 54, 63, 78–9, 83, 86–7, 96, 155, 185
  see also visor
masque, court 26, 72
Massinger, Philip
  The Parliament of Love 176

Massys, Quinten
  An Old Woman ('The Ugly Duchess') 99, 100
Matthew of Vendome
  Ars versificatoria 98–9
Maus, Katherine Eisaman 51
Mazzio, Carlo 195n.91
measles 105
mechanical philosophy 3, 35–40, 54–5
medicine 1, 46, 183, 190n.14, 226n.118
Medusa 103, 106
melancholy *see* Burton, Robert
Melbourne, Jane 65, 67, 202n.99 and n.103
Mellinkoff, Ruth 58
menstruation 6, 75, 101–7
The Merry Dutch Miller 102–3, 137
Michelangelo 195n.79
Middleton, Thomas
  The Changeling (with William Rowley) 69–70, 80, 83–93, 200n.56
  The Ghost of Lucrece 184
  Women Beware Women 115
Milton, John
  Paradise Lost 11, 51, 119, 132–3, 213n.141
Minois, Georges 108
Mintz, Susannah B. 220n.8
Miso-Spilus
  A Wonder of Wonders 134, 158
mole 20, 34, 45, 155, 176, 205n.52
monster 2, 20, 23, 27, 36–7, 75, 106, 115, 122, 125, 133, 190n.16, 196n.96, 197n.112 and n.126, 198n.131, 205n.48 and n.51
monstrosity 18, 73, 95, 106, 159
monstrous birth 19, 31, 34, 37, 39, 159
  see also conjoined twins
de Montaigne, Michel
  'An Apology for Raymond Sebond' 16
  'On the Lame' 16–17
  'On a Monster-child' 20
  'On Physiognomy' 77, 78, 83–4, 89
Montuori, Deborah 202n.99 and n.100
'Moor' *see* black body

Moore, Richard
  Ho thesaurus en ostrakinois 204n.27
mother
  birth 45, 97, 99, 132
  maternal body 6
  maternal imagination 159–60, 220n.7
  see also monstrous birth
mouth 17, 22, 48, 59, 98, 102, 114, 125, 127, 128, 131, 141, 173, 182
  see also lips; teeth
Munday, Anthony
  The Defence of Contraries 142–3
mutilation 16, 29, 67, 101, 129, 159, 158–88
  self-mutilation 7, 18, 158–88

Nashe, Thomas 201n.70
  Nashes Lenten Stuffe 143
  The Terrors of the Night 54, 56
de Navarre, Marguerite
  The Heptameron 173
Neoplatonism *see* Platonism
Nicol, David 92
Norden, John
  The Labyrinth of Man's Life 118
Nordenfalk, Carl 202n.88
nose 15–16, 17, 21, 22, 25, 43, 54, 59, 78, 86, 98, 102, 103, 107, 108, 121, 125–6, 128, 137, 141–2, 145, 153, 154, 168, 172, 173, 181, 183, 184
snot 128, 141, 144, 145
Nussbaum, Felicity 93–4, 159, 160, 197n.120, 204n.28, 207n.89

obesity 2, 46, 77, 78, 95, 115–22, 125, 128, 142, 153, 212n.109, 213n.133, 214n.147
  see also belly; lean
O'Connor, John 196n.107
odiousness 40, 70, 75–6, 101, 129, 132, 144
old age 2, 3–7, 4, 20, 45, 75–6, 86, 98–9, 102–16, 127–30, 134, 137, 138, 139, 147
The Olde Bride, or The Gilded Beauty 102, 111, 113

Oldham, John
   'To the memory' 154–5
'opaque' body 3, 6, 35, 39, 54, 66, 67, 69, 80–93, 141, 163
Overbury, Sir Thomas
   A Wife 191n.10
Ovid
   Metamorphoses 162

painted face *see* cosmetics
Painter, William
   The Palace of Pleasure 160, 173–4
pale 2, 46, 47, 104, 118, 125, 127, 128, 136, 164, 204n.27
   wan 2, 104, 118, 164
   see also white body
palm-reading *see* physiognomy
Panofsky, Erwin 203n.10, 215n.13
paradox 13, 20, 27, 61, 72, 107, 113, 120, 129, 139–50, 170, 177, 184, 216n.32
Park, Katherine 22
Parker, Patricia 213n.142, 214n.150
Parrott, T. M. 222n.41
Passion, The 27–9
passions 2, 22, 46, 48, 49, 51, 56, 59, 66, 70–1, 75, 77, 80, 89, 95, 119, 122, 124, 126–7, 129, 173
Paster, Gail Kern 102
Peacham, Henry
   The Compleat Gentleman 46, 53
Peacock, John 195n.78 and n.79
pearl 101, 131, 141, 144, 154, 155, 203n.17
Pender, Stephen 4–5, 93, 190n.16 and n.18
Pepys, Samuel
   The Diary of Samuel Pepys 21–2
Peru 16
Petrarchan poetry 5, 7, 101, 115, 121, 140, 144–6, 150, 154–5, 186, 217n.60, 218n.79
physiognomy 5, 34, 39, 48–64, 69–71, 80–2, 85, 90, 93, 128
   palm-reading 54, 70
pimple 24, 125, 128, 134, 141, 152, 219n.112
plague 66, 101, 104, 106, 152

Platonism 48, 71, 79, 151, 180–1
   Ficino, Marsilio 71
   Neoplatonism 12, 14–15, 18, 41–3, 46, 71–2, 133, 154, 179–81, 185
   Plotinus 18, 42, 180
pleasure 14, 16, 19, 21–34, 74, 92, 120, 129, 139, 174
Plotinus *see* Platonism
poison 18, 46, 57, 66, 89, 90, 103, 105, 118, 133, 160, 165, 178, 183, 184, 185
Polinska, Wioleta 222n.48
Pollard, Robert
   Choyce Drollery (with John Sweeting) 119, 142, 147
Porter, Martin 53, 190n.17
Porter, Roy 1
pox *see* smallpox; syphilis
praising ugliness 7, 20–1, 27, 113, 131–57, 158–87
Prestwich, Edmund
   'On an old Ill-favoured Woman' 102, 104, 105, 111
   'To Almanna' 150
prodigy 21–2, 34, 37–40, 45, 55, 67, 103, 165
proportion 13–14, 17, 18, 22, 38, 43, 45, 46, 48–9, 55, 65, 72, 81, 116, 117, 140, 142, 161
   symmetry 18, 19, 35, 145, 159
Protestantism 29, 34, 44, 51–2, 63, 69, 72–7, 79–80, 83, 105, 118, 170–1, 173, 178, 189n.4, 225n.97
   Church of England 29, 43, 58, 63, 72, 74
   Puritan 73, 75, 103, 119, 223n.60
   see also Calvin, John
Puritan *see* Protestantism
Purkiss, Diane 171
Puttenham, George
   The Arte of English Poesie 18

Quarles, Francis
   Argalus and Parthenia 186
   Hadassa 73–4, 203n.24

R., M.
   The Mothers Counsell 75–6, 82

Rabelais, Francois
  Gargantua and Pantagruel 78–9
race 21, 188
  see also black body
Randolph, Thomas
  'Upon a very deformed Gentlewoman' 107
rape 113, 162, 168, 173–4, 183–4, 226n.121
Reformation *see* Protestantism
regicide 63
Reynolds, Edward
  A Treatise of the Passions 22
Reynolds, John
  The Triumph of God's Revenge 118
Rhodes, Neil 117, 201n.70, 214n.149
Roman Catholicism 29, 49, 72–4, 119, 223n.60
  Jesuit 53, 201n.67
  see also Henrietta Maria
Rosslyn, Felicity 92
Rowlands, Samuel
  'The Devil's Health-drinker' 118
Rowley, William
  The Changeling see Middleton, Thomas
  The Witch of Edmonton see Dekker, Thomas
ruby 72, 154
Russo, Mary 158–9, 207n.2

de Sade, Marquis
  The 120 Days of Sodom 22
Sadler, John
  The Sicke Womans Private Looking-glasse 34, 198n.109
St Agatha 170, 222n.52
St Bonaventure 23
St Brigid 222n.52
St Margaret 168, 169–70
Sanderson, Sir William
  Graphice 17, 43, 116
Sandwith, F. M. 219n.104
satire 20, 31, 65, 85, 99, 180
Saunders, Corinne 169
Saunders, Richard
  Physiognomie 48–9, 49, 70

Sawday, Jonathan 190n.11
scabies 103, 209n.39
scar 25, 29, 127, 151–7, 163, 175, 178–87
Scarry, Elaine 171–2
Schiesari, Juliana 214n.165, 215n.177
Schmitt, Charles B. 201n.67
Schoenbaum, Samuel 180
Schoenfeldt, Michael C. 46, 204n.36
Schulenburg, Jane Tibbets 169
science *see* mechanical philosophy
Scott, Sarah
  Agreeable Ugliness 2, 94–5, 151, 194n.66
  Millenium Hall 162–3
self-mutilation *see* mutilation
Selleck, Nancy 46, 48
Semonin, Paul 196n.96, 197n.112
sepulchre 2, 136, 164
Shakespeare, William
  As You Like It 161
  The Comedy of Errors 48, 120–1, 163–4, 172, 186
  Hamlet 1, 140, 205n.52, 221n.16
  1 Henry IV 46, 118–20
  2 Henry IV 117, 119, 121
  King John 45
  Love's Labours Lost 140
  Macbeth 5
  Othello 51, 79–80
  The Rape of Lucrece 162
  Romeo and Juliet 117
  Sonnets 7, 140
  The Taming of the Shrew 167–8
  The Tempest 108, 205n.48
  The Tragedy of King Richard III 80–3, 160, 166–7
  Venus and Adonis 163
shame 31, 60–1, 95, 147, 150, 162, 181, 183–4
  see also guilt
Sheppard, Samuel
  'An old Woman Letcherous' 103–4
Shildrick, Margrit 198n.131
Shipman, Thomas
  'Beauty's Enemy' 153, 155–6

Shirley, James 34, 197n.111
  The Dukes Mistris 20, 139, 180, 181–2
  'One that loved none but deformed women' 150
  'To a Beautiful Lady' 27, 139, 14
  'To the Proud M.' 102, 107
shrew 104, 167–8
shroud 2, 164
Sidney, Sir Philip
  An Apology for Poetry 31, 133–4
  The Countess of Pembroke's Arcadia 131, 133, 142, 178–87
Silenus 3, 5, 69, 77–80, 129, 163, 182
Skelton, John
  Elynour Rummynge 103
skin 14, 17, 29, 44, 46, 52, 57, 65, 76, 89, 98, 101, 105–6, 111, 114, 115, 116, 118, 123, 125–8, 131, 136, 137, 140, 144, 151–7, 160, 163, 169, 172, 176–8, 181, 184, 221n.22 and n.23
  skin-deep 3, 5, 12, 56, 80, 84
  tanned 16, 125
  see also boil; complexion; pimple; pale; scar; ulcer; wart; wen; wrinkle
slut 99, 125, 137, 142
smallpox 105, 111, 117, 151–7, 163, 219n.96, n.107 and n.112, 220n.115 and n.123
smell 6, 49, 71, 75, 103, 104, 115, 125, 127–8, 133, 214n.170
Smith, Nigel 223n.60
snot *see* nose
social class 2, 5, 12, 23, 27, 31, 35, 39–40, 41, 53, 55, 70–1, 77, 94–5, 99, 102–3, 106, 119, 121, 151–4, 188
Socrates 52, 78–9, 201n.60
  see also Silenus
Specht, Henrik 44, 190n.13, 209n.39
Spencer, John
  A Discourse Concerning Prodigies 35–40, 55
Spenser, Edmund
  The Faerie Queene 73, 99
  'An Hymne in Honour of Beautie' 42–3
spider 36, 94

Spierenburg, Pieter 223n.65
Stachniewski, John 200n.56, 206n.86
stain 45, 46, 47, 49, 51, 61, 101, 154, 172, 177, 183–6
Stallybrass, Peter 102, 207n.4
Stampino, Maria Galli 216n.32, 217n.50
star 53, 57, 61, 72, 98, 150, 154, 155, 171, 183, 205n.52
starvation 117, 119, 141, 171, 222n.48
stigma 58–61, 105, 108
Stott, Andrew 206n.87
Stubbes, Phillip
  Anatomy of the Abuses 73, 172
sublime 22, 77, 194n.61
Suckling, John
  'The Deformed Mistress' 141–2, 144, 150
Summers, David 193n.42
Sutton, Katherine
  A Christian Womans Experiences 106
Sweeting, John *see* Pollard, Robert
Sydenham, Thomas
  The Compleat Method 152–3, 219n.96, 219n.112
symmetry *see* proportion
Synnott, Anthony 203n.9
syphilis 105, 153, 182–4, 226n.114 and n.118

Tartarkiewicz, Wladyslaw 25
Taverner, Richard
  Proverbes and Adagies 133
Tayler, Edward William 215n.6
Taylor, Charles 69, 81, 205n.62
teeth 16, 31, 98
  black 16, 104, 125, 128, 140, 142, 181
  rotten 103, 105, 125, 127, 209n.41
  protruding 48
Tempesta, Antonio
  The Twelve Principal Roman Heroes and Heroines 31, 32–3, 146, 148–9
Tennenhouse, Leonard 224n.69, 226n.121
Thane, Pat 211n.80
thin *see* lean
Thomson, Philip 195n.77

Thomson, Rosemarie Garland 197n.116
Tilmouth, Christopher 122
Titian
   The Flaying of Marsyas 163, *164*
   Isabella d'Este 134, *135*
toad 18, 36, 66, 88, 108, 166, 178
Torrey, Michael 81, 190–1n.23
torture 29, 129, 169, 170–2
Tournon, André 224n.76 and n.77
Trapnel, Anna 171, 223n.60
Trobiner, Alice 210n.68 and n.73, 211n.75
Turkish 16, 170
Twyne, Laurence
   The Patterne of Painfull Adventures 117

ugly beauty 139, 155, 212n.97, 216n.32, 217n.60, 218n.79
   see also deformed mistress
ulcer 75, 84

Vasari, Giorgio 26, 195n.79
Vaughan, Virginia Mason 176
Veevers, Erica 72
Venus 16, 20, 106, 127, 131, 155, 163, 176
Vetruvius 27
Vickers, Brian 191n.23, 198n.132
Vickers, Nancy J. 186, 217n.68
Villiers, George
   A Character of an Ugly Woman 101–3
violence 7, 63, 66–7, 73, 97–8, 107, 108, 127, 129, 137, 153, 158–87
virago 6, 108, 115, 117, 125, 130
virginity 85–6, 124, 159–60, 162, 168–79
virgin martyr *see* martyr
visor 77, 83, 86–7, 206n.74
   see also mask
vomit 97, 102, 104, 123
de Voragine, Jacobus
   The Golden Legend 169–70, 222n.52

waist 98, 116, 125, 132, 142
wan *see* pale
Ward, Edward
   'Club of Ugly Faces' 20–1, 22

Warner, Lyndan 211n.85
wart 5, 22, 24, 128
Webster, John
   The Devil's Law-Case 175–7
   The Duchess of Malfi 45, 53, 111
   The White Devil 160, 167, 177–8, 225n.91
wen 22, 37
Wesley, Samuel
   'On a Discourteous Damsel' 99, 104
Westra, Laura 226n.108
White, Helen C. 224n.72
white body 15, 20, 73, 80, 116, 136, 146, 154, 161, 176–7, 186, 219n.112
   see also fair; pale
whore 53, 66, 86–7, 107, 137, 172
   Whore of Babylon 73, 153, 203n.17
widow 103, 108–9, 124, 152, 171, 211n.85
William of Auvergne 11, 17
Williams, David 197n.126
Williams, R. Grant 122–3
Williams, Raymond 190n.20
Wisdom 44
witch 5, 7, 54, 56, 86, 89, 107–8, 121, 125, 207n.5
witchcraft 82, 181–2
Wither, George
   'Deformitie within may bee' 110
Wolf, John E. 190n.14
womb 37, 45, 105, 121
wonder 34, 35, 38, 40, 45, 87, 102, 150, 158, 197n.116
The Wonders of the Female World 76–7
Wood, Anthony 34, 197n.111
wound 29, 37, 67, 91, 127, 168–9, 171–2, 186
Wright, Thomas
   The Passions of the Minde 49–53, 70–1, 119
wrinkle 54, 63, 76, 81, 90, 99, 107–8, 114, 125, 128–9, 137, 147

Ziolkowski, Jan 199n.23
Zunker, Mark J. 196n.98

EU authorised representative for GPSR:
Easy Access System Europe, Mustamäe tee 50,
10621 Tallinn, Estonia
gpsr.requests@easproject.com

www.ingramcontent.com/pod-product-compliance
Lightning Source LLC
Chambersburg PA
CBHW020122240426
43673CB00038B/561